India's *Ad Hoc* Arsenal
Direction or Drift in Defence Policy?

India's *Ad Hoc* Arsenal
Direction or Drift in Defence Policy?

Chris Smith

OXFORD UNIVERSITY PRESS

1994

Oxford University Press, Walton Street, Oxford OX2 6DP
Oxford New York Toronto
Delhi Bombay Calcutta Madras Karachi
Kuala Lumpur Singapore Hong Kong Tokyo
Nairobi Dar es Salaam Cape Town
Melbourne Auckland Madrid
and associated companies in
Berlin Ibadan

Oxford is a trade mark of Oxford University Press

Published in the United States
by Oxford University Press Inc., New York

British Library Cataloguing in Publication Data
Data available

Library of Congress Cataloging in Publication Data
Smith, Chris, 1955–
India's ad hoc arsenal:direction or drift in defence policy?/Chris Smith.
"SIPRI"
Includes bibliographical references (p.   ) and index.
1. India—Military policy. 2. India—History, Military—20th
century. I. Stockholm International Peace Research Institute.
II. Title.
UA840.S624 1994 355′. 033554—dc20 93–44216
ISBN 0–19–829168-X (alk. paper)

Typeset and originated by Stockholm International Peace Research Institute
Printed in Great Britain
on acid-free paper by
Biddles Ltd, Guildford and King's Lynn

Contents

Preface

During recent years and especially since the end of the Persian Gulf War, international concern over the flow of military technology from North to South has risen dramatically. Increasingly, however, there is a growing awareness of our inability to understand why developing countries invest scarce resources on such a scale in ambitious and often destabilizing defence programmes. While there is now a widespread understanding that at the East–West level defence and security policies were influenced as much by internal, domestic considerations as by the reactions to the actions of perceived enemies, our understanding of what motivates developing countries was and still is much less clear.

This book on the dynamics of India's defence policy since 1947 is an attempt to explain why India has invested considerable resources in its armed forces since independence and markedly during the 1980s. It is the first in a series of SIPRI publications on the domestic influences on the defence policies and postures in developing countries.

Over the past two years, India has seen economic and political sovereignty slip slowly but undeniably from the grasp of national decision makers, largely as a result of increasing intervention by multilateral aid agencies. The ideals which influenced political economy for decades are now a memory. Ironically, in its attempts to ensure national security, regional hegemony and simultaneously make a mark on the international stage, the inflated defence budget has contributed to the loss of precisely what Indians have consistently voted for and worked towards preserving—security and sovereignty. National security has been acquired at the expense of economic security.

This is a dilemma which many countries are being forced to confront. The problems call for broad political debate on the fundamental principles which guide defence and foreign policies. While all nation states have the right to acquire the means to national security, there should always be close consideration of how much is enough and at which point the means defeat the ends.

In this book, SIPRI hopes to stimulate debate on the direction which Indian defence policy has taken over the past four decades. Many other countries will have to consider their own in the coming years. More of the same will not bring India increased security, in the broadest sense. Nor will it acquire for India either the security or the international prominence the nation so obviously deserves.

Adam Daniel Rotfeld
Director of SIPRI
January 1994

Acknowledgements

This book is the culmination of several years' work on South Asian security issues. Over this time, many people from several countries have helped me in various ways to acquire information and improve my understanding of Indian defence issues. Financial support has come from a number of sources.

In the United States I would like to thank Walter Anderson, Richard Cronin, Pranay Gupte, George Perkovich and, especially, Stephen Cohen for their help and advice. In Canada, Lorne Kavic spent a good deal of time with me discussing the 1947–62 period and his comments were invaluable for what turned out to be a very difficult chapter.

In Britain, I have received a great deal of support from friends and colleagues at the Science Policy Research Unit of the University of Sussex between 1980 and 1983: the Technology and the Arms Race seminars were an important influence during the planning and preparation of this book. The Institute of Development Studies, also at the University of Sussex, provided me with an excellent research environment between 1985 and 1991: Bruce Claxton and James Manor were very helpful in different ways during much of the later research and writing. Since 1992 the Centre for Defence Studies, King's College, University of London, has provided me with a wonderful intellectual environment and I am very grateful to Mike Clarke and Professor Lawrence Freedman. Elsewhere in Britain Professor Neville Brown, Professor Barry Buzan, Harry Dean, Bernard Harbor, Bill Haywood, Professor James O'Connell, Malcolm Spaven, Irene Williams and Professor Steve Smith have either commented on drafts or discussed parts of the project with me or offered general encouragement on several occasions. The late Lady Blackett kindly gave me access to her husband's papers in the Royal Society archives.

In Sweden, Tomas Ohlson and Rita Tullberg were very helpful to me during a research visit in 1986. The SIPRI arms trade files were an extremely useful resource and the editorial team—Peter Rea, Eve Johansson and Billie Bielckus—put a great deal of effort into improving the quality of the text. Ian Anthony and Ravinder Pal Singh read the whole text and made a number of extremely useful comments.

In India, the period I spent between November 1983 and March 1985 as a fellow of the United Nations University sub-programme on Peace and Global Transformation was productive and stimulating. The UNU provided me with a fellowship, research facilities and travelling expenses without which my field work and interviewing would not have been possible. I greatly appreciate the support of Janusz Golebiowski and Professor Kinhide Mushakoji from the UNU in Tokyo, Shekah Shah from the Ford Foundation in Delhi, and Professor Giri Deshingkar and Professor Rajni Kothari who ran the programme in Delhi. Also in Delhi, my friends and colleagues from the Centre for the Study of Developing Societies provided me with an stimulating intellectual environment during my time in India.

Many people in India took the time and effort to discuss the project with me: some requested off-the-record interviews. B. D. NagChaudhri and D. Raghunandan shared with me their experiences and recollections of the Indian defence industry. Ghayar Alam, G. Balachandra, Praful Bidwai, John Fullerton, K. S. Katoch, Rita Manchanda,

K. Subrahmanyam and Bharat Wariavwalla were helpful on many occasions. Countless other people in India provided me with help and hospitality.

Over the years the project has been funded from several different sources. The Joseph Rowntree Charitable Trust, the Barrow and Geraldine S. Cadbury Trust, and Heinz and Anna Kroch Foundation, the University of Bath, Nicholas and Ruth Gillett and Phillip Radley provided the initial finance for me to complete my PhD, which formed the first stage of this project. Nicholas Gillett was extremely helpful and supportive. Most recently, the Harold Hyam Wingate Foundation and the Nuffield Foundation awarded me a scholarship and a grant respectively to cover the costs of a visit to India and a final draft.

Finally, I appreciate the encouragement and support of many friends and relatives. In particular, Giri Deshingkar has been a constant source of information, inspiration and encouragement.

Nevertheless, all mistakes and errors remain my own.

Chris Smith
London
January 1994

Acronyms and abbreviations

AAC	Army Aviation Corps
ADA	Aeronautical Development Agency
ADV	Air Defence Variant
AEW	Advanced early warning
ALH	Advanced Light Helicopter
APC	Armoured personnel carrier
ARDE	Armament Research and Development Establishment
ASLV	Augmented space launch vehicle
ASW	Anti-submarine warfare
ATF	Advanced Tactical Fighter
BAe	British Aerospace Ltd
BJP	Bharatiya Janata Party
CANDU	Canadian deuterium-uranium (reactor)
CDS	Chief of Defence Staff
CENTO	Central Treaty Organization
CEP	Circular error probable
CIS	Commonwealth of Independent States
CKD	Completely knocked down
CSC	Chiefs of Staff Committee
CTBT	Comprehensive test ban treaty CTBT
CVRE	Combat Vehicle Research Establishment
C^3I	Command, control, communications and intelligence
DCC	Defence Committee of the Cabinet
DGCA	Directorate General of Civil Aviation
DMC	Defence Minister's Committee
DoDP	Department of Defence Production
DRDO	Defence Research and Development Organization
ECC	Emergency Committee of the Cabinet
ECM	Electronic counter measures
FRG	Federal Republic of Germany
GE	General Electric
GNP	Gross national product
GTRE	Gas Turbine Research Establishment
HAL	Hindustan Aeronautics Limited
HDW	Howaldtswerke-Deutsche Werft
IAEA	International Atomic Energy Agency
IAF	Indian Air Force
ICS	Indian Civil Service
IDS	Interdictor Strike

IDSA	Institute for Defence Studies and Analysis
IMF	International Monetary Fund
INA	Indian National Army
INC	Indian National Congress
IRBM	Intermediate-range ballistic missile
ISC	Inter-Service Committee
ISRO	Indian Space Research Organisation
JIC	Joint Intelligence Committee of the Cabinet
LCA	Light Combat Aircraft
LTTE	Liberation Tigers of Tamil Eelam
MBT	Main battle tank
MEA	Ministry of External Affairs
MoD	Ministry of Defence
MoU	Memorandum of Understanding
MQM	Mohajir Qaumi Mahaz
MRCA	Multi-Role Combat Aircraft
MTCR	Missile Technology Control Regime
NAL	National Aeronautics Laboratory
NAM	Non-aligned movement
NATO	North Atlantic Treaty Oganization
NEFA	North-East Frontier Agency
NPT	Non-Proliferation Treaty
OECD	Organization for Economic Co-operation and Development
OPEC	Organization of Petroleum Exporting Countries
PAC	Public Accounts Committee
PACC	Political Affairs Committee of the Cabinet
PPRC	Policy Planning and Review Committee
R&D	Research and development
RAPP	Rajastani Atomic Power Plant
RDF	Rapid Deployment Force
SAARC	South Asian Association for Regional Co-operation
SALT	Strategic Arms Limitation Talks
SAM	Surface-to-air missile
SEATO	South East Asia Treaty Organization
SLOC	Sea lines of communication
SLV	Space launch vehicle
UN	United Nations

1. Introduction

During the mid-1970s, military expenditures in and arms sales to Third World countries began to rise significantly. Conflicts in the Middle East had persuaded the Organization of Petroleum Exporting Countries (OPEC) states to use oil pricing as a weapon against the West to offset continued economic, political and *matériel* support for Israel. The result was a massive increase in wealth for the OPEC states, and countries such as Iran and Saudi Arabia significantly increased their military expenditures and arms purchases. In addition, the Western clearing banks, fearful of a liquidity crisis brought on by the mounting deposits of petro-dollars on the one hand and domestic stagflation on the other, began to increase their lending to non-OPEC Third World countries.

The majority of Third World countries were at that time operating defence equipment that was obsolete, second-hand and, usually, impaired by excessive wear and tear. The credit boom offered an excellent opportunity to upgrade defence equipment, particularly as Western suppliers were increasingly keen to export state-of-the-art equipment to offset domestic economic decline and balance of payments difficulties, both exacerbated by rising oil prices. By the late 1970s, commercial banks had become the most important source of finance for arms sales.

Arms imports and military expenditures rose as a consequence throughout the Third World. According to one estimate, 20 per cent of the debt crisis in the early 1980s can be explained by credits for arms imports.[1] The exception to the rule was the Indian sub-continent. Procurement was low through the 1970s in both India and Pakistan. They underwent dramatic modernization programmes throughout the 1980s, however, during which time most countries were cutting back on arms imports, and between 1987 and 1991 India imported $17.5 billion of defence equipment, $7 billion more than the second highest importer, Saudi Arabia.[2]

Accompanying these developments was a shift of attention by the research community. Throughout the 1950s and 1960s, concentration had focused upon the role and importance of military institutions, with particular reference to the development process. Abruptly, the emphasis changed and centred upon the role of arms sales in the post-war world and the relationship between military expenditure and underdevelopment. There was however little attempt to disaggregate to the country level.

[1] Brzoska, M., *Military Trade, Aid and Developing Country Debt. Report*, prepared by the SRC Department of the World Bank Research Symposium on Military Expenditure (World Bank: Washington, DC, Dec. 1990), p. 44.
[2] Anthony, I. *et al.*, 'The trade in major conventional weapons', *SIPRI Yearbook 1992: World Armaments and Disarmament* (Oxford University Press: Oxford, 1992), p. 273. Billion is used throughout to mean 1000 million.

As a result, little is known about the motivations which underpin procurement drives in non-industrialized countries. In the post-cold war era, the full heterogeneity of the erstwhile Third World has received new attention from research and policy-making communities. Following the collapse of the bipolar world order, individual countries and the regions in which they exist are becoming better understood in their own right—Middle Eastern states are a case in point.

Inadequate knowledge of what drives the demand side of the international arms trade is a major lacuna in the field of international security studies. There is a tendency to understand the dynamics in terms of regional politics, enmity between nations and sub-imperial strategies. Yet, when the same questions are asked of industrialized countries, the terms of reference are very different and tend to incorporate internal, domestic, technological, bureaucratic 'push' factors as much as the external, defence-orientated 'pull' factors. The majority of underdeveloped countries do have enough of a political-bureaucratic process to justify increased attention to the detail of their policy making.

This is made all the more pertinent by a growing acceptance within the international community that the international arms trade must be subject to greater control, especially following the mounting evidence of Iraq's ability to trawl the international defence market for more or less everything it required, up to and including the technology required to produce weapons of mass destruction. Yet, in part because so little is known about demand-side dynamics, there is an inbuilt tendency to dwell unduly upon supply-side initiatives and methods of control.

Important though this is, it overlooks why developing countries strive to build up their armouries and why certain types of weapon are sought over and above others. In general, the majority prefer to procure the most capable systems the exchequer is prepared to afford, despite the economic opportunity costs, the lost opportunities for development and the drain on foreign exchange reserves. Several countries can afford advanced military technology, but many cannot.

What then drives different countries to purchase weapons and what determines which weapons are chosen? The question can be easily answered at the level of generality—threat perceptions, force levels, prestige, technology acquisition, corruption, and so on. Yet what motivates Iraq is different from what drives Argentina, Malaysia, Morocco or Nigeria. All countries have their particular sets of reasons for acquiring defence technology, even though there may be common threads running through the defence process, as can be detected in the West.

Moreover, if arms imports really are detrimental to development, why have states not sought cost-effective solutions to regional defence problems? Is it because there are no cost-effective solutions to the problem of an enemy equipped with advanced technology? Has nobody bothered to investigate and, if not, why not? Who then comes in for blame if defence has a negative impact upon development, the 'merchants of death', senior members of the armed forces, senior bureaucrats, politicians, or a public which sees no reason to accept second best and is prepared to foot the bill?

This book attempts to answer what seems at first sight a series of straightforward questions. Why has India spent $17.5 billion in recent years on arms imports? What lies behind India's nuclear weapon programme? Why has India not achieved more in the drive towards self-sufficiency? Who supports such expansive defence programmes? In sum, what drives India's defence policy in the directions it has taken over the past 40 years?

The study is of particular interest because of recent events. Despite, or because of, such an ambitious programme, India has failed to maintain optimum levels of defence preparedness. Around the turn of the decade, the defence budget came under severe pressure as external indebtedness rose and foreign exchange reserves dwindled. The modernization programme started in the early 1980s ground to an ignominious halt amid stories of logistical shortages which could only amount to a reduction in defence capability.

Nevertheless, this does not seem to matter a great deal. New Delhi is not overly concerned that enough spare parts cannot be bought or even that defence debts cannot be serviced. This has not led, for example, to an upsurge in demands for nuclearization to compensate for the loss of conventional capacity. All in all, the country seems fairly calm as stories and rumours mount. There is no real feeling of increased insecurity. The government is not under challenge for failing to guarantee defence preparedness. Given the traditional fear of attack from China and Pakistan and the memory of four wars since 1947, this is noteworthy.

The following chapters attempt to analyse the national security process in India. India's external security problems are identified, and the question of who is responsible for responding to these threats is addressed. The result is not a rationalized, well-informed or streamlined decision-making process. The key actors are various and common interests few and far between. Despite the institutionalization of rolling five-year defence plans, the process is chaotic and lacking in vision—weapons are procured as much on an *ad hoc* basis as on the strength of informed debate, forethought and planning. Above all, the waste of resources is considerable and the level of public acceptance exceptional.

2. India: regional security from Aryan times to the present

I. From the Aryans to the British: the legacy of invasion

Security concerns in the Indian sub-continent have been significantly influenced by a long history of waves of immigration and invasion which stretch back over some 4000 years. Throughout this period northern India in particular was subjected to successive incursions by warring tribes and invasion attempts from the north-west; some were successful, others were not.

First and foremost, there was a period of successful colonization by the Aryan tribes from about 1500 BC. Formerly it was thought that the Aryans, who originated in the region of the Caspian Sea and the southern Russian steppes and reached India in search of pasture, marked the virtual beginning of Indian history, and that this was implicitly reflected in Hindu mythology. As late as the 1920s, however, archaeology revealed the existence of pre-Aryan settlements in the north-west of India, the Indus Valley civilization, which had declined and almost completely disintegrated by 1500 BC. The Aryans, descendants of the Indo-Europeans, migrated into northern India via the passes of the Hindu Kush from Bactria, a Greek kingdom to the west of the Hindu Kush, and the north Iranian plateau. By 800 BC the Aryans were moving south, clearing forests and establishing their cultural roots in the sub-continent. The indigenous peoples settled in northern India, the Dasas and the Panis, were of some concern to the Aryans who were compelled to use considerable force to overwhelm the Dasas and then to stop the Panis from cattle stealing, a basic source of wealth for the semi-nomadic pastoralists.

The Aryan influence was extremely important. Not only did it exert a strong influence upon Indian culture, socio-political organization and the religious life of the native population; it also conflicted, both socially and politically, with the indigenous Dravidian culture. This encounter may have been an initial catalyst for the unique Indian system of caste. It may also have laid the cultural foundations for a divide between north and south by pushing the Dravidians to the south.

Following the Aryans came the Greeks. In 327 BC Alexander of Macedon entered the Indian provinces of the Achaemenid empire centred around the Hindu Kush, an incursion facilitated by the Aryan movement to the east which left the north-west open and unattended. Alexander's invasion was somewhat opportunistic and, although he left governors to rule where his invasion had been successful, little impact was made and the Greek presence quickly collapsed once Alexander's back was turned.

As the presence of the Greeks faded away so opportunities opened up in the north-west for nomadic tribes from central Asia. After the death of Alexander and the end of Achaemenid rule in Iran, several independent kingdoms sprang up in Iran and neighbouring areas, including the kingdoms of Bactria and Parthia. The Bactrians then moved towards the sub-continent, in a south-easterly direction, to occupy what is now modern-day Afghanistan and the Makran areas.[1] This was followed by a further movement to the south and east into the Punjab and down the Indus valley into Kutch, thereby establishing Indo-Greek power in the north-western region as far east as Delhi. By the second century BC the kingdom of Bactria was successfully threatened by nomadic tribes from central Asia, especially the Scythians who also overran the Parthians but had themselves been displaced from modern-day Uzbekistan. The Scythians, or Shakas as they were known in India, poured through the Bolan Pass near Quetta and into the Indus valley.

For the next few hundred years there was a respite from external invasion, once the Gupta dynasty had gained control over northern India. However, during the 5th century AD the calm was shaken by the Huns who fought a hard and successful campaign of attrition during the latter half of the century and brought with them into India several central Asian tribes, such as the Gujaras. Relatively half-hearted attempts by the Arabs to move beyond the Indus valley were easily frustrated. Thereafter, conflicts in the sub-continent were fundamentally 'domestic' until the arrival of the Turkish–Afghan sultans, followed by the Portuguese, the Moguls and, finally, the British.[2]

The raids carried out by Mahmud of Ghazni and Muhammad Ghuri brought Turkish–Afghan interests and religion into the sub-continent around the 12th century. Centred in Delhi and overseen by sultans, their influence on Indian political, cultural and religious life was pervasive, although much less definitive than that of their Islamic successors, the Moguls. This was followed in the 15th century by the arrival of the Portuguese. In 1487 Bartolomeu Dias travelled to the wealthy trading ports of the Malabar coast in present-day Kerala and returned to Lisbon with stories of wealth on the one hand and vulnerability on the other. The Portuguese duly arrived around the coast of Gujarat in 1498 with a fleet commanded by Vasco da Gama seeking to establish trading posts and small colonies. Although prevented from doing so in this quarter by the invasion of the Moguls in the 16th century, the Portuguese were able to establish bolt-holes in the south and the west, Goa in particular. Yet again, India had to absorb another culture and another religion—at first sight modern-day Goa seems to have more in common with South America than South Asia.

The influence of the Moguls, after they established their empire in India, was immense, and as important and enduring as that of the Aryans; indeed it has even been suggested that the unity imposed upon India by Britain and the

---

[1] The area of Makran straddles the south of both Iran and Pakistan. It is a mountainous coastal region to the north-west of the Gulf of Oman.

[2] Thapar, R., *A History of India,* vol. 1 (Penguin: Harmondsworth, 1966), pp. 28–36. See also the excellent annotated bibliography for further reading.

efforts of the country's nation-builders after 1947 would have been that much more difficult without the organization and administration introduced by the Moguls.[3] The Moguls were followed by French and British trading companies which appeared in several areas, notably Pondicherry and Calcutta. Eventually the sub-continent fell to British colonialism and was transformed into the Indian Empire.

Several thousand years of foreign domination and invasion had a considerable and indelible impact upon Indian civilization, particularly in the north and later in the south as well. The effects are various and often extremely subtle. On the one hand, the extent and duration of foreign domination, specifically in the north, has refined perceptions of threat and the ability to calibrate insecurity over a lengthy period of history, although surprisingly little was actually done to protect the vulnerable gateways in the north-west—the Bolan Pass and the Hindu Kush—during the protracted period of upheaval in central Asia which led to the building of the Great Wall of China. The probable reason is that although India's southern states were sufficiently culturally and politically homogeneous, northern India was the complete reverse, a shifting collection of interlopers with more interest in exploiting the wealth of the kingdoms than in maintaining the security of the region—moving on was always an option.

On the other hand, Hinduism and, consequently, India had proved adept at absorbing and assimilating foreign influences in a particular way which both minimizes conflict and gives the society the ability to retain key aspects of religion and culture. Ironically, it was the continuing ability to absorb foreign influences which eventually created the weaknesses which allowed a foreign mercantile country to attain complete domination over the region in the short space of 80 years.[4]

Hinduism, a term which has come into common usage during the past 100 years, is unique among religions of the world in its degree of catholicity and capability for assimilation. Thus, invasions of India and conversely Hindu 'colonization' in South East Asia were rendered much less traumatic by a very advanced degree of cultural elasticity, particularly among the Brahmins, the religious caste which traditionally assumed responsibility for the legal, religious and cultural aspects of Hinduism. With the exception of the Moguls, the majority of the invaders arrived with relatively weak theological traditions of their own, which made confrontation less likely and assimilation more to the cultural and religious advantage of the native population. However, the gulf between Hindu and Muslim failed to diminish over time. One effect was the emergence of Sikhism which attempted to bridge the gap. Given the history of other regional crossroads, such as Central Europe, or the colonial history of South America and Africa, the historical record and the evidence of elasticity and assimilation are both fascinating and remarkable.

---

[3] Spear, P., *A History of India*, vol. 2 (Penguin: Harmondsworth, 1965), p. 51.
[4] Spear (note 3), p. 106.

During the period of Muslim rule in India, there was a clear divergence of security perspectives between the Muslim rulers and the Hindu subjects. The former perceived threats to their empire from the north-west as well as from the Hindu rajas established within the sub-continent. The latter only perceived a threat to their way of life from the aliens who kept arriving from the north-west. It was only with the coming of the British that both became aware of the threat from the sea.

For racial, cultural and economic reasons the Hindu/Indian reaction to the British was in the beginning benign, but over time became more fractious. Initially, the British were welcomed and the indigenous population was grateful for the establishment of law and order; although Robert Clive may have acted like a robber baron, Lords Hastings and Cornwallis offered form, cohesion and organization. Within the social grid the British were treated as a kind of *Kshatriya* (the warrior and aristocracy caste) which again emphasizes the Hindu capacity for assimilation. The first British to reach India were also more accommodating and less racially conscious than were succeeding generations. During the early phase of colonization both parties were therefore capable of a form of integration. At one time it was not uncommon for the *angrez* (English) to marry local women, wear traditional Indian dress and even worship Hindu deities which signified a near complete break with European culture. This changed later when the sea route was shortened by the opening of the Suez Canal, increasing numbers of European women came to settle in India and more direct lines of authority were opened up from London.

In the 19th and early 20th centuries the presence of the British in India completely altered the security configuration in the Indian sub-continent. India had been made into the British Indian Empire, and Indian leaders and opinion shapers were no longer concerned about external security decisions. All decisions concerning security from invasion were taken in London or by the British Viceroy in Delhi. Policy implementation was the task of both the military and the civilian British bureaucrats in the sub-continent, despite the growing acceptance of Indian nationals into senior ranks of the bureaucracy and armed forces. Consequently, throughout modern history up until World War II, the development of Indian political culture was such that external issues and security considerations had little influence upon the emerging nationalist ideology, even though the geography of the sub-continent offered an element of identity which was often missing in other colonies. The British presence in India reinforced this tendency in another way. The collective political mind of India concentrated itself upon the British and the need for independence, particularly during and after the Hindu and Muslim intellectual revivals of the 19th century which culminated in the creation of the Indian National Congress (INC) in 1885.[5] In one sense, the presence of the British in India even reduced the importance of communal tensions in the sub-continent—to the British all Indians were

[5] Calvocoressi, P., *World Politics Since 1945* (Longman: London, 1977), p. 239.

'native' subjects and, from the other direction, Indians were able to find a common cause against the British, which encouraged nationalist sentiments.

The lack of attention to events and trends outside the Indian sub-continent was an important if understandable oversight on the part of the Indian nationalists. The geographic involvement of the Indian sub-continent in an emerging international system had come about almost a century earlier with the Treaty of Tilsit in 1807. This treaty represented an attempt by Napoleon Bonaparte to eliminate Russia from the European balance of power. In order to consolidate and preserve the Napoleonic empire, he had to isolate Britain, which could be done most effectively by diverting Russia away both from events in Europe and from a possible alliance with Britain. Consequently Napoleon persuaded Tsar Alexander I to accept the illusion that he could become Emperor of the East providing France did not interfere. In return, Alexander would allow Napoleon to consolidate his empire in the West.

The direct importance of the Treaty of Tilsit for the Indian sub-continent was negligible. However, it was not without indirect significance for two reasons. First, although Britain was able to check Alexander's expansion eastwards towards Persia and the sub-continent, the geopolitical importance of Russia for India became an established fact which has barely altered since. Second, the sub-continent became for the first time an integral part of a wider geopolitical framework. Hitherto India had been a largely imperial prize by virtue of its size, remarkable wealth, raw materials, indigenous products and enviable markets. Essentially, the Indian sub-continent was an end in itself. The rise of Russia and its role in the European balance of power, coupled with its geographic position and potential for expansion to the east and the south, implicated India in international political developments beyond South Asia. By the initial decades of the 20th century the Indian intelligentsia had started to respond to geopolitical developments. External issues were far less subtle than before and the interpreters within the INC more receptive than their predecessors.

II. Independence, partition and the war of 1947

During World War I Indian troops contributed to the British effort on the Western Front and also served in Egypt and Iraq. The cost was considerable: 62 056 Indian troops were killed during the war; fewer than 1000 were officers.[6] The educated officers, at least, had some sense of why the British Empire was at war with Germany and of the role of India, whereas the *jawans* (infantry soldiers) would have had little political understanding as to why, against whom and for what they were fighting. However, a significant gain during this period for India was that the British rulers were forced to accept the importance of the consent of their Indian subjects in the running of the Indian

---

[6] *Statistics of the Military Effort of the British Empire During the Great War* (War Office: London, 1922).

Empire. India had little choice as to whether or not it became involved in the war, although its contribution earned for India a promise of *swaraj*, or 'home rule', over the course of the conflict. Yet it is a moot point whether or not this was intended as a reward and compensation or as an inducement for further, increased contributions to the vast resources of manpower needed to fight the war. Nevertheless, Indians had heard by this time about the revolution in Russia and the 14 points of President Wilson. His discourse about rights and self-determination contrasted strongly with the views of the British. The Indian intelligentsia had also seen Britain seriously weakened and almost subdued: hereafter, the momentum for independence grew dramatically.

Despite attempts at prevarication, the British Government in 1918 published the Montagu-Chelmsford Report which was intended to establish the principle of self-government for India and hasten the Indianization of the Indian Army. Its recognition that 'home rule' was inescapable was however offset by a marked ambivalence over the question of, and the undeniable ramifications for, the future of the Empire. In the meantime, opinion in favour of complete independence grew in India with each passing year between the two world wars. By 1935, Britain was ready to pass the Government of India Act which gave a great deal of domestic autonomy to India but kept defence matters in British hands.

The outbreak of World War II sharpened nationalist sentiments within the INC. However, this was not enough to prevent the incumbent Viceroy once again involving India in a war without prior consultation with Indian ministers, who on this occasion promptly resigned, even though Japan's entry into the war made India's involvement inevitable. In the event, the extreme resentment of the Indian élites made little overall difference to the British agenda, in part because economic conditions in India had deteriorated so badly during the 1930s. In spite of rising nationalist sentiments, recruitment for the Allied war effort was relatively successful across the whole country. Nationalist sentiment had grown stronger and more concerted at the local/regional levels, but the national linkages were relatively weak. It was Mahatma Gandhi who subsequently strengthened these links. Over the course of the war the INC secured a firmer grip on the political situation within India and managed to channel nationalist sentiment into the Quit India Movement, which grew in numbers and appeal. Moreover, it was generally thought that Japan's intention to invade was fundamentally linked to the British presence or, to put it another way, that if the British could be swiftly removed Congress might do business with Japan to extricate itself from a conflict the roots of which were irrelevant to India.

Although the Quit India Movement of 1942 was suppressed, London could no longer avoid or prevaricate over the question of Indian independence. Britain, fighting a two-front war against Germany in Europe and Japan in Asia, and that too with a large number of Indian troops, was particularly exposed at that time within India. This strategic vulnerability was further compounded by the generous credit arrangements Britain was able to extract from India during the war years, the source of the post-war sterling imbalances.

The end of the war and the election of a Labour Government in Britain in 1945 lent new impetus to the British commitment to independence for India. In addition, India was in a far stronger position politically, organizationally and economically. The Attlee Government sent three Cabinet ministers to India to iron out the growing differences between Britain and the two major political groupings in India—the Muslim League, which had developed the notion of an independent state for Muslims to be called Pakistan, and the INC. The mission proved to be impossible and partition became inevitable. Over the course of the war relations between the INC and the Muslim League had deteriorated markedly. Britain's attempts at arbitration were nullified by the Muslim leader Muhammad Ali Jinnah's conviction that Britain was partial to the INC. By 1946 Jinnah had inaugurated a programme of direct action to establish a separate, sovereign state for Indian Muslims. Communal violence in late 1946 forced Viceroy Wavell to recommend that his Government either maintain power for a further decade, or transfer it piecemeal to the provinces.

In the event the British Government did neither. Attlee retired the incumbent Viceroy and gave Louis Mountbatten the onerous task of partitioning India and granting independence to two sovereign states in the Indian sub-continent. The projected date for independence was June 1948. It quickly became clear to Mountbatten, however, that the time span involved was too long; his assessment of the severity of communal violence was that India was close to civil war. The British Government duly brought forward the date to August 1947.

That Mountbatten could effect a transfer of power in such a short space of time was a remarkable political achievement. However, in the time available, administrative shortcuts were unavoidable. Given that the British Government was in effect creating two new nation states, the territorial issue was paramount, sensitive and divisive. A representative boundary commission was formed and chaired by Sir Cyril Radcliffe to consider Bengal and the Punjab, where the numbers of Muslims and Hindus were more or less equal. The equal balance of votes as between the representatives of the two communities meant however that Radcliffe was frequently left with a casting vote and often took decisions on the basis of insufficient information and, sometimes, downright ignorance.

Of particular importance for the future was the commission's indecisiveness over the northern state of Kashmir. At the time of partition Kashmir had a Hindu ruler but the state was predominantly Muslim. The hereditary Maharaja, Sir Hari Sing, could not decide in which direction to move; joining forces with Pakistan would most certainly have lost him his throne while in the other direction lay the possibility of considerable resentment on the part of his subjects. As a result, in the interests of a rapid settlement the Radcliffe Plan left open the future allegience of Kashmir.

The two-way diaspora which developed around the time of independence for India and Pakistan resulted in confusion, insecurity and atrocious bloodshed. The process of partition resulted in the death of half a million people. The violence of partition exacerbated the existing atmosphere of mistrust, and additional resentment in Pakistan grew over India's *de facto* control of the valley of

Kashmir. In October 1947 tribesmen from Pakistan invaded Kashmir with a view to liberating the Muslims of Kashmir from the Hindu Maharaja. When the raiders reached the valley of Kashmir the Maharaja appealed to New Delhi for help, but the Indian Government refused to commit troops until he ended his procrastination and formally acceded to India. The Maharaja's subsequent period of deliberation and New Delhi's inaction permitted the tribesmen to move right up to the capital of Kashmir, Srinagar. By the time the Indian Government felt able to commit troops, Srinagar was already occupied. The Government had to organize a major airlift of troops, to capture first Srinagar airport and subsequently some portions of the valley.

In early 1948 Prime Minister Nehru referred the Kashmir issue to the United Nations Security Council, although the UN was to recommend a plebiscite in 1949 which would certainly have seen Kashmir leave the Indian Union. (For resolutions and decisions of the UN Security Council on India and Pakistan, see appendix A.) Before a cease-fire could be agreed, on 1 January 1949, Pakistan had committed Army units to Kashmir with sufficient success to occupy a significant proportion of the state in the west, Azad Kashmir, a position from which it has never retreated.

The first Indo-Pakistani War, often referred to as the 'First Round', was the direct result of partition. Since that time relations between India and Pakistan over Kashmir have been acrimonious and embittered—the more so in recent times. One short-lived exception was the agreement arrived at between India and Pakistan in 1972 at Simla in the wake of Pakistan's defeat in the 1971 war, which resulted in the creation of Bangladesh. It included provisional lines of demarcation in Kashmir. In general, however, Pakistan has never been prepared to surrender the territory annexed in 1947–48 and, for its part, India has never intended to fulfil its promise to honour the UN Security Council recommendation for a plebiscite in Kashmir, which is why Kashmir remains a disputed territory. Compounding these problems is the fact that the state of Jammu and Kashmir is strategically important but troublesome in the Indian Union. The state government has frequently expressed opinions which deviate from the preferred position of the centre. Of late, the state has seen the emergence of a strong and committed independence movement, which has required considerable use of force and brutality on the part of the Sikh and Hindu troops against Kashmiri Muslims, to the extent that Amnesty International has been banned from the area.[7] An Amnesty International Report published in March 1992 severely criticized India for its human rights record.[8] Nor is the situation likely to improve during the current rise in Hindu chauvinism which is sweeping through Indian society. Political intervention from New Delhi in Kashmir's affairs is routine and no Indian Prime Minister would risk a plebiscite, such is the degree of mutual mistrust between state and centre.

[7] McKirk, T., 'The vicious little war in India's Camelot', *The Independent,* 17 Sep. 1991.
[8] Amnesty International, *India: Torture, Rape and Deaths in Custody* (Amnesty International: London, Mar. 1991).

III. Statehood and insecurity

The creation of Pakistan affected India in a more profound way than is immediately evident from a historical account of the First Round. The partition of the Indian sub-continent created two nation states whose very existence created for each a national security problem. The war of 1947 merely confirmed what was already suspected in New Delhi and Islamabad, namely that there would be near permanent hostility between the two states into the foreseeable future and probably beyond.

For India, partition had both direct and indirect effects upon national perceptions of security and created a very particular security dilemma.[9] The circumstances of independence and the very creation of Pakistan, in the prevailing atmosphere of suspicion, left a deep sense of insecurity and raised pertinent questions of territorial integrity, national security and sovereignty. First and foremost, it was the prelude to the dispute over Kashmir, which would always be a difficult circle for India to square following the UN resolution. The acceptance of *de facto* borders, effectively ceding at least Azad Kashmir to Pakistan, would amount to a considerable loss of regional prestige for India, international opinion notwithstanding. In addition, to lose all of Kashmir would constitute a loss of security. Given the prevailing regional security equation, it would add to the size and potential resources of Pakistan and alleviate in part Pakistan's primary strategic weakness—a conspicuous lack of defence in depth. Above all, it would cut off India's important supply route to Ladakh, which is fundamental for defence against China.

Henceforth the security configuration in the sub-continent was conditioned by the existence of two nation states whose creation and existence stemmed from religious antipathy, by the 'two nations' theory which held that Hindus and Muslims could only co-exist in separate nation states, and by profound mutual mistrust bordering on hatred. Partition was neither a complete nor a compulsory process. A large number of Muslims remained in India—currently some 80 million—and Indian leaders have habitually assumed that the primary allegiance of the Muslim minority was towards Pakistan. They thus constituted an internal threat and a potential fifth column. This idea has become lodged in the public imagination. Indian voters are quick to use Muslims as a scapegoat for many of the country's internal, domestic problems, as is in part reflected in the rise of the Bharatiya Janata Party (BJP), a radical Hindu party, the growth of strident anti-Muslim sentiments and anti-Pakistani rhetoric in the speeches of Indian politicians.

The Indian élites may have harboured a cultural sense of insecurity following a long history of invasion from the north-west. Prior to the arrival of the British, Indian culture had evolved a unique system for assimilating successful 'invasions', but the period under British rule and subsequent independence had

---

[9] A particular security dilemma but not unique—there is a striking resemblance here to the Middle East and the Arab–Israeli dispute.

moulded India into something approximating a nation state which superseded this well-tried and partially successful cultural mechanism, and independence had created the salient problem of 'national security' which virtually excluded innovation in or alternative views of foreign and defence policy.

Pakistan posed security problems in another sense. Its existence threw into sharp relief the unresolved debate between the theological/Islamic and the ideo-logical/nationalist-secularist definition of nationhood.[10] This is an aspect of South Asian political culture which has taken a particular twist both with the emergence world-wide of Islamic fundamentalism and, in India, with the recent growing popularity and measured electoral success of the BJP.

The very fact of partition overshadowed the political euphoria of indepen-dence for the Indian Congress Party. Having been traditionally the party in favour of a free but undivided India, partition and the very existence of Pakistan were to an extent symbols of what could not be obtained from Mount-batten and the British Government, and therefore a manifest symbol of failure. It was also the partition of a 'motherland' complete with a particularly strong sense of religious geography.[11]

IV. Indian security perceptions and international politics

The rapid crystallization of India's perception of Pakistan took place against the background of an unfolding cold war between the USA and the USSR. The development of Forward Defence Areas and the policy of containment brought Pakistan into the purview of US foreign policy, albeit uneasily, and resulted in sizeable shipments of military aid to facilitate the modernization of a defence force which barely existed after partition. For Pakistan, it was a means to acquire rapidly economic and military capability that would not otherwise have been forthcoming. However, US attempts to encircle the USSR also destabil-ized South Asia by bringing the region into the force field of the cold war. It added a new and dangerous dimension to existing tensions in the region and in part laid the *matériel* foundations for the continuing arms race between India and Pakistan.

In May 1954 Pakistan signed an agreement with the USA which opened the way for military aid on the condition that Pakistan accepted co-operation in a regional defence network directed against the USSR. Pakistan's geographical position was of critical importance to the containment strategy. Apart from Pakistan's borders with Afghanistan and its control over the strategically important Hindu Kush mountain ranges, it was also situated favourably, split as it was between East and West Pakistan and between the regions from which the member countries of both the South East Asia Treaty Organisation (SEATO)

[10] Deshingkar, G., 'Civilisation concerns', *Seminar,* no. 256 (1980), pp. 4–6.

[11] Bhargava, G. S., *South Asian Security after Afghanistan* (Lexington Books: Lexington, Mass., 1983), p. 111.

and Central Treaty Organization (CENTO) were drawn.[12] In September 1955 Pakistan joined CENTO and by the end of the same year it had also joined SEATO.

US President Eisenhower went to considerable pains during 1955 to justify to India the wider rationale for the military aid to Pakistan, but his overture fell on deaf ears. Nehru and key opinion shapers in New Delhi saw the aid as a direct and aggressive move designed to compromise India's foreign policy based upon non-alignment. This resulted in conciliatory statements from the US President and a marked rise in US economic aid to India, again to little effect. Between 1954 and 1964 Pakistan received some $1.5 billion of military assistance from the USA. India received $95 million in military aid, but far greater economic assistance;[13] however, no amount of economic aid could offset the strident remarks from Secretary of State Dulles, who in 1954 considered the Indian policy of non-alignment to be 'an immoral conception'.[14] Nor did policy makers in New Delhi ignore the view held by Vice President Richard Nixon during the same period that a defence alliance with Pakistan would provide 'a counter-blast to the confirmed neutralism of Nehru's India'.[15] Add to this India's extreme reluctance to accept food aid from the USA under Public Law PL480, and the foundations for a mistrustful and awkward relationship were firmly in place by the 1950s.

More to the point, perhaps, US military aid to Pakistan significantly affected the regional military balance. In a sense, a continuing Indian military superiority might have been more successful in preserving whatever regional security existed at the time, if unfairly. All three services in Pakistan benefited substantially from the military aid package, particularly the Air Force. For example, the Army received 460 M-47 and M-48 Patton battle tanks between 1955 and 1965; the Navy received coastal mine-sweepers, two 'CH' class destroyers and, of great importance at the time, a Tench-class submarine in 1964; although it was on loan it was the first acquisition of its kind by a South Asian country; and Air Force strength was increased significantly with the acquisition of 120 F-86F fighters between 1956 and 1958, 26 Martin B-57B Canberra long-range bombers and later, in 1962, the Lockheed F-104 equipped with Sidewinder air-to-air missiles.[16]

Third, the military alliance between Pakistan and the USA, however cosmetic, mutually opportunist and, for the USA intended primarily to deter the expansionist aims of the USSR, pushed India's security problems into another dimension. Henceforth any attempt to steer clear of or rise above the ebb and flow of cold war politics was impossible for India. Conflict and war between

---

[12] CENTO, founded in 1955, at this period consisted of Iran, Iraq, Pakistan, Turkey and the UK. Iraq withdrew in 1959. SEATO was founded in 1954 and at this period consisted of Australia, France, New Zealand, Pakistan, the Philippines, Thailand, the UK and the USA.

[13] George, T., Litwak, R. and Chubin, S., 'The place of India in US foreign policy', in International Institute for Strategic Studies, *India and the Great Powers* (Gower/IISS: Aldershot, 1984), p. 168.

[14] SIPRI, *The Arms Trade with the Third World* (Almqvist & Wiksell: Stockholm, 1971), p. 493.

[15] SIPRI (note 14), p. 493.

[16] SIPRI (note 14), p. 836–37.

India and Pakistan would be more than a regional issue once Pakistan became assimilated into the containment process; India was now unwittingly integrated into the 'seamless web' of international politics. Nevertheless, the process was not entirely in Pakistan's favour, as Islamabad discovered when arms embargoes were applied in 1965 and 1971. In addition, the military aid relationship between China and Pakistan after the 1962 war pushed India indirectly into the proximity of the major dispute between China and the USSR.

This is the background to India's security perceptions *vis-à-vis* Pakistan in the period between 1947 and 1965, 1965 being the date of the second Indo-Pakistani War.

V. Territorial integrity and the threat from the north-west

Having mapped out the historical development of India's external security environment *vis-à-vis* Pakistan, it is now appropriate to measure more precisely where the points of actual insecurity currently lie. A basic rationale for India's security problem is the possibility of future conflict along the Indo-Pakistani border, which is approximately 1100 miles in length, although the Sino-Indian border dilemma is sometimes used as an argument. The Indo-Pakistani border can be divided into five distinct theatres: the Siachin Glacier, Jammu and Kashmir, the Punjab, the Rajasthan desert and the Rann of Kutch.

The Siachin Glacier

The Siachin Glacier is situated to the very north of the *de facto* border between India and Pakistan, within the Karakoram mountain range (for a map of the area see figure 2.1). The strategically important area within Jammu and Kashmir, Azad Kashmir, lost to Pakistan in 1947, consists of about one-third of the state to the north. Within this disputed area, the central focus is the small town of Gilgit. The 1949 Karachi Agreement which brought active hostilities to an end, and the 1972 Simla Agreement (see appendix B) delineated a cease-fire line, now referred to as the Line of Control, which terminated at the Karakoram Pass. The status of the area to the north was never delineated, however, because of the enormous problems which military operations north of Thang have always posed to both sides. Apart from the logistical problems of moving food, fuel and equipment in mountainous regions as high as 6000 metres, temperatures during the winter can drop as low as −40°centigrade and bad weather lasts from October until May. At the time of partition, expending time and energy over the demarcation of such a desolate border made little sense; military technology had not developed sufficiently to warrant the boundary commission's close consideration of the area. Military operations only began during the early 1980s when the appropriate equipment became available to both sides. Because both sides had engaged in a process of using mountaineering expeditions to

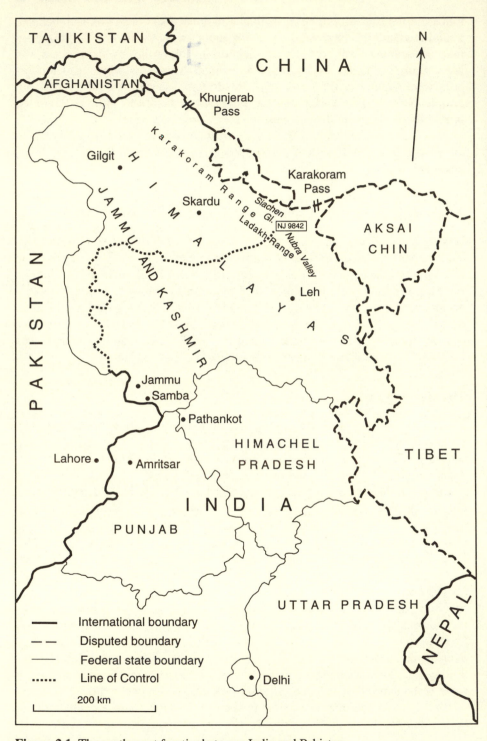

Figure 2.1. The north-west frontier between India and Pakistan

make claims on undemarcated areas of territory on the glacier, however, in 1982 it was recognized by both sides that the cease-fire line should be extended in a straight north-easterly direction to a point immediately south of the Karakoram Pass.

Once it was established, both sides appeared to respect the cease-fire line— until 1984, when Indian troops took possession of the northern end of the glacier, well above the newly established cease-fire line and a *de facto* incursion into Azad Kashmir. In June, India repelled an attack by the Pakistani Army and talks held in 1986 concluded in stalemate. Indian strategists now argue that occupation of the Saltoro heights is no longer negotiable. From this position Indian forces can dominate the landscape and can spot and react to any Pakistani attempt to move towards the Nubra valley, possession of which would allow Pakistani forces to cut off the road from Leh to the Karakoram Pass.[17] The Indian Government now argues that the line of control should go through the Saltoro ridge, which is significantly to the north of NJ 9842 and effectively creates a disputed area of some 10 000 square km.

India's rationale for digging in well beyond the Line of Control agreed in 1982 was not so much the regaining of inhospitable tracts of Kashmir but the potential for closer logistical links between China and Pakistan in the event of a conflict—Tibet borders the entire region which is in dispute. In addition, following the Chinese occupation of the uninhabited Aksai Chin region, India has shown a marked sensitivity to developments or changes in any region, whether inhabitable, inhospitable, or otherwise. Concerns about a further erosion of the government's hold over Kashmir are probably a *post hoc* justification for continued activity in the hardest of environments to minimal effect: once Indian troops had dug in beyond the 1982 line, the issue became one of losing or maintaining face rather than of military advantage, and the posture has proved expensive to maintain in both human and economic terms.

Strategically, there is something to be gained here for Pakistan but, again, it is doubtful whether the advantage is worth the engagement in a conflict of attrition. Pakistan's inherent strategic weaknesses *vis-à-vis* India, which range from a severely underdeveloped resource base to a chronic lack of defence in depth, can be partially offset by the threat of involving India in a two-front war with China. Acquisition of the Siachin Glacier not only places a formidable logistical obstacle behind the Pakistani border; it also increases the common border between Pakistan and China. In the words of an Indian general, 'the strategic Tibet–Sinkiang [Xinjiang] road passes through territory captured by China east of Siachin [in 1962]. Northwards we have a new road from Pakistan going through the Khunjerab Pass. These form a noose [a]round India's jugular. If they took Siachin, they would be holding a dagger to our backs in the Nubra Valley'.[18]

---

[17] Singh, R., 'Siachin Glacier: breaking the ice', *India Today*, vol. 14, no. 13 (15 July 1989), p. 79.
[18] 'Gunfire on the glacier', *India Today*, 31 July 1985, p. 79.

More likely, however, is that the intentions are more limited—Pakistan is scoring some valuable propaganda points and gaining some military experience in high-altitude warfare, whereas the Indian Army is facing a limited conflict of attrition. Pakistan's success in this quarter will increase the importance of the control and sovereignty of the Siachin region for India. It is an area of dispute which could precipitate a full-scale conflict under certain political conditions. Moreover, when placed in historical context, any threat of territorial loss in this region assumes exaggerated dimensions. It would be costly and imprudent for either side to raise the conflict onto another level. Certainly, there is a growing feeling among decision makers in Islamabad that the expense of the campaign is too much and the mood is changing towards compromise if not submission.

Jammu and Kashmir

Further south along the cease-fire line the fundamental problem facing India would come from an unconventional, low-intensity conflict. The provision of aid and arms by Pakistan to the Kashmiri tribesmen could tie down a number of Indian forces in an economical and attritional fashion, although guerrilla-type warfare in this theatre has traditionally never met with great success.[19] Of late, however, the Indian armed forces and the central government have been presented with a series of awkward internal security problems in Kashmir which have been unresolved since the level of repression and violence increased considerably in 1990 and 1991. In February 1987 India evacuated a number of villages along the Kashmir border with Pakistan following shelling by the Pakistani Army. At a point when confidence-building measures in this theatre appeared to be working, anti-government agitation erupted among Kashmiri militants and forced the Indian Government to deploy troops which eventually totalled 300 000, and whose discipline and behaviour caused increased tension and anger. By mid-1990 it seemed that the Kashmir situation might spark another Indo-Pakistani war, and this was probably only avoided because of the level of political and economic risk which both sides would have faced.

In the rest of Jammu and Kashmir, India faces one other threat from Pakistan. The concern is India's strategic weakness around the Samba–Pathankot corridor, which lies to the very south of the state. At the narrowest point of the corridor a mere 90 kilometres (56 miles) separate Pakistan and the steeply rising Himalayas. Above the corridor lies the whole state of Jammu and Kashmir. India fears a surprise attack from Pakistan in this extremely vulnerable area. Such an attack on the corridor could cut off India's rail and road access to the rest of the state. After declaring a cease-fire, Pakistan could open negotiations and offer back to India the seized territory in exchange for the valley of Kashmir, thereby solving the dispute over Kashmir in its favour.[20]

[19] Cohen, S., *The Pakistan Army* (University of California Press: Berkeley, Calif., 1984), p. 147.
[20] Deshingkar, G., 'Can Pakistan take us on?', *The Illustrated Weekly of India,* 5 Aug. 1984, p. 9.

The Punjab

South of Jammu and Kashmir lies the state of Punjab, which presents a completely different set of security problems for India, particularly since the Army action against the holiest of the Sikh shrines, the Golden Temple in Amritsar, in June 1984. The Punjab, which is the home of the Sikhs, is the most productive and wealthy state of the Indian Union—it is often referred to as the bread-basket of India. Lately, it has become the centre of India's most contentious, long-drawn out and violent internal security problem which stems from the Sikh claim to an independent homeland, Khalistan. Sikh militants have proved able and willing to engage in terrorist activity outside the sub-continent, most notably, allegedly, in the bombing of an Air India flight over the Atlantic. In 1990 over 3500 people were killed in related incidents in the Punjab.[21] Here Pakistan holds numerous options for destabilization, which New Delhi claims Islamabad has exploited in recent years. The Indian Government has produced the testimonies of several captured Sikh militants which state that the Pakistani Government has permitted terrorists to establish training and supply camps over the border and few observers now doubt that Pakistan's support for the Sikh cause is a fundamental reason for the latter's success and longevity. This allows the terrorists a crucial advantage which military strategists consider to be essential for the success of this type of long-term operation, namely the existence of a friendly border and access to bolt-holes beyond the reach of counter-insurgency forces, witness the important roles played by Cambodia (for the Viet Cong), Costa Rica (for the Sandinistas) and Iran (for the Kurds) in recent decades. In early 1993 the Indian internal security forces achieved a number of important and seemingly definitive victories against the Sikh militants. Violence in the state is now at its lowest level for several years.

In principle the Punjab could be the staging area for a Pakistani attack upon India, but in practice this is unlikely to be the case. Traditionally, Pakistan has stressed fixed defences in the form of two deep and wide trenches around Lahore, which suggests defence, not attack. India has also built significant fixed defences near the border backed by very elaborate defence-in-depth arrangements. For Pakistan, the capture of Amritsar during a war would be of great psychological importance, but to move beyond the Punjab the Pakistani armed forces would have to cross two major rivers.[22] Given the cost and inherent difficulties of mounting such an operation, it is unlikely to be a realistic choice.

The Rajasthan desert

Further south of the Punjab lies the Rajasthan desert, an area in which much of the armoured fighting between India and Pakistan has taken place in the past.

---

[21] Bedi, R., 'India's reluctant police', *Jane's Defence Weekly*, vol. 16, no. 1 (6 July 1991), p. 22.
[22] Rikhye, R., *The Indo-Pakistan Ground Balance: A Preliminary Analysis* (Centre for the Study of Developing Societies: Delhi, mimeograph, 1984), p. 124.

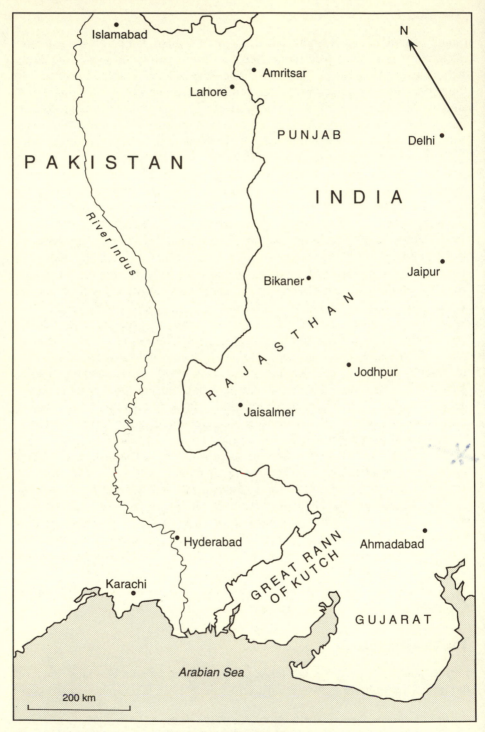

Figure 2.2. The Rajastan desert and the Rann of Kutch

The arid and semi-arid environments lend themselves well to armoured man-œuvre. Here the strategic advantage lies with India, not Pakistan. In this theatre India would seek to advance to the Indus River, capture the road and rail links between north and south, separate the vital port of Karachi from the north and effectively cut Pakistan in two. This was precisely the scenario Pakistan feared during the Indian military exercise of October 1986 to February 1987, code-named Operation Brasstacks, when the Indian Army opted to test its mecha-nized forces in the Rajasthan desert some 60 kilometres from the border across which Pakistan was similarly engaged in winter exercises. (One contentious and probably overstated view holds that Brasstacks was in fact designed to pro-voke a war against Pakistan: through a massive diversion of Pakistan's attention to the Sindh theatre an opportunity would present itself for the libera-tion of Skardu and Gilgit in Azad Kashmir.[23])

Pakistan's options are less straightforward. It would take a long and resourceful campaign to make a major impact beyond the Rajasthan desert by capturing, for example, Jodhpur or Jaiselmer; and a long and resource-intensive campaign is precisely the type of warfare which Pakistan is least equipped to undertake. It would also be necessary to cross the Indira Gandhi Canal. Even an attempt to humiliate India by cutting off the Valley of Kashmir would lead to counter-attacks in other theatres, which Pakistan could certainly not sustain for long without external assistance. Consequently the Pakistani military has few illusions as to how it should conduct a campaign against India; defence doctrine has always stressed the need for rapid results and is now centred upon 'offensive defence' which has replaced the doctrine of 'layered defence', in which military commanders had less faith, the former being the only perceiv-able means of countering India's strategic and *matériel* advantages.[24] Con-versely, the only way Pakistan can counter an Indian attack in force across the Rajasthan desert is by threatening India elsewhere. This is what it chose to do during Operation Brasstacks, but the Punjab border was included as well for good measure.

The Rann of Kutch

Finally, the most southern stretch of the border between India and Pakistan and the least likely theatre of attack is the Rann of Kutch. This area is a large salt waste, equally hazardous and wearing for soldiers and mechanized equipment alike. It is most unlikely that Pakistan or India would see much profit in mounting an attack in this region, although skirmishes did occur in the events leading up to 1965, this also being an area where borders were ill-defined.

[23] Rikhye, R., *The War That Never Was: The Story of India's Strategic Failures* (Chanakya Publications: Delhi, 1988). See also the critical review of this book by a retired Head of Military Intelligence: Sinha, S. K. (Lt Gen.), 'Hawk's eye view', *Indian Express Magazine*, 13 Nov. 1988.

[24] Hussain, M., 'The strike of a True Believer: Pakistan tests new doctrine', *Jane's Defence Weekly*, vol. 12, no. 22 (2 Dec. 1989), pp. 1230–31.

VI. Pakistan: limitations and capabilities

India's security concerns *vis-à-vis* Pakistan should also be seen in relation to the capabilities of the latter. Pakistan is a weak country, both economically and strategically. It would have great difficulty in prevailing in a war against India—resources, both military and civilian, are too limited, international support insufficient and the political and economic costs too high, even if there existed a chance of success in Kashmir.

Pakistan is an extreme example of a state in search of an identity. First and foremost, it is far from certain whether or not Pakistan should ever have existed as a state in its own right, particularly in the configuration of East and West Pakistan. However much internal domestic politics might have necessitated the imposition of borders to separate Hindus and Muslims, it is reasonable to question whether or not the states comprising East Pakistan, now Bangladesh, and (West) Pakistan could not have enjoyed a better future as a represented part of the Indian Union, rather than as a beleaguered state with a continuing and profound sense of insecurity positioned at the crossroads of one of the most strategically important regions of the world. Although India's 80 million Muslims have started to feel the brunt of Hindu chauvinism, this is recent. Certainly, tensions have always existed not far from the surface, but Muslims in India have fared surprisingly well over the past four decades—indeed, their material successes could in part lie behind the renewed animosity from the Hindus. Nevertheless, Pakistan does exist, albeit having suffered the ignominy of partition, and it continues to do so in a state of broad-based and chronic insecurity.

Economically, Pakistan has always been a curious country. It is known for being poor, yet in many respects it is a wealthy country. Following a period of uncontrolled growth in the 1960s economic power became severely concentrated; at one point 22 families controlled 66 per cent of industrial assets, 80 per cent of the banks and 70 per cent of the insurance companies.[25] Pakistan's gross national product (GNP) per capita is one-third higher than India's and the infrastructure—roads, transport and telephones—is the most advanced in South Asia. Although there were set-backs during the Bhutto period his successor, General Zia, presided over annual growth rates of over 6 per cent. The succeeding civilian regimes have been less successful. Agriculture has been a successful sector in recent years, returning annual growth rates of 4 per cent, above population growth.

Indeed, Pakistan has been likened to Israel: it is politically beleaguered by large and powerful countries, but it has been built by migrants with almost as much entrepreneurial spirit as the Jews of Israel. The economy has been growing by an average of 7 per cent per year while population growth is a mere 2.9

---

[25] Vas, E. A., 'Pakistan's security futures', ed. S. P. Cohen, *The Security of South Asia: American and Asian Perspectives* (University of Illinois Press: Chicago, Ill., 1987), p. 88.

per cent.[26] Migrant workers in the Persian Gulf and other non-resident Pakistanis repatriate large quantities of their earnings in foreign exchange, although remittances have been severely curtailed since the onset of the conflict in the Persian Gulf. As with other South Asian economies, however, the impact of the Persian Gulf crisis was considerable, with an estimated 2.4 per cent negative impact on GNP, which followed a period of low oil prices.[27]

Although domestic debt is rising, public investment, education, infrastructure and industry are badly neglected.[28] Government is borrowing heavily from the national banks in anticipation of the introduction of Islamic rules—*sharia*—to control the country's banking system. Pakistan is both indebted and a high military spender: defence expenditure and debt servicing account for 80 per cent of government expenditure. Aid continues to flow into Pakistan but with increasing misgiving.[29] In 1991 Pakistan was instructed by the International Monetary Fund (IMF) to reduce its military expenditure by 9 per cent if future loans were to be forthcoming. Equally damaging, the German Economic Co-operation Minister, Carl-Dieter Spranger, announced in November 1991 that bilateral aid to Pakistan (and India) would be cut by 25 per cent in 1992 because of 'excessive armament'.[30]

In contrast to Israel, there appears to be a lack of commitment to national development or indeed to national democracy. Corruption is rampant— Karachi, for example, is now understood to be ungovernable, hence the recent efforts by the Army to break the power of the Mohajir Qaumi Mahaz (MQM) party and the rural dacoit groups in Sindh.[31] Levels of violence and extortion throughout the country have certainly been rising and small arms proliferation is uncontrolled and has been exacerbated especially by the store of weaponry that found its way into the northern parts of the country as a result of the US response to the Soviet invasion of Afghanistan. Such is the availability of surplus stocks since the Soviet withdrawal that it is now possible to purchase virtually anything on the black market, up to and including sophisticated weapons. Drug trafficking has become a major social and political problem. Industrialists are wary of investment lest elected leaders repeat the profligate and irresponsible nationalization favoured by Bhutto, despite a more open economy than exists in India. These worries are compounded by the appalling state of the nation's infrastructure. As is the case with India, many of Pakistan's best and brightest are working abroad, but the reservoir of talent is much smaller. The Government admits to spending 40 per cent of its revenue on defence, but the

[26] 'Pakistan: living on the edge', *The Economist*, 17 Jan. 1987, pp. 3, 4.

[27] Overseas Development Institute, *The Impact of the Gulf Crisis on Developing Countries* (Overseas Development Institute: London, Mar. 1991), p. 1.

[28] Under Islamic banking laws the charging of interest is forbidden.

[29] 'Pakistan', *Journal of Defense and Diplomacy*, vol. 8, no. 7/8, (July/Aug. 1990), p. 31.

[30] McDonald, H., 'Arms audit: Germany, Soviet Union deliver double shock', *Far Eastern Economic Review*, vol. 154, no. 48 (28 Nov. 1992), p. 20.

[31] Gupta, S., 'Pakistan: changing power equations', *India Today*, vol. 17, no. 18 (16–30 Sep. 1992), pp. 14–20. MQM is a prominent political party.

total is undoubtedly higher.[32] Rich nationals keep a nest-egg of money outside the country.[33] Successive governments, especially military ones, have returned some of the worst human rights records in South Asia. Despite opportunities and potential, there have been as many failures as there have been successes in Pakistan, witness the disappointing and ignominious failure of Benazir Bhutto's Government.

Strategically, Pakistan's situation is more straightforward to assess. To the north, Pakistan faces both Afghanistan and the former USSR. Relations are not normally warm with either of these countries, and during the Soviet occupation of Afghanistan the Government was forced to keep two of its 15 Army divisions in the north, and its strategic problems were further compounded by a mammoth influx of some three million Afghan refugees. To the south, the country is dwarfed by India—one elephant among six pygmies—which has consistently intimidated and, on one occasion, divided Pakistan. Successive governments have been forced to plan around the ever-present possibility of armed conflict with India that would have the effect of weakening the already fragile economic and political cohesion of the country. Conceivably, an aggressive Indian government could plan to drive Pakistan into a state of non-viability without actually facing the problem of absorption.

Since Pakistan's creation its key ally has been the USA, although there have been isolated attempts by the USSR to forge better links. Relations with the USA have never been reliably good and diplomatic problems are rarely far from the surface. Although in recent years Pakistan has received two massive tranches of military and economic aid from the USA, which together amount to almost $8 billion (about 40 per cent of it for military equipment), the relationship is a complex one. First, political and military leaders in Pakistan never fully internalized their role as a client and cold war accomplice. Second, the recently curtailed aid agreement was based upon the dictates of the final chapter of the cold war and the erstwhile Soviet occupation of Afghanistan. It is therefore somewhat unlikely that Pakistan will receive another opportunity of this kind to exploit the key tenets of US foreign policy in the foreseeable future.

Although relations with the Reagan Administration were good, Pakistan failed to convince US President George Bush that they were worth the political and financial investment expended by his predecessor, even though military aid is currently being repaid at 14 per cent interest. Once the USSR withdrew from Afghanistan much, if not all, of the rationale for such high levels of military aid virtually disappeared. The USA will therefore eventually no longer require a consistent conduit for channelling arms to the *mujahideen* and the appropriate means to transport these weapons, namely the Inter-Service Intelligence (ISI) agency. Indeed this may be seen as a significant liability given the level of militarization in the region and the serious decline in law and order. Nor will

---

[32] Wickramanayake, D., 'Indian threat makes defence more important than food', *Defence,* vol. 22, no. 7 (July 1991), p. 14.

[33] 'Pakistan: living on the edge', *The Economist,* 17 Jan. 1987, pp. 3, 4.

the continued conceptual rehabilitation of Pakistan as a Forward Defense Area be possible in the future.

President Bush may also have been more cautious about friendship with present and future leaders of Pakistan than was President Reagan with Zia because of his assessment of military aid in the context of Pakistan's nuclear aspirations. It is conceivable that military aid through the 1980s was based upon more than an attempt to fortify Pakistan as a Forward Defence Area *vis-à-vis* the USSR—that it was also intended to relieve the pressure upon military planners in Islamabad. The severe military imbalance *vis-à-vis* India contributed significantly to the momentum building up behind the nuclear weapon programme. The fact that the US reappraisal appears to have met with a degree of cynicism in Islamabad added weight to the Bush Administration's decision in October 1990 to cross the Rubicon and declare to Congress that, for the first time, the Administration could not certify without equivocation that Pakistan does not possess a nuclear weapon. In November 1990, Congress duly cut the Bush Administration's 1991 overall foreign military aid request, including all aid to Pakistan, which had requested $574 million in foreign economic aid and $228 million in military aid.

Pakistan requires the support of a major power such as the USA primarily because it is an artificial country, created by bureaucrats rather than by history or geography. It is surrounded by hostile neighbours, two of which are more powerful and, moreover, putatively involved with each other in a treaty of co-operation and friendship.[34] This encirclement is to some extent offset by Pakistan's relationship with China, although these links have never been very easy to assess, and its net value of course decreases with the level of *rapprochement* which obtains at any given time between China and India. Currently, the Sino-Pakistani relationship is robust. On the one hand, Pakistan has ceded territory to and has bought defence equipment from China, both in significant quantities; and on the other hand, China is widely alleged to be assisting Pakistan with its nuclear weapon programme, possibly with the testing and handling of fissile material at the criticality stage, but there is as yet no firm evidence for this.

The benefits for China from the sharing of nuclear technology with Pakistan are difficult to discern, particularly given the declared Chinese policy of not sharing nuclear weapon know-how with other countries. Most certainly, the threat and implications of exposure would seem to outweigh the political gain for China against India and the former USSR, especially during the pre-Tiananmen Square period when China was attempting to adjust its external image to facilitate the import of civilian and military technology from the West. Nevertheless, there are several observers, some of whom claim to be in possession of classified information, who are convinced that nuclear collaboration is occurring. However, if China was reluctant before 1989, it may now feel less

[34] Pakistan and Iran were alleged to be potentially successful theatres of attack for the Soviet Union's Operational Manoeuvre Group. Though unlikely, this gives some idea of the type of scenario Pakistan has had to take into consideration. See Bellamy, C., *The Future of Land Warfare* (Croom Helm: London, 1987), pp. 113–24.

restrained; given the level of international disapprobation which the state has since invited it may feel that it can hardly do much more to create offence. To some extent, this is reflected in its arms export policy, which is consistent with the 'nothing to lose' policy of a pariah state, for example, the decision in 1993 to defy the international community's attempts to eliminate the further horizontal proliferation of nuclear-capable missiles by selling M-11 missiles to Pakistan. On the other hand, China's decision to accede to the Non-Proliferation Treaty (NPT) will push in the opposite direction, as will the imposition of sanctions by the USA.

Above all, however, Pakistan's strategic weakness stems from the fact that it is topographically very difficult to defend. It is a narrow country and most of the industrial centres and major cities lie unfortunately close to the Indian border, on which there are no geographical impediments such as a major river or a mountain range to slow advancing forces. Karachi, Pakistan's only major port, is relatively easy for India to blockade, especially given its naval superiority and Fleet Air Arm. Those responsible for defence in Pakistan therefore confront the problem on two fronts, land and sea, and are forced to consider the protection of 90 per cent of the population and the greater part of the infrastructure and economic assets.[35] Pakistan's vulnerable strategic position and economic weakness have forced defence planners to adopt a policy based upon offensive defence; quite simply the armed forces can never allow themselves the option of ceding territory in order to regroup. Thus, during a crisis, Pakistan is likely to be the first to escalate to armed conflict and, moreover, will employ heavy force in order to gain an initial advantage. Such a small country cannot trade space for time, nor can it sustain a war that lasts for longer than 10 or 14 days without massive resupply—here again, the parallels with Israel are considerable. (Pakistan is also heavily reliant upon US defence equipment and it is US policy to keep its clients on a short leash so that Washington is able to determine, or at least influence significantly, the outcome of any armed conflict in which client states become involved.)

Equally important to Pakistan is the stress upon superior generalship and the high performance of its weapon systems.[36] Therein, however, lies something of a paradox for the country's decision makers. Given the declining interest on the part of the USA, which would probably have occurred over time with or without the mounting evidence pertaining to the nuclear weapon programme, Pakistan cannot afford to induct the type of sophisticated equipment it needs to maintain a doctrine based on offensive defence. The alternative is to revert to 'Lanchester's Law' which states that in the face of superior weaponry it is necessary to outnumber the enemy by a factor of between two and four. In view of India's considerable quantitative and qualitative advantage over Pakistan, this would require a massive rearmament programme, albeit involving less sophisticated equipment, and it is highly unlikely that international finance organiza-

[35] Tellis, A., 'India's naval expansion: reflections on history and strategy', *Comparative Strategy*, vol. 6, no. 2 (1987).
[36] See Cohen (note 19), p. 142.

tions would turn a blind eye, given the inevitable rise in procurement costs and the increasing interest on the part of those organizations in military expenditures.

Both before and after 1971, the date marking the creation of the state of Bangladesh, Pakistan has always been a weak and exposed state. At no point, except perhaps during the Kashmir operation of 1948, has it been able to pursue a defence policy and posture any more ambitious than that of maintaining a capability which will raise significantly the cost to India of an attack. Indeed, even Pakistan's pursuit of a nuclear option can be seen in this way.

These views are rarely shared by policy makers in New Delhi. Given the country's natural disadvantages and weak economy, it is difficult to see from which direction, bar regional *détente*, Pakistan will acquire the type of security it needs to work towards political and economic development. If India's foreign and defence policy towards Pakistan really is geared towards forcing it to spend beyond its means, with all the associated political, economic and social problems that this entails, the strategy has met with a reasonable amount of success. However, it is also the case that Pakistan has itself made the task that much easier for decision makers in New Delhi by failing to redress the deep-seated generic problems of corruption, poor governance and unbalanced civil–military relations, to which must also be added a consistent failure to recognize geopolitical facts of life, namely India's natural supremacy; a nation in search of peace should hardly be quite so supportive of neighbouring terrorist organizations.

Indian decision makers do not believe that Pakistan is capable of unpicking or even unhinging the Indian Union through military operations in Kashmir or elsewhere, although successive governments have traditionally gained enormous political capital from a stress upon the military threat from the north-west and the linkages to the wider East–West conflict. In particular, during the final months of Indira Gandhi's last term of office, the Government was all too quick to spot 'gathering war clouds' on the Indo-Pakistani border or 'foreign hands' at work inside the country—witness the tone of government press releases and partisan media statements over this period.

The real threat from Pakistan for India is much more complex and inchoate. India's real regional vulnerability stems not from a great power presence in the Indian Ocean or from Pakistan or China *per se*. The threat lies in India's own structural political weaknesses and the potency of centrifugal forces which run through the whole country, in Nagaland, Manipur, the Punjab, Goa, Tamil Nadu and Darjeeling, for example. What really concerns the more sober and thoughtful Indian security analysts is the link between partition in 1947 and the potential Balkanization of the Indian Union. Pakistan is an example of a minority that has achieved separation. Are anti-centre sentiments in the Punjab and Darjeeling symptomatic of the same basic problem which led to partition in 1947? Could one charismatic leader or more from one or several of these rebellious outposts, with sound financial resources and organizational skills, succeed in doing to the Indian Union what Pakistan could never hope to do itself but would probably enjoy witnessing?[37] Indeed, was the partition of Pakistan in 1971, in which India played such a catalytic role, a part of the same process? Consider also the inordinate and destabilizing effect on the Indian polity of the assassinations of Indira and Rajiv Gandhi; both assassinations were linked to separatist militant groups.

At one and the same time Pakistan is both tied to India's internal weaknesses and an external security threat. The fact that Pakistan can to some extent aid the centrifugal forces, particularly in the Punjab and Kashmir, and gain relative strength from the weakening of the Indian Union is an integral part of the security equation in the region. Moreover, this is more likely to happen to a state which increasingly lacks both popular legitimacy and substantial economic and military resources, a scenario which many might argue is India's medium-term future if some form of political and economic recovery fails to take root before the turn of the century. Terrorist organizations have perhaps grasped this concept.

Independence required India to become a nation state in contrast to the more fluid and absorbent political culture which obtained for centuries before the arrival of the British. The nation state was an alien and untried political format which exaggerated the authority and rule of the centre and, furthermore, presented the new Government in 1947 with the unusual problems of nation statehood, of which territorial integrity was an example. In essence, the relationship between the British Indian Empire and the kingdoms was somewhat benign, founded as it was upon a mutuality of interests or exploitation. Because India became a nation state at independence with a federal constitution which institutionalized centre–state relations in a different way, based more upon Western political culture, the power relationship changed. Legislative rather than cultural mechanisms, such as the imposition of a common language (Hindi) and revenue disbursements from the centre to the states, were used as a means of binding the 'nation' together to a degree which had no precedent. The conflicts and frictions which have resulted are a considerable source of confusion for India.[38] In addition to these structural conflicts there are majority–minority conflicts and Hindu–Muslim tensions especially. The speed and ease with which the current anti-Muslim campaign has taken root is evidence of this. Significantly, any dispute involving the Muslim minority in India always generates protests in Pakistan.

From these perspectives it is possible to understand better why Indian opinions, particularly those based upon Hindu chauvinism, still consider Pakistan to be a salient security threat, even though both the 1965 and 1971 wars (the Second and Third Rounds) went in India's favour, the latter in particular. Pakistan may not pose a significant military threat to India, and probably never

[37] External financial assistance is an important but neglected factor. Disaffected minorities have tended to migrate which over time yields sources of income for weapons and propaganda, witness the help available for Croats, Israelis, Punjabis and Tamils.

[38] For a perceptive discussion of state formation in India see Rudolph, L. I. and Rudolph, S. H., *In Pursuit of Lakshmi: The Political Economy of the Indian State* (University of Chicago Press: Chicago, Ill., 1987), pp. 60–98.

will on account of its strategic and economic weakness. Instead, Pakistan poses an altogether different type of threat, much less quantifiable than those which are rooted in strength, power and territoriality. It is the view of many decision makers that if Pakistan cannot be controlled and the power relationship maintained, the internal centrifugal forces could proliferate and bring about further acts of partition. Conceivably, with sufficient support and encouragement, Muslims and Sikhs could provide a Trojan horse on behalf of the Pakistani Government which could break up the Indian Union and thereby reduce the security problems for Pakistan. Khalistan would provide a useful buffer state and continuing friction between Kashmir and New Delhi does Pakistan little harm at all. It is particularly relevant to note the difference in India's approach to China, which had the distinction of inflicting on India its worst national humiliation in 1962 and possesses the military means to humiliate India in no uncertain terms, including a nuclear strike. Pakistan has no such capability yet, but it is always considered within India to be a far greater threat to security than China, even when Sino-Indian relations are at low ebb.

VII. India's national security problems and Sri Lanka

The complex relationship between internal and external security can also be clearly identified in relations between Sri Lanka and India. The population of Sri Lanka comprises a mixture of the indigenous Sinhalese (74 per cent) and the Tamils who originate from the south Indian state of Tamil Nadu. Tamils in Sri Lanka fall into two groups. First, there are those who emigrated to Sri Lanka over the course of several centuries and, second, there are those who were brought in by the British to work the tea plantations and who still see India as their homeland.

Separatist troubles have simmered since the mid-1960s but became particularly acute in the 1980s. Because of the mounting number of Tamil casualties the Indian Government inevitably became involved, and relations between the two governments deteriorated. In 1986 Rajiv Gandhi's Government adopted a two-pronged policy of limiting the effectiveness of the Tamils by closing down bases in Tamil Nadu while simultaneously placing pressure upon the Sri Lankan Government to improve the existing devolution offers to the Tamil Tigers. These attempts failed and led to a marked increase in violence and bloodshed. As Sri Lanka slipped towards anarchy in 1987 the Indian Government intervened decisively. Rajiv Gandhi and Prime Minister Jayawardene managed to reach an accord which was rejected by both Sinhalese and Tamils. As the violence increased still further the Indian Government took a major decision and sent a peace-keeping force, which eventually reached a number larger than that of the Sri Lankan Army. In 1990 Indian troops were withdrawn, having achieved little.

The Sri Lankan problem failed to go away, however. As long as Tamil Nadu remained a base and training ground for Tamil separatists, the Indian

Government was inextricably involved. Moreover, by the 1990s the Tigers had established more of a stronghold than a bolt-hole in Tamil Nadu. This included their own communications network, a virtual government in the camps and open defiance of customs and immigration laws. State leaders were unwilling to interfere with Tamil operations because they were popular, and the imposition of President's Rule (direct rule from New Delhi and a suspension of the state legislature) also had little effect. The more Sri Lanka slid into a state of anarchy, the more complex and intractable the problems became for New Delhi; all attempts at reconciliation, accord and conflict resolution seemed to fail, and as militancy on both sides in Sri Lanka became more widespread so the chances of success and compromise receded.

A turning-point was reached with the assassination of Rajiv Gandhi when he was electioneering in Tamil Nadu. The assassination was undoubtedly the work of the Tamil Tigers and produced considerable anti-Tiger feeling in all Tamil states. The motive for it is interesting where security issues are concerned. There were three possible motivations. First, it is possible that Rajiv Gandhi reiterated the Congress(I) Party's manifesto—which stated that Sri Lanka's Tamils should be prepared to live in Sri Lanka but with greater autonomy and thereby surrender claims to independent statehood—during a cordial meeting with Kasi Anandhan, a Liberation Tigers of Tamil Eelam (LTTE) central committee member. Such a policy was anathema to the Tigers, and Rajiv Gandhi would almost certainly have been the next Indian Prime Minister. Second, during the negotiations surrounding the 1987 peace accord, Rajiv Gandhi placed the Tamil leader Parbhakaran under house arrest until he signed the accord. The assassination could thus have been founded on a long-standing grudge. Third, and of greatest significance, the Tamil Tigers may have judged that India's short-term unity lay largely in the hands of Rajiv Gandhi and that with the Congress dynasty firmly in place an independent Tamil state—Eelam—was impossible.[39] In recent months, the Indian Government has moved against the LTTE camps in India. In May 1992 it declared LTTE an illegal organization in India and has closed down its bases in Tamil Nadu. The fact that this occurred almost a full year after the assassination of Rajiv Gandhi says much about the difficulties facing the Union Government.

VIII. Bangladesh and the Himalayan kingdoms

Indian governments have traditionally given priority to the security threat from the north-west, often if not always to the exclusion of other concerns. Before 1971, East Pakistan (now Bangladesh) was not considered salient; from an economic, political and military point of view it was never seen as a threat even when it was a part of Pakistan, and much less so after 1971. Bangladesh is neither a grave security threat to India nor a theatre which has any strategic or

---

[39] Gupta, S., Viswanathan, A. and Shetty, K., 'Assassination probe: fitting the pieces', *India Today*, vol. 16, no. 12 (16–30 June 1991), pp. 35–36.

economic interest. Essentially, and unfortunately, it is composed of a massive delta which links the sub-continent's major rivers to the Bay of Bengal. The Brahmaputra runs from north to south and cuts the country approximately down the middle and is joined from the east by the Meghna. The country is divided yet again in the west by the Ganges.

Despite Bangladesh's dreadful poverty, which is made annually worse by extreme population increase and environmental damage, the country has shown a remarkable cohesion and resilience. The population of over one million is almost heterogeneous—the vast majority are Bengalis and 90 per cent of the population is Muslim. Following the 1971 war and the creation of Bangladesh, relations with India were initially cordial. However, anti-Indian sentiments grew over time, possibly nurtured by the military regime, until the late 1970s when tension erupted over the Farakka Barrage—an attempt to unsilt the Hoogly river and increase the water flow into Calcutta port—and claims to *chars,* the fluvial islands which rise up in the delta from time to time. In particular trouble mounted over claims to the Purbasha Char, due to rumours of oil potential.[40] The recent decision by India to lease a corridor of territory to Bangladesh to provide access to the sea indicates how superficial security concerns are in reality. However, the recent influx of Bangladeshi refugees may well be a considerable irritant if it proceeds unchecked.

Whatever the current and potential disputes with Bangladesh, be they closer links with India's adversaries, assistance to secessionist factions in the Indian states to the east of the country, or territorial contests, Bangladesh can hardly face up squarely to India. Its armed forces are largely starved of equipment—Bangladesh rarely spends more than 2 per cent of GNP on defence—although they are well catered for in their cantonments, which is a means of ensuring minimal interest in the affairs and workings of state. India may be frequently annoyed by Bangladesh but it has never felt insecure, nor is this likely to happen in the future.

It is also possible to exclude the security threat posed by the other small states such as the Himalayan kingdoms. Although the South Asian Association for Regional Co-operation (SAARC) process may in time evolve to offer these countries a less impotent role, they barely figure in India's security calculus. Bhutan has been loosely integrated into India's defence system. Relations with Nepal have been more fractious, witness a recent dispute which engendered a firm response from New Delhi. Following an arms deal between Nepal and China, India rescinded the bilateral trade and transit agreement which was a crucial economic agreement for landlocked Nepal. Although relations soon returned to normal in 1989, this only came when Nepal tacitly acquiesced to a more accommodating arrangement which both benefited Nepal and underlined India's strategic preponderance in the region.

[40] Rizvi, G., 'The role of small states in the South Asian complex', eds B. Buzan and G. Rizvi, *South Asian Insecurity and the Great Powers* (Macmillan: London, 1986), pp. 131–36.

Sikkim, east of Nepal, was until 1975 a protectorate of India and is now the twenty-second state of the Indian Union. Between Sikkim and Tibet there are several passes which can be used throughout the year. Furthermore, Sikkim is rich in timber and mineral resources and is close to Tibet in terms of culture and ethnicity. The strategically important Chumbi valley lies between Sikkim and Bhutan but is a part of Tibet. It is often described as a dagger pointed at India. Further south lies the Jalpaiguri district, a narrow corridor between Nepal and Bangladesh. This area is only 150 miles from the Chumbi valley and links all the north-eastern states of India to the rest of the country.[41]

IX. The China question

In the late 1940s China underwent tremendous internal upheaval which culminated in the dominance of communism. Until then China posed no threat either to South Asia or to the buffer states which separated the two major Asian powers. Initially, the state of complacency continued; during the 1950s, Mao Zedong was concerned with the major powers, the Korean War, internal consolidation and retrenchment. Consequently, Nehru did not consider China to be either an immediate threat or a serious security consideration, although after China's entry into Tibet in 1950 he took rapid steps to include Nepal in India's defence perimeter and extend Indian administration into Tawang, a monastery town beyond the MacMahon Line, the border recognized by the governments of India and Tibet but not by China in 1914.

In addition, the mid-1950s was the Bandung period and the spirit of non-alignment influenced India's perception of Chinese communism.[42] The Indian Government saw in Bandung not only a spirit of general non-alignment and neutralism but also a special relationship with China, the other major Asian power. *Hindi-Chini Bhai Bhai* (the brotherhood of Indians and Chinese) became the slogan of the day. Perhaps the goodwill between Beijing and Delhi was based on pragmatism as well, for the evolution of a 'third force' in international politics could barely succeed without the participation of both.

In later years the spirit and intention of non-alignment and neutralism continued, albeit in a battered form. Cordial relations between India and China did not. Immediately after the success of the Chinese revolution, India was one of the first countries to recognize communist China and extend goodwill. The dispatch of one of New Delhi's most able diplomats to become ambassador in Beijing was intended to show how well-disposed India was to communist China. However, reciprocation on the part of Mao was hardly fulsome; Peking initially referred to the Indian Government as both a 'puppet' of imperialism

---

[41] Bandyopadhyaya, J., *The Making of Indian Foreign Policy* (Allied Publishers: New Delhi, 1979), pp. 34–36.

[42] The Bandung Conference (1955) was the first large-scale gathering of Asian and African states, and led to the creation of the Non-Aligned Movement.

and an obstacle to movements of national liberation.[43] It was only when India proved its neutrality in the Korean War that China grudgingly accepted India's anti-imperialist credentials. Towards the end of the 1950s, Sino-Indian relations deteriorated rapidly.

Ideology aside, China's policy towards India concerned Tibet, a desire for a permanent incorporation of Tibet into China and a concomitant fear of Indian objections and even covert support to Tibetan independence. For China, the annexation of Tibet was the final stage in the unification of the 'five races' in China. However, such a move would give India and China a shared and 'live' frontier. The Chinese therefore had to legitimize and control the situation. The process was a crude one; the 'liberation' of Tibet was accompanied by the denigration of India, particularly after the Dalai Lama fled to India.

Despite the initial impulse of Beijing to create an atmosphere of hostility, Nehru refused to be drawn. India's, or rather Nehru's, foreign policy was conditioned by the belief that China would not threaten India directly because Beijing was preoccupied with both internal and external problems. Thus, Nehru felt that a policy of friendship would best serve India's ends and that the 'third force' was worth a great deal to India's security in both the long and the short term. India could not afford either a war or a policy based upon deterrence through strength.

As a result, Nehru pursued a distinct policy of appeasement towards China on the Tibet question. Ideally, Nehru would have preferred China to accept a low-profile relationship with Tibet based upon a system of suzerainty guaranteeing extensive autonomy for Tibet. To this end, during the discussions over the Sino-Indian treaty on Tibet, the Indian negotiators accepted the inclusion of a reference to the 'Tibet region of China'. Nevertheless, towards the end of the 1950s, a dispute over the Sino-Indian border arose and rapidly became intractable. Nehru continued to hope for a solution in India's favour based upon diplomacy but the Chinese Government wanted a package deal which included concessions by both sides. When Nehru's Government expressed its complete inflexibility on the issue, the Chinese resorted to meaningless polemic, holding 'the Indian bourgeoisie and their expansionist tendencies' responsible for the impasse.

For India the Himalayan frontier is of critical strategic importance in relation to China. This has been the case since the time of the British Indian Empire. In addition, the creation of a buffer zone in Tibet is particularly important given the complicated geopolitics of the area which comprises today's northern and eastern India, northern Pakistan, Tibet and the Chinese province of Xinjiang, Bhutan, Sikkim and Nepal.

To the extreme north-west the part of Kashmir controlled by Pakistan is contiguous with the Xinjiang province of China and close to Tajikistan. The area separating Tajikistan and Pakistan is the Wakhan corridor, which has been

[43] Thomas, R. G. C., *The Defence of India: A Budgetary Perspective of Strategy and Politics* (Macmillan: Delhi, 1978), pp. 40–41.

largely depopulated since the Soviet invasion of Afghanistan. Linking Pakistan to China is the mountain pass which now carries a highway through the Karakoram mountain range linking Gilgit to Kashgar in Xinjiang.

East and a little south of this point is the Aksai Chin area which is occupied by China but claimed by India. Further south there is a narrow parcel of land controlled by India which borders Tibet but has no natural communications features. South of Ladakh there is a short border between Himachal Pradesh (India) and Tibet which contains the strategically important Spiti Pass and below this area is the even more significant Shipki Pass, which used to be an ancient trade route but now links up to the Xinjiang–Tibet Highway. The northern border of Uttar Pradesh also borders Tibet with several passes that are also in proximity to the Xinjiang–Tibet Highway due to a complex network of ancient trade routes. Further south Nepal and Tibet share a border. There are several passes which can be penetrated. The Nara Pass, the Kodari Pass and the Rasa Pass are all points of access for China into Nepal and it is the exposed plains of Nepal which run into the Indo-Gangetic plain, the heartland of eastern India.

After backing down over the question of China's suzerainty over Tibet and by tacitly accepting the Chinese Government's claims to 'liberate' Tibet, India lost the Tibetan buffer and sought thereafter to reach a working agreement with communist China over the MacMahon Line. The attempts failed and throughout the late 1950s relations with China grew steadily worse. India, to bolster its claims on the ground, adopted a 'Forward Policy' which put Indian troops behind Chinese positions. In 1960 and 1961, sporadic border incidents occurred and grew more frequent. In April 1962 the eight-year agreement over Tibet between India and China expired and Chinese activity in the disputed region intensified. In September 1962 war broke out and the Indian Army suffered its worst and most humiliating defeat in an area in which it had long shown neglect and uninterest. The ramifications of defeat in this war are considered in chapter 4 in relation to defence policy and posture.

X. The Indian Ocean

When India became independent all security threats were deemed to come from the north-west. Indian policy makers never appeared particularly concerned about threats from the sea. This was in part because the Indian Ocean was still patrolled by the British Royal Navy. Indian defence decision makers however also decided to avoid too great an emphasis upon naval power because of the resources required to build up a blue water navy capable of projecting power throughout the Indian Ocean.[44] In later years, particularly during the 1980s, this policy was reversed as policy makers came to see a much greater need for naval deterrence.

---

[44] Alternatively, a 'brown' water navy is capable of little more than coastal defence.

The Indian Ocean is the third largest ocean in the world, after the Pacific and the Atlantic; it extends over 75 million square km. India is one of the most geopolitically important littoral states in the region. It lies at the very centre of an immense 'bay' reaching from the Cape of Good Hope around to the Australian city of Perth. Immediately after World War II it was the Atlantic and Pacific Oceans which attracted the attention of defence planners in the major powers, mostly because of the cold war and the proximity of the superpowers to both oceans. The Indian Ocean was still considered to be a British 'lake', for good reason. After the war the UK maintained a considerable naval interest in the region and among certain littoral states, such as Aden (now Yemen), Malaysia and Singapore. Over 100 000 British troops were stationed in the littoral islands and over 10 per cent of the UK's defence expenditure was earmarked for operations in the Far East.[45] Under these conditions India had little to be concerned about in this theatre. Pakistan had no real naval capability until the 1960s and China had no access—in order to reach the Indian Ocean the Chinese Navy would have been forced to go through the Straits of Malacca and/or Sunda, thus placing itself in direct confrontation with the UK.

In the 1960s Indian policy makers recognized the need for a more conscious maritime strategy and policy changed significantly. By the early 1960s it became evident that Indonesia considered itself a significant maritime power and, moreover, laid claim to the Nicobar Islands which were under India's control. A marked decline in relations between India and Indonesia was arrested only when the Sukarno Government collapsed in 1965.

Equally important for India was the British Prime Minister Harold Wilson's decision in late 1967 to withdraw armed forces from all points east of Suez. Wilson wanted to direct more attention and resources to Europe and was equally aware of the growing fragility of the British economy. This effectively created a power vacuum which was filled primarily by the two superpowers. By the mid-1970s the region had become of particular significance for both powers. Apart from the retreat of the UK and the felt need to compete for new strategic advantage, the superpowers had other reasons for reassessing their position in the Indian Ocean.

For the USSR, involvement in the Indian Ocean theatre and efforts to curry favour with several littoral states, India included, represented an attempt to cancel the successes of the US strategy of containment. In addition, ideology was important. Along the littoral there were many states, including India and Indonesia, which could be coaxed close to the Soviet camp. These were countries which displayed a leaning towards socialism even if their own communist parties were ignored and marginalized.

The question which is rarely asked inside or outside New Delhi is where Indian security interests and the presence of major naval powers in the Indian Ocean conflict. Over the past decade the Ministries of External Affairs and

---

[45] Braun, D., *The Indian Ocean: Region of Conflict or 'Zone of Peace'?* (C. Hirst: London, 1983), p. 93.

Defence have voiced criticism and concern about the increase in non-Indian defence capability in the Indian Ocean. However, few have asked how much these developments actually impinge upon the security interests of India. Nor has there been any appreciable attempt at an official level to fit naval threat perception to appropriate response in this particular theatre. The advantage to India in having the US presence in the region to guarantee the uninterrupted flow of oil from the Gulf is similarly overlooked. India too needs to import oil from the Persian Gulf and the international community's treatment of oil reserves as sacrosanct may in the future benefit India as it now does most Organization of Petroleum Exporting Countries (OPEC) countries, for India too has potentially enviable oil reserves within striking distance of many Islamic countries.

There are two ways to assess India's insecurity from the direction of the Ocean. First, what is the possibility that India might be invaded by an enemy approaching from the Indian Ocean? Second, how much are India's regional and international interests threatened by the recent activities of certain major powers in the Indian Ocean?

From a purely military perspective India does have a sense of weakness in the south. Ironically, it suffers from a marked surfeit of defence in depth. India's defence arrangements traditionally concentrate the country's defence in the north, although a Southern Command has recently been established and the Government has been inclined to draw some of its military capabilities further to the south, out of the range of Pakistan's air power. The national capital is well to the north, and its position is important for a country with a poor infrastructure. Furthermore, there is a cultural and political divide separating north and south which might complicate the Indian response to an invasion from the south.

However, it is difficult to conceive of a situation in which India would be threatened by outright invasion from this direction. New Delhi has created of late a blurred image of a threat from the ocean but it is no more than that. The only theoretically conceivable threat is from the USA, but to most observers outside India, and to many inside as well, there is no circumstance in which India could be threatened from this quarter. It is difficult to see why foreign policy and defence planners see such a degree of insecurity in this theatre. It is perhaps for this reason that the threat is articulated in the vaguest of terms.

Second, India's perspective on the Indian Ocean raises some interesting questions. The foreign nationals of Indian descent who reside in island or littoral states in the Indian Ocean number approximately 4.6 million.[46] However, the Indian Government has shown no particular strength of feeling when it comes to the often disturbing status of these minorities in East Africa (Uganda and now Kenya), Burma and Malaysia, for example. In the late 1980s, the plight of Indians in Fiji and Sri Lanka has caused much greater concern but

---

[46] Elkin, J. F., 'New Delhi's Indian Ocean Policy', *Naval War College Review*, vol. 15, no 4/3 (autumn 1987), pp. 52–53.

mainly for political, not humanitarian, reasons. Nevertheless, there are other factors which a government might consider important. Many of these migrants are traders, often from Gujarat and Tamil Nadu. As such they establish good links with Indian businessmen, thereby increasing India's trade advantage in the region. Some are comparatively wealthy and through kinship ties they repatriate considerable sums of foreign exchange to India.

Raw materials are also important. Since the early 1980s India has developed its oil industry and the newest fields are located off Bombay High and the Orissan coast, and the areas off the Kerala coast and around the Andaman Islands offer good potential.[47] Existing oilfields provide a good proportion of India's fossil fuel requirements and are essential to economic development and to the military's petrol, oil and lubricant requirements. Furthermore, India has a substantial merchant navy and the Indian Ocean is potentially rich in mineral deposits, such as manganese and other metallic nodules.

These commercial and economic attributes clearly add up to something worth protecting. However, translating the protection of these assets into a part of the security equation is difficult. The treatment of Indian nationals in countries such as Fiji, Kenya and Uganda has not by and large drawn a particularly militant response from the Indian Government. In reality, the Indian Government is impotent to act outside the sub-continent, just as Western governments can do little about the harsh legal penalties imposed upon Western narcotics smugglers convicted in Asia. The protective wall of sovereignty is difficult to breach, short of invasion. One exception was Sri Lanka, where 70 000–100 000 Indian troops were stationed during the late 1980s. In addition, in 1988 an Indian task force successfully prevented a *coup d'état* in the Maldives. In the same year unsubstantiated but probably exaggerated reports emerged suggesting that the Government was considering sending a naval task force to Fiji in a display of forceful protest against the disenfranchisement of Fijian Indians.

Nor can it be convincingly argued that India faces the prospect of a resource war within its Exclusive Economic Zone. Its off-shore oilfields constitute only a partial source and are not likely to attract aggressive foreign exploiters. In the case of mineral reserves, conflicts over these will be contested in international courts of law and United Nations forums, not the ocean itself. In this respect, the naval presence of the superpowers and the increasing strategic importance of the region will serve as an unintended benefit for India. A country such as Indonesia would be very reluctant to wage a regional resource war in such a sensitive area and the international community would be keen to prevent a collision between regional powers.

Despite the undeniable fact that India is a rising middle-rank power, it has little to fear in either a territorial or an economic sense from the present configuration of power in the Indian Ocean. Unless India seeks to extend significantly

[47] Sidhu, W. P. S. and Katiyar, A.,'Bidding for black gold', *India Today,* vol. 14, no. 18 (16–30 Sep. 1991), pp. 51–52.

its sphere of interest, military activities in the Indian Ocean short of nuclear war will not affect dramatically the health and welfare of the Indian state.

Finally, given the remarkable changes in international affairs in 1990, which continue at the time of writing, it is relevant to question how the Indian state may be affected following the end of bipolarity, the crisis in the Gulf and the ascendency of the USA to an unparalleled position of international power.

At this point the Indian Government has taken little notice of the way the evolving international system might affect the sub-continent. The main reason for this is the parlous state of India's economy and the massive political changes which have occurred since the assassination of Rajiv Gandhi. Although the Congress(I) Party has been re-elected, its hold on power is weak. Coupled with the country's declining economic fortunes, attention to foreign affairs has been relatively subdued in recent months. The political impact upon India of the Persian Gulf crisis was not great, although the economy suffered considerably, many Indian nationals became refugees following the invasion of Kuwait, and the knock-on effects of higher oil prices and reduced remittances should not be ignored. Prime Minister Chandra Shekhar was forced to reverse his decision to allow US aircraft to refuel at Bombay because of a surprising amount of support for Iraq throughout the country; this may have been as much anti-USA as it was pro-Iraq.

XI. Domestic, regional and international: India and the seamless web of security

An essential aspect of the regional security problem for India lies in the historical development of the Indian state. External observers often fall into the trap of analysing Indian security perspectives from two positions which both lack the required depth. First, there is a tendency to adopt a tidy but ahistorical approach which ignores the elements of continuity and discontinuity which may exist between the major periods of Indian history. The complex and unique development of the Indian nation state and the relationship to contemporary foreign and defence policies is overlooked. Certainly the development of India's security dilemma can be dated from independence and partition. The response of India the nation state to external threats may be in part both shaped and complicated by what existed before. Second, analysts tend also to see the Indian nation state as a convenient but superficial unit. Internal contradictions may not be inextricably linked to external perceptions but there is a relationship between the two, which is becoming more permanent.

That security problems exist for India, or more precisely the Indian Union, is not in question. Although the state is relatively safe from external invasion, and has been since 1947, its very survival is in part threatened by events and entities inside its borders, particularly Sikh extremism until recently. Furthermore, these internal contradictions have made an impact upon, and are linked to, India's relations with other South Asian countries. Thus, for as long as marked centrifugal tendencies exist internally, India will be less secure within South Asia. Conversely, to a certain degree the Indian Government requires an external threat in the shape of Muslim Pakistan or communist China as a part of a negative nation-building process. At critical points external threats may create a form of internal, domestic political cohesion, which is far from evident in contemporary India under normal conditions.

The troublesome aspects of India's security problems are twofold. First, the resolution of South Asia's security problems in general seems at present to be infinitely more complicated than the type of 'security dilemma' which exists in the West. For the future, the tenuous 'no war, no peace either' stalemate will depend largely on the ability of the Indian state to understand, manage and control its domestic problems. Yet there does not appear to be either the political capability or the political will to grasp this particular nettle; never before has Indian politics seemed so bereft of purpose. As so many conflicts between the centre and the state governments become time-honoured and reluctantly accepted by the polity as unfortunate facts of contemporary life, solutions will become more difficult and the tendency to use regional problems to explain domestic crises will be more tempting; the automatic reaction of blaming Pakistan for the March 1993 bombings in Bombay is a case in point.

Second, and equally problematic, there is the Indian Government's response to its security problems. Essentially, complex and deep-seated political problems are side-stepped and this process of prevarication is masked by a series of military–technical fixes, which bear little relation to the true nature of India's security problems yet strain the exchequer sufficiently to engender security problems in other non-military spheres, such as food and economic security. Why, for example, does India require a 3:1 conventional superiority over Pakistan, a neighbour which it has successfully partitioned and whose weaknesses are evident? Moreover, this scale of domination emerged well before Pakistan's nuclear ambitions became evident. Why too is India concentrating so much upon the threat from the Indian Ocean which at best is grossly exaggerated and at worst is beyond India's control and direction? Why is the political response to China so different from the response to Pakistan? True, the threat from Pakistan is made all the more worrisome by the Muslim population in India, Kashmir and the bitter memory of partition. It is also true that the least activity by China in border areas creates panic in India, witness the sharp dip in bilateral relations which occurred in 1986, for few good reasons. China, it seems, has never lost its status as both a long-term and a serious threat to India but, overall, the attempts at reconciliation and normalization in this quarter are more sincere—witness the series of confidence-building measures agreed between the sides in September 1993. Where possible the China problem is tackled at the diplomatic level, quite successfully in recent months, but the threat from Pakistan is habitually explained in military terms.

Clearly there are other factors to be considered and investigated. Is the combination of Pakistan and other security issues as critical for India as levels of defence preparedness would suggest? Just how insecure is India? If it is not insecure, then what precisely are the driving forces behind India's search for military power? Although the response to external threats may be primarily military, it is not necessarily the case that military activities are the outcome of external threats. This is the case in other countries, particularly among Organization for Economic Co-operation and Development (OECD) countries, and it could well be the case in India.

To several observers both inside and outside India the configuration of Indian defence policy appears to make little sense because it relates so unevenly to India's insecurities, although this is an area of enquiry which has received less attention than it deserves. In the following chapters the mismatch between defence policy and external security threats will be explained. Defence in India will be seen to have a logic of its own, however destructive this may turn out to be in both an economic and a political sense.

3. Defence policy and practice, 1947–62

I. Introduction

Until the 1971 war with Pakistan, the 1962 war with China had been the most significant factor in India's short history as an independent nation state (see chapter 4). Since that humiliating defeat successive Indian governments have purposefully given defence a high profile to ensure that among both the voting public and regional adversaries there is sufficient confidence that India is well defended. In the immediate aftermath of the 1962 war, decision makers and the Government's critics concentrated upon three sets of reasons for the failure to prevent defeat, the abortive attempts to check the apparent scale of the humiliation and the ineptitude of the defence effort.

First, Prime Minister Jawaharlal Nehru was severely criticized for misreading Chinese intentions and failing to prepare for war. This failure was seen to be a by-product of non-alignment, but this was a rather simplistic interpretation of a very complex situation which, as discussed earlier, turned on India's economic weakness and determination to remain politically independent in a competitive bipolar system.[1]

Second, Krishna Menon as Defence Minister was criticized for under-equipping the armed forces, although this too was at best a simplified and misleading view of what Menon was attempting to do—if India was to become a significant defence producer it was inevitable that defence resources would have to be reallocated to boost domestic efforts to both the temporary and the long-term detriment of imports. During his tenure as Defence Minister, Menon's left-wing views changed the emphasis of defence policy, but his root and branch reorganization of the defence sector engendered considerable ill-feeling among senior members of the armed forces. His service promotions were considered to be politically motivated and led on one occasion to the attempted resignation of General Thimayya, the Army Chief of Staff. However, against this must be set the antipathy of most high-ranking senior officers to Menon's approach to defence production, although he did find enthusiastic support from bureaucrats such as H. M. Patel[2] and some of the younger senior officers, such as P. C. Lal. In addition, Menon's arrogant handling of the defence portfolio made him unpopular in several quarters and a natural target for both parliament and the press in the embittered post-war atmosphere.

Third, received wisdom widely considered the country to be underdefended.[3] Indian leaders were assumed to have lacked the political will to ensure adequate

---

[1] Rana, A. P., *The Imperatives of Non-Alignment* (Macmillan: Delhi, 1976).
[2] Conversations with the author, Vidyanagar, Gujarat, 14 May 1991.
[3] For a comprehensive coverage of these issues see Thomas, R. G. C., *The Defence of India: A Budgetary Perspective of Strategy and Politics* (Macmillan: Delhi, 1978).

defence arrangements between 1947 and 1962 to guard against the threat from the north-east. As a result, when China attacked India after several months of low-level conflict and skirmishing, the armed forces proved incapable of mounting a defensive campaign.

This alleged lack of preparedness prior to the 1962 Sino-Indian War is the subject of this chapter. Surprisingly, given the national importance of this war, the question has only been lightly covered by Indian defence analysts. Conclusions rest more on assumptions and received wisdom passed down through the years than on empirical research. The question is generally considered to be unimportant because during this period defence expenditure was extremely low, procurement modest and, more generally, defence was the junior partner of development on the one hand and non-alignment on the other. In fact, this was not the case. Defence had a life of its own and was a significantly more prominent sector than most, if not all, analysts have thus far suggested. This can be illustrated by looking beyond what India was spending and acquiring for defence purposes: it can be shown that the period between 1947 and 1962 was extremely important, both qualitatively and quantitatively. It was during this period that many of the key debates concerning future defence and foreign policy were decided upon and, contrary to popular opinion, it appears to be the case that Indian decision makers were more ambitious than they were cautious, especially on the procurement side. This entailed rather more expenditure than is immediately obvious from the observable allocations to the defence sector. It also required the sanctioning of key defence missions, which added up to a defence posture which conflicted with the statements made by Nehru and others during that period, however weak the country may have been in one particular theatre.

II. Defence before independence

Prior to independence, defence was a neglected aspect of thinking among the leaders of the Indian National Congress (INC). References to defence in early INC resolutions and policy documents are very limited. When defence issues did emerge this was usually in the context of industrialization strategy: a free India would strive to develop defence industries under public ownership subject to the ability of the state to mobilize sufficient resources and capacity.[4] Generally, the INC collectively assumed that a free India would be relatively secure from attack and invasion on the basis of its natural frontiers and its neutral and peaceful status. Following so many years under the yoke of the British Indian Empire, independent India would emerge as a model and an example of a new nation which no major power would consider worth the risk of invading—the political cost would be too high and, initially, the economic returns far too low. This propensity to ignore defence was strengthened by the

---

[4] Indian National Congress, *Resolutions on Economic Policy and Programme: 1924-54* (All India Congress Committee: New Delhi, 1954), p. 32.

primacy of non-co-operation and non-violence in Indian thinking, and the overwhelming concentration on the struggle for independence as an end in itself. Furthermore, Pakistan was not a consideration until the eve of independence, and few senior INC members foresaw major tensions emerging with other countries, such as the USSR, or direct threats to Indian sovereignty; the major powers were certain to be exhausted by World War II or too wary of each other to move militarily on a country of independent India's geopolitical importance.

When Nehru became a prominent member of the INC he shared many of his colleagues' assumptions concerning the future defence of independent India. At the same time, however, he attempted to inject more thinking and sophistication into planning for future defence needs and foreign policy goals, albeit at the broadest possible levels, which gave prominence to the former rather than the latter. In line with orthodox INC thinking, a free India, he maintained, would be well protected by the balance of power in the world at large. None of the major world powers would be prepared to permit the invasion of the sub-continent on account of its geo-strategic, political and economic potential and importance once the British had left. During the 1930s Nehru wrote frequently on the foreign policy issues an independent India would have to deal with in the future.[5]

In so doing, however, Nehru had no real platform to build upon. Mahatma Gandhi gave little thought to the national defence issue but wished to institutionalize non-violence when India became independent, which would certainly have had major implications for future defence plans. In stark contrast to the prevailing Gandhian ethic based upon non-violence, non-cooperation and anti-militarism, Nehru and Subhas Chandra Bose, subsequently the leader of the Indian National Army (INA), gradually developed their own independent views on defence and both argued for the creation of a military capability based on a defence industry under solely public ownership.[6] As early as 1928 Nehru stated his position on defence on several occasions without equivocation—for example: 'When freedom comes, we shall develop our army and strengthen it and make it more efficient than it is today.'[7]

This stress upon development, strength and efficiency, albeit at a highly generalized level, was complemented by Nehru's support for science policy, remarkable for a Third World leader but not perhaps for the first Prime Minister of India.[8] Nehru was fascinated throughout his life by modern science and its potential role in an independent industrial India: 'It is science alone that can solve the problems of hunger and poverty, of insanitation and illiteracy, of vast

[5] See for example Nehru, J., *India and the World* (Allen & Unwin: London, 1936).

[6] The INA was formed in 1941 when captured Indian soldiers drawn from defeated units of the British Indian Army in the South East Asian theatre were organized by the Japanese invading forces into an army which would fight alongside Japan for the 'liberation' of India. Subhas Chandra Bose revived the INA in 1943, to great effect.

[7] Bright, J. (ed.), *The Speeches of Jawaharlal Nehru* (Indian Printing Works: Lahore, 1946), p. 152.

[8] Vishvanathan, S., *Organizing or Science: The Making of an Industrial Research Laboratory* (Oxford University Press: Delhi, 1985).

resources running to waste, of a rich country inhabited by a starving people . . . The future belongs to those who make friends with science.'[9]

Nehru envisaged a major partnership in the future between the scientific community and the armed forces in the same way as he worked towards similar partnerships for economic development. Indeed, the establishment of 'mother industries' to produce the means of production under public ownership was a key tenet of INC policy. In 1946 Nehru also informed another audience in Bombay that India would defend itself by all the means at its disposal and apparently implied clearly that this did not exclude nuclear weapons, or atomic weapons as they were termed at that period.[10] However, as became clear in later years, in many instances politicians and soldiers often remained remarkably ignorant as to the full and enduring effects of nuclear weapons, witness the tendency of many war planners to imagine that a nuclear war would in effect be a rerun of World War II writ large.

III. Independence and the formation of defence policy

Beyond the occasional reference to defence and security the INC came to power in 1947 without a defence policy of much substance—the goal of independence and the accompanying sentiment of nationalism seemed to have absorbed the energy of the movement at the cost of virtually everything else. However, once independence had been achieved, Nehru was confronted with the task of moulding India post-partition into a viable nation state. Partition and the impact of the First Round had highlighted the problems of defence and sovereignty and had given both a sense of urgency. In this context, Nehru had three major problems to confront.

First, a legacy remained from the INA, although it had been emasculated by the British some years before independence and Bose died in 1946. The ideas and example of Bose appealed to those concerned with direct action and ethnic unity. Although Congress had great credibility with the former, it commanded less respect among the latter, particularly since it had failed to prevent partition, though not necessarily through any fault of its own. Furthermore, the INA had been a popular force in the struggle for independence and its suppression by the British had increased its appeal among the rank and file, particularly with the extremist elements. What transpired over this period was thus a split among the forces and groups responsible for the leadership of the independence movement.

Bose had attempted to align himself with the Axis powers during the war and peddled a political philosophy which conflicted directly with the teaching and example of Gandhi: 'Bose viewed the INA and its officers in highly political

[9] Vishvanathan (note 8). Quoted originally in Ram, A., 'A few thoughts on applied science in India', *CGCRI Bulletin,* vol. 13, no. 4 (1966), pp. 1–8.

[10] Kavic, L., *India's Quest for Security: Defence Policies 1947–1965* (University of California Press: Berkeley, Calif., 1967), p. 27.

terms. Like the military of totalitarian states, the INA was regarded as a center (or one of the main centers) of politics and national regeneration. It was the model of an Indian "people's army", a military organization truly representative of the nation, the focus of national attention, the servant of a neototalitarian ideology.'[11]

For the Congress leadership the INA represented a total antithesis of both the ends and the means of the movement for independence. Yet, paradoxically, it was at the same time extremely popular and potentially a threat both to the hegemony of the Congress Party and to the very process of representative government. It was a difficult circle for the Congress to square. First, the INA unequivocally and deliberately compromised the ethic of non-violence and much of what the INC stood for. Second, it would have been a substantial political risk for the Congress to alienate such a powerful group. Third, the INA had challenged, albeit without success, the monopoly of the INC as the body which had achieved independence.

Somewhat fortunately for the INC, Bose's death deprived the movement of charismatic leadership. After World War II, many of the INA officers were shot, the troops demobbed and the INA gradually faded away as a political force. However, the threat of resurgence and the existence of an old guard remained as problems. In order both to reward and to emasculate the movement, the remaining ex-INA members of sufficient status were dispatched to various corners of the world as high-status ambassadors, who could not criticize their own government. Others were given positions at home on a deputy minister level.[12]

This process of assimilation without marked alienation or threat was, according to Stephen Cohen, 'an act of great political skill', a judgement with which it is difficult not to agree.[13] However, although the INA had been dissolved, Nehru would undoubtedly have been mindful of the popularity and prestige Bose had commanded. With the INA's high profile among the Indian public, the spectre of militarism had emerged within India bringing with it the possibility, if distant, of an active role for the military in the Indian political process.[14] In addition, the Army was the most powerful and well-organized institution in the country even though it was not controlled by INA members or sympathizers. Indeed, Cohen has also argued that the low-profile defence policy eventually adopted by Nehru was a direct result of the popularity of the INA and there may well have been a connection between Nehru's outward policy

---

[11] Cohen, S., *The Indian Army: Its Contribution to the Development of a Nation* (University of California Press: London, 1971), pp. 162–63.

[12] Cohen (note 11), p. 165, fn. 51.

[13] Cohen (note 11), p. 163

[14] India is often if not always thought to be one example of a developing country where the military is content not to intervene in the political process. However, in the late 1950s and early 1960s commentators on India and Pakistan, such as Hugh Tinker, were suggesting that if public order in India degenerated as it had done in Pakistan the Army might intervene, given that it was the real power behind the state administration. The confidence shown towards the Indian military as an apolitical force is more recent.

framework and the legacy of the INA.[15] So too might this have been a motivation for not having a defence chief of staff.

Throughout his short career Bose spoke and wrote at some length about the issue of defence in a free India, even though like others he managed to say little of substance about policy. For Bose the Indian Army was a symbol of both past subjugation and complete independence in the future. During the Round Table Conference sessions, between 1930 and 1933, Bose was openly critical of Gandhi's failure to voice without equivocation the demand for full control over the Indian armed forces. Then, in 1933, the British Government issued a White Paper which stated that the Governor General, rather than elected bodies, would have control over the 'independent' defence forces.[16] Quite understandably, Bose read into this an attempt by the British Government to retain an option to maintain its monopoly over organized force, which could be exercised at will so as to nullify the political achievement of representative government. For Bose, firm control over a strong defence force and independence were two sides of the same coin:

India wants the status of a free country, with her own flag, her own army, navy and defence force, and with her own ambassadors in the capitals of free countries . . . Independence which India aspires after, today, is not 'Dominion Home Rule' as we find in Canada or Australia, but full national sovereignty as obtains in the United States of America or in France . . . Building up a national army will be a . . . difficult task. . . . the dearth of Indian officers of high rank remains and will present some difficulty . . . In this connection India's chief problem will be to train up a large number of officers of all ranks within a period of ten years—and thereby complete the formation of the National Army. Along with the Army, [the] Navy and Air Force will also have to be built up . . . [17]

Somehow, therefore, Nehru had to develop a defence policy which did not appear to take too many leaves from the INA's book, a difficult task considering the erstwhile convergence of Nehru's and Bose's defence views prior to independence and the fact that Bose was correct on several counts.

The second problem which influenced defence policy after 1947 was partition. Naturally, early policy makers had no idea that partition would accompany independence. Still less were they prepared for the bloodshed which accompanied partition or the atmosphere of profound mistrust and hatred between India and Pakistan which resulted. Partition also readjusted completely the former policy based upon India's relative power in the region, about which the INC leadership was so confident before independence. Through partition India lost the deep-water port of Karachi—strategically important for naval docking purposes—and many of the natural features which could have inhibited territorial invasion, although India's geopolitical importance remained largely

---

[15] Cohen (note 11), p. 176

[16] Amita, S., 'Subhas Chandra Bose: a light on his political ideas as related to the problem of Indian defence', *Asian Affairs*, vol. 6, no. 1 (Jan.–Mar. 1984), p. 90.

[17] Bose, S. C., *The Indian Struggle* (Asia Publishing House: New Delhi, 1964), pp. 366, 453–54.

unchanged. In addition, India acquired a significant additional security problem in the form of Pakistan which promptly resulted in both a war and a significant loss of territory in Kashmir.

The third problem which influenced defence policy in the formative period was that the creation of a new state in the region provided an extra avenue for major powers to project power and influence and an opportunity for competition by proxy; the history of superpower influence in South Asia would have been markedly different without the creation of Pakistan. Nehru made a conscious attempt to sidestep the cold war and avoid being dragged into the force field of superpower politics. India's experience during the two world wars would also have been at the forefront of Nehru's mind and he wanted to avoid putting his country in a position whereby it could be drawn into a war without its prior consent. Coupled with India's extreme weakness, this led initially to a policy of neutralism which later became more active in the form of non-alignment.

Here, Nehru and Menon were being primarily pragmatic. If the Congress Party was to survive the early years of independence, it was essential for it to meet at least some of the increasing expectations of the masses following the departure of the British. However, involvement in superpower politics would have led inevitably to rising defence expenditures even with grants and aid from, say, the USA. Increased defence expenditures during this period would have affected significantly the resources available for development. This is not to doubt the sincerity of Nehru's foreign policy, his commitment to a 'third force' and his role within the United Nations, but pressing domestic concerns were also a factor which influenced the evolution of foreign policy—a 'guns without butter' routine for India could have been political suicide for the Congress Party.

During the first decade of independence, Nehru was determined to industrialize the Indian economy and bring millions above the poverty line, all within the framework of democratic socialism. In order to achieve this end, Nehru realized that defence expenditure had to be subject to the strictest control. Consequently, between 1947 and 1962, defence expenditure was low, averaging no more than 2 per cent of GNP per annum. During this period the net national product increased unevenly and the rate of growth fluctuated between 1 and 4 per cent per annum. Allowing for an increase in population of over 2 per cent per annum, very little was left over for increases in standards of living, investment, or indeed, improvements to the national security apparatus.[18] Furthermore, Nehru prompted a political debate regarding the effect of high defence expenditure upon national development.

Consequently, when designing a policy for defence, Nehru seemed keen to ensure three basic conditions. First, the armed services and the threat of militarism had to be kept in check. Second, given the nature of the relationship

[18] Figures taken from Chaudhuri, P., *The Indian Economy: Poverty and Development* (Crosby Lockwood Staples: London, 1978), p. 52.

between defence and foreign policy, the attainment of self-sufficiency in defence production coupled with independence from the superpowers became two important criteria. Third, over the course of the nation-building programme, expenditure on defence should not reduce significantly the resources available for investment.

IV. The Blackett Report

In practice, it seems that Nehru lacked the expertise to translate his broad policy aims into a strategy for long-term military coherence in general and arms procurement in particular. Neither he nor his civilian advisers understood sufficiently the intricacies of military technology and strategy, and the advice of the service chiefs alone would have been inappropriate and insufficient. In addition, there existed gaping holes in the decision-making process. It was only during World War II that Indian Civil Service (ICS) officers were deputed into South Block (of the Ministry of Defence) where defence decisions are taken and implemented, this being the decision of Field Marshall Sir Claude Auchinleck, the Commander-in-Chief in India.[19] Moreover, it took a long time to change the Department of Defence into anything more than a post office. Prior to independence all decisions were ultimately taken in Whitehall. ICS people had little involvement in the decision-making process—defence expenditure was non-vote, that is, not requiring a Parliamentary vote, and there was little need for trained personnel to justify and account for expenditure. Immediately after partition, when the Defence Department became the Ministry of Defence (MoD), the ICS was faced with a bureaucratic vacuum as permanent regulations became outmoded in practice because they had always been framed with reference to British authority.[20] Moreover, many British officers remained after partition to help with the transference of power and authority and many proved extremely unwilling to respect and take notice of MoD bureaucrats.[21] The result was a process of confusion and breakdown.

Consequently, Nehru sought the advice of an outside expert, a famous British physicist, P. M. S. Blackett, who later became the President of the Royal Society. Nehru asked Blackett to prepare a report outlining the measures necessary for India to become near self-sufficient in defence production over a period of approximately seven years (the time-scale appears to have been arbitrary), but at the same time to retain adequate defence and security. During the second half of 1948, Blackett assessed India's economic, industrial and technological capability in a geopolitical framework. The result was a short report submitted to the Indian Defence Minister, in which Blackett attempted a study of how

---

[19] H. M. Patel, conversations with the author, Vidyanagar, Gujarat, 14 May 1991.
[20] Venkateswaran, A. L., *Defence Organisation in India* (Ministry of Information and Broadcasting, Delhi, 1967), pp. 115, 117.
[21] H. M. Patel, conversations with the author, Vidyanagar, Gujarat, 14 May 1991.

India could 'best cut her defence coat according to her scientific, financial and industrial cloth'.[22]

In 1948 India's per capita income totalled less than one-tenth that of the UK and industrial production was a mere 2 per cent of the UK's. Blackett endorsed the need for self-sufficiency but he framed his recommendations in the context of available resources. The Blackett Report followed an earlier report by another British adviser, Wansborough Jones, who had previously submitted a paper on the scientific and organizational measures required to make India a self-supporting defence entity.[23] The paper was commissioned by the Interim Government prior to independence in 1947 and formed the basis for defence science organization in India. In this report Wansborough Jones outlined four central roles for the Indian armed forces: (*a*) to secure the land frontier against raids from border tribes or from attack by a second-class army; (*b*) to support civil power; this role was later dropped and tactfully ignored by Blackett; (*c*) to provide a small expeditionary force capable of protecting India's regional interests; and (*d*) within available financial resources to develop a force capable of taking the field in a first-class war. With the exception of the second element, Blackett followed these guide-lines.

From the outset Blackett worked from the assumption that India was a new nation which wished to stand unaided in defence issues. This was in direct contrast to a previous, pre-1947 conception held by Britain that India would look towards the Commonwealth of Nations for protection in the event of hostilities, particularly in relation to naval assistance. Blackett realized that defence policy had not yet acquired either a traditional pattern or entrenched bureaucratic interests—policy shifts would be very difficult once final decisions become increasingly characterized by bureaucratic–political criteria.[24] Ample opportunity existed for an innovative approach to both defence doctrine and policy. Above all, Blackett advised the Indian Government not to prepare to fight World War III, which he considered both irrelevant and impossible anyway: India's defence needs were primarily related to threats from the northwest. Technical planning for a small-scale war was the fundamental requirement, although this did not eliminate exploring the basic concepts of a more sophisticated defence profile in the future.

Blackett's starting point for his defence plan was India's extreme economic weakness. On this basis he outlined the choices open to the Government. In order to become self-sufficient a strong economy and industrial base were essential. The importing of sophisticated defence equipment would drain foreign exchange reserves and slow the rise in national income through industrialization and improved agriculture, upon which any future rise in military

---

[22] Blackett, P. M. S., *Scientific Problem of Defence in Relation to the Indian Armed Forces: A Report to the Hon'ble the Defence Minister* (New Delhi, 10 Sep. 1948).

[23] The Blackett Report on defence should not be confused with a later report he compiled on the National Physics Laboratory.

[24] For an excellent explanation and analysis of bureaucratic politics in the US context see the unparalleled essay by Allison, G. T., *Essence of Decision: Explaining the Cuban Missile Crisis* (Little Brown & Co.: Boston, Mass., 1971).

expenditure would itself be based. In fact Blackett recommended initial *reductions* in defence expenditure to encourage growth in other sectors.

In relation to choice of technology, Blackett recognized the inevitability of foreign imports but suggested a strategy for minimizing the impact of defence imports on foreign exchange reserves. He proposed the division of procurement into *competitive* and *non-competitive* weapons. In so doing he kept in mind India's likely enemies and, as well, the likelihood that the major powers would not be drawn into an intervention in the event of a regional conflict. To some degree, this protected India's regional interests. Moreover, even if India was in possession of extremely advanced military equipment, it would be unlikely to be quantitatively sufficient to offer many independent options against a major power given the posture India could afford in the foreseeable future.

Competitive weapons were the type of front-line weapon platform which relied upon state-of-the-art technology for optimum performance during engagement with enemy forces—fighter aircraft, heavy tanks or an aircraft-carrier task force, for example. Non-competitive weapons were those which were used in roles which did not require optimum performance in order to be effective, such as small arms, field guns, motor transport and night bombers. Both the USA and the UK possessed large *matériel* stockpiles following the end of World War II. If India bought up some of these surplus stocks, if it avoided where possible high-performance weapons and chose instead low-performance weapons in non-competitive areas, and, further, linked defence planning to relevant scenarios, a measure of self-sufficiency was possible in the future.

If surplus weapons were available Blackett saw only three reasons for importing new and improved models: (*a*) in the case of a highly competitive weapon; (*b*) if a non-competitive weapon system offered such a markedly improved performance over its predecessor as to justify the capital cost by reducing running and maintenance costs; and (*c*) in order to supply training schools with single models to keep the services in touch with modern developments. Furthermore, Blackett argued that self-sufficiency would create freedom of choice in foreign policy rather than strategic isolation. Although Blackett did not place particular stress upon this observation, it was in fact of immense importance because therein lay the link between a preferred, affordable and independent defence policy and posture, as outlined by Nehru, and the policy of non-alignment.

With regard to the composition of the three services, Blackett made a series of specific recommendations. Wisely, he paid considerable attention to the missions of the armed services as well as the type of equipment each should be seeking.

The Indian Navy was ascribed three central missions:[25] (*a*) the protection of coastal shipping against mining, submarines, surface and airborne attack, with

---

[25] The Blackett Report contains far more detail on naval policy and is quite weak on considerations for the Army. This is undoubtedly because Blackett was a naval officer during World War II and had relatively little knowledge of ground forces and tactics.

the capability to respond in kind; (b) escorting and protecting a small number of ocean convoys between Aden (now Yemen) and Singapore but no further; merchant shipping was always going to be a valuable national asset for India and important for the development of trade; and (c) co-operation with the Army and Air Force in repelling enemy landing operations and advances along coastlines, and to be able to undertake similar operations against the enemy.

Given the general principles from which he was working, Blackett argued that the acquisition of cruisers was inadvisable because of their cost and vulnerability; the deep draught of a cruiser rendering it vulnerable to mines and submarines. With the exception of convoy protection, the advice was invariably the same—opt for small, cost-effective and non-prestigious systems for the central missions and generally. Surprisingly, in view of the costs involved, the acquisition of a small escort carrier for convoy protection was recommended and justified on the basis that it would have greater utility than the cumbersome cruiser. However, Blackett also pointed out that such a mission was far too expensive for India at that time and that 'India's assumed opponent'—that is, Pakistan— would be unlikely to acquire the type of bomber with the range and capability required to attack convoys in the foreseeable future.

In his discussion of the future of the Indian Air Force (IAF), Blackett's recommendations were much more guarded. First, he ruled out a long-range bombing role on the basis of cost and efficacy. Blackett was also strongly opposed to strategic bombing on humanitarian grounds, following the destruction of German cities by the Allies during the last stages of World War II.[26] In particular, he argued that India could not hope to acquire a precision bombing capability, so that any long-range bombing mission would have to be countervalue strikes directed against civilian population centres. Apart from the doubtfulness of any military gain, such action might lead to a campaign of mutual destruction, even without nuclear weapons: 'In view of the high density of India's own cities and the impossibility of affording an adequate defence against enemy air attacks, it would seem a great mistake for India to initiate such a campaign of mutual destruction, and probably even a mistake to retaliate in kind even if so attacked.'[27]

Where India could profit was through the acquisition of smaller, single-engined fighter-bombers which would not need fighter escort and would offer an adequate if not an optimum strike capability. Blackett was also unconvinced that the IAF required jet fighters. Apart from the need to evaluate carefully the suitability of, for example, Vampires and Meteors for the arid and semi-arid conditions of north-west India, involving problems of dust and high ambient temperatures, jet fighters were also too fast to offer joint Army–Air Force target identification missions. Nevertheless, Blackett endorsed fully the procurement of night fighters, photo-reconnaissance aircraft and trainers, and he recom-

---

[26] Zuckerman, S., *Nuclear Illusions and Reality* (Collins: London, 1982), p. 111.
[27] Blackett Report (note 22), p. 12.

mended a major boost to the Hindustan Aircraft Factory at the earliest possible moment.

Blackett's report was much less comprehensive on the future role of the Indian Army, perhaps because he agreed with others that the Army had to be firmly controlled. However, he did highlight the potential for relatively rapid progress towards self-sufficiency which would be made less difficult by the prior existence of ordnance factories established by the British. In addition, the Army was the best possible candidate for the exploitation of non-competitive equipment. The only specific recommendation was for the development of highly trained anti-aircraft units to protect airfields, factories and other key targets.

Finally, Blackett considered the role and organization of defence science in India. This contribution was perhaps the most relevant in the report, particularly in relation to self-sufficiency. First, Blackett dismissed India's potential for developing an indigenous capability in the more advanced fields of defence technology, such as chemical and biological warfare, high-performance aircraft, guided missiles, atomic warfare, millimetric radar and large ship design. Instead, the preferred route towards self-sufficiency should be in increasing the efficiency of weapon systems which were tried and tested and familiar to both the armed forces and defence scientists. Thus, both servicemen and scientists could usefully collaborate on radar tracking, interception, bombing accuracy and air attacks on ships. Equally, the scientific community should be given the space and resources to nurture a research and development (R&D) capability that was relevant to India and that would keep abreast of developments elsewhere by covering in detail the published literature on defence science and technology. This called for a considerable increase in funding, sound organization under the Scientific Adviser to the MoD and carefully controlled collaboration between the Government, the armed forces and the science community. Indeed, Blackett received enthusiastic advice from Homi Bhabha and S. S. Bhatnagar, who later sat on the Defence Science Policy Board, and Professor D. S. Kothari, the first Scientific Adviser to the MoD.[28]

The Blackett Report appeared to be accepted by the policy makers of the day. In February 1949 Blackett received a letter from the incumbent Defence Secretary, H. M. Patel, the creator of the Indian MoD, which read: 'I am glad, however, to be able to inform you that *the Government have accepted your report practically in its entirety*. The only important point of difference related to your recommendations for the Navy, but the difference is not, to my mind, one of great substance' (emphasis added).[29]

Despite Patel's comments to Blackett and the realistic and affordable policy options offered to India, Blackett's recommendations were either ignored or very poorly implemented. Thereafter, Blackett's contribution to science and technology in India came only in the form of proposals to reorganize the

[28] Venkateswaran (note 20), p. 281.
[29] Letter from P. M. Patel to P. M. S. Blackett, D.O. No 62/5/49 (Ministry of Defence: New Delhi, 10 Feb. 1949). (Royal Society archives: London.)

National Physics Laboratory, the task for which he is best remembered.[30] He is also remembered for his enthusiastic endorsement of the Indian nuclear energy programme.[31] However, according to one former decision maker, Blackett moved from defence to non-military science policy primarily because he considered his efforts in the former to have been a failure, whereas he certainly had more success in more formal science policy.[32] Although the report remained both well known and well read by policy makers, it also became an unpopular document in later years. At a press conference to celebrate the silver jubilee of the Defence Research and Development Organisation on 12 January 1984, the incumbent Chief Scientific Adviser to the MoD, Dr V. S. Arunachalam, was openly critical of Blackett's 'ruse' to retard the development of India's indigenous defence capability.

Inevitably, although he was not without his supporters, Blackett did encounter opposition within India, particularly from the armed forces, which is understandable and predictable considering his recommendations concerning non-competitive equipment, economic and industrial development before defence, indigenous production, and reductions in defence expenditure. In effect, Blackett was attempting to downgrade the relative importance of the armed forces in favour of economic growth, and his report left all three armed services with the need to protect a considerable amount of bureaucratic turf. Furthermore, all or most of the advice he gave cut against the grain of military professional interests which had been so successfully transferred from the UK to India, but which, after 1947, required a prince's purse from a pauperized polity. Among his private papers there are signs that his attempts to rationalize defence policy met with stiff resistance from the service chiefs:

At my first meeting with the Defence Minister, I asked, as a starting point for my thinking . . . to be told the military plans of the three armed forces . . . The next day the Service chiefs produced their future plans. It only needed a short perusal of these documents to see that the total proposed packages of the three services nearly reached the total Indian Central Budget.[33]

Elsewhere in his papers there is a transcript of an interview given in Delhi. Over the course of the interview Blackett reiterated his reservations about the recommendations of the service chiefs:

I usually managed to speak to the Joint Chiefs of Staff meeting. But I am not of any official status in defence matters. I found it very interesting and I think it was useful getting to know a country which has got independence. You got certain advice from the old British advisors, which may or may not suit the occasion. Then there was very dangerous advice, it was hard to get objective advice and I had a lot to do . . . I think I saved India a lot of money by discouraging her from some of the wilder ideas that the

[30] Vishvanathan (note 8).

[31] H. M. Patel, conversations with the author, Vidyanagar, Gujarat, 14 May 1991.

[32] B. N. NagChaudhri, conversations with the author (15 Oct. 1984, Delhi).

[33] Blackett, P. M. S., Blackett Papers G-29 (Royal Society Archives, London), p. 3.

Chiefs of Staff had when I went there . . . I once wrote a paper which was read, I was told, by new ministers coming in for the next ten years.[34]

Despite the 'wild' advice of the chiefs of staff, the Indian Cabinet did indeed take a decision in 1949 to adopt a narrow and circumspect defence policy with the defence of the north-west as a priority. The policy was based upon the assumption that, in the event of a war, Pakistan would have the initiative in launching an attack on Kashmir. In such a situation the Indian Army divisions in Kashmir would attempt to hold the attacking forces while the rest of the Indian Army advanced towards Lahore and Sialkot. A decisive defeat of the Pakistan Army, coupled with the occupation of Lahore, was considered sufficient to bring Pakistan to the negotiating table. At the diplomatic level, the Indian Government would work to prevent Pakistan from receiving war credits from external powers, which would enable it to continue fighting the war. If these efforts failed to halt the war, the Government would mobilize international support for a negotiated settlement.[35]

No moves were made to make anything more than a token defence in the North-East Frontier Agency (NEFA) against a potential threat from China—the diplomatic process was considered sufficient. Nehru was in fact aware that the logic of accepting that an exceptional threat from China existed would have demanded a very much more expensive defence policy.[36] In principle, therefore, early defence policy was the result of Nehru's attempts to contain defence expenditure and find a reasonable fit between India's defence and foreign policies.

Without doubt, the Blackett Report was a document of exceptional insight which could have been particularly useful to Indian defence policy makers and may even have had some influence upon early policy formation; discussion on the report certainly took place in the Defence Committee of the Cabinet.[37] Without losing sight of the central problem of defence, Blackett offered India a means to relative security which contained four important ingredients. First, the report emphasized the need for self-sufficiency. Second, the defence policy proposed was consistent with the foreign policy of non-alignment. Third, it would have been relatively cheap to implement. Fourth, the armed services would have been controlled, both politically and financially.

The policy adopted in 1949 was also encouraging. Indian policy makers appeared to recognize that India was unable to fight anything like a major war, and they adopted instead a policy that was both sensible and affordable. Furthermore, through the stress upon negotiation and the exploitation of international opinion, there was a conscious attempt to link defence policy to foreign policy.

---

[34] Transcript of radio interview with P. M. S. Blackett, Blackett Papers G-12 (Royal Society Archives, London), pp. 2–3.

[35] Kavic (note 10), p. 37.

[36] I am grateful to Lorne Kavic for this insight. Conversations with the author, Vancouver, July 1988.

[37] H. M. Patel, conversations with the author, Vidyanagar, Gujarat, 14 May 1991.

Nevertheless, it is axiomatic that policies do not succeed on paper alone; they require successful implementation. Although Nehru may have attempted to restrain the role of the military and to cap defence expenditure, it is by no means clear that he succeeded. Nor is it clear that Nehru fully came to terms with the implications of the principles he valued. There is little disagreement as to the general direction of *declared* defence policy between 1947 and 1962. However, so far there has been no real attempt to investigate whether or not the Indian Government attempted to implement the policy described above, or succeeded in so doing if such an attempt was made.

In order to understand this more clearly it is necessary to look closely at India's defence policy in practice, that is, at the importing and production of weapon systems based upon the defence missions which evolved during the period 1947–62.

V. The Indian Army

As a result of the policy adopted soon after the attainment of independence, the Indian Army maintained its position as the focal point of defence. During this period over 75 per cent of the defence budget was allocated to the Army but, at the same time, equipment modernization was perfunctory because of the government's unwillingness to expend limited foreign exchange reserves, which were stretched to the limit to pay for the modernization of the other two services and for non-military requirements. Much of the budget was given over to pay and pensions, which always account for a large proportion of the Indian Army's annual budget on account of the country's tradition of maintaining an extremely large standing army. Consequently, until 1962 the Army could only allocate 50 per cent of its budget to capital expenditure.

In 1950 Nehru reduced the size of the Army by 50 000 men to approximately 300 000, in an attempt to make economies and simultaneously to transform it into a more mechanized rather than an infantry force. However, the cuts were made in places where they scarcely amounted to anything of military significance, and a proposal to cut the Army by a further 100 000 men in 1951–52 was abandoned.[38] Despite the apparent wish for mechanization, Army procurement during this period was relatively insignificant in terms of major weapon systems, but quite comprehensive in terms of stores and ammunition, which allowed adequate stockpiling for defence but not modernization.

Given India's limited resources, the evolution of defence policy and posture should certainly have favoured the Army. At independence the country possessed a well-organized and professional Army, by far the senior service. By contrast, the Navy and Air Force were both much smaller and younger. Under British rule, their roles were insignificant, particularly that of the Navy. In addition, there was a natural fit between what the Army could provide, what decision makers felt they wanted from defence, the resources available for

[38] Kavic (note 10), pp. 84–85.

defence and current threat perceptions. Without any serious change in organization the Army could provide a defence against Pakistan based initially upon a relatively cheap and labour-intensive form of security. Increasing the material strength of the Army would not require excessive imports or major structural changes to the composition of the armed forces. However, against this must be set the political objections to and fears of increasing the strength of the Army.

Between 1947 and 1958 India made little effort to acquire modern infantry weapons, but the emphasis changed in 1958 when Krishna Menon took over the defence portfolio. The Army retained in service the mortars, artillery and howitzers from World War II and, for many years after 1947, the Enfield .303 rifle, a weapon of World War I vintage.[39] However, towards the late 1950s, after the scale of US military aid to Pakistan became evident, tank procurement increased, the most notable acquisition being the purchase of over 200 Centurion tanks from the UK between 1956 and 1957.[40]

The somewhat mediocre fortunes of the Army should also be seen against the backdrop of three significant constitutional and governmental changes by which the Indian Government sought to limit the Army's power and authority. First, on the very first day of independence, the separate post of Commander-in-Chief was abolished and the title was given to the President of India, which transformed it into a largely ceremonial post. Ostensibly this was to promote balance between the three services but the move was also intended to minimize the possibility of a challenge to civilian authority from the Army. Second, the MoD came to be dominated by the civil service and thereafter expanded its capacity to control information and make decisions on military matters, although successes appear to have been minimal.[41] Third, for several years after independence the Government gradually changed the Warrant of Precedence[42] which substantially reduced the Army's prestige and its pay, and further emphasized the principle and practice of civilian control.[43]

VI. The Indian Air Force

The 1949 policy guide-lines adopted by the Cabinet dictated that the Army become the pivotal service, with the Air Force and Navy ascribed little more than a supporting role. However, between 1948 and 1956, the IAF received, by any standards, sufficient hardware to constitute an independent buildup, far beyond the role of support alone. Starting with 100 Spitfires and Tempests in 1948, the IAF took delivery of an unspecified number of De Havilland Vampire F3 fighters in late 1948, 52 Vampire FB9s and Vampire NF54s in 1949–50 and

[39] SIPRI, *The Arms Trade with the Third World* (Almqvist & Wiksell: Stockholm, 1971), p. 475.

[40] Evidence of tank purchases varies considerably. According to SIPRI (note 39) India bought 180 Sherman, 210 Centurion and 40 AMX-13 tanks, but according to Kavic (note 10) the figures are 30, 200 and 150 respectively.

[41] The civilian control of the MoD also harks back to the famous dispute between Kitchener and Curzon in the 19th century. See Cohen (note 11), p. 25.

[42] The legislative order which defines levels of hierarchy within the state.

[43] Cohen (note 11), pp. 171–73.

71 French Dassault MD–450 Ouragan fighter-bombers in 1953–54.[44] Following a decision in principle on 1 April 1956 to procure the English Electric Canberra, 10 months later the Government ordered 54 B(1).58 light bombers, eight PR57 photo-reconnaissance aircraft and six T4 dual-control trainers. Deliveries began in the early summer of 1957. The inventory of Canberras was further increased by 20–30 units in 1961/62. In mid-1955, the Government was considering the purchase of 80 Dassault Mystère IVA interceptors or the licensed production of the British Folland Gnat. At a later date the Government placed orders for another 33 Dassault Ouragans, replaced its earlier Ouragans with 110 Mystères and extended negotiations with Folland for the Gnat, which eventually went into production. As the IAF was taking delivery of these French aircraft in mid-1957, and Hindustan Aeronautics Ltd (HAL) was beginning production of the Gnat in Bangalore, the Government ordered 160 Hawker Hunter Mk.56 FGAs (ground attack fighters) and 22 Mk.66 trainers from the UK.[45]

By the late 1950s, through the procurement of the Canberra, the IAF had a strategic bombing role *vis-à-vis* Pakistan.[46] All the models of the Vampire procured by the IAF had only recently entered service with the Royal Air Force (RAF) in the UK. The Vampire F3, for example, a tropicalized version of the FB5, was developed by the UK for deployment in the Far East. Although India purchased the system between 1949 and 1950, it did not enter RAF service in the Far East until January 1952. Much the same is true of the Canberra (see table 3.1). Furthermore, the relative capability of the Canberra should not be overlooked. In its time it was considered a remarkable aircraft, capable of extremely high altitudes and, during the period in question, it was an extremely advanced weapon system.[47]

---

[44] When matched against Pakistani procurement prior to the aid agreement with the USA, the acquisition of the Ouragan may seem profligate, particularly so many units. However, correspondence between high-ranking members of the British Air Ministry in 1952 provides a possible explanation: 'I am led to believe that the Indian Air Force will do its best to convince their Government that the French product is the better bet. Behind their conviction is the thought that the Ouragan can be made readily available to them in the numbers they require, and also the desire not to place all their orders for aircraft in a single country. . . . The Indians are of course looking for their "top cover". They are quite happy with the Vampires as ground attack aircraft and also as day interceptors of piston engined opposition, but they are also conscious of the unbalanced nature of this fighter force and want an aeroplane that can tackle a really high level opponent whether he be a bomber or a top screen. *As they spend most of their time looking over the fence at Pakistan, I would imagine they are not thinking in terms of any very large numbers, but have perhaps heard of UK offers of the Canberra to Pakistan.*' (Emphasis added.) Public Record Office, London, Ref: 371/1011211 110720.

[45] Kavic (note 10) pp. 102–104.

[46] Although the rate of technological change over the past three decades makes comparison difficult, it was the equivalent of India purchasing the Tornado Multi-Role Combat Aircraft in 1983.

[47] The Canberra was later adapted by the USA for extremely high altitude photo-reconnaissance in the form of the famous U-2.

Table 3.1. Selected Indian Air Force and Royal Air Force procurement, 1946–61

Make/model	RAF front-line service/squadron service[a]	Withdrawn by RAF	Procured by IAF
Tempest IV (tropical version?)	Dec. 1946	Mar. 1950	1948
Vampire F-3	FL service Apr. 1947; squadron service 1948; Cyprus 1949	1952	Apr. 1948
Vampire F.B9 (tropical versions of F.B5 in service)	FL service Nov. 1951 (Malta)	FL service 1956 (remained in 2nd line until 1960–61)	1949/50
Vampire NF.54 (export version of NF.10[b])	July 1951	1954	IAF received 15 units in 1957–59
Canberra B(1)-58[c] (export version of B(1).8)	May 1961 (Germany)	June 1972	July 1955– late 1956[d]

[a] For training purposes the date of squadron service is about six months later than the date of front-line services.

[b] The NF-24 was a private venture intended for the export market. An arms export ban in 1950–51 prevented the sale of NF-24s to Egypt. Instead the units were taken by the RAF as an interim measure because of production delays on other versions of night fighter.

[c] A central mission for the B(1).8 was low-level nuclear strike.

[d] One Canberra was exported to India directly from the first production batch, the thirteenth from an initial batch of 30. Between August 1956 and September 1958, 16 units reached India directly, the bulk arriving in late 1956.

Source: Armament and Disarmament Information Unit resource base, Science Policy Research Unit, University of Sussex, UK.

These procurement details seem to reflect a departure from the policy adopted in 1949 in which the Cabinet essentially committed India to a defence policy based upon a strong Army and relatively little else. Nor is it not possible to detect much of Blackett's influence here either. What too of the Government's intention to procure new aircraft equipment at the slowest possible rate?[48] To all intents and purposes, the IAF became henceforth an independent service with a role that exceeded support.

The rate of aircraft procurement either represents an astounding institutional victory for the IAF throughout the 1950s, or a significant policy change on the part of the Government during the implementation process. Certainly, procurement details suggest that neither Blackett's recommendations nor the policy guide-lines adopted in 1949 were followed with any great enthusiasm, even

[48] H. M. Patel, conversations with the author, Vidyanagar, Gujarat, 14 May 1991.

though the practical problems associated with competitive and non-competitive weapons are most pronounced in the field of aeronautics, which was in a rapid state of evolution during this period. The fact remains that the IAF managed to ensure that all or most of the weapon systems it required were forthcoming even before the ascendancy of Krishna Menon, the Defence Minister renowned for his support of the IAF. The expansion also preceded the consolidation of the US–Pakistan military aid agreement, even though Indian intelligence sources may have anticipated such an agreement several years earlier. IAF procurement signified, therefore, a widening gap between public defence policy and actual defence posture.

VII. The Indian Navy

At independence the Indian Navy was a meagre force comprising 32 obsolete vessels primarily intended for coastal patrol, including four sloops, two frigates, one corvette and 12 minesweepers—nothing of any great worth.[49] In addition, for reasons which are unclear, the British had tended to recruit primarily Punjabi Muslims into the lower ranks of the Navy, and they went to Pakistan in 1947. This left India with a very small number of ratings after partition.[50]

Initially, Britain attempted to persuade India to build up a Navy which could integrate itself into a larger force based upon the Commonwealth navies. However, Indian decision makers were adamant that India should control a strong and independent Navy commensurate with the country's size, long coastline, geopolitical location and potential wealth. As a result, the Indian Government laid down plans for a *strategic* role for the Indian Navy after 1947. In response to a Government directive in late 1947, before Blackett arrived on the scene, the Indian Naval Headquarters drew up a 10-year plan of naval expansion under the direction of Vice-Admiral Parry, seconded from the Royal Navy.[51] The proposed programme envisaged the development of a carrier force comprising two light fleet aircraft-carriers, three light cruisers, eight to nine destroyers and the necessary support vessels. If implemented, this programme would have represented a quantum increase in naval capability.

The expansion programme commenced in 1948 and within two years a light cruiser and three 'R' Class destroyers had been purchased from the UK. A Directorate of Naval Aviation was also formed in 1948 with a remit to develop plans for a Fleet Air Arm. The procurement of two aircraft-carriers from the UK was planned for 1955 and 1957, by which time India would also have obtained 300 modern naval fighters, fighter-bombers and anti-submarine aircraft.

In the event, the ambitious scope of this programme was severely affected by uncertain market conditions stemming from the Korean War, the formation of NATO and the ensuing rise in domestic demand among the major defence

[49] Larus, J., *The Indian Navy: The Neglected Service Expands, Modernizes and Faces the Future.* Foreign Policy Perspectives: US and India Seminar, Bangalore, 25–29 June, 1978, p. 1.

[50] Kathari, Admiral R. D., *A Sailor Remembers* (Vikas: New Delhi, 1982), p. 62.

[51] Kavic (note 10) p. 117.

exporters. In particular, the British were unable to commit themselves to a sales package of this magnitude; during this period the UK was India's main and pre-ferred source of defence equipment, particularly for the Navy. However, the situation then was somewhat different from what it is during the present era. Immediately after the end of World War II the UK had very little surplus capacity in the defence sector and the sale of equipment to countries such as India and Pakistan often involved juggling between the needs of the domestic forces and overseas customers; latterly the UK has become much more reliant upon the Third World export market and is often prepared to meet requests from overseas buyers before its own armed forces have acquired all the units on order. Meanwhile, the Indian Government reconsidered the naval programme and concluded that it was beyond the country's means, irrespective of supply shortfalls. Nevertheless, new plans for a small carrier force were drawn up in 1949 and revealed in January 1950. The scheme was marginally revised in 1953, resulting in decisions to purchase a fleet replenishment vessel from Italy and to borrow three ex-escort destroyers of the Hunt Type-2 class from the UK. In addition, a light cruiser and two inshore minesweepers were also purchased from the UK in 1954 and 1955.

As part of the expansion plan, a six-year naval programme was revealed in 1955 with the vessels to be built in British shipyards. Actual procurement was cut back significantly because of a foreign exchange shortage in 1957–58, fol-lowing a balance of payments crisis which led to deficits of $650 million. However, the financial crisis did not prevent the purchase of the British light fleet carrier, *Hercules,* in 1957 and its modernization in Belfast, or the purchase of Sea Hawks and Alizes aircraft for the Fleet Air Arm. The carrier, renamed the INS *Vikrant*, was bought from the UK in January 1957, was commissioned in March 1961 and received its full complement of naval aircraft five months later.[52]

In the case of the Indian Navy the situation is relatively clear. Both the Government and the services intended India to have a blue water navy with an ability to operate in the ocean reaches to the south, east and west. However, a lack of foreign exchange coupled with the non-availability of British vessels for purchase prevented the immediate attainment of such a capability. The Navy had to be the first casualty of financial stringency, despite Blackett's recom-mendations for significant expansion; the bottom line on defence policy was an adequate land–air based defence against Pakistan, and the naval role in such a posture was limited. In the event of a war with Pakistan the Navy was respon-sible for bottling up the Pakistan Navy in Karachi harbour and to a lesser extent at Chittagong.

Nevertheless, it is somewhat misleading to describe the Navy as India's 'forgotten service',[53] even though it received very small budgetary allocations during this period—a mere 4.7 per cent of the total defence budget and 13.3 per

[52] Kavic (note 10), pp. 116–25.
[53] Larus (note 49).

cent of capital expenditure of the defence budget, even in the 1962/63 budget. Both the Army and the Air Force received over 40 per cent of defence capital expenditure, which was under 10 per cent of the entire defence budget.[54] The reason for this apparent 'forgetfulness' was that India could always have turned to the UK in the event of a pronounced security threat from the Indian Ocean. During this period the Indian Ocean was still a 'British lake'—Britain had not yet withdrawn from east of Suez and links between the two countries were, as they are now, cordial.

VIII. Actors and institutions: the dynamics of defence policy

The evolution of defence policy in the years following the attainment of independence is so confusing as to prompt the question whether there was any policy at all. From the information available and presented here it would appear that Nehru's well-documented wish to restrain defence expenditure was ignored, both directly and indirectly, despite the 1949 policy directives from the Cabinet. The resources committed to the Indian Army were broadly in line with Nehru's defence policy and with the recommendations of Blackett. However, the arrangements made for the other two services, notably the speed and scale of procurement, connote the adoption of far-reaching missions, even given the need to increase the strength of both to balance that of the Army. This suggests that either Nehru had much less control over defence policy than is generally accepted or, alternatively, that under pressure from the service chiefs he willingly acquiesced to what amounted to a significant deviation from declared policy.

Although the allocations to the Navy were low during the first two decades of independence, there was a firm intention on the part of the key decision makers to build up a strong naval presence in the Indian Ocean. It is clear that the naval programme was restrained through necessity rather than choice; the Indian economy was not growing at a particularly rapid rate during the period in question. But for the domestic foreign exchange crisis and the contraction of supply on account of the Korean War, the naval programme could well have been more dynamic. Even so, the acquisition of an aircraft-carrier, light cruisers and the Fleet Air Arm less than 15 years after independence amounts to something very different from neglect.

The development of the IAF is even more at variance with declared policy. According to the Cabinet's policy guide-lines adopted in 1949 and not changed subsequently, the task of the IAF was primarily to support the Army in the event of a land war against Pakistan. The Chief of Air Staff affirmed this in the aftermath of the 1965 war: 'The task of the Air Force is to give effective support to [the] army, and during the 1965 operations we were able largely to achieve that'.[55]

[54] Thomas (note 3), table 4, p. 147.
[55] Thomas (note 3), p. 176.

The procurement of defence equipment suggests otherwise. The Canberra and the Hunter, for example, had little to do with either supporting the Army or countering the acquisitions of Pakistan, even after the signing of the 1954 military assistance pact with the USA; either they were designed for missions not included in declared policy or they were purchased for the sake of national prestige.[56] Furthermore, the Air Force may have been used primarily to support the Army during the 1965 war but it is important to differentiate between the complete spectrum of activities and options at the disposal of an armed service and its activities in a specific conflict. For example, during the Viet Nam War the US Air Force (USAF) did not use nuclear weapons, but there was no suggestion that the USAF had lost any of its institutional strength. Much the same can be said of the British Royal Navy task force during the Falklands/Malvinas conflict.

With both the Navy and the Air Force it is more important to understand their institutional development in terms of missions, rather than to look exclusively at procurement and expenditure. In particular, the development of both a blue water navy and a strategic bombing capability, whether deliberately or almost casually undertaken, implies that both the IAF and the Navy fared much better in their mission-directed institutional development than is traditionally assumed. Once missions have been established they are relinquished or reversed with extreme reluctance; they invariably reflect or reinforce key tenets of foreign policy, major perceptions of threat, or institutional interests, both military and civilian.[57] Furthermore, once a mission has been established it must be followed by procurement. Otherwise, by definition, a country is not adequately defended.

In contrast to the situation in the USA, for example, it is difficult to define with documented precision the contours of decision making and bureaucratic infighting which led during this period to the departure from declared policy. (Whether one policy replaced another is debatable but certainly defence posture changed significantly.) This is due in large part to the considerable amount of secrecy which surrounds issues relating to defence within India and in part to the unusually small number of actors involved. For a decade Nehru and Menon had primary control over both defence and foreign affairs; the defence portfolio was invariably given to junior ranking Cabinet ministers and was not considered a prestigious post. Cabinet debate on key issues was lacking, and as Cabinet Secretary H. M. Patel found it extremely difficult to inject smoothness and cohesion into the decision-making process, because of a combination of Nehru's style of government, the closed nature of the debate, and legislative and bureaucratic ignorance.

From an examination of the rate of procurement by the Indian armed forces and the abiding sense of equivocation which emerges when defence policy

[56] SIPRI (note 39), p. 475.

[57] The development of a nuclear weapon option may be said to reflect a civilian rather than a military predilection. The Indian armed forces have been traditionally cautious of the nuclear option, possibly because in time of war decision making will become much more of a political than a military process.

during the period in question is placed under the microscope, it appears that the received wisdom is significantly misinformed. Much of the evidence and many of the relevant policy moves have been misread: India did not proceed along a defence path characterized by policy restraint nor does it seem that defence policy was sufficiently well linked at the conceptual level to foreign policy; the fate of Blackett's recommendations is evidence of this. The armed forces may have been demoted in relation to their civilian peers but, when resources permitted, they received the equipment they wanted.

How then can this period be understood? The evidence points persuasively if not conclusively to a defence policy which drifted rather than evolved. While it is probably incorrect to accept one particular explanation there are four possible ways to read the evolution of India's defence policy between 1947 and 1962.

The first explanation is that the decision-making process tilted in favour of the long-term ambitions of the Indian élites. They believed that India was destined to become a nation of considerable power and influence in both South Asia and the Indian Ocean. This affected the defence thinking of those who made and implemented policy from the outset, and caused them to lay the foundations for a blue water navy and a land–air strength of impressive proportions, encouraged undoubtedly by high-ranking military officers. The continuing ambiguity of policy on nuclear weapons, both before and since independence, reflects well the duality of defence policy, as does the rate of Naval and Air Force procurement after 1947. In particular, the procurement of both an aircraft-carrier task force and strategic bomber squadrons indicates that defence policy reflected a more ambitious and comprehensive defence posture than Nehru had led both the Indian nation and the rest of the world to believe. Thus, in tandem with other influential policy and opinion shapers, Nehru the international statesman, Gandhian and democratic socialist may have pursued a very different agenda for his country from the one he publicly avowed.

The second possibility is that Nehru may not have understood or recognized the growing drift in defence policy. It is well known that Nehru was impatient with policy detail even though he exercised considerable control over the foreign and defence portfolios—he neither knew much about defence nor took much interest in it.[58] His excessive workload and the overall diversity of the problems he elected to confront—international, regional and domestic—may have permitted a situation in which an altered defence policy could emerge. In addition, Nehru harboured a pious objection to becoming involved in the workings of defence and was well known for his general impatience with the minutiae of policy, which led him to leave policy *implementation* to others.

There is no evidence that Nehru's ministers and gatekeepers were in any way disloyal. Krishna Menon may have upset the armed forces during his period of tenure as Defence Minister, and he may also have misjudged the 'forward policy' against China, but he adhered broadly to declared policy. Within that he was committed to increasing the efficiency of professional leadership among

[58] H. M. Patel, conversations with the author, Vidyanagar, Gujarat, 14 May 1991.

the armed forces; this led to the famous dispute with General Thimayya over promotions. Second, he was committed to increasing India's capacity to produce indigenous defence equipment. Both missions sat comfortably with declared defence policy, although the impetus on Menon's part may have stemmed from his more narrow political ambition.

Nor is there any evidence to suggest that the professional bureaucrats in the MoD were intent on subverting the policy laid down by Nehru. Blackett appeared not to find any antagonism to Nehru's self-sufficiency directive among the members of the MoD he encountered; on the contrary, he appeared to strike a warm rapport with characters such as H. M. Patel and D. S. Kothari. On the other hand, the service chiefs were less enamoured of the attitudes of the bureaucrats, witness the complaints of the first Chief of the Navy Staff:

wise counsel . . . helped me to exercise restraint in periods of frustration. These frustrations arose chiefly from the bureaucratic machinery. Bureaucrats fall into two categories. There were those who knew all about everything, including operational and technical matters, and those particularly of the Finance Ministry, who did not seem to care what harm they did to the service so long as they saved money for the exchequer. There was a third neuter group whose effective contribution was minimal. The basic fault lay in the system of functioning of the ministry whose officials played no part in the initial formulation of plans, thus depriving themselves of the opportunity to appreciate both the professional considerations and requirements as well as financial and practical limitations that are involved in any proposal. They preferred to remain the ultimate arbiter.[59]

A third possibility is that the three chiefs of staff were the key to the yawning gap between formulated policy and its implementation. Their opposition to the Blackett approach has already been considered. Is it possible that the authority of these actors extended to redefining the policy of Nehru, the key architect of defence policy? Here it is necessary to consider the way in which policy decisions were formulated between 1947 and 1962.

Immediately after independence a number of committees were set up to advise the Government and the Defence Minister on defence problems, particularly in relation to Pakistan. The structure comprised the Defence Committee of the Cabinet which was underpinned by a series of other committees, of which the most important were the Defence Minister's Committee, the Chiefs of Staff Committee, the Joint Intelligence Committee and the Joint Planning Committee. The Defence Committee comprised the Prime Minister, the Defence Minister, the Foreign Minister, the Finance Minister and other important Cabinet ministers. On all the other committees designed to underpin the Defence Committee of the Cabinet sat members of the armed forces ranging from the chiefs of staff (Defence Minister's Committee, Chiefs of Staff Committee, Joint Planning Committee) to the directors of intelligence of the three services and the representatives of the chiefs of staff (see figure 9.1).[60]

---

[59] Kathari (note 50), p. 63.
[60] Rao, P. V. R., *Defence Without Drift* (Popular Prakashan: Bombay, 1970), pp. 307–308.

Consequently, at the formal decision-making level, the chiefs of staff constituted a ubiquitous presence either directly or by proxy. In practice, Nehru would have been constantly bombarded during policy planning sessions by the views of the service chiefs, many of whom were contemptuous of the views of bureaucrats. Moreover, not only were non-military views in the minority but, because of poor technical and operational knowledge, they were probably less persuasive as well:

In the opinion of H. M. Patel, a former Defence Secretary, the policy organization of the Defence Ministry was 'sufficiently flexible to ensure that every relevant point of view has a chance of being presented at appropriate level if necessary'. The theory is rarely if ever translated in practice, however . . . The ability of the average civilian official to make such decisions . . . must be judged against Patel's own admission that the ignorance of civilian officials (to which may properly be added that of the politicians) is so complete as to be a self-evident and incontrovertible fact.[61]

Before independence, the Commander-in-Chief was also the War Member on the Governor General's Executive Council. All proposals requiring decisions were sent first to the Military Finance Department and if the proposal was accepted the file was sent to the Defence Department for implementation. Under this system, the armed forces took whatever decisions they could and saw no need to consult the Defence Department.

Obviously, this situation was untenable after 1947, particularly as the three service chiefs were under the control of the Defence Minister and MoD and both needed to know a great deal about what was going on. In 1949, over the course of the defence review, new rules governing decision making were brought in. A list of the most important areas of decision making was drawn up and the Service Headquarters were instructed to send anything relating to this list to the MoD in the first instance. The Ministry would then examine the request from all the relevant angles and any differences of opinion were taken up in meetings.

Nevertheless, although the MoD slowly built for itself a base of expertise and knowledge, it could not acquire the required skills quickly enough to confront the armed forces on equal terms. Moreover, in 1958, Krishna Menon reversed the new procedures and gave the power of decision making back to the service chiefs. Thus, at the Secretariat level, the MoD became, or remained, little more than a post office and a much less attractive area of the bureaucracy in which to work.[62]

The initial system of decision making was set up by Lord Ismay, an adviser to Mountbatten. However, over time the formal committee structure disintegrated: the Defence, Chiefs of Staff and Intelligence Committees were effectively telescoped into one and decisions were increasingly considered on an *ad hoc* basis by the Prime Minister, the Defence Minister, the Chief of Army Staff and

[61] Kavic (note 10), p. 217.
[62] Venkateswaran, A. L., 'Why a defence ministry?', *Indian Express*, 25 May 1984.

some senior Army officers.[63] For example, in January 1948, prior to leaving for Washington to take up the task of advising Sir Gopalaswamy Ayyangar, the leader of the Indian delegation to the UN Security Council concerned with the Kashmir dispute, B. M. Kaul, then a low-ranking military officer, was called to Nehru's residence. Referring to a recent discussion between Air Vice Marshal Mukerji and himself, Nehru asked Kaul to explore the possibility of purchasing the Mitchell bomber while in the USA. Kaul did so but his request was eventually turned down primarily because of the unorthodox approach, but also because of the failure of the Indian Government to inform either the US State Department or the UK Government, which was the customary supplier of defence equipment to India.[64] In another more serious incident Krishna Menon worked through friends and personal contacts to secure a bulk sale of disposal stocks of jeeps and engendered at the same time a great deal of parliamentary disapproval which contributed significantly to his departure. Such informal methods of decision making would have further excluded non-military decision makers.

It is also necessary to consider the possibility that the level of military ignorance among both Government and bureaucracy may have allowed the armed forces to get their way through incremental changes. It is true that only the armed forces were able to link defence policy to technological needs, by virtue of the ubiquitous ignorance that existed elsewhere. However, the notion that the armed forces conspired against their civilian counterparts for enhanced allocations or unnecessary equipment contradicts all that is known about both sides. Nehru was the shrewdest of politicians and it is extremely unlikely that his political instinct would have permitted defence policy to develop in a direction of which he did not approve. Moreover, the nature of the *ad hoc* policy-making machinery described above, suggests that the Army would have fared much better if it had enjoyed undue influence during this era. The logical conclusion is that the increased strength of the armed forces came about with Nehru's approval.

Fourth, it is conceivable that defence policy went through several redefinitions as a result of the strained relations with Pakistan over Kashmir and, in addition, the establishment of a bilateral economic and military aid agreement between the USA and Pakistan. Despite Nehru's attempt to isolate his country from the impact of the cold war and the inevitable domestic consequences, he was unsuccessful for reasons over which he had little or no control.

During the early 1950s the USA pursued a collective security policy based upon the creation of an interlocking series of alliances designed to hem in the USSR and prevent communist expansionism. Pakistan became a member of the Baghdad Pact in September 1955 and later that year joined SEATO. Although talk of arms transfers had been in the air for several years, when the agreement was struck Pakistan concentrated upon using the aid to create a multi-service

---

[63] Rao (note 60), p. 309.
[64] Kaul, B. M., *The Untold Story* (Allied Publishers: New Delhi, 1967), pp. 97–98.

capability to resist external attack, from India in particular.[65] Consequently, the Government of Pakistan paid special attention to the development of the Pakistan Air Force through the acquisition of the F-86 Sabre, the B-57 Canberra and the F-104, equipped with Sidewinder air-to-air missiles. The Army received heavy artillery, Patton (M-47 and M-48) tanks and M-24, M-4 and M-41 tanks.

The motivation on the part of Pakistan was undoubtedly to counter India's growing military strength and the gradual erosion of the only advantage Pakistan enjoyed, that of superior firepower. Moreover, Pakistan was convinced that the UK favoured India when it came to deliberations concerning arms transfers and the military balance. If Pakistan was to continue to dispute Kashmir, therefore, it had to find economic and military-political aid from somewhere. In the event it somewhat reluctantly pandered to Secretary of State Dulles's policies opposing Soviet expansionism. Nor did the aid arrive without conditions: Pakistan was compelled to offer its airfields as an alternative escape route for US spy planes flying over the USSR, and to permit the construction at Peshawar of a communications base which became an important intelligence centre.

There are three important points to recognize concerning the effect upon India of US aid to Pakistan. First, although it did have an impact upon India's security perspective, the latter's defence policy and posture were not fundamentally altered. India's rearmament programme was well in motion before the mid-1950s, and the argument that there was an 'action–reaction' process which compelled India to change its defence policy has been overstated. Second, the 'action–reaction' cycle can act both ways, and it is more likely that Pakistan's decision to seek military and economic aid was a reaction to the erosion of its firepower capability *vis-à-vis* India. As table 3.2 and figure 3.1 indicate, India appears to have been intent on seeking a significant advantage well before the aid agreement was signed. Many but not all of the acquisitions which arrived after 1955 were planned and/or ordered well before. Moreover, although the records are both poor and patchy, it would seem that India consistently outspent Pakistan in absolute terms on defence by an approximate factor of three. Third, despite reservations about India's non-aligned foreign policy, the USA also provided small quantities of defence equipment to India in the mid-1950s. This of course implies that in the event of renewed fighting between India and Pakistan, problems would occur for US policy makers over which side to support. This is precisely what happened in 1965. The USA embargoed both sides, thereby making a victory for Pakistan very unlikely, if not impossible.

[65] SIPRI (note 39), p. 494.

Table 3.2. Military expenditure and procurement of sophisticated armament in India and Pakistan, 1948–62. Military expenditure is expressed in local currency (current prices).

Year	India mil. ex.[a] (mn rupees)	Pakistan mil. ex.[b] (mn rupees)	Indian Air Force	Pakistan Air Force	Indian Army	Pakistan Army	Indian Navy	Pakistan Navy
1948			100 Spitfire & Tempest (fighters) ? de Havilland Vampires F3 (fighters)					
1949			52 Vampires	10 Sea Fury (fighters)				
1950			F.B9 and NF-54 (fighters)				3 R Class destroyers	
1951	2105			36 Vickers Attacker (bombers)				1 0 Class destroyer
1952	2054							
1953	2138		71 MD-450 Ouragan (fighter bombers)		180/30 M-4 Shermans		3 Hunt Class Escort destroyers	
1954	2163		10 Vampire NF-54 (fighter bombers)			? M-24 Chaffee 200 M-4 Shermans 50 M41 Bulldogs		
1955	2137							
US Aid in Pakistan commences								

Year								
1956	2321		50 Vampire T.55 8 Seahawk (fighters)	120 NA F-86 (fighters)	210 Centurion			2 Battle Class destroyers 1 Dido Class light cruiser
1957	2832		182 Hawker Hunter F.56 & T.66 (fighters) 33 MD450 Ouragans		40 AMX-13		1 Colony Class cruiser	
1958	3106	952	74 Canberra B(1) 58 & PR 57 (bombers/recce)	32 Martin Canberra B-57/Bs and RB-57s		460 M-47 and M-48 Pattons[c]	1 Leopard Class anti-aircraft frigate	4 CV and CH Class destroyers
1959	3065	1063	110 Mystère IVA (interceptors)					
1960	3225	1210	100 Folland Gnat (fighters)			M-113	2 Whitby Class anti-submarine frigates	
1961	3545	1208					1 Majestic Class aircraft-carrier	
1962	4951	1178		14 F-104A and F-104B Star-fighter (fighters)				

[a] Recalculated to calendar year from fiscal years, starting 1 Apr.
[b] Recalculated to calendar year from fiscal years, starting 1 July.
[c] Delivered between 1955 and 1960.

Sources: Kavic, L., *India's Quest for Security: Defence Policies 1947–65* (University of California Press: Berkeley, Calif., 1967); military expenditure data from SIPRI worksheets.

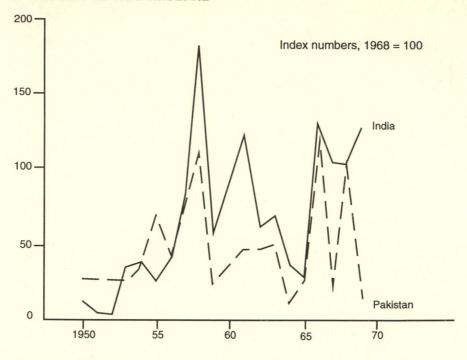

Figure 3.1. Comparison of the rise and fall in major weapon supplies to India and Pakistan, 1950–69

Note: Total major weapon imports to India in the period 1950–69 were $2000 million. Total major weapon imports to Pakistan in the period were $500 million.

Source: SIPRI, *The Arms Trade with the Third World* (Almqvist & Wiksell: Stockholm, 1971), p. 472.

The real cost of growth in the defence sector was largely hidden. In the immediate post-war period, India did not need to draw on its foreign exchange reserves, as it obtained most of its defence equipment from the UK. It was able to pay for much of its defence equipment by drawing heavily on the sterling balances representing the debts incurred by Britain during World War II when many of the latter's costs in India were paid in rupees. This was an extremely useful situation for India, as the British Prime Minister, Winston Churchill, recognized when he alluded to the dilemma it posed for Britain in a memorandum circulated to his Cabinet:

It must be remembered that these two countries [India and Pakistan] may go to War with one another and that is the only object for which they seek arms. Unfair balance was shown to India in the arrangements made at the time of partition and the balance might be slightly redressed in favour of Pakistan. On the other hand we place ourselves in a very questionable position of arming both sides with no other object than long-term advantages of keeping up the United Kingdom manufacturing potentials. For

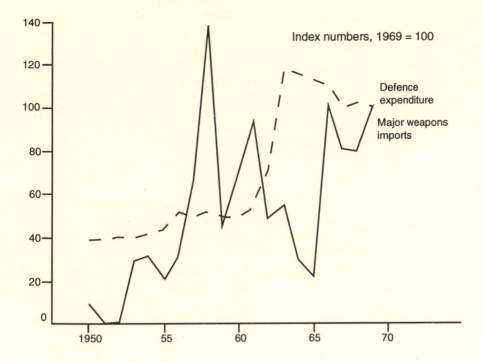

Figure 3.2. Comparison of the rise and fall in major weapon supplies and defence expenditure in India, 1950–69

Note: Total Indian defence expenditure in the period 1950–69 was $16 355 million (at 1960 prices and exchange rates). Total major weapon imports were $2007 million.

Source: SIPRI, *The Arms Trade with the Third World* (Almqvist & Wiksell: Stockholm, 1971), p. 473.

instance, forty-two bombers for Pakistan raises the query 'who are they going to bomb?' Obviously the cities of India. This involves us in serious responsibility. We are like an arms merchant supplying both sides in a possibly impending struggle. There is of course this difference that we do not get paid anything. All that happens is that the amounts are marked off the so-called 'sterling balances' . . . A refusal to continue supplies would not prevent them from obtaining at any rate some of their requirements from elsewhere. This would almost certainly be from outside the sterling area and would thus impose a further strain on the foreign currency reserves of the sterling area as a whole.[66]

In addition, the Indian Government also used the sterling balances to pay pensions to retired service personnel resident in the UK.[67]

In absolute terms and as a proportion of GNP, defence expenditure was low, although the defence burden as a percentage of central government expenditure

[66] 'Supply of arms to India and Pakistan'. Memo from Prime Minister Winston Churchill to Cabinet. Public Record Office, London, Ref. CAB 129/49.
[67] H. M. Patel, conversations with the author, Vidyanagar, Gujarat, 14 May 1991.

was high; in 1950 the Government allocated 29 per cent of current expenditure to defence.[68] The costs in terms of foreign exchange have been estimated at approximately $50 million in 1950, rising to $210 million in 1959.[69] The gap between procurement and expenditure is further borne out by figure 3.2. As procurement increased dramatically between 1956 and 1957 defence expenditure remained relatively constant and did not rise significantly until after the Sino-Indian war of 1962. India received virtually no military aid during this period.

IX. Conclusion

On the basis of the evidence it is possible to conclude that India had embarked upon a significant defence buildup well before both the establishment of the US–Pakistan military aid programme and the 1962 war. The background to this policy can be examined from three angles.[70]

First, it is inconceivable that Nehru was completely unaware of the defence buildup. More likely the duality of defence policy during this period stems in part from, or was facilitated by, the inherent contradiction between Nehru the idealist, international statesman, pacifist/Gandhian and democratic socialist, and Nehru the realist and leader of a large, newly independent country with the potential for real international power and significance. Although by instinct Nehru preferred to use political power and diplomacy rather than force, he may also have realized that a shallow defence capability would severely compromise India's future greatness. In addition, many of the hopes for regional stability were disappointed and from the 'First Round' onwards India sought at least to match and in the event greatly to exceed the military capability of Pakistan. At the same time, Nehru had to be seen to be placing maximum emphasis upon economic and social development, which ruled out expenditure and investment for future international power. The confused defence policy which emerged was a tortuous attempt to find a fit between the present and the future, the domestic and the foreign, and the regional and international influences bearing upon the Prime Minister, who himself was torn between idealist aims and realist instincts.

Second, the role of the armed forces should not be underestimated. Although they were weakened in relative terms after 1947 they still managed to score many institutional successes. This was in part because they had a monopoly of the information and knowledge required to link policy, strategy and technology. It was also because of their steadfast refusal to break conceptually with the Sandhurst legacy; as soldiers schooled in the British tradition they clung tenaciously to the European/Western way of defence despite the costs and

---

[68] Kavic (note 10), appendix I.

[69] Terhal, P., 'Foreign exchange costs of the Indian military, 1950–1972', *Journal of Peace Research*, vol. 19, no. 3 (1982), table I.

[70] I am grateful to Lorne Kavic for his comments on this part of the analysis. Conversations with the author 26 July 1988, Vancouver.

dependency which such a process entailed. Or, to put it another way, they were clever enough to offer no attempt to assist Nehru with the design of a defence policy which would have reflected the key tenets of non-alignment and would have built upon the ideas put forward by Blackett. They simply ignored the contradictions between actual and declared defence policy and readily accepted the considerable rewards of a confused defence policy.

Finally, despite Nehru's best intentions, policy making and implementation were a ramshackle process and remain so to this day. Although the need to deter further threats from Pakistan in Kashmir was accepted by all concerned, the lack of debate, discussion and clear thinking resulted in a confused policy based upon a covert acceptance of realism on the one hand, and the occasional genuflection to idealism on the other. Nehru may have been too preoccupied to orchestrate and follow through a debate among experts, while the armed forces stuck rigidly to their traditionalist views, which eventually prevailed. As it became clear that procurement reflected a slow and moderate growth towards eventual great power status, with all the attendant regional and economic ramifications, the armed forces were content to profit from the drift which others were ill-equipped to halt. Thus, although all agreed that the country had to purchase enough to retain an edge over Pakistan, only the armed forces could differentiate precisely between adequacy and excess. As with other countries the 'how much is enough' problem proved to be an insoluble dilemma for policy makers because the policy process never squarely investigated, debated or rationalized the moves required both to deter Pakistan and to retain the key tenets of Nehru's idealism.

4. From humiliation to regional hegemony: the maturing of defence policy, 1962–80

I. The Sino-Indian War of 1962

The 1962 Sino-Indian War was both a surprise and a disaster for India and the ramifications were numerous and far-reaching. With the benefit of hindsight the conflict seems almost to have been inevitable. During the historic Bandung Conference in 1955 Zhou Enlai and Prime Minister Nehru were by far the major actors. Given that it was fundamentally questionable whether or not the concept of non-alignment could co-exist with communist China, future rivalry between the two great Asian states seemed unavoidable. Although Nehru was sympathetic towards the new China of the 1950s, China made it clear that it had repudiated a number of existing boundaries, including those which had separated Tibet and India since colonial times. Then in March 1959 the Dalai Lama fled to India and set up a Tibetan Government-in-exile in Dharamsala, which China took to be interference by India with its internal affairs. When China then suggested a conference to review their joint frontiers and India retaliated by reiterating the validity of the MacMahon Line, the stage was set for conflict, although Nehru chose to misread most of the warning signals with a curious consistency.

Nehru and his advisers had placed little emphasis upon the threat to NEFA (the North-East Frontier Agency, now renamed Arunachal Pradesh). As suggested in the previous chapter, this may have been in part because to recognize China as a threat to India's security would have involved the Union Government in a much more significant defence effort than was deemed expedient or affordable, over and above the arrangements which had already been made for defence in the north-west. Second, Nehru's idealism and the importance of China to the non-aligned movement made it desirable that the two Asian giants should be seen to be on the best possible terms. Consequently India's policy towards China was invariably forgiving and, wherever possible, Nehru attempted to find foreign policy solutions to bilateral problems, even though his policy led on several occasions to loss of face. For example, Nehru was weak over the independent status of Tibet and little protest was made over the several references to Nehru in Chinese political writings as an 'imperialist running dog' and a 'member of the political garbage group in Asia'.[1] When relations with China eventually became excessively strained the Government's reaction was one of indecision and prevarication.

---

[1] Sardesai, D. R., 'India and Southeast Asia', ed. B. R. Nanda, *Indian Foreign Policy: The Nehru Years* (Vikas: Delhi, 1976), p. 85.

The drift towards war began in 1960 when the Chinese made limited advances into areas around Ladakh. Neither the Nationalist Government of Chiang Kai-shek nor the communist Government which replaced it were prepared to accept the *status quo*. Each served notice on India that China would challenge the legitimacy of the MacMahon Line, the border between Tibet and India which had been recognized by both parties in 1913–14. Both Chinese governments had committed themselves to the restoration of China's former historical power. To this Mao Zedong added his own particular revolutionary perspective. While the Indian Government was relatively complacent regarding the aggression of the Kuomintang Government, over suzerainty over Tibet for example, the accession of a communist Government created some alarm. Furthermore, after 1949 several Maoist communist groups emerged on the Indian political scene and the potential threat of a fifth column would certainly have increased the concern engendered by the accession of Mao Zedong. Nevertheless, Nehru calculated—wrongly—that China could not threaten India so soon after such a long and destructive civil war.[2] Indeed, although Nehru thought that a limited war was possible in the north-western theatre, he thought it impossible between India and China.[3]

Nehru and his advisers continued to misjudge fundamentally Chinese intentions. In 1960 the Chinese Government began to question blatantly the legitimacy of the MacMahon Line by sending patrols into disputed areas. In 1961 the People's Liberation Army occupied Dehra Compass and established a border post on the Chip Chap river which brought the Chinese to their 1960 territorial claim line. The Indian Government began to respond in kind by establishing outposts throughout the disputed areas, for both military and political ends. By mid-1961 the Indian Government considered the position to be relatively stable and balanced, concluded that it was time to challenge the Chinese outposts and severed their lines of supply and communication. On 30 November the Chinese delivered a written warning to India: 'The Chinese government would have every reason to send troops across the so-called MacMahon Line and enter the vast area between the crest of the Himalayas and their southern foot'.[4] In April 1962 the eight-year agreement over Tibet between India and China expired and Chinese activity in the disputed region intensified. By mid-1962 Nehru was still claiming that his China policy had been a success but Beijing retaliated by increasing the number of patrols in the area and attacking India aggressively in newspaper editorials.

In July both sides met eyeball to eyeball when Chinese troops surrounded an Indian border post; the Chinese eventually retreated when the Indian troops stood their ground. Interpreting the Chinese action as a 'blink', the Indian Government became more strong-willed and began to challenge forcefully

---

[2] Kavic, L., *India's Quest for Security: Defence Policies 1947–1965* (University of California Press: Berkeley, Calif., 1967), pp. 41–43.

[3] Vertzberger, Y., 'India's strategic posture and the border war defeat of 1962: a case study of miscalculation', *Strategic Studies*, vol. 5, no. 3 (Sep. 1982), pp. 370–92.

[4] Khera, S. S., *India's Defence Problems* (Orient Longman: New Delhi, 1968), p. 171.

China's movements into NEFA. By September the border dispute appeared to be on the verge of unravelling. Throughout the month the two sides clashed sporadically. By mid-October Nehru let it be known to the press that the Army had been instructed to eject the Chinese troops from NEFA. After further skirmishing the Chinese mobilized along the borders of Sikkim, Bhutan and NEFA. By 20 October the conflict had started and the Chinese advanced on both the Ladakh and the NEFA fronts.

In the Ladakh theatre India proved just able to prevent a complete rout, although by mid-November the Chinese Army was in possession of all the territory its Government had previously claimed. In NEFA the Indian Army fared much worse. In the face of a forceful assault by the Chinese, the Indian defence effort collapsed, the morale of the troops was crushed and the Army leadership disgraced. General Kaul, who had been sent to organize the defence of NEFA, was posted to the Punjab and General Manekshaw took over, while the Chief of Army Staff, General Thapar, opted for indefinite 'sick leave'. With the Chinese within 40 miles of Tezpur (now in Assam) and 100 miles from the Digpoi oil fields, both the military and the Government were in complete disarray.

Although the Indian Army possessed considerable reserves and resources during the early 1960s, its weapons and ancillary equipment were dated, its troops disorganized and, as an institution, the Army was still in a state of transition because it had previously clung too tenaciously to the traditions of the Raj. Furthermore, the defence of NEFA had been overlooked and neglected. After several years of procrastination at the political level throughout the mid-1950s, a suitable strategy for the defence of NEFA was denied either consideration or resources until 1960 when General Thimayya conducted a study of high-altitude defence organization and tactics in the Italian Alps. Thimayya's recommendation for a strategy based upon lightly equipped and mobile infantry in the forward areas and backed by a strong and highly mechanized force on the plains was rejected by Nehru for three interrelated reasons. First, he felt that the Chinese did not constitute a sufficient threat to warrant such a dedicated strategy. Second, the implications for defence expenditure were considerable. Third, he did not want to jeopardize his carefully constructed foreign policy.[5]

On 20 November the Chinese Government announced a unilateral withdrawal to points where it considered the territorial boundaries should be. The Indian Government objected vehemently but there was little it could do except appeal for a withdrawal and a reversion to the *status quo ante*. To all intents and purposes India had lost the war and was forced to face the implications of both territorial loss and national humiliation on a grand scale.

The scale of the defeat and the culpability of both the civilian and military institutions cannot be underestimated. In terms of national identity the 1962 war had an impact upon India similar to the US defeat in Viet Nam. An even greater loss of international prestige was avoided only by the occurrence of the

---

[5] Kavic (note 2), p. 96.

Cuban Missile Crisis at the same time, which kept the rest of the world greatly concerned and fully occupied. From a military standpoint the armed forces proved to be utterly incapable of defending India's territorial integrity in the east and the implications of the débâcle were not lost on those who were concerned for the future of Kashmir.

Although it is generally agreed that the Indian armed forces fared very badly, there are differences in the judgements of exactly how poorly they performed which range from total non-performance to marginal defeat. Over the course of the war only the Army was actively engaged. The Navy could not have played any part in the conflict. The Air Force was scarcely used, for four possible reasons. First, there were technical difficulties involved in operating in Himalayan altitudes, particularly when the aircraft were fully armed, and when the problems became evident military leaders became reluctant to use air power.[6] Second, the threat from the Chinese armed forces was exclusively ground-based because they too sidelined the Air Force. This reinforced the hesitance of the Indian leadership, though much might have been gained from ground attack missions against an opposing army which lacked air cover. Instead, the role of the IAF was limited to supply and transport duties, and even these perfunctory tasks were complicated by a limited number of poor-quality landing strips at Leh in Ladakh and Chusul in NEFA. Third, the Army's reluctance to call upon the IAF was possibly due to traditionalism and inertia where inter-service co-operation was concerned.[7] Fourth and more likely, however, the Army may have decided to sideline the Air Force as a way of downplaying the importance of airpower during a period when the IAF as an institution was in the ascendancy (see chapter 3, section V). Had the Army performed better it could have increased the legitimacy of its claim for increased capital expenditures following a period when its own fortunes had been meagre.

Following the termination of hostilities the Government commissioned an enquiry by Lt-Gen. Henderson-Brooks. This remains classified, and since the war successive Indian governments have refused to release this and other documentation pertaining to the conflict with China. Most of the information available is to be found either in autobiographical accounts from high-ranking officers involved in the war or from commentators who have used either these sources or their authors for primary source material.

The most popular and enduring explanation for the Indian defeat charged Krishna Menon with almost total blame, although the significance of the 'Menon factor' is unclear. In many ways it does seem that Menon had a poor record in certain areas of security planning, particularly with regard to the Army and his alleged attempts to build a separate political base through promotions. In fact, although a significant amount of advanced new equipment was absorbed by the armed forces during Menon's term, for the most part it had

---

[6] Subrahmanyam, K., 'Nehru and the India–China conflict of 1962', in Nanda, B. R., *Indian Foreign Policy: The Nehru Years* (Vikas: Delhi, 1976), p. 119.

[7] Thomas, R. G. C., *Indian Security Policy* (Princeton University Press: Princeton, N.J., 1986), pp. 145–46.

been ordered before he took control of the defence portfolio. With the exception of the Hunter deal, Menon generally attempted to acquire a reputation as an economy-minded rather than as a profligate Defence Minister.[8] Equally Menon was the politician senior Indian Army officers loved to hate and the crushing defeat by China offered an opportunity to place total blame on Menon's shoulders and mount a full-scale campaign to have him removed from office. Over time the constant and unrelenting criticism of Menon from the press, the armed forces and the Congress Party created a situation which led directly to Menon's resignation. It also created a convenient atmosphere in which any other explanation for defeat became inconceivable.

Vertzberger has traced the roots of the 1962 failure to bureaucratic mismanagement and dereliction of duty on the part of the key decision makers.[9] In contrast, Lt-Col J. R. Saigal, a senior Army officer who experienced at first hand the rout in NEFA, has argued that excessive corruption and incompetence in the higher echelons of the Army during the early 1960s were to blame. He also asserts that India's defences in NEFA crumbled from the very start of the war.[10] Nehru himself remained loyal to Menon and only demoted him under extreme pressure, preferring instead to blame defeat upon intelligence, equipment and logistical failures.

The causes of the 1962 defeat remain, therefore, somewhat confused. Clearly, the defence effort was deficient and it is likely that the war was lost through a combination of political miscalculation, inadequate security arrangements, intelligence failures and military error, in that chronological order. The ramifications of the 1962 defeat were, however, more important than the defeat itself. The outward sense of optimism which had characterized defence and foreign policy making at the political level between 1947 and 1962 never returned. Thereafter, politicians from all parties were at one in arguing that, in the future, expenditure on defence should be a first charge on the exchequer.

In the aftermath of the humiliating defeat, Nehru admitted to a failure in defence planning claiming that 'military weakness has been a temptation, and a little military strength may be a deterrent'.[11] In October 1962 Menon was demoted within the Cabinet and the Government lost not only a remarkable if controversial political figure but also a decision maker with a genuine commitment to self-sufficiency in the defence sector, which, as will be seen, was very significant for India over the long term. Following pressure from senior members of the Congress Party Nehru took up the defence portfolio himself and moved Menon to a newly created but insignificant Cabinet post of Minister for Defence Production, a position which deprived him of much of his earlier influence.

[8] Kavic (note 2), fn. 33, pp. 155–56.

[9] Vertzberger, Y., 'Bureaucratic-organizational politics and information processing in a developing state', *International Studies Quarterly*, vol. 28, no. 1 (Mar. 1984), pp. 69–93.

[10] Saigal, Lt Col J. R., *The Unfought War of 1962: The NEFA Debacle* (Allied Publishers: New Delhi, 1979). As a Lieutenant Colonel Saigal ranked seventh in the Indian Army chain of command and rank structure.

[11] Kavic (note 2), p. 192.

Once Menon had been sidelined the Cabinet set about redressing what it considered to be one of the former Defence Minister's key failures, namely a lack of defence preparedness. Whether or not this charge against Menon was justified, it had the effect of concentrating the Government's attention on technological rather than institutional solutions to the country's insecurities. Indeed, the former virtually cancelled out the latter: an under-equipped army is not necessarily inefficient or the victim of poor foreign policy, military, intelligence and political decision making. Nehru and the rest of the Cabinet were admitting the wrong mistake. As has been argued in the previous chapter, India was not a militarily weak country overall, even though the eastern borders may have been poorly defended and these problems compounded by an inhospitable terrain and acute logistical shortcomings.[12] The modernization programme of the 1950s had given India a defence posture of some significance, inappropriate perhaps for defence against China and biased towards the Air Force but, nevertheless, India could hardly claim to be militarily weak.

In the years before the war the armed forces had been given a relatively free hand in the interpretation of defence needs. In so doing and together with the politicians, they had virtually ignored the prospect of a conflict with China, although they did demand a change of policy when it became evident that the defence of NEFA was inadequate given Chinese intentions. For the armed forces and, indeed, Nehru and his advisers, the threat to India's security was in the north-west and their reasoning was much more subtle than politics and defence, as Kavic has recognized:

In the absence of a clearly identifiable threat from China until the later 'fifties, Pakistan provided an expedient strategic rationale without which, given the pronounced nonaligned posture of the government, sound and efficient military policies would have been difficult to formulate and implement. The civilian fear and distrust of Pakistan thus appeared as a 'blessing in disguise' in preventing even greater economies in defence outlay and was used to good effect.[13]

II. Defence policy

In the aftermath of the 1962 war the Indian Government and polity were united in the need to commit increased resources and effort to upgrade the country's defence capabilities. The first budget after the war in 1963 planned for a near doubling of defence expenditure from the Rs.473 crores allocated in 1962/63, which included an emergency allocation of Rs.100 crores for the war effort, to Rs.867 crores.[14] In the following year India increased the percentage of GNP spent on defence to 4 per cent per annum, a massive 32.5 per cent of total gov-

[12] According to Raju Thomas, a shipment of small arms was rapidly moved from the Western to the Eastern sector when hostilities began but took six weeks thereafter to reach the front line: Thomas (note 7).
[13] Kavic (note 2), p. 153.
[14] Thomas, R. G. C., *The Defence of India: A Budgetary Perspective of Strategy and Politics* (Macmillan: Delhi, 1978), p. 106. A crore is 10 million.

ernment expenditure. At the same time, all debate at any level on the required scale of defence expenditure disappeared. Instead, the primary question became one of how best to allocate the quantum increase in defence allocations.

The rise in defence expenditure after the war led to a rigorous upgrading of defence capability. The result was a five-year plan for defence made public in early 1964 and implemented immediately. The plan had six objectives: (*a*) the creation of an 825 000-man army and the modernization of its weapons and equipment; (*b*) modernization of the IAF and its stabilization at 45 squadrons; (*c*) the modernization but not expansion of the Navy; (*d*) an increase in the domestic defence production base; (*e*) infrastructural improvements in the border areas; and (*f*) the expansion of R&D.[15] However, it is interesting to note at this point that the modernization programme represented essentially more of the same. Nehru and his successor, Lal Bahadur Shastri (Nehru died in May 1964), committed India to a full-scale modernization programme with a renewed emphasis upon the threat from China, but neither considered a defence *review*. Nor, parenthetically, was there much desire to seek fully the opinions of the legislature through parliamentary debate. At no point, it seems, was the question addressed why India failed to defend itself adequately against China, given the resources it had at its disposal overall. Consequently, failures at the level of strategic planning, intelligence and military performance were subsumed under a more general acceptance that whatever resources the Indian armed forces had at the time were insufficient to meet the security threats on all the relevant fronts.

Coupled with the commitments already made to defence between 1947 and 1962, some of which had not come to fruition by 1962, the five-year plan amounted to a significant increase in India's defence capability. Nevertheless, there were inherent and persistent weaknesses. Despite the commitment to increased defence production, the armed forces remained heavily and unduly dependent upon imported military technology, which increased proportionally as imports rose. A clear strategy for reversing this situation was nowhere in evidence, in stark contrast to Nehru's stated commitment to indigenization and the 1964 Defence Plan. Not only did this place increasing pressure upon foreign exchange reserves, which eventually led to substantial delays in procurement, it also begot political obstacles as the country automatically became hostage to the vagaries of the bi-polar international system.

III. The 1964 rearmament programme

The new defence plan began in April 1964 and was designed to extend over a three-year period. It concentrated primarily upon re-equipping and strengthening the Army following a period of restraint before the 1962 war. The Army programme was specifically directed towards meeting the Chinese threat and Nehru went to considerable pains to assure the Pakistani President, Ayub Khan,

[15] Kavic (note 2), pp. 192–93.

that the programme was designed for defence against China rather than belligerence against Pakistan.

As a first step India appealed for military aid, despite the consensus over the need to raise defence allocations, and the response was a good one. This also contradicted India's policy of non-alignment. The USA and the UK both extended equipment grants of $60 million and Canada, France and Australia contributed supplies to the value of about $10 million.[16]

In March 1962 the budget for the Army stood at Rs.245 crores; in the budget following the war allocations more than doubled to Rs.571 crores.[17] Together with the aid packages this rise facilitated a major re-equipment programme and an organizational and training review.

On *matériel*, the replacement of the Lee-Enfield .303 rifle by the semi-automatic Ishapore was speeded up, heavy mortars were procured from France together with an agreement on licensed production, the ordnance factories were instructed to develop a mountain howitzer and the production of Japanese Nissan trucks was increased.[18] The Avadi Heavy Vehicles factory in Madras delivered 70 medium tanks to the Army in 1965, the Sten machine gun was replaced by the more modern Sterling, the .303 was rebored to a new standard, and improved types of communications equipment were sought from both foreign and domestic sources. Efforts were also made to upgrade the quality of the vehicle fleet by discarding vehicles after less use and acquiring better licensed production arrangements.[19]

The size of the Army was increased from 10–11 divisions to 21 divisions and stress was placed upon the development of mountain divisions and the recruitment of hill peoples such as Gurkhas and Nagas. Troop training for jungle and mountain warfare was stepped up, largely through the expansion of the High Altitude Warfare School. Some attempt was made to overcome the extreme reliance upon conventional tactics, particularly with regard to mobility, which made the Indian Army so vulnerable to the unorthodox procedures employed by the Chinese communists, the result of the distinctive approach to warfare developed by Mao Zedong. On the organizational front new logistical guide-lines were introduced and similar efforts were made to make better use of intelligence.[20]

The acquisition of armoured fighting vehicles had been largely decided upon before the war and little was accomplished between the termination of the Sino-Indian War and the outbreak of the 1965 war with Pakistan. Even the acquisition of the Soviet PT-76 light tank dates back to 1955 and the agreement to procure 225 T-55 main battle tanks between 1968 and 1971 also pre-dates the 1962 war.

[16] SIPRI, *The Arms Trade with the Third World* (Almqvist & Wiksell: Stockholm, 1971), p. 477.

[17] Thomas (note 14), p. 151.

[18] SIPRI (note 16), p. 477.

[19] Kavic (note 2), p. 195.

[20] Kavic (note 2), pp. 183–84, 195.

For both the Air Force and the Navy there was less that could be achieved directly because the blame for defeat and thereafter the emphasis upon modernization was placed squarely upon the Army. However, this did not prevent the Air Force from receiving a substantial increase in planned strength, although not all for front-line equipment. Contained within the plans for expanding the Air Force to 45 squadrons were proposals for a strengthening of ground-based air defence, increased transport capacity, to be financed from US military aid, and Soviet and French helicopters in the form of 50 Mi-4s and 20 Sud Alouette IIIs. The Government also reached agreement with France over the licensed production of the Alouette III and between 1966 and 1973 120 units were produced at Hindustan Aeronautics Ltd (HAL), allegedly with an indigenous content of 90 per cent.[21] Another fillip to the indigenous defence effort came with the redeployment of the team working on the Kiran jet trainer over to the HF-24 fighter project, although in the event the hopes for the swift upgrading of the aircraft to a supersonic version came to little. Indeed, the procurement of 160 Hawker Hunter F.56s through the 1950s to replace the Vampires, Ouragans and Mystères was seen as an interim measure pending the completion of the HF-24 project, which perhaps indicates the lack of faith of the defence planners in the capabilities of HAL (see chapter 7).

The Navy received even less in the modernization programme. Although overtures were made towards the Swedish and Japanese governments concerning possible collaborative ventures, it is likely that the moves were made to unsettle the UK's confidence in future orders and thereby to up the ante—a ploy which was used again to good effect in the 1980s. The strategy quickly showed results when the UK offered the Indian Government credits totalling £4.7 million for the construction of three Leander Class frigates, an offer that was swiftly accepted. Both the UK and the USA refused to accede to India's request for three destroyers and the UK was also equivocal over requests for production facilities for the Oberon Class submarine following the Indian Government's acceptance of the Navy's argument for a submarine arm. However, the Government did manage to augment the capability of the *Vikrant* and establish bases on the Andaman Islands and at Vishakhapatnam, which also became a major dockyard.[22]

IV. The strengthening of Soviet–Indian relations

Perhaps the major shift in government policy over this period concerned the consolidation of cordial relations with the USSR and, to a much lesser extent, the development of a supplier–recipient relationship with the USA. The flirtation with the USSR was primarily intended to provide the quantity of defence equipment which India's meagre foreign exchange reserves could not cover if

[21] SIPRI, *Arms Trade Registers: The Arms Trade with the Third World* (Almqvist and Wiksell: Stockholm, 1975).

[22] Kavic (note 2), pp. 201–202.

all the equipment was procured from Western sources. It was also ideologically more acceptable to a ruling party which espoused and practised, technically at least, the tenets of democratic socialism.

The burgeoning relationship with the USSR in fact went back to the mid-1950s and does not date from the cooling of Sino-Soviet relations in the early 1960s, as might be expected. A major turning point came as the USSR moved away from the isolationist policies adopted in the 1940s under Stalin in favour of a more active foreign policy under First Secretary Nikita Sergeyevich Khrushchev. Even before the crucial Twentieth Congress of the Communist Party in 1956, the USSR was eyeing India as an ally. As early as August 1953 the Chairman of the Soviet Council of Ministers, Georgi Malenkov, made a straightforward bid for friendship:

The position of so large a state as India is of great importance for strengthening peace in the East. India has made a considerable contribution to the efforts of peace-loving countries aimed at ending the war in Korea, and relations with India are stronger; cultural and economic ties are developing. We hope that relations between India and the Soviet Union will continue to develop and grow, with friendly cooperation as the keynote.[23]

A trade agreement in 1953 was followed by an unofficial visit in the same year by Nehru's daughter, Indira Gandhi, who became the next but one Prime Minister. The unprecedented visit to Moscow by Nehru in June 1955 was followed by the visit of Soviet Prime Minister Bulganin and Khrushchev to Delhi five months later. The material benefits which India derived from the relationship were considerable. In 1953 trade turnover between the two countries was only $1.6 million, a total lower than it had been during the last days of the tsars. However, by 1958 trade had increased to $94.6 million and by 1965 India had become the largest non-communist trading partner of the USSR. Up until the late 1980s the rupee–rouble trade continued to be of considerable benefit to India, particularly as a means of acquiring defence equipment.

The relationship was also significant in other ways. Whereas Western suppliers often prevaricated over the transfer of capital goods, the USSR wasted no time when it came to turnkey projects such as the Bhilai steel mill, because bureaucratic–ideological factors overshadowed commercial interests, both long-term and short-term. In 1960, the USSR began to provide India with cheap crude oil. On all transactions India was able to pay either with rupees or in goods, which permitted it on occasion to export manufactured items which could not be sold in the West. However, this benefit was partially offset by the Soviet penchant for reselling certain Indian goods in Europe to help its own foreign exchange problems. This subsequently drove down the value of Indian exports. Finally, economic aid was given on extremely favourable terms, generally with an interest rate of 2.5 per cent over 12 years with payments beginning only when the project was completed. In contrast, offers from

[23] Menon, K. P. S., *The Flying Troika* (Oxford University Press: London, 1963), p. 58.

Western governments were in the region of 4.5–6.3 per cent over a shorter length of time, with repayments in hard currency.[24] Given the potential volume of trade in both civilian and military goods, this was an offer India could hardly refuse.

However, head and shoulders above all other benefits, the USSR began to export defence equipment on equally favourable terms. In 1960 both sides reached agreements on military credits and in the followings years up until 1965 the transfer of helicopters and aircraft (Mi-14, An-12, MiG-21), Atoll air-to-air missiles for the MiG-21 and light tanks proceeded apace. This equipment came cheaply and permitted India the opportunity both to diversify and to increase its overall defence capability. Moreover, the USSR proved a useful ally in other, related ways. When India invaded the Portuguese enclaves of Goa, Damon and Diu the USSR used its power of veto in the UN Security Council to minimize the scale and impact of international condemnation. As relations between China and India grew worse prior to the outbreak of war the USSR adopted a neutral position which was as much a disadvantage for Beijing as it was an advantage for New Delhi, although during the early stages of the conflict the USSR appeared to favour 'brotherly' China over 'friendly' India, albeit temporarily.[25] Nevertheless, the Indian Government managed to extract the most advantageous conditions from the USSR in part because it successfully played off the two superpowers against each other; after all India was a potentially huge market and a notable ideological prize.

Throughout the period leading up to the MiG deal, the Indian Government actively entertained the idea of a significant procurement of advanced military technology from the USA. For example, throughout early 1964 the Government appeared to be negotiating with the USA for the commercial sale of finished and unassembled F-104s (including a plant to be built in India by the USA), the F-101 Voodoo, the F-102 all-weather interceptor—the system most comparable to the MiG-21—and three to five squadrons of F-51 Skyray and F-5B Freedom Fighters, both equipped with Sidewinder missiles.[26] However, negotiations came to nothing. In theory, a defence agreement with India would have been in the best interests of the USA as a further bolster against the communist bloc. (Even though tensions between China and the USSR had already occurred, the full significance of the Sino-Soviet split was recognized somewhat slowly in Washington.) At one point it looked as though India might acquire a 20-year credit arrangement with the Export-Import Bank for a part of the transaction, but its inability to finance such a major deal was fairly evident from the outset. The flirtation with Washington was quite probably a well-disguised attempt to create concern in Moscow and offset Soviet attempts to curry favour with Pakistan during this period. What the Kremlin was hoping to achieve was to deprive both China and the USA of a useful and strategically important ally. Furthermore, during the period when the MiG deal was under consideration,

[24] Horn, R. C., *Soviet–Indian Relations: Issues and Influence* (Praeger: New York, 1982), pp. 1–15.
[25] Sandhu, B., *Unresolved Conflict: India and China* (Sangam Books: London, 1988), p. 175.
[26] Kavic (note 2), pp. 198–99.

Moscow was by no means convinced that India should become the favoured state in South Asia.

As the inter-war (1962–65) rearmament process continued, the scale of diversification became clear, as did the Government's willingness to consider acquiring military technology from practically anywhere. Basically, India had started to move away from reliance upon the UK for defence equipment, and turned to both Eastern and other Western suppliers to ensure that no one country or power bloc could be in a position selectively to deny defence equipment and thereby influence either defence or foreign policy. In effect what this amounted to was a form of negative non-alignment. Nevertheless, the strategic wisdom of this policy is open to question, as was the degree of success. Diversification without doubt makes for an excellent political choice, particularly when a country's foreign policy is based upon the principle of non-alignment, which is so difficult to practise in many areas. However, from a logistical perspective the acquisition of equipment from so many different sources with such little interoperability must have created some extremely time-consuming and expensive problems, particularly *vis-à-vis* spare part inventories and maintenance. These problems would have been compounded by India's geographic size, the need to deter on two fronts after 1962 and its underdeveloped infrastructure; it only needs to be remembered how much concern there has been in NATO over interoperability to appreciate the problems for a country such as India which operates both Western and Soviet equipment.

V. The 1965 Indo-Pakistani War: consolidation and a new direction

In 1965 Pakistan and India clashed again (the 'Second Round'), but India had relatively little difficulty in asserting its undoubted quantitative military superiority. Since independence, the boundaries in the inhospitable area of the Rann of Kutch were ill-defined, and during 1965 several skirmishes occurred. Pakistan's success in this quarter encouraged it to take the conflict to Kashmir to exploit India's political weakness following the death of Nehru. Because the Kashmir issue was internationally sensitive India could ill afford a drawn-out conflict and mounted a massive three-pronged attack across the border towards Lahore. When China threatened to open a second front in support of its ally, Pakistan, the superpowers intervened and forced both to a ceasefire and a return to the *status quo ante*.

During the conflict it was more a case of Pakistan performing badly than India performing well. The Pakistani Air Force was in principle much better equipped than the IAF following the recent acquisition in significant numbers of the F-104 and F-86 from the USA and, indeed, it managed to conduct some successful operations. The Pakistani pilots, however, found the F-104s extremely difficult to handle and throughout the conflict they were deployed with less efficacy than the Indian Gnat, which performed to a much higher level than expected. Much the same was true of Pakistan's Patton tanks whose crew were unable to come to terms with the automatic fire controls.[27] All in all, the conflict was short-lived and relatively fruitless. Pakistan's attempt to spotlight the Kashmir problem on the world stage by provoking action by Muslim freedom fighters across the UN cease-fire line was rather futile. Similarly, India's attempt seriously to weaken the Pakistani defence effort through attrition on the ground was hardly a resounding success either, even though the Indian armed forces did prevail following both counter-attack and invasion.[28]

Coming so soon after both the 1962 Sino-Indian War and the death of Nehru, the 1965 war prompted a serious political debate within India over the credibility of non-alignment as a means towards security. Nehru had always possessed a wider vision of the positive role and indeed the nuisance value of neutralism and non-alignment. However, the effect and impact of his foreign policy was experienced principally beyond the region of South Asia and, furthermore, non-alignment did not seem to deliver the requisite security closer to home. Within the space of three years India had been attacked by both China and Pakistan, both of whom were edging closer together diplomatically, and India held territory claimed by both. Neither the superpowers nor the UK seemed to possess either the loyalty or the influence to prevent an attack by either China or Pakistan. Still less could be done to prevent a united front. Without doubt, non-alignment was the preferred foreign policy for India but the new Prime Minister, Indira Gandhi, was faced with the problem of finding a fit between foreign policy, security and defence in the absence of both healthy foreign exchange reserves and alignment with a major power.

In the wake of the 1965 war Indira Gandhi sought to consolidate India's regional position after two decades of flux in defence and foreign policy coupled with an uncertain domestic political environment. First, however, she addressed the complex and troublesome domestic front, an inevitable prerequisite for future activity at the regional level. In the late 1960s she split the Congress Party and in so doing unexpectedly consolidated her political position and guaranteed her immediate political future by alienating the right with the backing of the left and centre of the party. This gave the Prime Minister an increasingly firm grip upon the political process and gave her a much sounder political power base.

Between 1965 and 1971 activity on the defence front was low-key. Without doubt, the new Prime Minister's concern to ensure her own political future distracted her attention from regional issues, particularly after the successful conclusion of the 1965 war. It was also the case that Indira Gandhi had two major problems to confront which slowed the rate of further defence procurement; the first concerned internal economic problems, the second a pronounced dip in relations with the USSR.

During the late 1960s the Indian economy started to show signs of stagnation. Until 1965 economic progress had been reasonably good. The industrial

[27] SIPRI (note 16), p. 75.
[28] Kavic (note 2), p. 189.

base had grown significantly between 1950 and 1965, particularly after the balance of payments crisis in 1957, which led directly to severe import controls. Government investment in the capital goods sector and the intermediate sectors, such as iron and steel, had been considerable and with development expenditure, the demand for these goods increased. During this period industrial output grew by about 7 per cent a year. Agricultural output increased by 2.8 per cent a year and the annual GNP growth rate was in excess of 4 per cent. Furthermore, the battle within the Congress Party during the first few years of independence between the more conservative groups aligned to business interests, led by Vallabhbhai Patel and Prakesh Tandon, and the democratic socialist/development lobby led by Nehru had been resolved in the latter's favour. During this era it seemed as though India could possibly find answers to its enormous and complex problems of poverty and underdevelopment, even though really effective wealth redistribution was lacking—the lower 40 per cent of the Indian population experienced little benefit from these economic improvements.

Instead, at the very point when the Indian economy should have experienced take-off it drifted into a decade of stagnation caused by a combination of the appalling droughts of 1965–66 and 1966–67, a sharp decline in foreign aid and growing contradictions within the economy. As the numbers employed in the industrial sectors increased, by 6 per cent between 1960 and 1965, agricultural production declined. Although food aid created initial stability, agricultural prices increased one-third more quickly than the price of manufactured goods between 1960 and 1964. Basically, the Indian agricultural sector was failing to keep pace with growth rates in other parts of the economy, which caused both inflation and an undue and unpopular reliance upon food aid.[29]

The Indian economy became vulnerable as, during the Third Five Year Plan, industries expanded, consumer incomes rose and the Government encouraged exports.[30] There were increasing problems over the nature and direction of foreign assistance, particularly from the USA, and the Government was unable either to raise taxes further or to push public sector industries to produce their own savings. The increasing lack of fit between agricultural and industrial growth presented the Government with impossible choices which were compounded by the opposition of farmers to compulsory state procurement at fixed prices and the taxation of agricultural income.[31] The choices open to the Government were either to extract savings from the economy and suffer the political consequences or to push for substantially increased foreign aid both to tide the economy over and to stimulate exports and agricultural growth. However, whichever strategy was chosen, good harvests were needed to relieve the aid burden and this is precisely where the economy came unstuck when

[29] Mellor, J. W., 'The Indian economy: objectives, performance and prospects', ed. J. W. Mellor, *India: A Rising Middle Power* (Selectbook Service Syndicate: Delhi, 1981), p. 100.

[30] Weiner, M., 'Assessing the political impact of foreign assistance', ed. Mellor (note 29), pp. 49–68.

[31] Rubin, B. R., *Private Power and Public Investment in India: A Study in the Political Economy of Development* (unpublished PhD dissertation, University of Chicago, Ill., 1982), p. 182.

failed harvests and famine struck India in the two-year period 1965–67.[32] All in all the economy did not recover for almost a full decade.

The onset of agricultural problems and the economic crisis did not lead directly to a reduction in defence allocations but it certainly led to their stabilization. Between 1965 and 1971 total defence expenditure never actually went down, although it fell as a percentage both of total government expenditure and of GNP. From a high point in 1965–66, when defence expenditure totalled 4 per cent of GNP, it declined to under 3.5 per cent before rising again temporarily between 1971 and 1973 to a fraction under 4.0 per cent.[33] During the period after the 1962 war, the growth in defence expenditure was compensated for by corresponding tax increases. However, the raising of taxes to fund increased defence expenditure did not increase the resource base available for investment in the public sector, and this inevitably added to the economic problems which the Government had to face.[34]

The second factor which influenced defence policy and posture was increasing uncertainty regarding India's relationship with the USSR. The motivations on the part of both sides during this period were extremely complicated and have much to do with the international geopolitical web involving China, the USSR and the USA on the one hand, and India and Pakistan on the other. The common denominators throughout this period were China and the attempts by both superpowers to alter the balance of power in Asia and globally by either including or excluding China.

The interest in China followed two unrelated events, the Sino-Soviet split and President Nixon's decision to withdraw from Viet Nam. For the USSR, China presented a major problem. Unable and unwilling to mend the rift that had opened up in the late 1950s, the USSR sought to isolate communist China and prevent if possible the growing *rapprochement* between China and the USA. After 1962, India became a natural ally in this process but, for unrelated reasons, Soviet-Indian relations deteriorated over the late 1960s. First, the USSR was disappointed when India failed to sign the NPT, which was opened for signature in July 1968: the treaty was clearly unpopular in India. Second, internal developments within India, prior to Indira Gandhi's consolidation of power, appeared to the Kremlin to be moving too far to the right and frequent references to Indian 'monopoly capitalism' in the Soviet press widened the rift, as did calls for increased nationalization. The USSR was also critical of progress on some of the major turnkey projects it had developed in India. Nor was the situation improved by New Delhi's cautious but unequivocal condemnation of the Soviet invasion of Czechoslovakia in 1968 and the brutal suppression of the Prague Spring. Third, New Delhi objected to the publication of Soviet maps of South Asia which placed the Sino-Indian border more or less in its *de facto* position.

---

[32] Mellor (note 29), p. 103.
[33] Thomas (note 7), table 5.5, p. 184.
[34] Rubin (note 31), p. 184.

Above all, however, New Delhi was dismayed by Soviet efforts throughout the last half of the 1960s to drive a wedge between China and Pakistan by successfully developing closer relations with the latter, which was in part motivated by Moscow's belief that India was too independent an ally to trust completely—at one point India even considered offering an olive branch to China to ensure New Delhi's independence of action. The most important activity between Pakistan and the USSR following the economic aid packages of the early 1960s was the successful conclusion of an arms transfer agreement in 1968. For Pakistan, the deal was designed to fill the vacuum created by the US embargo in 1965 which, although partially lifted in 1966, had created great problems owing to Pakistan's erstwhile near complete reliance upon US defence equipment. The arms actually transferred were barely significant and did not include, for example, missiles, and also came with a proviso which prevented their use against India.[35] However, it was the political context which concerned India. Not only did the deal coincide with a further weakening of US–Pakistani relations following the premature cancellation of the US lease on Peshawar, but around the same time Western newspapers reported discussions between Pakistan and the USSR over refuelling rights in East Pakistan; India had earlier refused to consider a similar request.[36]

The combination of economic and internal political problems and a cooling of relations with the USSR severely restricted India's ability to continue the modernization of its armed forces; the Government was simply unable to acquire defence equipment on the open market from the UK, the USA and other major Western suppliers. Arms transfers from the USSR did not cease completely during this difficult period but the lack of commitment was evident. In September 1964, Moscow agreed to provide India with an additional 38 MiG-21s as well as SA-2 Guideline missiles for air defence. In 1968 the transfer of 100 Su-7B fighters costing $1 million each began and continued until the end of the decade. India also received 40 T-54 tanks in 1968 and 1969 and, perhaps most significantly, three F Class submarines during the same period.[37] Nevertheless, much of the equipment received had been agreed upon during a period when relations were much less strained and India's economy less precarious—the announcement that India would request Soviet submarines, for example, came in early 1964 following the US delivery of a submarine to Pakistan.

For the Air Force and Army the period between the two wars with Pakistan, 1965–71, was largely given over to operational improvements rather than procurement. After both the 1962 and 1965 wars it was evident that the Army had not exploited the potential military utility of air power. Although the problems

---

[35] Reports differ as to what the agreement entailed. *The Statesman* (Calcutta) (12 July 1968) suggested that the transfer consisted of spare parts for the dilapidated tanks (T-59) and aircraft (MiG-19) Pakistan had received from China, whereas SIPRI suggests that the transfers were tanks and aircraft spare parts. See SIPRI, *SIPRI Yearbook of World Armaments and Disarmament 1969–70* (Almqvist and Wiksell: Stockholm, 1970), p. 25

[36] SIPRI (note 35), p. 499.

[37] SIPRI (note 16), pp. 833–36.

in 1962 were both technical and institutional, it was only in 1965 that the Army considered using the country's considerable air power for tactical combat support when it found itself under extreme pressure. For the most part the Army and Air Force fought separate wars. In 1969, however, the command and control boundaries between the two services were redefined to facilitate co-ordination and the benefits of this move were reaped in the 1971 war.[38]

What India appears to have experienced during this period was significant assimilation problems.[39] After more than a decade of frantic procurement for the Air Force in particular, minimal attempts appear to have been made to exploit effectively all aspects of the technology on offer—the full potential of the equipment was not recognized or, if it was, the military leadership failed to master the new-found capability.

A very different picture obtained for the Indian Navy between the 1965 and 1971 wars. As with the Air Force, the Navy saw little in the way of active duty during the 1962 and 1965 wars, in part because the wars were land based and the naval threats were minimal, but also because the Indian military leadership failed to request naval assistance for blockades, for example.

The Indian Navy's blue water role had been established nearly two decades earlier and during the late 1960s the chiefs of naval staff, Admiral Chatterji and his successor Admiral S. M. Nanda, co-ordinated a high-profile debate on raising the status of the Indian Navy. Arguing that the country's naval power should be increased was however made all the more difficult by the relative absence of a serious threat from the Indian Ocean. In recent history the most significant event which the key opinion-shapers could allude to were the reports during the 1965 war, later confirmed in the memoirs of a Pakistani air marshal, that Indonesia's President Sukarno had offered to divert India's attention and resources by seizing the Andaman and Nicobar Islands which lie roughly between the two countries.[40] Another consideration was the growing dependence of China on oil imports and the military advantage which could be gained by restricting Chinese shipping, thus relieving the pressures on India's northern landward defences.[41]

The naval debate centred upon the British decision taken in 1966 to withdraw all forces east of Suez and surrender the control of the Indian Ocean. The prospect of a power vacuum in the region and the entrenched belief among Indian strategists, notably K. M. Pannikar, that whoever controls the Indian Ocean has India at its mercy, opened up an opportunity for naval planners to argue that the country should extend its naval influence.

A report undertaken by the naval study group at the Indian Defence College in early 1969 mooted the idea that India should take the initiative to form a strong military alliance with 'other' South-East Asian countries and/or one of

---

[38] Thomas (note 7), pp. 152–53.

[39] For a useful explanation of the assimilation concept see Dupoy, T. N., *The Evolution of Weapons and Warfare* (Hero Books: Fairfax, Va, 1984).

[40] Thomas (note 7), pp. 152–53.

[41] This was the view of Capt. D. R. Mehta, quoted in Harrigan, A., 'India's maritime posture', *Military Review*, Apr. 1969.

the two superpowers. In open defiance of existing foreign policy, the study group argued the need to contain China by superior strength and this entailed a departure from non-alignment until such time as India's industrial and economic base was sufficiently strong to support independent action, which would be unlikely until around 1980.[42] The incumbent Defence Minister, Swaran Singh, rejected the report, as did Indian Army strategists who argued that India should have a brown not a blue water naval strategy.

Nevertheless, the British withdrawal from East of Suez provided momentum for the debate over allocations to the Indian Navy, much of which was articulated via the influential Madras newspaper, *The Hindu*.[43] Moreover, the Navy found a measure of support in parliamentary circles, particularly among élites which shared the long-term view of India becoming a world power of some significance. A parallel debate also emerged in the USA with a suggestion that it should protect India's maritime interests until such time as it could fully afford to operate independently, which also fitted well with the foreign policy designs of the era: 'the United States should underwrite the maritime security of India and the emergent nations of South and South-East Asia, whose limited resources can then better be used for the development of their armies and air forces for effective deployment in the immediately threatened areas of their territories.'[44]

Even without the acceptance of this grand design, Indian naval planners argued that naval allocations had to increase to overcome the growing problem of obsolescence. There was, therefore, a straightforward case to be made in favour of modernization. By the late 1960s, for example, the Sea Hawks allocated to the *Vikrant* were obsolete yet the carrier's decks were too small for more modern aircraft. Although replacement was beyond the country's means, greater attention to modernization was urgently required.[45]

Despite the Government's reservations concerning the cost and desirability of implementing the requests of the naval lobby, it proved to be not wholly unsympathetic. Throughout the last half of the 1960s allocations to the Navy grew steadily at the expense of the Air Force, from 7.8 per cent of defence capital expenditure in 1966–67 to 34.3 per cent in 1970–71.[46] The capital-intensive nature of naval equipment notwithstanding, this was a significant institutional victory which was underlined in 1968 by the elevation of the Chief of Naval Staff to the rank of Admiral, thereby bringing the post in line with the equivalents in the other services.

In terms of equipment, the favourable mood in New Delhi and increased allocations actually brought very little. Apart from the equipment received from the USSR, in 1968 the Navy received the first Leander-class frigate from Mazagon Docks in Bombay and Alouette helicopters from HAL in Bangalore.

[42] *The Times*, 13 May 1969.
[43] Thomas (note 14), p. 206.
[44] 'India as a prospective partner', *US Naval Institute Proceedings*, vol. 90, no. 9 (Sep. 1964), p. 109.
[45] 'India's naval role takes shape', *US Naval Institute Proceedings*, vol. 94, no. 9 (Aug. 1968).
[46] Thomas (note 7), table 5.9, p. 192.

A year later, India received from the UK Hunt Escort Type destroyers, which had long been obsolete in the Royal Navy, and a new helicopter squadron was constituted. In addition, there were proposals and promises to establish a new naval base in the Bay of Bengal and that at some time in the future the likely replacement for the *Vikrant's* strike-force would be the V/STOL Harrier.[47]

Prior to the successful 'liberation' of Bangladesh, India's regional position threatened to become far from secure as the USSR continued its flirtation with Pakistan as a means of pursuing its by now long-standing conflict with communist China. Nevertheless, a combination of both nimble and heavy diplomatic footwork by New Delhi in 1969 in effect assured Indian freedom of action thereafter and, in addition, paved the way for an enduring political relationship with the USSR from which the Indian defence sector was the principal beneficiary.

By early 1969 the USSR showed little sign of back-pedalling over arms supplies to Pakistan even though it increasingly required a sympathetic voice from India on China, the more so as Pakistan showed little predilection to lean to one side and reduce its ties with China. Instead, Pakistan agreed to a road-building programme to link China and Pakistan via the old Silk Route and through territory claimed by India. Indeed, as a direct affront to the USSR and Indira Gandhi, the Pakistani Government offered to open border talks with China with no preconditions in an obvious gesture of defiance and irritation.[48]

In New Delhi, Prime Minister Gandhi was running dangerously short of options and desperately needed the support of the USSR which could only be achieved by brinkmanship, which in turn necessitated threatening the Soviet position in South Asia. The US withdrawal from Viet Nam and President Nixon's announcement that henceforth the USA would expect Asian countries to look after their own security meant that for India there was little immediate chance of securing concessions from the USSR by currying favour with or, perhaps, acquiring arms from the USA. The Kremlin must have accepted the risk involved in alienating India, but as problems emerged between East and West Pakistan the extent of the gamble must have become clearer—effectively Moscow risked losing all its influence in South Asia if it alienated India and if Pakistan became too difficult an ally.

VI. The 1971 Indo-Pakistani War: the Third Round

The growing problems between East and West Pakistan were rooted in economic disparities which stemmed from the inordinate economic and political power wielded by the Punjabi ruling classes and the military. The manifestation

---

[47] Thomas (note 14), pp. 214–15.

[48] The anti-Soviet nature of this gesture is underlined by the observation that the Indian Prime Minister could not offer talks without preconditions—the original Sino-Indian border is enshrined in the Indian constitution and, as such, any resolution of the long-standing dispute requires a change in the Indian constitution and a two-thirds majority in parliament which no Prime Minister before Rajiv Gandhi had ever possessed.

of the problems between East and West centred on issues which seem to have an echoing ring in South Asia; East Pakistan complained that it received too little benefit from its jute and tea exports, foreign aid tended to be selectively distributed, and the Bengali majority in the East resented the imposition of Urdu as the official language.

During the 1960s the level of discontent in the East grew, and the country's problems were compounded by a 1000-mile corridor separating the two wings with a cultural gap at least as wide. Unity and cohesion were impossible to maintain and conflict between East and West became inevitable, particularly given the level of inequality between the two wings and the unwillingness on the part of the state to redress the situation. In all likelihood Pakistan would have divided itself, even without the assistance of India. However, the 'liberation' of Bangladesh offered a considerable regional prize for India and virtually negated the political effects of the 1962 war.

Following the 1970 election in Pakistan, the leader of the Awami League, Sheikh Mujibur Rahman, took control of East Pakistan, which constituted one of the five provinces in Pakistan. Zulfikar Ali Bhutto won a less decisive victory than predicted but became Prime Minister. The strength of Mujibur's support in the East forced Bhutto into talks with the provincial leader which quickly came to nothing. In addition, East Pakistan was reeling under the effects of an appalling cyclone which claimed 200 000 lives and the problems were compounded by the inability of relief organizations to cope with the disaster and, allegedly, a dilatory response on the part of the West. The deteriorating situation led to an intensification of activity on the part of the Mukti Bahini (freedom fighters), trained and supported by India, which managed to co-ordinate a campaign involving conventional warfare, guerrilla resistance and a campaign of civil disobedience. In the face of appalling repression by the Army, approximately 10 million Hindu refugees and fugitives from the internal fighting that had erupted spilled over into India.

Seizing the opportunity to weaken Pakistan irrevocably, India invaded East Pakistan, swiftly overran its defences in the space of two weeks, captured 90 000 prisoners and killed up to 10 000 troops. During the course of the entire struggle, some three million lives were lost—the equivalent of the entire population of Wales.[49] In the west, India moved into the Rann of Kutch and regained a slice of Azad Kashmir to the north, although the conflict was more even in the west than in the east.

The effect of the long-drawn out conflict between East and West Pakistan and the reorganization and synchronization of the Indian armed forces bestowed upon New Delhi two decisive advantages, and both were successfully exploited. The event was marred for the Indian Government, however, by the appearance of the USS *Enterprise* and several escort ships in the Bay of Bengal. This symbolic and traditional gesture of 'speak softly but carry a big stick' in support of Pakistan was not lost on the Indian élites and the event still

---

[49] Arnold, G., *Wars in the Third World Since 1945* (Cassell: London, 1991), p. 467. (Arnold's figure was drawn from a Minority Rights Report.)

figures frequently in foreign and defence policy debates—it has become an extremely potent symbol. Although Indian leaders have always seen this as a threat of intervention to control the pace and intensity of conflict in the region, US motivations were in fact more complex. Preventing the onset of total chaos in South Asia was only one item of President Nixon's and Henry Kissinger's agenda, which included relations with China and superpower responses to conflicts in not just South Asia but also the Middle East and Indo-China:

What made the [1971] crisis so difficult was that the stakes were so much greater than the public perception of them. The issue burst upon us while Pakistan was our only channel to China; we had no other means of communication with Peking. A major American initiative of fundamental importance to the global balance of power could not have survived if we colluded with the Soviet Union in the public humiliation of China's friend—and our ally.[50]

Nevertheless, by the end of the year India had presided over the most humiliating defeat of Pakistan and, moreover, had implemented the first example of the dismemberment of a Third World state.

VII. The Soviet Union and India: burgeoning dependency

The decade of the 1970s was the most turbulent independent India has yet experienced, a period of both political and economic chaos. Throughout the early 1970s the economy went from bad to worse. The fourth Five Year Plan (1969–74) was characterized by reckless deficit financing. In 1972–73 the important growing season which occurs during the monsoon, the *kharif*, was largely a failure, and this setback was swiftly followed by rises in oil prices following moves by OPEC during the Yom Kippur War. Between January 1972 and January 1974 the price index rose by 40 per cent.[51] The political coalitions which Indira Gandhi had so successfully engineered a decade earlier along class lines began to break up as disenchantment appeared among the ranks of organized labour, students and the intellectual left. The growing tension between these groups and the Government was exacerbated by strike-breaking, rises in the base lending rate and other measures designed to decrease dissent, increase savings and investment and reduce the flow of credit in the economy. Although some of these measures improved the Prime Minister's popularity to some extent, they did not prevent the imposition of a State of Emergency. This resulted from the Allahabad High Court's indictment of Indira Gandhi on charges of electoral malpractice, which led to her receiving a statutory disqualification from political activities for five years. Although the Supreme Court granted a stay pending appeal, the Prime Minister declared a

[50] Kissinger, H., *The White House Years* (Weidenfeld and Nicolson and Michael Joseph: New York, 1979), p. 911.
[51] Jha, P. S., *India: A Political Economy of Stagnation* (Oxford University Press: Bombay, 1980), p. 135.

State of Emergency two days later, swiftly arrested large numbers of political opponents and imposed Draconian censorship measures.

Started in June 1975, the Emergency lasted for nearly two years, until eventually the Janata Party won an historic election in 1977 and Morarji Desai became Prime Minister. However, as soon as the new Government took power the inevitable splits in the fragile coalition occurred. This allowed Indira Gandhi to resume power three years later after winning the 1980 election.

The complacency with regard to security brought about by the dismemberment of Pakistan, the parlous state of the Indian economy and the general level of political turmoil pushed defence and, to a lesser extent, foreign affairs into the background. Moreover, the aftermath of the war was mixed for India. Although regional hegemony and additional security were recognizable gains, sufficient problems occurred during the 1970s to diminish considerably the gains from the war.

First and foremost, the complex diplomatic game involving China, India, Pakistan, the USSR and the USA proceeded apace. Although the USA continued with its arms embargo on South Asia and generally concentrated upon extricating itself from the Viet Nam War, the movement towards China was unmistakable. This process reawakened Soviet interest in Pakistan, to drive a wedge between China and the USA. Since many of the problems of political instability in South Asia which emerged in the 1960s had been resolved, ironically by India for the most part, the USSR had more options.

Although Soviet policy was open to opportunities to weaken China through overtures to Pakistan, the Kremlin nevertheless did its best to fulfil all its political obligations to India under the 1971 Treaty of Co-operation and Friendship. In 1972 Moscow gave the Indian Foreign Secretary T. N. Kaul and Planning Minister D. P. Dhar warm receptions on separate visits. Both these events led to increased diplomatic support and assistance for India's ailing economy. Also in 1972 Admiral Gorshkov visited India to encourage the expansion of the Indian Navy as an additional counter to the burgeoning US naval buildup in the region, aware no doubt that the Paris Peace Talks were nearing a solution which would offer Nixon the opportunity to implement his 'grand design'. While the Nixon Doctrine (1970) signalled an end to containment and a marked reduction in US global commitments, the US Navy used the opportunity to transform itself from a service focused largely on the South Pacific and East Asia to a new organization with global pretentions.[52] During the same year Moscow offered New Delhi another Petya Class frigate. In October 1972 General Secretary Leonid Brezhnev visited Delhi and the occasion was given a very high profile in Moscow as part of an attempt to reactivate interest in an Asian security complex to form a power bloc against China.

Despite the USSR's equivocation over whether or not to pursue friendly relations with Pakistan and India's countering by either cooling its rhetoric or threatening to play the China card, which entailed a normalization of relations

[52] Shurman, F., *The Foreign Policies of Richard Nixon: the Grand Design*, Research Series no. 65 (University of California: Berkeley, Calif., 1987), pp. 161–95.

intended to isolate the USSR, the underlying strength of bilateral relations remained until the mid-1970s. However, after the 1971 war the Kremlin barely raised the issue of military aid and arms transfers, although it is unclear how interested the Indians were in further agreements. Until 1975, procurement from the USSR was low-key and amounted to little more than the transfer of facilities to produce improved versions of the MiG-21. On the Soviet side the level of antipathy may have been a manifestation of the developing *détente* between East and West and, given the US arms embargo on the region, which remained in place until 1975, the desire not to upset the regional balance.

In New Delhi two arguments may have applied: (*a*) the Government was becoming aware that dependence upon the USSR was uncomfortably strong. By the early 1970s, arms imports from the communist bloc represented an inordinately high percentage of military imports. In 1961 imports from these sources amounted to a mere 10 per cent of total military imports; in 1971, 1972 and 1973 the level was consistently 90 per cent;[53] (*b*) the decision makers in New Delhi undoubtedly came to the conclusion that further modernization was too expensive and unnecessary, from a regional political perspective at least. Even though Moscow accepted payments in rupees and goods, the benefits were frequently negated by 'switch trading' whereby East European countries would export goods previously given to the USSR for payment by India as a means of raising foreign exchange. Payment to the USSR in exportable goods may not have actually reduced levels of foreign exchange but would have cut considerably the potential for earning hard currency during a period when India's reserves were extremely low.

Nevertheless, on the question of Soviet defence equipment the pattern of Indian behaviour was contradictory for the first half of the decade. On the one hand there was a growing awareness of and concern about dependency. In addition, during this period there were several suggestions that the Indian armed forces were dissatisfied with the quality and flow of equipment from the USSR. The Foxtrot submarines, originally designed for cold war operations, gave recurring problems in tropical zones. Over 30 Su-7 fighter-bombers were lost during the 1971 war in part because their slow rate of climb made them vulnerable to ground fire.[54] Because of centralized production schedules Soviet spare parts were taking up to 37 months to come through.[55] On each given system spare parts requirements would have been greater for the Indian armed forces on account of the inevitable increase of workload due to smaller inventories—for example, an Indian MiG-21 requires more frequent tyre and brake-pad renewals as each system would be used more frequently than its Soviet counterpart.[56]

[53] Terhal, P., 'Preliminary estimate of foreign exchange use of the Indian military, 1950–72', Discussion Paper no. 63 (Centre for Development Planning, Erasmus University: Rotterdam, 1982), table 6, pp. 14–15.

[54] Rikhye, R., 'India unhappy over Soviet arms', *Armed Forces Journal International,* Mar. 1975, p. 14.

[55] *The Times,* 3 July 1970.

[56] Dr G. Alam, conversations with the author, Delhi, Dec. 1984.

On the other hand, New Delhi had nowhere else to go for defence equipment during a time when the mounting bill for foodgrains, fertilizers, oil and steel had virtually wiped out the country's foreign exchange reserves. This was also a period when the international arms trade had entered a new phase of commercialization which consolidated after the 1973 oil crisis. For example, interest in the Harrier to replace the obsolete Sea Hawks for the *Vikrant* dates back to at least mid-1973. It came to nothing as the cost would have amounted to foreign exchange worth at least Rs.100 crores.[57] Reports that India would acquire the Soviet Yak-36 strike fighter instead to refurbish the Fleet Air Arm were never substantiated. Thus, in the quest to expand the Navy, India was forced to continue its dependent relationship with the USSR. By the end of the decade, therefore, following great political and diplomatic manœuvring, India had acquired an array of modern naval equipment from the USSR, including eight F Class submarines, 10 Petya II frigates, 3 Nanchuka corvettes equipped with SSM and SAM missiles, 16 of the Osa Class missile patrol boats, which had performed so well in the 1971 war, coastal patrol boats and minesweepers.[58] However, in keeping with the naval expansion policy seven Il-38 Mays were procured for long-range reconnaissance and in 1974 the USSR undertook to refurbish completely the naval base at Vishakhapatnam.

For the Air Force, further expansion and modernization was barely possible in the early 1970s. Although there was a widespread desire to replace the Canberra bomber and the Hunter, the USSR was unable to fill the gap and other systems were considered too expensive. In fact, interest in the Anglo-French Jaguar as a potential follow-on system emerged as early as July 1968 following an offer by the British Aircraft Corporation which included licensed production rights of the plane when it was at the design stage.[59] Nevertheless, the increasing age of India's long-range strike force and the implications thereof were not lost on defence planners. In addition, the obsolescence of other aircraft, coupled with the rumour in the mid-1970s that Pakistan might augment its inventory of Mirage-3/5 fighter-bombers with a shipment of similar aircraft from Libya, introduced the option of acquiring a long-range fighter bomber.[60] In addition to the Jaguar other similar aircraft which came under consideration were the MiG-23, the Swedish Saab-37 Viggen and the French F-1 Mirage.

In the period between the 1971 war and the Janata ascendancy, the Army fared badly with regard to the import of equipment but much better in relation to indigenous production. However, its relative share of the defence budget declined. During the 1960s the Army received on average 77.7 per cent of the annual defence budget but by 1973–74 this had declined to 71.1 per cent.[61] Moreover, soaring inflation and rising manpower costs further eroded the Army's purchasing power. Thus, by 1973–74 capital expenditure for the Army

[57] Malhotra, I., 'Hankering after the Harrier: wrong approach to naval defence', *Times of India*, 6 Sep. 1973.

[58] International Institute for Strategic Studies, *The Military Balance 1979–80* (IISS: London, 1980).

[59] 'India Considering Jaguar Production', *Flight International,* 8 Aug. 1968.

[60] Thomas (note 7), p. 169.

[61] Figures extrapolated from Thomas (note 7), table 5.9, p. 192.

had fallen to 38 per cent, some 10 per cent less than for the Navy, as against a mean of 53.4 per cent during the 1960s.[62] Consequently, little in the way of planned or actual procurement occurred during the 1970s.

In summary, therefore, it seems that throughout the 1970s India's defence procurement policy was low key, especially with regard to the Army. The only realistic source of equipment given the foreign exchange crisis was the USSR. Although it was well recognized that the country required a more modern deep-strike capability, the availability of hardware from the USSR was limited and the foreign exchange costs of purchases from elsewhere prohibitive. Where a commonality of interests did occur was in the mutual desire on the part of the USSR and India to see a stronger Indian blue water navy. For the Soviet Union this was a means of retaining influence with India, partially countering the US naval buildup in the region, avoiding a strain on US–Soviet relations which might have been caused by disturbing the fragile Indo-Pakistani balance of power through the transfer of ground and air forces, and, perhaps, laying the foundations for gaining access to the strategically sited naval base at Vishakhapatnam. For India, it was an opportunity to build upon its dormant blue water strategy, increase naval power and capitalize upon, but not fill, the power vacuum that had emerged following Britain's retreat East of Suez.

VIII. The Janata period: reduced dependency and increased procurement

Although it was clear that India could ill afford to modernize parts of the Air Force, a head of steam had nevertheless built up under discussions for modernization. Replacement discussions were well advanced when Morarji Desai came to power in 1977. Years before, Desai had held the finance portfolio in the Nehru Government and he was well known for his reluctance to expend resources on defence, until after the 1962 war.

Politically, the Janata Government framed its policies in a reactive fashion. It was essentially a loose-knit coalition which owed its existence to both Indira Gandhi and the Emergency. Once both had disappeared (Indira Gandhi, however, kept up an extremely good public profile which later served her well), an ideological vacuum occurred which was filled with responsive gestures rather than with a vision of where realistically the new Government could take India in the crucible of international politics. The policies which emerged were very much the antithesis of Indira Gandhi's. First, Desai rejected India's equivocal nuclear policy and pledged not to pursue the nuclear option, although this fell well short of signing the NPT. Second, the new Government attempted to reduce the dependence upon the USSR, a policy which was facilitated by a dramatic rise in foreign exchange reserves. In November 1976 reserves stood at Rs.2403 crores but exactly two years later they more than doubled to Rs.5153

---

[62] Thomas (note 7), table 5.9, p. 192.

crores.[63] Third, and related to previous policy, the government attempted to re-establish India's credibility as a non-aligned power.

The new Government continued some of the policies of its predecessor and kept alive the prospect that India would acquire a deep-strike penetration aircraft some two generations beyond the Canberra and the Hunter. Prior to the election of Janata a Defence Plan for 1976–81 had been adopted, which the new Government honoured. With foreign exchange reserves much higher, the Government could afford actively to consider the Jaguar deal. This had been on ice for a decade, and was only revitalized in theory as a result of Pakistan's procurement of the Mirage 3/5.

In addition, India could also play the market and force the major European arms exporters to compete against each other. In February 1978 Defence Minister Jagjivan Ram announced that India was considering the Saab-Scania Viggen, the Dassault-Breguet Mirage F-1 and the Anglo-French Jaguar. From the Soviet side an offer of the MiG-23, the Su-20 and the Su-22 had been considered but was rejected because none of the aircraft were suitable for the intended missions, and questions had been raised about their performance capabilities. The factors which influenced decision makers were unit costs, terms of payment, delivery schedules, licensed production options and offset arrangements.[64] Although it is thought that the IAF favoured the Swedish Viggen in all its variations (reconnaissance, high-altitude, interceptor and strike), this option was blocked by the USA. The plane was powered by a Pratt and Whitney engine (a US corporation) which gave the US Government the power of veto.[65] The Mirage was turned down, probably on the grounds of the French relationship with Pakistan.[66] In February 1978 British Prime Minister James Callaghan visited India with the thinly disguised intention of securing the Jaguar deal and an order for six cargo ships.[67] The visit was preceded by a visit in January from the US President, Jimmy Carter, when the US veto was probably discussed in detail. However, by June it was becoming clear that the Indian Government was coming down in favour of the Jaguar. Ostensibly this was because of the system's low-level navigation capability, range and avionics equipment;[68] more likely, however, the Government was faced with a single option for political rather than technical reasons, primarily a desire to move

[63] Thomas, R., *India's Emergence as an Industrial Power—Middle Eastern Contracts* (C. Hurst: London, 1982), appendix I, p. 113.

[64] Offset arrangements have increasingly become a part of most arms deals in recent years. Basically, the system works in the following way. Country A will sell to country B and include licensed production arrangements. Country B will include in the deal the option to produce more than is required for domestic purposes and sell the surplus spare parts either to a third country operating the same system or back to the original supplier. In this instance an element of the offset deal involved the UK buying back India's obsolete Canberras and Hunters once the Jaguar entered service (*Air International,* Dec. 1978, p. 254). For an analysis of the more recent offset trend see Neuman, S., 'Offsets in the international arms market', *World Military Expenditures and Arms Transfers* (US Arms Control and Disarmament Agency: Washington, DC, 1985), pp. 35–40.

[65] Nagchaudhri, conversations with the author, New Delhi, Mar. 1985.

[66] For an overview of this relationship during this period see 'Armed forces modernisation', *India Backgrounder,* vol. 4, no. 17 (23 July 1979).

[67] *Far Eastern Economic Review,* 17 Feb. 1978, p. 5.

[68] 'Britain poised to win £1bn. Jaguar order from India', *Financial Times,* 28 June 1977.

away from dependence upon the USSR although the choice of alternative suppliers was extremely limited once French and Swedish options were ruled out. In October 1978 the Government announced its selection and at the cost of $2.2 billion agreed to purchase 200 Jaguar International aircraft—40 to be purchased outright and the rest to be built in India.[69] The announcement came as a relief to both sides. As one source commented, somewhat wryly, 'Serious negotiations began in 1972 or 1973 and it has been hot and cold ever since, largely on the question of financing.'[70]

The importance of the Jaguar deal was that it signified the end of India's low-key procurement, heralded the onset of a large-scale modernization programme and, furthermore, indicated that India was henceforth prepared to buy from whatever source provided the most relevant and superior technology. Or, put another way, India now felt able to reduce its dependency upon the Soviet bloc for defence equipment.

Although little else appeared to be under consideration for the IAF but the MiG-23 to augment the Jaguar DSPA strike force, in early 1979 a high-powered Indian defence team toured Europe to gather information concerning further modernization of the Navy.[71] In particular, the team assessed four European shipyards for the ability to provide India with some 20 submarines to replace the eight Soviet Foxtrots currently in service. Uppermost in the minds of the team members was the desire to strike a deal similar to the Jaguar agreement involving outright purchase, technology transfer and offset options. For this, the Government was prepared to consider costs of between $700 and $1000 million.[72] In addition, interest in the Harrier V/STOL was rekindled, albeit with an upwardly revised price, and the deal was announced in October 1978.[73] In effect, the Government had no choice and the circumstances were similar to those which had obtained with the Jaguar. The Soviet equivalent of the Harrier, the Yak-36 Forger-A, was too much of an unknown quantity, the US Skyhawk was never a serious contender on account of US arms sales policy to the sub-continent, and no other system was suitable for the relatively short flight deck on the *Vikrant*, which, at the time, had not been fitted with a ski ramp.

Around the same period the Army was given the go-ahead to consider a new generation main battle tank. Although the West German Leopard II and the British Chieftain V were considered, competition with the Soviet T-72 never appeared really serious as 100 units had already been procured while the evaluation of the German and British tanks was in progress. Also under consideration during this period was a replacement for the Czech OT-62 armoured per-

---

[69] The Jaguar International is the export version of the Jaguar deployed by France and the UK. The key difference is that the International is powered by two Rolls-Royce-Turbomeca Adour Mk. 102 engines which contain 17 per cent more thrust than the standard Jaguar.

[70] 'India selects Jaguar International', *Aviation Week & Space Technology,* 16 Oct. 1978.

[71] Sharma, K. K., 'Modernising the military: Indian defence requirements' *Financial Times*, 12 Apr. 1979.

[72] Marshall, P., 'India is shopping for arms with list totaling $4 billion', *Washington Star* (9 July 1979).

[73] *Air International,* Dec. 1978, p. 254.

sonnel carrier, a decision which also came down in favour of the Soviet BMP-1 with the only close contender being the less well armed but faster and more expensive West German Marder.[74]

Clearly, the Janata Government was extremely serious in its attempts at an across-the-board modernization of India's defence capability. The motivation appears to have been primarily technological, although there were strong but unsubstantiated hints of corruption over the Jaguar deal, involving commissions totalling £56.8 million.[75] However, most of the allegations were made 10 days before Prime Minister Charan Singh sought a vote of confidence in parliament.[76] Unquestionably, there were few security considerations which required urgent attention and little attempt was made to justify the procurement process on these grounds:

The modernization programmes for the three services will take at least three years to carry out, but there is no hurry since India does not expect an immediate threat from across its borders. China is still showing signs of wanting to mend fences and the threat from Pakistan is no longer serious because internal upheaval rules out military adventures. The main purpose of the Defence Ministry's multi-pronged effort is to keep abreast of the latest advances in defence technology and to begin preparations immediately to face the expected strategic challenges of the 1980s.[77]

IX. Indian defence policy, 1962–80: answers in search of problems

During the 1960s and 1970s India's defence posture expanded significantly, allowing for the paucity of foreign exchange reserves, the parlous state of the economy and domestic political upheaval. However, as the defence postures evolved it does not seem clear as to what decision makers and planners were seeking—clear policy guide-lines appeared to be lacking.

First and foremost, the post-1962 political atmosphere left Indian leaders in no doubt that substantial changes were required in the defence sector. To allay public doubts and fears, remedial action in the form of extra allocations was an understandable gesture to ensure the political survival of the Congress Party. However, the new guide-lines of 1964 notwithstanding, Nehru appeared not to see the need for a wide-ranging defence review. India lost the 1962 conflict with China because of incompetence, both before and especially during the short war. The defence sector may have been lacking in certain areas which could otherwise have allowed the armed forces to fare less atrociously, such as better aircraft, infantry weapons and artillery. However, the root cause of the defeat was poor defence organization and a failure to ensure an adequate defence capability in the north-east, a lack of training for high-altitude warfare,

[74] India Backgrounder, 23 July 1979, p. 1802.
[75] Sharma, K. K., 'Jaguar deal "pay-off" claim', Financial Times (London), 17 Aug.1979.
[76] International Herald Tribune, 11–12 Aug. 1979.
[77] Sharma (note 71).

poor decision making at the political and intelligence levels, which resulted in the Chinese threat being taken altogether too lightly and, finally, inadequate combat capability.

In 1964 the Indian Government sanctioned and allocated resources for a new defence capability based upon high-altitude warfare training. It also endeavoured to reduce the institutional cleavages between the three services. Essentially, however, it looked for technical and *matériel* solutions to political and organizational problems. Instead of seeking the aid of the UN Security Council over the border dispute India sought military aid instead. True, any Security Council resolution would have been totally ignored by communist China, as its Government was not recognized by the UN during that time. The involvement of the UN would also have been embarrassing for India in view of its long-standing failure to comply with the UN ruling over Kashmir in favour of a plebiscite. However, in view of Nehru's predilection for the resolution of conflict by multilateral negotiating mechanisms, the failure to involve the UN and attempt a peaceful settlement in principle suggests double standards on the part of the Nehru Government. It seemed that Nehru's pleas for peaceful solutions to international conflicts did not apply in a regional setting. The benefit of involving the UN would have been more than cosmetic. By permitting an international bureaucracy to take its stand, India would have captured the moral high ground for the years to come, just as Pakistan had done 15 years earlier over Kashmir.

The defence buildup which followed the war essentially masked deeper problems and may even have created more. The weakness of foreign policy formulation and intelligence gathering were not given the attention they deserved. Within the defence sector itself, there were similar misperceptions. Rather than review defence policy with a view to ensuring that India was better defended, policy makers assumed that an increase in the strength of all the three services was the primary requirement. Conceivably, organizational changes and cost-benefit analyses could have led to a stronger defence and major rises in defence expenditure beyond the need to assuage public opinion could have been avoided. In the absence of a really effective policy-making process, the armed forces were permitted to preside over a rather haphazard rearmament process, just as they did in the years before the Sino-Indian War.

The full negative effects of the defence buildups both before and after the 1962 war were not felt for many years, although it has been argued that increased defence requirements after 1962 were the single cause of the largest growth in tax revenues since independence.[78] Problems first began to occur after the 1970s when the need for replacement and modernization became evident but the Government lacked the foreign exchange reserves and the political mandate to engage the country in a new defence buildup—the more so following the dismemberment of Pakistan. Consequently, Indira Gandhi was forced into the Soviet camp and finally into a Treaty of Co-operation and Friendship in

[78] Rubin (note 31), p. 183.

1971. In political terms the haphazard policy-making process in the years between 1947 and 1962 thus eventually compromised significantly the policy of non-alignment. It also led to a marked dependence upon the USSR and established a patron–client relationship of a similar intensity to that of the USA and Israel.

When the Janata Party came to power in 1977, it had no clear vision of which way to take defence policy after a decade of growing dependency upon the USSR, witness in particular the extreme confusion over India's nuclear weapon policy. While accepting the need for conventional defence modernization, the new Government was singularly unambitious and conservative. Once again the patterns of the past were repeated. There were no calls for a wide-ranging defence review. Parliamentary debate was lacking in the extreme. Nobody in parliament seemed to question the lack of fit between defence and foreign policy, or the imperative to modernize and spend against a backdrop of such unusual regional security. Moreover, as arms imports began to appear from a diverse array of suppliers to break the dependency upon the USSR, nobody questioned the economic costs or the potential operational problems which could emerge from a defence capability drawn from so many different sources.

In contrast, the élites of India, the press corps and all other interested parties seemed content to see the country move gradually towards the attainment of regional power status, even if this implied an increased reliance upon the USSR, despite an ambivalent attitude towards the communist bloc and most of that which it represented. The durability of the national consensus for medium-power status at least was fully borne out by the reaction to the nuclear test in 1974 (see chapter 8). Indira Gandhi's decision to carry out the test was a popular one, even though it cast the country so close to the periphery of the international community, whereas before India had been in the vanguard of the attempts to attain a more stable and less violent world order. The development costs entailed by foreclosing access to nuclear technology from what became the London Suppliers' Club were also considered to be worthwhile.

Throughout the years between 1962 and 1980 defence policy drifted further away from the basic need to acquire security into a poorly thought-out policy of acquiring the symbols required by a regional power. The naval buildup, for example, reflects well the policy of drift. Although an opportunity arose with the departure of the British Navy, India was ill equipped economically to undertake the blue water mission, with or without the backing of the USSR. Rather than heed the lessons of the 1962, 1965 and 1971 wars which indicated the marginal utility of either a brown or a blue water naval capability in a conflict with China either or Pakistan, the Indian Government pressed ahead during a period when the economy was weak and the international climate had ceased to favour military aid.

By the time Indira Gandhi was returned to power, it had become clear that all the three services were in need of further attention, despite or perhaps because of the rate of procurement over the 1970s. True, the Janata Government had put into motion a form of modernization but not, it seemed, after due policy debate, threat assessment and consideration of the short- and long-term policy implications. Prime Minister Gandhi merely picked up where Morarji Desai had left off and only after an agreement had been reached to modernize the armed forces did the Government begin to articulate new fears from new quarters, such as the superpower buildup in the Indian Ocean and the new cold war. As will be seen, the defence postures which followed were even more unwieldly and irrelevant than those of the 1960s and 1970s and seemed to become more geared to seeking problems to justify acquisitions, rather than *vice versa*.

5.   Indian arms imports, 1980–88

I. The new cold war and South Asia

The year 1980 was a watershed in post-World War II international affairs. The fragile *détente* which existed between the two superpowers during the late 1960s and early 1970s ended finally when the USSR invaded Afghanistan in December 1979. This was the first time that the USSR had invaded a nation state outside its recognized sphere of influence or in South Asia and the ramifications were extensive. Tension between the two superpowers and their allies was further exacerbated when a resurgence of trade union activism in Poland prompted a heavy-handed response from Moscow and an equally strident condemnation from the West. During the same period, China went to war with Viet Nam and the Iraq–Iran War erupted in the Middle East.

On the other side of the Iron Curtain a new radicalism emerged in the USA and, to a lesser extent, other NATO countries. Significant changes had already occurred in the late 1970s, particularly in the USA. President Jimmy Carter attempted to redress perceived weaknesses within NATO by demanding with some success that all NATO countries raise their defence expenditures by 3 per cent in real terms. An attempt was also made to bind the Western alliance together and simultaneously counter the Soviet deployment of SS-20 medium-range nuclear missiles by modernizing the NATO intermediate-range nuclear weapons with the Pershing II missile and the cruise missile. At the same time, in keeping with the 'dual-track' policy which stressed simultaneous acquisition and negotiation to eliminate these weapons, NATO tried to force the pace on arms control. Following the success of the Strategic Arms Limitation Talks (SALT II), NATO wanted the USSR to remain at the negotiating table over the short period when NATO would have enjoyed a clear nuclear superiority. However, after the Soviet invasion of Afghanistan, Congress refused to ratify the SALT II Treaty.

The humiliation and impotence felt by the USA during the internment of US hostages by the Khomeini Government contributed to a crushing electoral defeat for President Carter in the November 1980 US presidential election. The outcome of the election was far from just a victory for the Republican Party and Ronald Reagan. It was also a triumph for the New Right and an opportunity to reshape US foreign, defence and domestic policies following a decade or more of perceived decline and national humiliation—Viet Nam, Watergate and Iran.

The re-emergence of cold warriors in some of the major capitals of the Western world coupled with knee-jerk reactions by the USSR to its regional and peripheral problems had a profound effect upon not only East–West relations but the international system as a whole. In addition, the international debt crisis, a growing awareness of the extent of environmental problems, a crisis of multilateralism which left many major international organizations in disarray, broad-based economic recession which exacerbated the impact of the debt crisis, reductions in bilateral aid and the burgeoning budget deficit in the USA added to the level of concern over the state of the international system. In effect, during a period when multilateral solutions were required to solve the problems engendered within an increasingly interdependent international system, paradoxically, the international community relied more on unilateral and bilateral measures and the major powers to regaining security through the pursuit of relative military power, whatever the cost.

Against this bleak backdrop Indira Gandhi was re-elected in India following the collapse of the Janata Government. As with previous Indian elections, the external regional and international setting played a negligible part in the choice of candidate or party. Indian elections are extremely parochial events, the result as much of the complexity of the political culture within the country as of the relative ignorance of Indian voters on events outside national boundaries and the broad consensus on external threats. (Where awareness exists, there is a remarkable consensus on feelings about Pakistan, especially in the north of the country.)

However, the new cold war impinged upon the Indian sub-continent in three direct ways, forcing the new Government to respond. First, the Soviet invasion of a country within the sub-continent confronted India with some awkward policy choices, particularly given the level of international condemnation which the event engendered. Second, started under Carter but pursued with a great deal more commitment by the Reagan Administration, the evolution of the Rapid Deployment Force (RDF) and deployments at both Diego Garcia and several Indian Ocean littoral states presented India with new perceived security threats from the Indian Ocean. Third, the decline in East–West relations and the invasion of Afghanistan were accompanied by a revival of the containment and forward defence policies pursued in the 1950s. This led directly to the extension of a massive US economic and military aid package to Pakistan, the first tranche of it amounting to $3.2 billion.[1] Apart from securing the immediate political survival of President Zia, the aid package facilitated the procurement of advanced military technology, notably 40 F-16 air combat fighters and the Abrams MI main battle tank.

Although US military aid to Pakistan was primarily intended to deliver a strong political signal to Russia the US-sponsored defence buildup created intense suspicion in New Delhi. With some justification, few believed that the Kremlin intended Afghanistan to be the first step in either the acquisition of warm water ports or the initial step towards the subjugation of South Asia.[2]

---

[1] President Carter was only prepared to offer $400 million of aid, which President Zia rejected as 'peanuts'. His arrogance towards the USA indicates how much he recognized Pakistan's renewed geopolitical significance.

[2] The approach of those who read most into the Soviet invasion is succinctly summarized by Amaury de Riencourt: 'The Russian venture is one further step in a long-term process which aims at reaching the warm waters of the Indian Ocean. The prospects are even more tantalizing in the latter part of the twenti-

Given that Pakistan is a narrow country (see chapter 2), US and Pakistani protestations that the new defence equipment was intended solely for the defence of Pakistan's north-west border were greeted with scepticism within India—forward defence may have been uppermost in the minds of US decision makers but President Zia undoubtedly had India in mind. Nor was New Delhi happy with the fact that the F-16 is potentially capable of delivering nuclear weapons or that Pakistan received a controversial waiver on the Symington Amendment, which forbids Congress to extend military aid to a country which is known to be producing nuclear weapons. The failure on the part of the USA to recognize Pakistan's intentions in this direction was made all the more worrying for New Delhi as Islamabad made little attempt to conceal the military side of the country's nuclear programme. Indeed, in 1987 Pakistan's cavalier attitude to this sensitive subject was fully revealed when, immediately prior to Congressional agreement on the second tranche of military and economic aid, A. Q. Khan, the father of Pakistan's nuclear weapon programme, admitted in an interview that the nuclear establishment could offer General Zia a nuclear weapon if so requested.[3]

The Soviet invasion of Afghanistan presented Indira Gandhi with a considerable problem. With a forthcoming New Delhi meeting of the Non-Aligned Movement (NAM) scheduled for February 1981 and with herself in the chair, she could not be seen to support the USSR's actions, which thus required a forthright statement in the 1980–81 *Report* of the Ministry of External Affairs: 'India's position was clearly enunciated on several occasions—namely, that it was opposed to the presence of foreign troops and bases in any country and that all forms of intervention and interference in the internal affairs of Afghanistan must cease.'[4]

At the same time, however, the Prime Minister did not wish to alienate the Soviet bloc during this particular period. Apart from respecting the cordial relations which had gone before, Indira Gandhi was certainly aware that the completion of the defence modernization programme and the perceived need to counter the new-found friendship between Pakistan and the USA would require considerable assistance from the USSR. Nor could she have forgotten the magnitude of non-military Soviet aid entering India and the need for steady increases in the future.[5] Her response in 1980 was, therefore, measured. India's

eth century than they were in the nineteenth, in the days of Kipling's "Great Game"'. de Riencourt, A., 'India and Pakistan in the shadow of Afghanistan', *Foreign Affairs*, vol. 61, no. 2 (Mar. 1982), p. 431.

[3] Pakistan's behaviour on this question appears to many as reckless, considering the risk involved in losing billions of dollars' worth of military and economic aid. However, it is possible to see Pakistan's behaviour from another perspective, as a calculating and subtle attempt to legitimize by default a nuclear weapon capability and so move closer to the Israeli position on nuclear weapons. For an analysis of similar behaviour patterns during negotiations for the second tranche of military and economic aid see Smith, C., 'A policy of ambiguity? Nuclear proliferation in South Asia', *ADIU Report*, vol. 9, no. 4 (July–Aug. 1987), pp. 1–4.

[4] India, Ministry of External Affairs, *Report 1980-81* (Ministry of External Affairs: New Delhi, 1981), pp. iv–v.

[5] According to the US Department of State, economic credits and grants to India have increased dramatically in recent years. In 1983 the figure stood at $140 million but by 1986 it had risen to $2125

role in the NAM and its genuine antipathy to this type of force and subjugation (witness the policy adopted following the Soviet invasion of Czeckoslovakia in 1968) prevented a response in press statements and UN forums which could have been construed as acquiescent.[6] Equally, India adamantly refused to condemn Soviet actions outright. While gestures of support would have been wholly out of place, New Delhi reacted with forbearance to the invasion following what the Prime Minister referred to as 'a realistic look at the situation'.[7]

The new situation in South Asia, set against a series of disturbing developments between the two superpowers and around the sensitive region of the Persian Gulf, created a complex problem for New Delhi primarily because of linkages from the regional to the international level. First and foremost, the US interest in Pakistan had been revived and Zia could henceforth rely upon a wide-ranging defence modernization programme on reasonable terms. For India, the consolidation of US–Pakistani ties exposed the sub-continent to the vicissitudes of wider international events over which it had little or no control. Second, there existed the complex linkage between Pakistan and both Iran and Saudi Arabia. During the 1960s Pakistan greatly assisted the Gulf Emirates, Jordan and Saudi Arabia in defence training[8]—indeed, President Zia himself acted as an adviser to the Royal Jordanian Army between 1969 and 1981.[9] In return, Pakistan gained financially from its relationship with the Gulf States. At the same time, Zia was careful not to alienate Iran during the Iraq–Iran War as defeat for that country could have led to ethnic problems along the common border in the absence of strong central governments.[10] Moreover, the defeat of Iran would have left Iraq in too strong a position in the Gulf, an observation which was not lost on US policy makers a decade later.

Consequently, as Indira Gandhi sought to consolidate her power at home, a new set of foreign policy considerations emerged for Indian policy makers. Would Pakistan flex its new-found military muscle given the compliant attitude adopted by the Reagan Administration? If events in the Gulf were to take an adverse turn, would South Asia become involved in some way? Would the new cold war spill over further into the Indian sub-continent? How could India preserve its relative naval power and all it represented in the midst of an unprecedented superpower buildup in the region? Would the USA seek further

---

million. See US Department of State, *Warsaw Pact Economic Aid Programs in Non-Communist LDCs: Holding Their Own in 1986* (US Government Printing Office: Washington, DC, Aug. 1988), table 8, p. 9.

[6] For example, Wigg, R., 'Mrs Gandhi defends her policy on Afghanistan', *The Times* (3 Apr. 1980).

[7] Quoted in Horn, R. C., *Soviet—Indian Relations: Issues and Influence* (Praeger: New York, 1982), p. 183.

[8] By the mid-1980s some 30 000 Pakistani troops were stationed throughout the Middle East—10 000 in Saudi Arabia and the rest in Kuwait, Libya, Oman and the United Arab Emirates.

[9] *Who's Who in the World, 1982–83* (Marquis Who's Who Inc.: Chicago, Ill., 1982), p. 1174.

[10] Robertson, B. A., 'South Asia and the Gulf complex', eds B. Buzan and G. Rizvi, *South Asian Insecurity and the Great Powers* (Macmillan: London, 1987), p. 169–75.

basing rights in Baluchistan (Pakistan), Chittagong (Bangladesh) or at the tank farm in Trincomalee (Sri Lanka)?[11]

Indian decision makers certainly did respond to these changed conditions. In addition to the modernization programmes sanctioned by the Janata Government, procurement rose substantially and the export equipment available from several major suppliers in the West and the USSR underwent consideration and evaluation. Initially, continuity with the Janata Government was embodied in a Five-Year Defence Plan adopted in May 1980 and a major defence review in May 1981, shortly before the US Congress acceded to the Reagan Administration's proposed aid package to Pakistan, but not before it became evident that a substantial commitment was on the horizon.[12] The result was an open season for the defence sector during which India imported Western and Soviet defence equipment on an unprecedented level. It was a conventional defence buildup of enormous width and depth which proceeded apace largely unnoticed both within and outside India. Throughout the 1980s all the major defence exporters attempted to establish a toe-hold in the Indian market during a period when demand in other parts of the Third World was declining precipitously. Only in mid-1988 did it become apparent that the modernization programme which had endured for nearly a decade was on the decline. In the defence budget for fiscal year 1988/89, aggregate allocations were raised by only Rs.10 billion, which represented a nominal increase but a backward step in real terms. While all three services received overall increases in cash terms, combined capital outlay actually declined from Rs.39 777.9 million in the previous year to Rs.38 721.2 million;[13] additional resources would have been required for imported goods such as fuel and lubricants and armed forces pay awards.

II. The Indian response

India emerged from the 1971 war with a keen sense of destiny but without the foreign exchange resources to turn strategic opportunity and political vision into reality through the acquisition of the type of defence technology which would identify India as a major Asian power and the indubitable power broker in South Asia. In addition, much of the defence equipment deployed by India was in urgent need of modernization. Following economic recovery in the late 1970s, foreign exchange reserves became stronger and the Janata Government was able to bow to many of the pressures coming from the defence sector.

[11] In 1981 the US Secretary of Defense, Caspar Weinberger, visited both Pakistan and Sri Lanka; this fuelled suspicions that basing rights were high on the agenda. It was also alleged at the same period that an agreement had been reached between Sri Lanka and the USA to develop in Sri Lanka a 'rest and recreation' facility for the US Seventh Fleet. 'Big role for the navy envisaged', *Times of India,* 9 Aug. 1981.

[12] Negotiations for a military and economic assistance package were successfully concluded in Sep. 1981. Full details of the deal can be found in Cronin, R. P., 'Pakistan: US Foreign Assistance Facts', Congressional Research Assistance Issue Brief (Library of Congress, Congressional Research Service: Washington, DC, Mar. 1987).

[13] 'Marked slow-down in Indian defense spending', *International Defense Review*, vol. 21, no. 5 (May 1988), p. 478.

When Indira Gandhi was re-elected, and at least until the 1982–83 monsoon failure, which cut the annual growth rate of GNP to 1.8 per cent, the economy still appeared reasonably strong. In the previous two years, growth rates had reached 7.5 per cent in 1980/81 and 5.2 per cent in 1981/82.[14] However, against this must be set double-figure inflation during this period and a negative growth rate of –4.8 per cent in 1979/80.

Continuing relative economic strength permitted the Prime Minister to accept further defence modernization and realize more of the potential afforded by India's victory in the 1971 war. Yet there was a significant lack of fit between the new threats as defined in New Delhi, however vaguely, and the type of defence equipment sought by India, particularly with regard to naval expansion. Throughout the early 1980s Congress(I) politicians were persistently alluding to 'gathering war clouds', 'the imminent threat of war' and, of course, the responsibility of a 'foreign hand' in the destabilization of India and the sub-continent.[15]

In fact, the scale of the programme indicated more than modernization alone; the rationale was much wider and found expression in the so-called 'Indira Doctrine'. Since 1971 India had been the *de facto* regional power in South Asia but needed to express power as much as to consolidate it. This could come only by serving notice on the other South Asian countries and their allies that India would henceforth claim a vital interest in instabilities in South Asia and a right to intervene to protect India's secular identity from the potentially damaging spillover effects of ethnic disturbance and religious fundamentalism. Using primarily the euphemism of 'non-alignment', a mantle which India could not have worn in any convincing way since 1971, Prime Minister Gandhi set out an agenda based upon the illegitimacy of foreign bases in South Asia, 'demilitarization' of the Indian Ocean—a thinly veiled attempt to eliminate superpower presence in the region—and, most important, bilateralism as a means of undercutting relations between hostile neighbours and extra-regional powers, such as China and the USA. It was, in essence, a bid for great, even superpower status which entailed assuming the role nearly attained by the deposed Shah of Iran. At the same time it also required that a wedge be driven between the USA and Pakistan lest the relationship should both erode India's relative power and bring the armed forces of the other superpower into South Asia.[16] The extent to which India saw other South Asian countries as 'back-yard' problems is reflected in K. Subrahmanyam's attitude in 1984 to the ramifications of the emerging Sri Lankan problem:

[14] Thomas, R. G. C., *Indian Security Policy* (Princeton University Press: Princeton, N.J., 1986), p. 215.

[15] An excellent cartoon in the *Indian Express* around this period depicted a senior politician moving away from a microphone having just finished a campaign speech. Half-way back to his seat he turned back towards the crowd saying, 'And by the way, I forgot to mention, there's an imminent threat of war'.

[16] For an incisive and very critical review of Indira Gandhi's view of India's future role in South Asia and the political culture which underpinned it, see Nations, R., 'Pride and paranoia: a Hindu resurgence inspires the "Indira Doctrine"', *Far Eastern Economic Review*, no. 33 (16 Aug. 1984), pp. 23–28.

There is no possibility of Sri Lanka doing anything militarily against India. But there is the possibility of [Colombo] going to the US, Israel or Britain for various kinds of assistance or training of troops. And if we permitted this it would give the wrong kind of impression of how far Colombo can go in dealing with its Tamil problem.[17]

Such a policy could scarcely carry weight without the military symbols of great power status which, in this instance, required the latest military technology and weapon systems commensurate with international power—modern long-range bombers, aircraft-carriers, nuclear-powered submarines, even nuclear weapons. With the exception of the nuclear weapons, the acquisition of these was the task which the Prime Minister set herself in 1980 and 1981.

In May 1980, less than six months after her re-election, Indira Gandhi secured an arms supply agreement with the USSR which amounted to the transfer of $1.63 billion of defence equipment, giving India a two-year grace period and then 15 years to repay the aid (as opposed to the 10-year repayment period offered by Western suppliers), at an interest rate of 2.5 per cent. All repayments could be made in local currency or goods, whereas all other suppliers required payment in hard currency. The central feature of the deal concerned the T-72 tank and the MiG-25 Foxbat, probably in its reconnaissance version only, but also included air-to-air missiles, Petya-class missile patrol boats, anti-tank weapons and electronic equipment.[18] Negotiations on this deal were started by the Janata Government.[19] Apart from the enviable repayment conditions, the deal was characterized by an unusual willingness on the part of the supplier to discuss technology transfer. Equally important, this deal came at a time when Pakistan had received an offer of credit totalling a mere $400 million for arms repayable at 11 per cent interest.[20] Agreement on the massive economic and military aid package was nowhere in sight at the time.

The deal with the USSR was swiftly followed by a rare press conference given by the Prime Minister, during which she intimated that her Government was on the verge of a heavy defence spending programme.[21] In the next budget Finance Minister Pranab Mukherjee announced a 20 per cent increase in defence expenditure to be financed by increased taxation.[22] Soon after the budget the combined effect of these moves was to bring the representatives of all the major arms exporters from the West to New Delhi. From this point on the Indian Government manipulated what became increasingly a buyer's market with considerable finesse.

In October 1980 an Indian defence team visited the USA and the occasion was followed by speculative reports that a $340 million deal had been signed for the supply of 230 light-weight, long-range howitzers and a large number of

[17] Nations (note 16), p. 26.
[18] Honsa, C., 'India gets USSR arms at bargain-basement prices', *Christian Science Monitor,* 30 May 1980.
[19] *MILAVNEWS,* Apr. 1980, p. 16.
[20] Honsa (note 18).
[21] Sharma, K. K., 'Gandhi hints at heavier Indian defence spending', *Financial Times*, 11 Aug. 1981.
[22] 'Indian defence spending', *Financial Times*, 1 Mar. 1982.

TOW (tube-launched, optically sighted, wire-guided) missiles for the Indian Army.[23] Some months later it was rumoured in Delhi that India had turned down an earlier offer from the USA to supply India with the F-16 and co-production of the F-5G intermediate fighter. Although the USA had been interested in the Indian arms market for some time, nothing more was heard of or reported on this deal. The Government's intention was probably to serve unequivocal notice upon the USSR that the policy of diversity would continue.

In March 1982 Soviet Defence Minister Marshal Ustinov undertook a six-day visit to New Delhi. He was accompanied by the largest and most senior defence team ever to visit a country outside the Soviet bloc. The upshot of the visit was the promise of T-80 tanks and the MiG-27 Flogger tactical strike fighter. The real or purely provocative plan to consider importing US defence equipment coupled with the previous report that India was actively considering a number of arms deals with the French including the Mirage 2000 (comparable to the MiG-27), Exocet missiles and Super Puma helicopters appeared to have worked. During such a tense period in US–Soviet relations and given the USSR's spectacular lack of success in acquiring basing rights in the Indian Ocean to counter the USA, the Kremlin needed all the allies it could acquire, with massive arms deals or otherwise.[24] Soon after, in June 1983, Defence Minister Venkataraman visited Moscow to discuss the possibility of acquiring the MiG-29 interceptor as a counter to the F-16. The significance of the request rested in the fact that the plane had yet to enter Soviet service. Later reports suggested that the Soviet response had been favourable.[25] As and when details of the deal became more widely known it seemed that the Indian success went beyond the MiG-29 and also included a licensed production option on the T-80 tank and MiG-31 Foxhound fighter.[26]

Despite or even because of successes with the USSR, the Indian Government continued to entertain export offers from the West. In May 1984 a senior British sales team arrived in Delhi to attempt to sign a Memorandum of Understanding (MoU) and build upon previous successes with Westland, Rolls Royce and British Aerospace (BAe). The visit was not well timed, coming as it did during a period when foreign exchange reserves were low and the emerging consensus within the Government appeared to favour foregoing further diversification, albeit temporarily.[27] During the same period, however, a draft agreement between India and Italy was announced to open the way for collaboration in defence electronics.[28] A five-year MoU was signed in August covering the exchange of information, with a stress upon electronic countermeasures.[29]

[23] '$340 m. worth of US arms for India', *The Statesman* (14 Oct. 1980).

[24] For many years the USSR attempted to persuade India to permit it basing rights at Vishakapatnam, the naval base on the east coast of India which the it has twice helped India to modernize.

[25] 'India's Soviet windfall?', *Aerospace Daily,* 24 Oct. 1983, p. 282.

[26] 'Major Indian arms contract goes to Soviets', *Defense Week,* vol. 5, no. 8 (3 Feb.1984), p. 6.

[27] 'India decides to rely more on Russians as source of its weapons', *Washington Times,* 5 July 1984; Ram, M., 'Planes and boats and guns—the bill is growing', *Far Eastern Economic Review,* 31 May 1984, pp. 26–27.

[28] 'Italian–Indian Pact', *Jane's Defence Weekly,* vol. 2, no. 5 (20 Oct. 1984).

[29] 'Italo-Indian defense agreement', *International Defense Review,* Aug. 1985, p. 1346.

Similar discussions were held with Spanish representatives in March 1985 with talks covering advanced jet trainers, field artillery and other armaments.[30]

In October 1984 Indira Gandhi was assassinated by her Sikh bodyguards. Between October and the end of the year India remained suspended in political confusion until Indira Gandhi's son, Rajiv, won the most astounding election victory in India's independent history. The new Prime Minister made little attempt to redirect Indian defence policy. However, one key difference soon became evident. Unlike his mother, Rajiv Gandhi was well disposed towards the USA and from the outset he appeared more willing to consider US defence imports. This benign approach towards the USA did in time lead to defence orders but had less of an effect than expected; by the time the deals were agreed, a new *détente* between the two superpowers was well under way which lessened considerably the political capital which could be gained by playing one off against the other.

It was, therefore, continuity rather than change which characterized the defence policy of Rajiv Gandhi. One innovation however, was his technical expertise, gained during his training and experience as a pilot for Indian Airlines. This gave him the ability to discuss technical issues in much greater detail, an aspect of bargaining in which his mother took no interest.[31]

Although the new Prime Minister was willing to reduce the ties that bound India to the USSR, he was unable to move too far, too quickly. First, India did not have the economic base to ignore completely Soviet offers of military equipment in favour of Western suppliers; the ability to diversify was always constrained by limited foreign exchange reserves, and the new Prime Minister's insistence upon economic liberalism cost the country dearly in foreign exchange. Second, delivery lead times need to be considered. Much of the Soviet defence equipment which arrived in India after Rajiv Gandhi was elected was ordered during his mother's term of office and before. Third, the inherent differences between Soviet and Western technology made such a radical shift very difficult to execute in practice (although, at great cost and with the help of military aid, Egypt has made just such a transition on two occasions in the past). With tanks, for example, the USSR relied heavily upon quantitative rather than qualitative strength to gain the upper hand through rapid attrition. Such tactics evolved from the technological limitations which existed in the Soviet defence industry and its inability to match the pace of technical change which obtains in the West. However, in a planned economy long production runs were less difficult, so Soviet military planners were bound to exploit this comparative advantage. The transfer of Soviet military technology to Third World countries undoubtedly carried with it some doctrinal baggage which was bound to be influential in how the weapon systems were assimilated by the recipient armed forces.

---

[30] Taibo, X. I., 'Talks on Spanish–Indian ventures', *Jane's Defence Weekly*, vol. 3, no. 10 (9 Mar. 1985).

[31] Bobb, D., 'Moscow's new offensive', *India Today*, vol. 9, no. 16 (31 Aug. 1984), p. 84.

The use of relatively low technology compensated for by weight of numbers requires a specific set of tactical considerations quite distinct from those which would be required from technology which is more capable, more costly and more difficult to repair.

Rajiv Gandhi was eventually voted out of office, primarily on the strength of a growing body of evidence pointing towards his personal involvement in massive commissions paid by the Swedish ordnance company, Bofors, in its bid to secure the 155-mm artillery deal, worth over $1.3 billion. He was assassinated in 1991, on the eve of a national election which would almost certainly have seen him re-elected. However, during his four years in power it was barely possible to say what the Prime Minister believed in, or understood, in relation to India's global or regional role—there was no 'Rajiv Doctrine', nor would there have been. Certainly, Rajiv Gandhi lacked the political depth of both his mother and his grandfather. Although his initial impact upon the world stage was highly favourable, his popularity was short-lived and he was soon considered to be of little significance in the NAM or any other form of politics in the southern hemisphere.

On specific questions of defence policy and posture, rather than more general questions of foreign policy, Rajiv Gandhi changed little. On the foreign policy front his path-breaking visit to China, which took place in mid-December 1988, the Indian intervention in Sri Lanka (which was mooted in New Delhi as early as mid-1984), the brief intervention in the Maldives and a warming of relations between India and the USA were the dominant events. With Pakistan, Rajiv Gandhi maintained the mix of 'no war, no peace either', although there were attempts to change this following the election of Benazir Bhutto. On several occasions he acquiesced in the armed forces flexing their muscles on both the Chinese and the Pakistan borders.[32] Probably he had no specific antipathy to the course charted by his mother which appeared to be popular within Congress(I), with the public at large and, in particular, with the armed forces. The only perceivable policy adjustment appears to have been the desire to see the indigenous defence technology base develop at a much more rapid rate and to overcome the inertia which set in over the 1970s. Finally, although Rajiv Gandhi himself and some of his key advisers, such as Arun Singh, held the defence portfolio at various points, the emphasis was always on the internal security problem. In particular, there was concern that Pakistan's support for the Sikh terrorists might strengthen the latter's resolve and options, and that the critical logistical importance to them of Pakistan as a sanctuary might become a major source of bilateral tension.

---

[32] The most significant display came during the Operation Brasstacks military exercise. In addition to souring relations for some months, the exercise prompted a full-scale mobilization of the Pakistani armed forces and almost the outbreak of war.

III. The Indian Army

Over the past decade, the Indian Army has once again fared much less well than the other two services. During the late 1970s and early 1980s, the Army received a decreasing proportion of the overall defence budget. From receiving 74 per cent in 1970–71, by 1980–81 the figure had dropped to 66 per cent (excluding pensions). This trend was also reflected in capital allocations which declined from 51 per cent to 36 per cent during the same period. With manpower levels standing at 1.1 million, a very large proportion of the Army's allocations are absorbed by pay, pensions and stores and this has been the case since 1963–64,[33] which places inevitable downward pressure upon other budget heads controlled by the Army.

The Army did receive a significant share of the modernization package. However, in contrast to the other two services, much of the planned procurement was drawn mainly from Soviet or indigenous resources, which increased considerably its inventory but with a minimal drain upon foreign exchange.

The agreement signed with the USSR in May 1980 gave the Army a significant increase in firepower. The long-standing desire to replace completely the ageing Centurions and supersede the obsolete and troublesome Vijayanta MBT (main battle tank) was at last granted through the procurement of 800 T-72 tanks, 200 to be supplied directly, the rest built under licence. The Vijayanta was not in fact withdrawn and, by the mid-1980s, 1250 units were still in service.[34] Instead, the Army examined various proposals for retrofitting the Vijayanta including the installation of a new and more powerful engine, laser ranging and night-visual systems.[35] Moreover, by 1986 only 350 T-72s had been received.[36]

In addition, the Army was scheduled to receive anti-tank and surface-to-surface missiles. Also mooted at a later point was the potential acquisition of the T-80 MBT which had yet to come off the production line in the USSR.[37] The offer finally came during the Ustinov visit in March 1982, although the primary purpose of the visit was to dissuade India from purchasing the Mirage 2000 by offering the MiG-27 fighter-bomber.[38] When Venkataraman visited Moscow in June 1983, Army equipment was scarcely on the agenda, except for the request for an updated technology transfer package for the T-72 to include the new laser range-finder.[39] In early 1984 New Delhi placed a significant order with the USSR which reconfirmed that the Indian Army was in line for the

---

[33] Pensions are not included in defence expenditure figures.

[34] International Institute for Strategic Studies, *The Military Balance 1986–1987* (IISS: London, 1986), p. 154. The government also cancelled the proposed sale of Centurion tanks in December 1980 and decided instead to utilize 'the tanks and their firepower in a suitable way'. *Indian Express,* 10 Dec. 1980.

[35] 'Indian Army to upgrade the tank units', *Asian Defence Journal,* Nov. 1981, p. 36.

[36] International Institute for Strategic Studies 1986 (note 34), p. 154.

[37] Ram, M., 'India goes shopping', *Far Eastern Economic Review* (16 Oct. 1981), p. 27.

[38] Library of Congress, Congressional Research Service, *The Soviet Union in the Third World, 1980–85: An Imperial Burden or Political Asset?*, Report prepared for the House of Representatives Committee on Foreign Affairs (Library of Congress, Congressional Research Service, 23 Sep. 1985), p. 132.

[39] Bobb, D., 'The message from Moscow', *India Today,* 15 Aug. 1983, p. 41.

more advanced T-72M and the T-80. In addition it was also to receive more BMP-1 armoured personnel carriers, the BMP-2 air-portable version, the SAM 8 missile, a mobile field surface-to-air system, the SAM 5 long-range surface-to-air missile and long-range, dual-capable, surface-to-surface missiles.[40] Several of these acquisitions related to the decision in mid-1981 to modernize the air defence regiments under Army command.[41]

Other imports for the Army arrived in piecemeal fashion during the mid-1980s. In mid-1985 the Government placed an order with the Dutch Government for 250 Hollandse Signaal Flycatcher radar weapon systems for its air defence regiments and intended for use in tandem with the Contraves Super-fledermaus weapon control systems.[42] One year later 120 Simfire Mk II Extended Range-Improved Tactical and Gunnery Simulators were ordered from the UK for the Army's main battle tank fleet.

If the Indian Government appeared to err on the side of economy when it came to the modernization programme for the Army during the first half of the 1980s, it was undoubtedly due to the impending decision to procure a substantial number of 155-mm artillery systems following Pakistan's decision to buy 75 155-mm M-198 towed howitzers from the USA. Although Pakistan's howitzers arrived under the military and economic aid agreement, India had been investigating the procurement of a 155-mm system since 1977.[43] The Army requirement was for a medium gun capable of firing heavy artillery at a long range. The key targets for the artillery would be enemy armour, troop carriers, roads and bridges, and with a range of about 30 kilometres it could only be attacked by air. By early 1981, the choice had been narrowed down to four options with Austria, France, Sweden and a British–German–Italian consortium as the contenders for the contract. In March 1986 the contract for a maximum of 1500 artillery pieces costing $3.5 billion (although some sources put the cost much lower at $1.14 billion—possibly due to the first part of the contract requiring the import of 410 systems, the rest of the contract involved semi- and completely knocked-down (S&CKD) kits and, eventually, indigenous production) was awarded to Sweden, which came as a great surprise to many.

Soon after, the deal erupted into a major scandal involving the payment of commissions to middlemen and unnamed Congress(I) Party heads. Even the Prime Minister, who also held the defence portfolio at the time, was accused of being involved, partly through his dealings with the Swedish Prime Minister, Olof Palme, who visited New Delhi some two months before the deal was signed. It has also been alleged that the brother of Amitabh Bachchan, an MP-actor associate of the Prime Minister, handled much of the money in Switzerland. Although Rajiv Gandhi was officially cleared of receiving any part of the $30 million commission and wind-up fees, the event rocked the Government and led to the resignation of Vishwanath Pratap Singh as Minister of Defence,

[40] Furdson, Maj.-Gen. E., 'Huge order by India for Soviet arms', *Daily Telegraph,* 19 Jan. 1984.
[41] 'Air defence regiments to be modernised', *Times of India,* 13 Aug. 1981.
[42] 'India buys Dutch radar system', *The Statesman,* 1 Jan. 1986.
[43] Bobb, D. *et al.,* 'The Bofors blast', *India Today,* vol. 12, no. 9 (15 May 1987), p. 18.

who thereafter emerged as a formidable voice in opposition. However, at no point, it seems, did the scandal shake public confidence in the way defence decisions are taken—it was primarily a political issue which did not involve questions of national security.

To add to the massive deal with Bofors, in late 1986 India considered the purchase of a self-propelled 155-mm howitzer from the UK with the intention of utilizing the Vijayanta chassis.[44] Only weeks later Royal Ordnance, the UK Government-owned munitions and arms factory, won an order from India for 14 combat engineering tractors in a deal worth £40 million.[45]

In 1987 the Army came under criticism for its prevarication over which rifle to choose as a replacement for the indigenous Ishapore. (In mid-1993 the Ministry of Defence finalized tenders for 100 000 Ak 47 assault rifles and 50 million rounds of ammunition. However, this is supposed to be an intermediate step pending the indigenous development of 5.56 mm assault rifles.[46])

Surprisingly, a report in early 1988 indicated that a new modernization phase for the Army was under way. Plans were reported to include more and better MBTs, an infrastructure for overhauling T-72 and BMP-1 units and several areas of indigenous production[47].

In addition to increased procurement, the Army had another bureaucratic battle to wage through the 1980s. Since independence its status and role, in absolute terms and in relation to both the civilian bureaucracy and the other services, had gradually declined. Yet at the same time, the role of the Army in the sensitive area of internal security gradually increased until by 1980 the Army had been used on 375 occasions to assist the police in maintaining law and order over a four-year period.[48] Certainly, much of this was related to relatively minor disturbances, but Prime Minister Gandhi's decision in June 1984 to violate the Golden Temple in Amritsar (Operation Bluestar) presented a particularly difficult task for the Army. It lowered morale among the ranks and led to desertions and alienation among Sikh troops.

As the Army became increasingly indispensable to the central Government's drive to maintain law and order and reverse the centrifugal forces within the country—forces which stretched from Tamil Nadu in the south-east of the country to the Punjab in the north-west—its leadership began to request compensation in various forms. First, the Army successfully pushed for a degree of reorganization to reflect the decline in its relative dependence upon basic infantry strength. Between 1979 and 1983 the overall strength of the Army increased, over and beyond armament procurement. The total number of Independent Armoured Brigades was raised to seven from five and a

[44] 'India considers Vickers self-propelled howitzer', *Jane's Defence Weekly,* vol. 6, no. 25 (27 Dec. 1986), p. 1472.

[45] 'Royal Ordnance awarded £40m Indian order', *Financial Times,* 22 Jan. 1987.

[46] Bedi, R., 'Indian arms buys defy cash shortfall', *Jane's Defence Weekly*, vol. 19, no. 19 (8 May 1993), pp. 29–30.

[47] 'India begins Army modernisation', *Jane's Defence Weekly,* vol. 9, no. 9 (5 Mar. 1988), p. 390.

[48] Jacobs, G., 'India's army', *Asia Defence Journal,* no. 9 (Sep. 1985), p. 4.

Mechanized Division was created.[49] However, the continuing debate over whether or not to create a post of chief of defence staff has not been resolved in the Army's favour (see chapter 9).

Second, during the mid-1980s a separate debate emerged over the position and status of the Indian Army in society. By March 1986 the Prime Minister had ordered an enquiry into the continued degradation of defence service officers in the Warrant of Precedence (see page 56). A related issue emerged in the question of the Army's technical competence. Traditionally, the Indian Army is notable for its conservatism, but the Chief of Army Staff over this period, General K. Sundarji, attempted to do to the Army what Rajiv Gandhi wished to do with the rest of Indian society in relation to science and technology. In a letter to the officer corps, Sundarji made his preferences very clear:

Many of us have not kept ourselves professionally uptodate, doctrinally or technologically: we have felt that we have 'got it made', and rested on our oars: we do not read enough: we do not think enough, and some of course, have been promoted well beyond their capability. In the practice of our profession, we have not insisted on standards being maintained and turn our eyes away from irregularities.[50]

Apart from the attempt to capitalize upon the compromises engendered by a greater involvement in internal security issues and thereby to increase its size and status, the Army was also aware of a serious and increasing skills shortage. All in all, it was apparently becoming an unattractive career. Of the troops selected for training some 37.5 per cent deserted. At the other end of the spectrum the Indian Military Academy, the main feeder institution for the officer cadres, had become desperately short of worthwhile recruits, particularly in engineering. The shortfall was 18 per cent in 1976/77 and 75 per cent in 1982/83. In the same year the technical course on offer at the Officers' Training School was discontinued due to a lack of adequate response. In order to redress this marked decline the Army requested lump sum grants to young soldiers and special allowances for high-risk jobs. Other demands included more respect in civilian circles for Army personnel.[51]

Third, the Army sought expansion through the creation of an Army Aviation Corps (AAC). Such an organization was created in mid-1986 with the intention of providing the Army with at least 200 helicopters, including gunships. Eventually, however, it turned out to be a hollow victory when allocations for the AAC dwindled to virtually nothing during the late 1980s. In the 1988–89 defence budget the Army aviation wing received only Rs.0.2 million ($154 000).[52]

[49] Jacobs (note 48), p. 6.
[50] 'PM to probe defence "degradation"', *Indian Express*, 3 Mar. 1986.
[51] Gupta, S., 'The Indian Army: asking for more', *India Today*, vol. 10, no. 2 (31 Jan. 1985), pp. 94–99.
[52] *MILAVNEWS*, Aug. 1988, p. 17.

IV. The Indian Navy

During the 1980s, the long-standing commitment to an ambitious naval presence in the region finally came to fruition. A Government report in 1978 signalled the onset of a 20-year naval development programme designed to give the country an indubitable blue water naval capability.[53] In keeping with Indira Gandhi's view of the preferred defence policy for India, the naval modernization programme was unequivocally based upon power projection. The proposed role for the Navy went beyond sea denial and was intended to include both the complete control of the sea lines of communication (SLOCs) and the ability to come to the aid of small developing countries within the region.[54] The primary naval missions during this period were fourfold:

(*a*) protection of India's water frontiers and sea approaches to the country;
(*b*) protection of India's natural resources in the waters contiguous to the Arabian Sea and Bay of Bengal;
(*c*) protection of the country's foreign marine traffic; and
(*d*) utilization of the Navy to promote Indian political and national goals throughout the Indian Ocean and the Middle East.

As with other areas of defence procurement, many of the decisions regarding expansion were in fact taken by the Janata Government and implemented during the 1980s with several additional acquisitions, and were continued by Indira Gandhi because they suited so well the search for regional hegemony. The process of decision making also took a considerable amount of time, particularly with regard to the evaluation of competing systems available from West European suppliers.

Another striking aspect of the naval modernization programme was the determination to move away from the USSR as a sole source of supply. During the 1970s the state of the economy and the willingness of the USSR to supply naval equipment gave the Indian Government no choice but to accept the offers. In the 1980s India found itself able to afford a more independent naval buildup which could permit the Navy to develop independent missions without external constraint.

One of the first agreements in this direction was the decision to supersede India's eight ageing Soviet Foxtrots with SSK-1500 Type-209 hunter-killer submarines of West German design. The deal took over two years to confirm on account of stiff competition from the Kockums shipyard in Sweden. In addition to the two craft from the Federal Republic of Germany (FRG), it was agreed that India would produce at least two more units indigenously in a deal costing an initial $500 million. In some quarters the agreement was heavily criticized on account of the poor performance of the Type-209 and its ageing

---

[53] Tellis, A., 'India's naval expansion: reflections on history and strategy', *Comparative Strategy*, vol. 6, no. 2 (1987), p. 193.
[54] Jacobs, G., 'India's navy and the Soviet Union', *Jane's Defence Review,* Aug. 1983, p. 886.

design.[55] The deal was cancelled in 1988 when India alleged that the West German company Howaldtswerke-Deutsche Werft (HDW) had sold similar design plans to South Africa but not before at least one of the boats had been received.[56]

The West German submarine deal was followed by a procurement rush by India throughout the mid-1980s involving imports from both the USSR and West European exporters. Without doubt, the key beneficiary during this period was the Fleet Air Arm following the modernization of the *Vikrant* during the early 1980s to include a ski ramp to accommodate the Harrier V/STOL and other needs for the future. Initial offers were received from France, Spain and the UK.[57] In addition, the Government began to approach foreign firms to buy the plans for the production of a second aircraft-carrier.[58] Exactly where in India such an enormous vessel could be produced was not clear at that time.

India's first Sea Harrier FRS Mk.51 was handed over to the Indian Navy in January 1983. It was followed by another five front-line aircraft and two trainers. The order was expected to be followed by a request for more Harriers as six aircraft were obviously an inadequate complement for the *Vikrant*.[59] The aircraft were armed with Matra 550 Magic dogfight missiles and, in the wake of the Falklands/Malvinas War, the Navy seemed keen to acquire the Exocet for the Harrier's anti-ship role. In the event, however, India ordered the more sophisticated Sea Eagle anti-ship missile from the UK which the Royal Navy was acquiring to replace its Exocet missiles.[60] The Sea Eagle was also intended to arm the 12 Sea King helicopters ordered from the UK following the rejection of an offer by France to supply a package involving the Super Puma and the Exocet, primarily for the Godavari frigates which carry two helicopters.[61] The Sea King order was swiftly followed by a parallel order to MEL (UK) for a £9 million Super Searcher airborne surface search radar system. French and British companies also competed for the sale of the anti-ship missile to equip the 24 Dornier Do 228 aircraft purchased in 1985 and designed to enter coastal patrol duties in 1988, an order worth £60 million.[62] The Sea Skua air-to-surface missile was the eventual choice, in part because of its interface with the Super Searcher.[63]

Interest in a second aircraft-carrier took several years to bring to fruition. However, on 24 April 1986 India announced plans to purchase the British carrier HMS *Hermes* (renamed the *Viraat*) for a sum of $94 million, including

[55] Karnad, B., 'Sub-standard sub for the navy', *Hindustan Times*, 21 Nov. 1981.

[56] 'Indian submarine joins fleet', *Jane's Defence Weekly*, vol. 7, no. 14 (14 Mar. 1987).

[57] Mukherjee, S. J., 'India still undecided about aircraft proposals', *Jane's Defence Weekly*, vol. 4, no. 1 (6 July 1985), p. 14.

[58] Dua, H. K., 'Navy may get new aircraft carrier', *Indian Express*, 7 May 1981.

[59] 'Harriers join Indian Navy', *Daily Telegraph*, 17 Dec. 1983.

[60] British Aerospace Dynamics Group, 'First export sale of Sea Eagle new-generation anti-ship missile', *News Release*, 20 July 1983.

[61] *MILAVNEWS*, Aug. 1983, p. 17.

[62] Chuter, A., 'Indian navy to purchase anti-ship missile', *Jane's Defence Weekly*, vol. 4, no. 12 (21 Sep. 1985), p. 601.

[63] 'Indian Navy to receive Dorniers with Sea Skua', *Jane's Defence Weekly*, vol. 6, no. 12 (19 July 1986).

dry-docking, refit, spares and support. The ship had been laid up for two years after serving as the flagship to the Royal Navy task force during the Falklands/Malvinas War. As with the *Vikrant*, *Hermes* was laid down after World War II and would have been scrapped by the UK if India had not bought it.[64] Even with refitting, the vessel had a limited life in 1987. Inevitably, the agreement to purchase another carrier led to increased orders for the Harrier and other equipment relevant to the deployment and protection of an extra carrier. Shortly before the deal was announced, reliable reports suggested that the MoU signed with the UK had been revised to accommodate more Harriers and Sea Kings to equip the new carrier.[65] By mid-1985 further orders for the Sea Harrier looked likely, to bring the number of Indian purchases to 48.[66] In addition, the Chief of Naval Staff, Admiral R. H. Tahiliani, indicated that a third and possibly fourth aircraft-carrier to replace the ageing *Vikrant* would be required but that in future the vessels would be produced indigenously.[67]

Increasing interest in the naval equipment on offer from the West brought several offers from the USSR. In 1982 the Soviet and Indian navies underwent joint training exercises.[68] Rather than being a sign of success for Soviet attempts towards a collective security system in Asia, the exercises were probably designed to impress upon the Indian Navy the capabilities of ships such as the Kresta II-class anti-submarine-warfare (ASW) cruisers and the aircraft-carrier *Minsk* which visited Bombay in 1982, together with the cruiser *Tashkent*.[69] Nevertheless, the USSR was disappointed. In particular, it was reported that the Navy was largely dissatisfied with Soviet naval equipment. It was alleged that Soviet submarines had to be serviced too frequently and that the overhaul period was too long. The Natya Class vessels also had to be modified for stability when major defects became apparent on the delivery run from Vladivostok.[70] However, as the Kremlin saw its influence decline its offers became more attractive and included nuclear-powered attack submarines and the Kilo-type submarines which were under development when India ordered the Type-209 submarines from the FRG.[71] These offers met with some success. In 1986 the decision was taken to replace the Petya-type ASW corvettes with Nanuchkas or newer types.[72] At the same time it was announced that the fourth of the Rajput Class of guided missile destroyers (Soviet-built *Kashin*) had joined the Indian Navy.[73] This was swiftly followed by the first of six Kilo Class submarines to augment the acquisition of Type-209s which together

[64] 'Indian Navy buys British carrier', *Navy News and Undersea Technology*, vol. 3, no. 10 (9 May 1986); 'Hermes for scrap if India says no', *Jane's Defence Weekly*, vol. 3, no. 25 (22 June 1985), p. 1197.

[65] 'Indian follow-on order for Sea Harriers "imminent"', *Jane's Defence Weekly*, vol. 4, no. 12 (21 Sep. 1985), p. 605.

[66] *MILAVNEWS*, July 1985, p. 5.

[67] 'Indian naval construction set for major expansion', *International Defense Review*, no. 3 (Mar. 1986), p. 369.

[68] Jacobs (note 54), p. 886.

[69] Jacobs (note 54), p. 888.

[70] Tandon, B., 'Kremlin in chase for navy deals', *Daily Telegraph*, 5 Mar. 1988.

[71] *Pacific Defence Reporter 1985 Annual Reference Addition*, Dec. 1984/Jan. 1985, p. 208.

[72] 'Indian Navy to replace corvettes', *Jane's Defence Weekly*, vol. 6, no. 11 (20 Sep. 1986), p. 622.

[73] 'New destroyer for Indian Navy', *Jane's Defence Weekly*, vol. 6, no. 11 (20 Sep. 1986), p. 618.

replaced the Foxtrots.[74] All in all the naval equipment procured from the USSR during this period amounted to $750 million and formed a part of the $1.6 billion deal.[75]

The major agreement of the 1980s came in late 1987 when India announced that it would shortly receive a nuclear-powered submarine from the USSR. Early the next year the ship was identified as a Charlie I-type cruise missile carrier equipped with eight launcher tubes.[76] This was the first time that a nuclear-powered submarine had sailed under the flag of a non-builder and it caused surprise and confusion within the nuclear non-proliferation regime; it was initially unclear whether or not the transfer contravened the terms of the NPT (although it was later established that the transfer was legitimate). Although the transfer had been first mooted as early as 1984, it was still a great surprise to the West.[77] This deal might have been followed by the transfer of another four or five similar systems, a part of a package involving expenditure in the region of Rs.3000 crores.[78] The submarine has however since been returned and the procurement of nuclear-powered submarines looks unlikely in the foreseeable future. It was also anticipated that by late 1988 the very low frequency communication station started in 1984 (the same date that negotiations opened with the USSR over the nuclear-powered submarine) would become operational, thereby giving India a naval capability unmatched by any other Indian Ocean littoral state.

Coupled with an ambitious naval shipbuilding programme, the modernization programme of the 1980s has given the Indian Navy a substantial increase in its ability to patrol the reaches of the Indian Ocean. Although the Navy has yet to use its guns in anger since the 1971 war, the growing capability of the Indian Navy is slowly becoming evident. In 1987 Indian frigates were seen off the coast of Mozambique, although the purpose of the visit was unclear. In 1988 the Government was able to intervene in the Maldives to prevent a *coup* succeeding, an act condoned by the Commonwealth but greatly resented by many of the smaller states in South Asia, particularly Sri Lanka. Further afield, there were unsubstantiated reports during the same year that India was considering intervention in Fiji to protect the lives and property of dispossessed Indians. Although highly unlikely to develop into anything concrete, the propensity to think the unthinkable in certain circles in New Delhi is significant in itself with regard to the type of ambitions harboured in certain sectors of the political community. Quite how much further the Government is prepared to go in displaying its now formidable naval force is not clear. Nor is it apparent how

[74] 'India receives first "Kilo" class submarine', *Jane's Defence Weekly*, vol. 6, no. 12 (27 Sep. 1986), p. 670.

[75] ''First view of INS Ranvir with Ka-28', *Jane's Defence Weekly*, vol. 6, no. 21 (29 Nov. 1986), p. 1260.

[76] 'India's SSGN identified', *Jane's Defence Weekly*, vol. 9, no. 5 (6 Feb. 1988), p. 199.

[77] 'Indian SSN departs Vladivostok submarine base', *Jane's Defence Weekly*, vol. 9, no. 3 (23 Jan. 1988), p. 116.

[78] *India Today*, 31 Dec. 1987, p. 72.

free the Government was to operate the nuclear submarines without restrictions, particularly with regard to deployment and engagement.

V. The Indian Air Force

For both the Indian Government and the IAF, 1980 was a year of confusion. Following widespread allegations over corrupt practices surrounding the Jaguar deal (see chapter 4, section VIII) which was eventually signed during the Janata era, the new Government prevaricated over how to proceed. A key difficulty stemmed from the fact that some of the most vociferous critics of the deal were by 1980 in decision-making positions. Prime Minister Gandhi had criticized the deal on the basis of cost-effectiveness, alleging that the cost of producing the Jaguar domestically was twice that of buying it direct from the UK.[79] Nevertheless, in March 1980 she took the decision to proceed with the £1 billion deal with the UK.[80] Shortly afterwards she rejected the conclusions of an official enquiry which came as a surprise, as one of her key political opponents, Jagjivan Ram, held the defence portfolio during the negotiations and the calls for a probe were widespread.[81]

The major deal agreed with the USSR in mid-1980 led the Government to renegotiate the terms of the Jaguar deal. On offer from the USSR was the MiG-23 at one-third the cost of the Jaguar and with all the favourable repayment conditions. Instead of purchasing 40 Jaguar units outright before moving on to licensed production, the Government decided to double the quantity of units bought 'off the shelf' and cancel the licensed production agreement.[82] So confident was the British Government that the order would be taken up in full, or so desperate to see it go through, that cancellation penalties were not included in the contract.[83] Nor did the British Government expect its Indian counterpart to waste £30–50 million of industrial investment in the form of tooling up at HAL which would potentially go to waste with the cancellation.[84] However, even as late as mid-1982, the situation was still unclear when Defence Minister R. Venkataraman remarked that 'the manufacture of more Jaguar aircraft had not been ruled out'.[85]

Equally confusing was the explanation coming from the Government that the Jaguar order had been scaled down in favour of the MiG-23 when in fact the systems were not comparable. The former has a dedicated long-range strike role, whereas the MiG-23 is designed for ground support within a 150-km

[79] Anthony, I., 'Soviet–Indian defence cooperation', *Royal United Services Institute and Brassey's Defence Yearbook* (Brassey's: London, 1988), p. 229.

[80] Sharma, K. K., 'Gandhi confirms Jaguar deal', *Financial Times*, 14 Mar. 1980.

[81] *Flight International*, 5 Apr. 1980, p. 1048.

[82] *Sunday Times*, 22 June 1980.

[83] Reports as to the cancellation fee differ. The *Far Eastern Economic Review*, 1 Aug. 1980, reported *high* cancellation fees as a reason for continuation.

[84] *The Guardian*, 12 Aug. 1980.

[85] *MILAVNEWS*, May 1982, p. 7.

radius. Moreover, the latter is single-engined whereas the IAF prefer twin-engined aircraft such as the Jaguar.

Part of the confusion was explained by the mid-year news that France had emerged as a prospective supplier of front-line aircraft in the form of the Mirage 2000, an offer said to be 'irresistible' for India:

India has been promised 'exclusive' production rights for the area—including exports to the Gulf and South-east Asia, if any country there can eventually afford the plane—if India signs a sizable contract, say 150 planes to be built in the mid-1980s. However, France has let it be known that a refusal could result in the *Mirage* F 2000 going to Pakistan and that France is considering a Pakistani request for 35 of these planes.

Thus the French are trying to box in India with its own security considerations—principally the denial of this ultra-advanced technology aircraft to Pakistan.[86]

In addition Dassault offered India a place at the drawing-board on its new development, the Mirage 4000, an extremely advanced aircraft intended to compete with the Grumman F-14 Tomcat and the McDonnell Douglas F-18.[87] The offer came at a time when French defence exports were facing serious problems, which explains why Dassault should in effect bid against itself (Dassault had an ongoing interest in the Jaguar deal on account of its recent takeover of Brueget, BAe's collaborator on the Jaguar). The Mirage 2000 had largely failed to find a niche in the export market owing to the success of rival systems such as the F-16. At a later date, while the Indian Government equivocated over the option to produce the Mirage under licence, the French offered to tie the deal to the development of the indigenous Light Combat Aircraft (LCA) through 'unrestricted access' to the technology embodied in the Mirage 2000.[88]

The French negotiating team arrived in New Delhi in late 1981 for final negotiations over the Mirage 2000. Such was the concern in the Kremlin that a firm toe-hold in the Indian market was on the point of being lost that an offer of the MiG-25 air superiority fighter as a counter to the F-16 coincided with the French visit. In addition, it also became known that India had accepted an earlier Soviet offer to procure and produce under licence the MiG-27 Flogger J tactical strike fighter rather than the MiG-23 BN.[89] Also on offer from the USSR during this period were AN-32 transport planes and Mi-24 helicopter gunships.[90]

The Mirage 2000 deal was finally signed in February 1982 after negotiations slowed down following Indian demands for a more attractive technology transfer and follow-on package plus a more powerful engine (the Snecma M53 P2, capable of an increased combat range) and reduced interest rates. The first stage of the deal involved the outright purchase of 40 units, costing $1.3 billion at

[86] Mascarenhas, A., 'India lets Harrier option drop', *Sunday Times,* 20 July 1980.

[87] MacLachlan, A., 'Dassault wins Indian order for Mirage jets', *Defense Week,* vol. 2, no. 25 (26 May 1981), p. 1.

[88] *MILAVNEWS*, Dec. 1983, p. 16.

[89] *MILAVNEWS*, May 1982, p. 8.

[90] *Asian Defence Journal*, Nov. 1981, pp. 36, 38.

$32 million per copy, with an option to proceed to a second stage involving the licensed production of another 110 units.[91]

Amid the tension surrounding the negotiations with France, a British defence export team arrived in New Delhi with the intention of interesting the Indian Government in the air defence variant (ADV) of the Tornado Multi-Role Combat Aircraft (MRCA). The offer would have been extended to the Interdictor Strike (IDS) had the Government shown any interest. In the event, the team returned to the UK empty-handed and reports at the time suggested that the MRCA was too expensive.[92] However, a key argument put forward by the sales team was that the MRCA would in fact be less expensive than the Mirage.[93] It also became clear at about the same time that India was not interested in submissions by Northrop for co-production of the F-20A by India.[94] Even if the Indian Government had shown more than a perfunctory interest, any deal involving the F-20 would have required Foreign Military Sales funding, which would have been unlikely given Congressional concern over policies which had in the past led to the arming of both India and Pakistan.

The MRCA failure was partially offset by the Government's decision to revive the licensed production section of the Jaguar contract. Following speculation that all licensed production had been cancelled, it was decided to assemble 45 CKD units and assemble a third batch of 31 Jaguars with an estimated value to the UK of $290 million.[95]

With few exceptions, little of any great significance occurred for the IAF throughout the mid-1980s. Most of the key modernization agreements had been settled, with or without an indigenous production element, and it only remained for the IAF to assimilate the new weapon systems in a reliable fashion and redress one of the worst accident rates in the world. The accident rate for the Chetak helicopter, produced under licence from France, was 10 times the world average in 1985. Moreover, between 1977 and 1983 an air safety committee investigated 262 major and minor accidents including 31 write-offs, the causes being attributed to pilot error, recklessness and a deficiency in trained technicians.[96] Nor were these expressions of concern allayed when, in mid-1986, three Indian fighter aircraft crashed within 24 hours—two of the fighters were MiG-21s, the third was not identified.[97]

There were reports that India had shown interest in the Nimrod AEW3 (Advanced Early Warning) system in 1982 and again in 1986 after the British Government rejected it, but they came to nothing, possibly because the system embodied so much sensitive equipment. Nor did plans to use an appropriate

[91] Malhotra, I., 'India finally signs deal for Mirages', *The Guardian*, 13 Feb. 1982.
[92] Smith, C. and George, B., 'The defence of India', *Jane's Defence Weekly,* vol. 3, no. 9 (2 Mar. 1985), pp. 365–70.
[93] *Asian Defence Journal,* Nov. 1981, p. 38.
[94] *MILAVNEWS*, Feb. 1983, p. 17.
[95] *MILAVNEWS*, Mar. 1983, p. 15.
[96] *MILAVNEWS*, Oct. 1985, p. 18.
[97] *MILAVNEWS*, Aug. 1986, p. 14.

version of the Nimrod's avionics in a less expensive airframe, such as the HS 748, which HAL was already producing.[98]

In late 1983 speculation mounted about a possible agreement between the USSR and India over the supply of the new MiG-29 Fulcrum, complete with manufacturing rights.[99] The deal was finally announced in August 1984 and came as a great surprise to the West. The MiG-29, a major top-line, state-of-the-art fighter was only just entering service with the Soviet Air Force and had yet to be issued to Warsaw Pact allies. Moreover, the USSR was habitually cautious about sensitive technology transfer to countries with links to the West.

While the MiG-29 caused great interest in the West for primarily political reasons, indicating as it did the extent to which the USSR was attempting to head off India's successful diversification programme, it was not until mid-1988 that the full significance of the deal became apparent. In the very much more relaxed atmosphere of the new *détente* the MiG-29 appeared at the Farnborough Air Show and caused a sensation by outperforming the most up-to-date Western systems, particularly with regard to manœuvrability.[100] Since the defection of a MiG-25 Foxbat pilot to Japan in September 1976, Western observers had been convinced of the retarded standards of Soviet aeronautic technology. Although the MiG-29 does not incorporate the type of advanced electronic, 'fly-by-wire' technology which is now incorporated in state-of-the-art Western systems, this proved not to be detrimental to either the horizontal or vertical performance modes of the aircraft. Thus, India's acquisition of 40–45 MiG-29s is now seen as a much more significant event than it seemed in 1984. However, the USSR withheld from the supply and co-production contract the sophisticated look down/shoot down radar and the new AA-X-10 medium-range air-to-air missiles which were expected to be the Fulcrum's primary armament when in Soviet Air Force service. Instead, the more dated avionics installed in the MiG-23 will be used, together with the less sophisticated air-to-air missiles which arm both the MiG-23s and the MiG-21s.[101]

With the exception of reports that the IAF would procure the Soviet IL-76 Mainstays to satisfy the AEW requirement and the Yak-28 Brewer E light bombers for Electronic Counter Measure (ECM) duties, little else was reported for the IAF.[102] Instead, attention focused upon the needs of the Fleet Air Arm, particularly following the appointment of Admiral Tahiliani as chief of naval staff in late 1984, he himself being an ex-naval aviator. Also, considerable attention and resources were directed towards India's major indigenous project of the decade, the light combat aircraft.

---

[98] *MILAVNEWS*, Aug. 1982, p. 13.

[99] *MILAVNEWS*, Nov. 1983, p. 20.

[100] See, for example, the several articles on the event in *Aviation Week & Space Technology*, 12 Sep. 1988.

[101] *MILAVNEWS*, Nov. 1984, p. 14.

[102] *MILAVNEWS*, Apr. 1984, p. 5.

VI. Procurement in search of a policy?

During the course of the 1980s, India engaged in the most significant conventional defence buildup in its history, and within the Third World it has been rivalled only by the profligate expansion programmes of the OPEC Gulf states during the late 1970s. In 1987, for example, approximately 20 per cent of all the arms exported to Third World countries were sold to India.[103] Tainted with several hints of corruption and necessitating heady rises in defence expenditure to service increasing procurement debts, the modernization programme proceeded apace without policy reviews after 1981 and, it seemed on occasion, without strong direction.

Over a five-year period, 1982–87, Indian defence expenditure rose by 50 per cent. The 1987/88 defence budget alone increased by 23 per cent from the previous year, which had in turn increased by an unplanned 16 per cent. However, $190 million was diverted from the defence budget in late 1987 to alleviate the chronic drought conditions experienced in many parts of the country, especially Rajasthan. With the exception of the period following the 1962 war, defence expenditure averaged approximately 3 per cent of GNP over the 1960s and 1970s. It moved closer to 5.5 per cent during the late 1980s before reductions occurred.[104]

Clearly, much of India's defence equipment was in urgent need of modernization by the 1970s. The USSR provided the only source of military hardware during that decade owing to India's chronic economic problems and foreign exchange shortages. When the Janata Government came to power it created the opportunity not only to preside over a significant modernization programme but also to reverse the degree of dependency upon the USSR. The re-election of Indira Gandhi saw a continuation of the modernization programme, but she exploited the diversification policy to extract the maximum financial, technological and political advantage from a buyers' market on the one hand and a concerned USSR on the other.

Politically, Indira Gandhi and, later, Rajiv Gandhi handled the process well, witness the quality of front-line equipment currently deployed by the Indian armed forces. However, it is by no means clear that India required the scale of modernization for defence alone. Nor is it apparent that the choice of technology was particularly appropriate for anything beyond symbolism.

In the early 1980s India perceived three key areas of threat to its security—China, Pakistan and a more nebulous threat from the Indian Ocean. In addition there were perceived problems stemming from the Soviet invasion of Afghanistan, the renewed and much resuscitated relationship between Pakistan and the USA and, further afield, disconcerting developments in the Persian Gulf; however, while the overall effect may have been to alter India's security environment, direct threats to the country's territorial integrity or off-shore resources

[103] SIPRI arms trade registers and data base.
[104] Gupta, S. and Thakurta, P. G., 'Heading for a crisis', *India Today,* vol. 14, no. 4 (28 Feb. 1989), p. 43.

are difficult to identify. While the nature of the geopolitical environment may have changed, certain basic principles, such as those identified by Nehru, did not. India's size and geopolitical significance in a bipolar world provided its own form of security.

Even with the US military and economic aid package, which over the decade amounted to less than India currently spends on defence each year, Pakistan posed little threat to India. While there always existed the possibility of a lightning strike to increase territorial gains in Azad Kashmir, unprovoked action would certainly have jeopardized bilateral military and economic aid from the USA and multilateral aid from elsewhere—Pakistan is unequivocally dependent upon the USA. It would also have been likely to tip the balance in favour of those Congressmen who wished to penalize Pakistan for its nuclear weapon programme. With the Punjab well fortified for defence on both sides, Pakistan's only outlet for aggression lay in the Rajasthan desert—an unlikely option given India's overwhelming 3:1 conventional superiority.

Nor was there any reason to suspect that China posed the type of threat which existed two decades earlier. Apart from a quantum increase in planning and vigilance to absorb another attack by China, India could rely upon the post-Mao internal upheavals and the massive four modernizations programme occupying all Chinese efforts into the foreseeable future. Although Sino-Indian relations did dip markedly in 1986, with the result of fractious relations and border incidents, the tension was short-lived. Indeed, it is remarkable how, over the 1970s and 1980s, the threat from China became an increasingly diplomatic rather than a military problem for New Delhi to solve. Rajiv Gandhi's successful visit to China in 1988 and the successive rounds of talks over border issues reflect well the propensity on both sides to seek diplomatic solutions and avoid another conflict at all costs.

Even more tenuous were the perceived threats from the Indian Ocean. While there did exist a major superpower buildup in the region following the departure of the British, the emphasis was upon strategic factors which turned largely on the Iraq–Iran War and the rise of Islamic fundamentalism. Pakistan's role in this process was of concern to India but the idea of a threat to off-shore oil resources or outright invasion or blockade from either the RDF or the US Seventh Fleet was inconceivable. Indeed, the significance of Indian policy in this theatre lies in its vagueness. At no point was the generalized threat perception followed through to its logical and specific conclusion.

Equally significant was the cavalier approach taken by India to defence posture overall. During a period when large capital ships were increasingly seen as vulnerable and expensive, the Government opted for a second aircraft-carrier and announced plans to procure at least a third from indigenous sources. In the aftermath of the Falklands/Malvinas War, the key lessons gleaned by Indian strategic planners did not centre upon the fortuitous circumstances under which the British task force managed to acquit itself, or the limitations and vulnerability revealed by large ships which at the very least did not benefit from anti-missile systems. In fact, defence opinion shapers were becoming seriously disenchanted with large ships because of their high-value status as targets and their increasing vulnerability in the face of missile improvements. Instead, Indian policy makers were alerted to the importance of protecting extended coastlines which in turn justified the pursuit of naval power. At no point did the Indian Navy appear to define the operational context to justify not only two or more aircraft-carriers but, in addition, the extremely expensive V/STOL airwing to accompany them.

While the Indian Air Force may have required updating and modernization, particularly in the wake of the US–Pakistan aid agreement, the steps taken were open to question in many instances. Procurement of the Jaguar and the Mirage 2000 was offered a *post hoc* justification by the Pakistani acquisition of the F-16. Whether or not the Jaguar could successfully fulfil its main mission and destroy the Pakistani F-16 squadrons while they were still on the ground would depend wholly upon the political circumstances leading up to the attack: it would have to be a pre-emptive, surprise attack. If the F-16s took off success-fully, the Mirage 2000 would be entrusted with the task of interception. Given the numerous military and industrial targets throughout northern and central India within range for an F-16, however, the mix of strike routes would be too numerous for the Mirage to patrol.[105] Given the extremely high cost of the Mirage, could the defence of India have been better served by a greater empha-sis upon fixed air defences? Why did the Indian Government opt for a fighter that the French Air Force accepted with some reluctance, that the IAF was equally equivocal about, that had sold poorly on the international market and, furthermore, is a single-engined plane and thus extremely vulnerable in the environment of northern India where it will most certainly be deployed?

Similarly, no debate appears to have taken place about the overall direction of Indian defence. While the political benefits of diversification are self-evi-dent, how much are they counter-balanced by operational problems? For example, a squadron of F-4 Phantoms requires an inventory of 70 000 spare parts to be kept flying in wartime conditions.[106] Each successive generation of military technology justifies its existence in part by offering greater perform-ance capability and, in general, is a more complex system than its predecessor, which inevitably means that greater spare part inventories are required. Fault diagnosis and maintenance are also becoming much more complex, requiring sophisticated computers to trace faults (and spare parts), and these too must be well maintained.[107] Recent procurement by the IAF has increased the range of equipment to include French, British, Soviet and West German systems, which must require immense planning to design a logistical chain which can only ever be as strong as its weakest link.

---

[105] Palit, D. K., Maj.-Gen. (Ret'd), 'Mirage deal needs careful thought', *Times of India*, 30 Oct. 1981.
[106] Albrecht, U. and Kaldor, M., 'Introduction', eds M. Kaldor and A. Eide, *World Military Order: The Impact of Military Technology on the Third World* (Macmillan: London, 1979), p. 7.
[107] See, for example, Spinney's description of the maintenance requirements for the F-16. Spinney, F. C., *Defense Facts of Life: The Plans/Reality Mismatch* (Westview Press: London, 1985).

Nor does any debate appear to have taken place about the implications of the performance of major weapon systems in recent conflicts, such as the Falklands/Malvinas War and the range of engagements between Israel and its neighbours. During an era when the vulnerability of major weapon systems was increasing because of significant technical advances in missile technology, the Indian Government poured vast amounts of foreign exchange into the purchase of precisely the type of systems over which hung so many question marks.

Finally, and the subject of the next chapter, India's procurement policy during the 1980s can be questioned in relation to the time-honoured policy of working towards self-sufficiency in the defence sector. For example, plans to produce under licence both the Jaguar and the Mirage were abandoned over time, leaving the aeronautics industry with nothing more than basic assembly of these systems from CKD kits.

The speed and extravagance of the defence buildup, coupled with the continuing neglect of indigenization, leads to the conclusion that political rather than military considerations were uppermost in the collective mind of the Political Affairs Committee of the Cabinet, the final arbiter on procurement decisions. Without doubt the imported systems offered the country a quantum increase in defence capability and added to security to some degree. However, the efficacy of the modernization programme is so dubious as to suggest that the symbols of power rather than the principles of defence were responsible for defining what the country imported.

6. India's defence sector, 1988–91

I. 1988: the end of an era

During the 1980s the Indian Government found no reason to contain a rapidly rising defence budget. The economy appeared to be in reasonable condition and the threat assessment appeared to justify the scale of defence modernization. Both the upper and lower houses of the parliament were content virtually to rubber-stamp the defence budget each April and successive charges of corruption tended to raise political questions which stopped well short of a full public debate over defence and procurement policy.

After a decade of growth, however, serious problems began to emerge in the late 1980s. Basically, the defence forces had over-extended the modernization programme and, as economic conditions became more problematic for the economy as a whole, the defence budget began to look extremely vulnerable. However, when the cuts came they did so at an extremely difficult time because of the impact upon systems already procured but not yet paid for or, apparently, sufficiently well-armed.

Albeit with the benefit of hindsight, we can see that the modernization programme has been a débâcle. The inability to find sufficient foreign exchange to complete the process has all but negated the heady procurement which went before. Arguably, in terms of military preparedness India was less well armed than is generally accepted, despite—or perhaps because of—the import policy which underpinned the modernization programme. These problems will take years to rectify.

II. The Indian economy and the road to debt

The year 1984 was a turning point in India's history, the year when Indira Gandhi ordered the attack on the Golden Temple in Amritsar, followed by her assassination by Sikh bodyguards which unleashed communal violence and carnage on a scale that was shocking but not unknown for India. With the ruling Congress(I) party in complete disarray, the scale of communal tension brought the Union to the brink of chaos. By December 1984, control appeared to have been returned—Rajiv Gandhi had won an unprecedented landslide victory by appealing to the electoral heart as his mother's son and to the electoral head as a modernizer capable of ruthlessness and innovation in the country's economy. Somewhat surprisingly, Rajiv Gandhi really did personify the aspirations of the burgeoning middle class.

He rose to power from an unpredictable power base. Despite his mother's attempts to survive in office without the support of the putative socialist wing of the Congress Party, she did not succeed, whereas he was sufficiently fresh and inexperienced to be free of or unaware of the complexities of the Congress culture. Many of the policies he was to enact had been on his mother's agenda, but it took a sea change in Indian politics to provide the relevant opportunities.[1]

In this respect Rajiv Gandhi was more like his grandfather, Nehru—a sincere and energetic positivist. In government, he surrounded himself with technocrats, albeit from the private sector, and felt at ease with promulgating straightforward solutions to India's economic problems. Essentially he set out on a course of modernization and liberalization in the Indian economy. Barriers came down and the 'licence raj', a product of India's version of a command economy, seemed, at last, to be under threat. Technology would flow into India, high-class manufactured goods would flow out, the rupee would eventually become convertible and the power brokers would be replaced by economic not political entrepreneurs.

The new economic policy was designed to release the pent-up demand among the urban middle class, which was growing considerably in both numbers and wealth. In particular, import duties were either eliminated or reduced on an array of intermediate and capital goods. In addition, through tax cuts, the imposition of severe penalties for tax evasion—which required making an example of some well-known figures—and an attempt to end the lobbying system, the Prime Minister added medicine to the sweeteners.

However, Rajiv Gandhi underestimated entirely the inherent resistance within India to innovations such as these. Congress(I) politicians were unhappy to see a decline in the influence they were able to wield over producers and consumers, a ramification of the excessive level of state control which obtained before, and the bureaucrats dragged their collective feet—they too felt threatened by the market changes being introduced.[2]

Two years on it seemed as though the programme was well on course. As the debilitating effect of over-protection and extreme regulation came to be reversed, industrial growth rose to higher levels than in the previous two decades, which was largely due to a marked increase in capital output. However, there were two major qualifications to the otherwise rosy picture. First, although India was experiencing economic growth, so were other Asian countries. India lagged behind in microelectronics, which was the driving force behind technology changes, new systems of production and new products in East and South-East Asia.[3] Second, although liberalization permitted the unrestricted import of capital goods and foreign technology, this was not accompanied by an export expansion to match. Indian products continued to be overpriced and of poor quality, and too few exports contained added value: with an import boom and sluggish exports, India faced a growing foreign exchange

---

[1] Bhargava, A., 'Indian economy during Mrs. Gandhi's regime', *Journal of Asian and African Studies,* vol. 22, nos 3–4 (1987).

[2] Manor, J., 'Tried, then abandoned: economic liberalisation in India', *IDS Bulletin,* vol. 18, no. 4 (Oct. 1987), p. 41.

[3] Housego, D., 'India: in search of new impetus', *Financial Times (Survey),* 20 Dec. 1988.

crisis. The telecommunications and transport infrastructure also left much to be desired.[4]

This was the situation inherited by Vishwanath Pratap Singh, whose National Front coalition assumed power in 1989. Public opinion turned against Rajiv Gandhi, primarily for his alleged involvement in the Bofors affair but also for his increasing inability to understand the needs of his country. Eventually, the new Government was forced to attempt to address a growing balance of payments crisis. Imports of components used in automobile manufacture, electronic goods and consumer durables were cut back.[5] This was linked to the Reserve Bank of India's credit squeeze, which halted expansion plans, increased production costs and promised drastic production cutbacks.[6]

At a critical point in the recovery process, India was badly hit by several years of drought and then in late 1990 by the Persian Gulf crisis. The rising price of oil was a serious blow to India, which remains extremely dependent upon imported oil, even though per capita consumption is among the lowest in the world. In addition, the loss of exports to Iraq and Kuwait and the loss of expatriate earnings from that quarter amounted to a loss of Rs.600 crores per annum.[7]

The new Congress Government under Narasimha Rao was forced to take radical steps to stabilize an economy in free fall and much of economic policy became inseparable from the demands of international finance organizations. Devaluation of the rupee by over 20 per cent against the dollar was the first step. However, as the trade deficit continued to grow, foreign exchange reserves dropped to perilous levels, as low as two or three weeks according to some estimates. An approach to the IMF became unavoidable. By mid-1991 India had a debt service ratio of 30 per cent (the proportion of export earnings required to service past loans from abroad), a $7.5 billion government deficit and a staggering $80 billion in foreign debts.[8]

Whether the new Government pre-empted the imposition of reforms by the IMF or reacted to a series of confidential guide-lines is unclear, but in mid-1991 sweeping economic changes were introduced, in the form of a new industrial policy and a remarkable budget. This was clearly a bold and possibly final attempt to rescue the limited economic gains of previous decades.[9] Despite the inevitable negative effect upon the poor, which will be exacerbated if infrastructure and social welfare projects continue to be stalled in favour of continued subsidies to consumers, farmers and state enterprises, there is a real chance of a semi-liberalized economy emerging before the end of the decade.

[4] Chengappa, R. and Bhandarkar, G., 'Export or perish', *India Today*, vol. 16, no. 16 (31 Aug. 1991), p. 64.

[5] Thakurta, P. G., 'Cutting corners: desperate steps to improve balance of payments', *India Today*, vol. 16, no. 16 (Aug. 1991), p. 64.

[6] Taneja, S., 'The big squeeze', *India Today*, vol. 16, no. 12 (30 June 1991).

[7] Jagannathan, J. and Thakurta, P. G., 'Thank you, Saddam', *India Today*, vol. 16, no. 3 (15 Feb. 1991), p. 28.

[8] Desmond, E. W., 'Who will pick up the tab?', *Time*, 8 Apr. 1991, p. 33.

[9] Chakravarti, S. and R. Jagannathan, 'New economic policy: ending the licence Raj', *India Today*, vol. 16, no. 15 (15 Aug. 1991).

III. The defence sector in the late 1980s

Under the watchful eye of international finance organizations and given too the scale of the economic crisis, the defence sector was bound to be affected. Defence expenditure is a 'non-plan' expenditure, that is, it does not form part of the five-year spending plans, and is lumped together with interest payments and subsidies—the logic behind this differentiation is to give government more freedom to manœuvre on issues which are invariably responsive to unpredictable elements. The seemingly endless series of allegations concerning commissions on the sale of defence goods was also an important influence on attempts to scale down the costs and claims of the defence sector—the political fall-out from the Bofors scandal was at its most serious in late 1987.

The first real signal of what lay in store for the defence sector came with an emergency measure in late 1987 to boost the drought relief programme by Rs.2.5 billion, to be taken directly from the defence budget. Essentially, the gesture was of a political nature designed to provide Rajiv Gandhi's faltering government with a more human face. However, no real defence review accompanied the cuts, nor was there much indication as to which service would take the brunt of the cuts.

In the 1988/89 budget, defence expenditure was increased by only Rs.1000 crores to Rs.13 000 crores, despite continuing clashes on the Siachin Glacier and the commitment in Sri Lanka. The Sri Lankan exercise was estimated to cost Rs.3 billion.[10] Of particular interest, capital outlay for all three services was reduced, raising interesting questions about ongoing and future procurement commitments.[11] In 1989/90, defence expenditure was cut by Rs.200 crores, ostensibly as a sign of good faith towards Pakistan.[12] More likely, however, the signal was a statement of intent to the IMF. Nevertheless, the revised estimate reflected a sharp increase, from Rs.13 000 crores to Rs.14 500 crores, a rise of 10 per cent over the previous year's revised estimate.[13]

Defence allocations appeared to be stagnating, but the situation was somewhat blurred. The revised estimates were consistently higher than the budget estimate, to take account of inflation and exchange rate fluctuations, and, according to some, the real defence outlay was up to 20 per cent more than the budget estimate for several reasons: (*a*) the defence budget has apparently started to exclude the cost of running the MoD and service pensions, which have always been a high and inelastic element (every year 60–70 000 servicemen between the ages of 35 and 40 retire);[14] (*b*) no provision was made for the Border Security Force, Assam Rifles and the Indo-Tibet Border Police; (*c*) other cosmetic savings were gained by deferring the payment of bills,

[10] Chandra, P., 'India plans super military machine', *The Sentinel (Guwahati)*, 26 Aug. 1989.
[11] 'Marked slow-down in Indian defense spending', *International Defense Review*, vol. 21, no. 5 (May 1988), p. 478.
[12] Joshi, M. K., 'Directions in India's defence and security policies', ed. R. Babbage and S. Gordon, *India's Strategic Future: Regional State or Global Power?* (Macmillan: Basingstoke, 1992), p. 79.
[13] Joshi (note 12), table 4.1, p. 78.
[14] Zutshi, A., 'Rising demands of defence system', *Hindustan Times,* 14 June 1989.

moving fuel costs to public sector oil companies and freight charges to public sector airlines and deferring modernization decisions which had already been taken in principle;[15] and (d) it is commonly accepted that expenditure on missile technology and whatever nuclear programme exists will be charged to the departments of space and atomic energy respectively.

The first signs of trouble became evident in 1988. In July Defence Minister K. C. Pant admitted that the Seventh Defence Five Year Plan (1985–90) had not been given approval. Newspaper pundits in particular began to question the policies adopted in previous years. Having seen Pakistan suffer under the weight of debt repayments, the Union Government appeared to be experiencing similar problems:

Pakistan has unwittingly walked into a military debt trap, and its servicing of old military debts now exceeds the fresh inflow.

One reason why our foreign exchange reserves are looking so unhealthy this year is the growing problem of defence repayments. The details are secret and no official figures are available, but military debt servicing certainly runs to over Rs 1,000 crore per year.[16]

Another (ex-military) pundit was more blunt: 'Better house keeping and . . . elimination of corruption would save a lot of money'.[17]

By 1989 the overall scale of the problems facing the defence sector was becoming clear. Although the Five-Year Defence Plan was approved—four years after it began—the artificially low figure presented in the 1988/89 budget was beginning to take effect on the day-to-day running of the defence forces. The declining value of the rupee inflated scheduled payments for imports in 1988 by a massive Rs.1400 crores and the armed forces had to lodge several requests for deferment, even down to the rupees needed to pay the USSR.[18] In December 1988 the services had difficulty in paying salaries, the rental for communications systems went unpaid and new contracts for ration supply had not been granted.[19]

Moreover, serious problems with the modernization programme were also coming to the fore. In sum, it seemed that much of the weaponry which the Indian armed forces had received during the 1980s was offering less defence than imagined. The programme to make the Army 'leaner and meaner' through mechanization (RAPIDS—Reorganized Plains Infantry Divisions and RAMIDS—Reorganized Mountain Infantry Divisions) had ground to a halt. Many of the new weapon platforms inducted into the IAF and the Navy during the 1980s were practically unarmed, as the available finances did not stretch to ammunition and missiles. In May 1990 the Comptroller and Auditor-General revealed that the Mirage 2000 had been inducted into squadron service without

[15] Rikhye, R., 'Sleight of hand', *Illustrated Weekly of India,* 4 Dec.1988.

[16] Anklsaria Aiyar, S. S., 'The military road to debt', *Indian Express,* 9 Nov. 1988).

[17] Cariappa, Brig. A. C. (Ret'd), 'Wastage on an inevitable activity', *The Hindu,* 13 Oct. 1988.

[18] Gupta, S. and Thakurta, P. G., 'Defence forces: heading for a crisis', *India Today,* vol. 14, no. 4 (28 Feb. 1989), p. 43.

[19] 'Resource crunch stalls defence plan', *The Hindu,* 2 Jan.1989.

its principal weapons, long-range missiles and runway penetration bombs. Conceivably, when the Mirage escorted the air-drop over Jaffna in 1987 it was armed with little more than its integral cannon.[20] Despite the growing list of accidents among IAF pilots, which was in part blamed upon the absence of an appropriate third-stage jet trainer, procurement was shelved. Spare parts and ammunition shortages for the T-72 tanks had reduced significantly the numbers available for each regiment.[21]

The election of 1989 saw the Congress(I) Government unseated by a tenuous coalition organized around the Janata Dal party. After a classic power struggle, V. P. Singh, Rajiv Gandhi's former Finance and Defence Minister who resigned in 1987 in the wake of the Bofors scandal, became Prime Minister. V. P. Singh inherited a defence sector in crisis and, moreover, in deficit as well. On the one hand, Singh had a distaste for the profligacy of the years under the Gandhis; he accused Rajiv Gandhi of adventurism in foreign policy and committed himself to the pursuit of better and more equal relations with India's neighbours. On the other, he was significantly influenced by Gandhian intellectuals drafted on to the Planning Commission who argued forcefully for conscious links to be made between the country's poverty and underdevelopment and high defence expenditure.

Unfortunately, progress was minimal. A flare-up of violence in Kashmir and a marked deterioration in Indo-Pakistan relations forced V. P. Singh to reconsider the parlous state of the defence sector, or at least provided an opportunity to bring the sector back from the point of bankruptcy. Despite running the risk of seriously disappointing the World Bank and the IMF, the Government might also have feared a run on the substantial foreign exchange deposits of non-resident Indians if Indo-Pakistan relations were to lead to war. In advance of the 1990 budget, therefore, it became widely known that the Government intended to raise defence expenditure, which was duly increased by Rs.2575 crores, an increase of 8.6 per cent. Of this, nearly one-third was given over to the creaking capital outlay.[22] However, few within the defence community acknowledged that the increase was adequate, which set the tone for the public debate which followed: 'In sum, what the proposed defence budget may manage to do is arrest the ill-effects of neglect suffered by the Services since 1987, while trying to avoid the debt-trap.'[23]

After the budget, V. P. Singh adopted an unapologetic line, arguing that Rajiv Gandhi had pursued a harmful and 'woolly-headed approach to security'.[24] Certainly, the Government would have found the problems in Kashmir a useful justification for raising defence expenditure. However, the increase was in part to do with V. P. Singh's political fortunes, the need for leadership credibility and the growing spectre of a non-viable defence sector.

---

[20] 'Mirages came without missile system: CAG', *The Hindu,* 11 May 1990.
[21] Gupta and Thakurta (note 18), p. 43.
[22] 'Sharp increase in defence outlay', *The Telegraph*, 20 Mar. 1990.
[23] Pendse, Maj-Gen. K. S., (Ret'd), 'In defence of higher defence outlay', *Indian Express,* 6 Apr. 1990.
[24] 'V. P.: Rajiv harmed defence', *Hindustan Times*, 1 May 1990.

Where the Government did take positive action was in the appointment of General Rodriguez as Chief of Army Staff and in drafting Arjun Singh to chair a committee for the review of defence expenditure. Rodriguez was expected to further the mechanization of the Army, to take up where General K. Sundarji had left off. The Singh Committee was entrusted with the task of efficient deployment, manpower planning and reducing inertia within the armed forces.[25] More significantly, Singh's covert remit was probably to erode the vested interests of the three services. Meanwhile, defence expenditure was raised again in 1991 by Rs.1100 crores in the interim budget, primarily to cover commitments and obligatory payments, but reduced by Rs.500 crores in the July budget, due entirely to the influence of Manmohan Singh, the new Finance Minister. Normally, a 15 per cent increase would have been almost mandatory, to do no more than mark time, especially with a 20 per cent inflation rate.[26]

Discussions on the shape of the Eighth Defence Plan are already well advanced. Without much in the way of political or intellectual leadership from the Singh Committee, the policies are likely to stay much the same although economic pressures are likely to remain or increase. Expectations over funding promise a major bureaucratic battle in the future—the Defence Research and Development Organization (DRDO) requires Rs.168 000 crores, Rs.68 000 crores more than the Government is prepared to discuss.[27] This debate began in the shadow of a $4 billion loan agreement with the IMF and the need to pledge 46.8 tonnes of gold with the Bank of England as collateral.[28]

Somewhat predictably, the shortage of funds has continued to create difficulties for the armed forces. The squadron strength of the IAF dropped from 40 to 35. Foreign exchange shortages stopped the production of Jaguars in March 1991. HAL has been particularly hard hit and faces becoming little more than a service unit into the future. The 1991/92 defence budget gave too little for the repayment of loans for Army equipment: some 400 of the Bofors 155-mm guns may not materialize. Exercises and training have been cut to the minimum. Long-term modernization—command, control, communications and intelligence (C^3I), electronic warfare and force multipliers—so important as the justification for the induction of advanced and expensive front-line equipment, is now almost certain not to proceed. The naval modernization programme has been all but shelved. A third-stage jet trainer now seems extremely unlikely.[29] The nuclear submarine leased from the USSR has been returned, probably to save the annual cost of the lease, which amounts to Rs.120 crores.

[25] Gupta, S., 'Armed forces: change of the guard', India Today, 31 July 1990).
[26] Sidhu, W. P. S., 'Chinks in the armour', India Today, vol. 16, no. 21 (15 Nov. 1991), p. 129.
[27] Kothari, M. K., 'Pruning defence expenditure', Economic Times, 23 Aug. 1991.
[28] Bedi, R., 'Indian cash crisis brings more cuts', Jane's Defence Weekly, vol. 16, no. 6 (10 Aug. 1991).
[29] Sidhu (note 26), pp. 129–31.

IV. The end of the rupee–rouble trade

During periods of economic constraint India has traditionally relied upon the USSR for an enlarged proportion of defence imports. In general, the armed forces are less enamoured with Soviet equipment and prefer instead state-of-the-art *matériel* from the West. Politically, this is also a preferred solution because India has always been at pains to emphasize its independence *vis-à-vis* the USSR.

The two definitive hallmarks of Soviet–Indian relations have been soft loans on the one hand and military sales on the other. During the early 1980s, the USSR supplied both in abundance. For their part, Indian negotiators managed to strike the optimum balance between concern over the threat of diversification on arms imports and camaraderie for a beleaguered superpower, which resulted in the granting of a military wish-list beyond what most would have predicted.

During the mid-1980s, the relationship began to change. Soviet General Secretary Mikhail Gorbachev visited Delhi in December 1986, and underneath the blaze of publicity and popularity there were warnings to New Delhi on the sensitive subjects of nuclear proliferation, the economic effects of high defence expenditure and relations with China.[30] India, however, had not kept up with the times and had some difficulty in adjusting to the new regime, having for so many years taken for granted its ability to manipulate Soviet dogma almost at will.

Conceivably, the long-term future of Indo-Soviet relations dominated by Gorbachev could well have provided New Delhi with a much tougher diplomatic relationship than it had come to expect. Even before the collapse of the USSR, problems were apparent. Traditionally, the defence trade between India and the USSR has been considered a loss-leader for the USSR, given that soft loans were extended to India which gave 20 years to pay at a mere 2 per cent interest.[31] In the early 1990s, the popular myth that India had a distinct advantage in this quarter was under revision. It became increasingly clear that the USSR would eventually require India to trade in hard currency once the rouble became convertible. It was also becoming clear how much, contrary to all expectations, India was disadvantaged by the trading arrangements between the two countries.

India needed Soviet trade for defence equipment, petroleum, non-ferrous metals and fertilizers. In return, the USSR imported Indian tea, technology, clothing, consumer electronics and spices. The whole exchange was conducted in rupees and Indian exports to the USSR habitually outpaced Soviet exports to India—by Rs.2600 crores in 1990/91—partly because the rupee was massively undervalued against the rouble. In effect this has put up the nominal value of India's exports to the USSR and forced the Indian Government to grant loans to Moscow in the form of 'technical credit'. At the same time, India had separate

---

[30] Austin, G., 'Soviet perspectives on India's developing security posture', in Babbage and Gordon (note 12), p. 144.

[31] 'India: old friends out of kilter', *The Economist,* vol. 320, no. 7724 (14 Sep. 1991), p. 72.

loans with the USSR to pay for defence equipment (in rupees). India also faced the disadvantages that several of the items it traded, consumer electronics for example, contained imported components which were purchased on the open market with hard currency—as much as 80 per cent on some items. The USSR also sold on Indian goods into hard currency areas.[32]

Quite what direction this will take depends upon an array of complex issues. The potential for discord over the rupee–rouble trade is considerable in itself. In addition, both sides have seen considerable political change since 1990, which will introduce new actors and new priorities. Certainly, India did not get off to a good start with Boris Yeltsin after Narasimha Rao's clumsy endorsement of the Soviet coup in August 1991. Nevertheless, because both sides produce manufactured goods which invariably fail to reach world standards, a mutually supportive relationship will probably continue, with Russia at least. However, much will also depend upon how the states in the southern part of the Commonwealth of Independent States (CIS) progress in the future. India's fear of isolation amidst unstable Muslim states must be considerable.

Future relations will also turn on how the complex defence issues can be resolved. Clearly, India would like to produce Soviet/Russian equipment under licence for export. Russia may agree in some instances, such as the MiG-21 series, and willingness to allow India access to the most sophisticated technology will increase as Russia's own problems mount. Recently, there has been speculation that Russia has offered $850 million credit for India to purchase redundant Soviet equipment, together with a parallel offer to buy the Yak-141 jump-jet and the Su-27. Other CIS states are themselves extremely short of foreign exchange and arms exports are certain to be seen as an economic solution which India can exploit—the AN-32, for example, was produced in Ukraine and India is keen to acquire spare parts for its squadrons. The East European states might also enter the market. Nevertheless, the ties that once bound India and the USSR no longer exist, and India is still coming to terms with the implications of a unipolar world. If any CIS state seeks to sell arms to Pakistan or Sri Lanka, for example, New Delhi will be powerless to intervene, witness Pakistan's trawl among the states of Eastern Europe for T-72 tanks.[33]

V. India enters the arms bazaar

The majority of major arms producers are also active in the international arms market. Even for the superpowers, the motivation is primarily economic and industrial. In general, the cost of military technology limits domestic demand. The benefits of exports, particularly when sales are made to countries with no export policy of their own, are economies of scale, foreign exchange earnings, longer production runs and the phased introduction of new weapon systems.

---

[32] Kaushal, N., 'For a few dollars more: India and the USSR question the basis of their trade relationship', *India Today,* vol. 16, no. 14 (31 July 1991), p. 78.

[33] 'T-72 tanks for Pakistan: how it affects India', *Amrita Bazar Patrika* (Calcutta), 11 July 1990.

Despite possessing a considerable defence production base, India has not so far been involved in defence exports, for three reasons: (*a*) India has experienced too many problems with the production of indigenous equipment to consider defence exports. If a system is not totally indigenous, as is often the case in India, exports can only proceed with the permission of the licenser; (*b*) domestic demand has been relatively high; and (*c*) as a leading member of the non-aligned community, India would be forced to conduct a considerable internal debate over the rights and wrongs of selling arms for commercial ends, if only for the sake of its credibility in the South.

The posture adopted by India in the late 1980s over the question whether or not the country should enter the arms market as an exporter belies the fact that it is no stranger to the export market. In April 1972 the Government announced that henceforth it would enter the arms export market with a view to becoming a major actor. Until then, exports had been negligible and mainly concerned with supplies, such as the $370 000 of boots, uniforms and helmets exported to Jordan, Lebanon, Nigeria and Saudi Arabia.[34] However, little or nothing emerged in the aftermath, although the Government was extremely embarrassed when it became clear that ex-Indian Army Centurion tanks had arrived in South Africa in 1978, via arms dealers in Jordan and Spain. Later, in 1980, Sanjay Gandhi was at the centre of a scheme to export Centurion spare parts to Israel, via Canada, and was also in discussion with the same arms dealer who sold on Centurions to South Africa over the sale of 200 of the same.[35] These incidents, as much as anything else, persuaded many in politics that India should not involve itself in the international arms bazaar. However, there were minor low-key sales of patrol boats to Bangladesh and Mauritius, Alouette helicopters to Bangladesh, Ethiopia, Liberia, Nepal and the Seychelles, second-hand AN-12, Otter and Caribou aircraft to Bangladesh, HJT-16 Kiran trainers to Liberia, HTT-34 trainers to Ghana, second-hand 105-mm guns to Bangladesh and ammunition, small arms and transport vehicles to Jordan, Lebanon, Malaysia, Nigeria and Oman.[36]

Through the early 1980s, reports on Indian defence sales were infrequent; a Defence Export Promotion Council was set up in 1984 but had little impact. The USSR was reported to be interested in the Chetak helicopter but there were no subsequent reports to indicate whether or not a sale had been made.[37] During the same year HAL stated its intention to commence exports, in the form of the Kiran jet trainer and the Marut, but omitted to mention any orders.[38] HAL's sanguine approach to the export potential for the Advanced Light Helicopter in

[34] Sarkar, J., 'India: arms for sale', *Far Eastern Economic Review,* 19 Aug. 1972.

[35] Niesewand, P., 'India in secret tank deals', *Guardian Weekly,* 31 Sep. 1980.

[36] Brzoska, M. and Ohlson, T. (eds), SIPRI, *Arms Transfers to the Third World 1971–85* (Oxford University Press: Oxford, 1987), appendix 3, p. 298.

[37] Ved, M., 'USSR likely to buy Chetak copters', *Hindustan Times,* 11 Jan. 1984.

[38] 'Indian firm to enter export market', *Aviation Week & Space Technology,* 24 Sep. 1984, p. 24.

1986 was also rather premature, although an HTT-34 turboprop trainer was demonstrated in Ghana and Nigeria.[39]

Towards the end of the decade, government policy changed dramatically, in direct response to the growing anticipation of a debilitating resource gap. In October 1988, Defence Minister K. C. Pant, the architect of the new policy, stated that the Government was receiving an increasing number of requests from foreign sources for spare parts and other types of equipment, such as clothing. In January 1989, Defence Secretary T. N. Seshan explained the policy:

we are reviewing how we can export Indian defence items, without compromising on certain basic principles . . . We don't want to add to local conflicts and so on. At the same time, industry, public and private sector, can benefit from exports . . . But I don't think we'll ever achieve the kind of aggressive marketing practices which some other countries have achieved.[40]

To add to this, K. C. Pant announced the creation of a task force to be headed by a senior officer and mooted several potential defence markets, such as Iran, Iraq, Libya, Malaysia and Viet Nam.[41]

Although it is probably correct to state that the breakthrough on arms exports never occurred and is unlikely to occur in the foreseeable future, the new policy did return some success. HAL came close to reaching an agreement over the sale of the Dornier 228 executive jet to Nepal, not a military system but useful for the balance of payments nevertheless.[42] In June 1989 a Saudi defence team visited India to discuss an officer training scheme.[43] In a similar vein, India was contracted to help Tanzania establish its first military college in Fort Ikoma.[44] It has also been rumoured that members of the military wing of the African National Congress received training in India. In late 1989 Zambia was poised to become the first serious customer. A military adviser's post had been set up in the Indian High Commission in Lusaka and on the agenda were transfers of armoured personnel carriers (APCs), artillery, rifles, semi-automatic weapons and MiG-21 aircraft. Because of Zambia's foreign exchange crisis, however, any deal would be unlikely to involve hard currency.[45]

There were similar export opportunities in 1990. Several public sector units participated in the Aerospace '90 Exhibition in Singapore.[46] Mauritius bought the Dornier 228.[47] Viet Nam investigated, but never followed through, the purchase of the production lines for the MiG-27 ground attack aircraft, the T-55

[39] Brown, D. A., 'India identifies large market for advanced light helicopter', *Aviation Week & Space Technology*, 19 May 1986, p. 69.

[40] Rao, N. V., 'Ambivalence on arms exports', *Indian Express,* 27 Jan. 1989.

[41] Ved, M., 'Task force for defence export', *Hindustan Times,* 2 Feb. 1989.

[42] 'HAL to sell aircraft to Napal', *Hindustan Times,* 10 Mar. 1989.

[43] Khergmvala, F. J., 'Saudi team visiting military facilities in India', *The Hindu,* 24 June 1989.

[44] 'Tanzanian war college established', *Jane's Defence Weekly,* vol. 12, no. 6 (12 Aug. 1989).

[45] Mukherjee, S., 'India set to sign Zambia in sales push', *Jane's Defence Weekly,* 16 Sep. 1989, p. 536.

[46] 'India to transfer technology with friendly countries', *Amrita Bazar Patrika* (Calcutta), 27 Feb. 1990.

[47] 'New feather in HAL's cap', *The Statesman,* 5 Mar. 1990.

and armoured personnel carriers.[48] In fiscal year 1990/91, defence exports totalled Rs.80 crores.[49]

In 1991 Bharat Electronics returned good results for the export of high-technology communications equipment, totalling about $14 million.[50] Bangladesh was offered Indian services to improve and modernize its defence forces, following a visit by the Chief of Army Staff.[51] India was invited to tender for a requirement from Mauritius for a single medium-size off-shore patrol vessel.[52] In 1992 the MoD announced that it was considering selling off 1500 pieces of artillery, worth about Rs.8 billion, together with scrap and ammunition worth another Rs.2 billion.[53]

Of somewhat greater concern since the change of policy have been the reports of sales of nuclear and chemical materials. In 1988 a (peaceful) nuclear accord was signed with Viet Nam.[54] In 1990 India made available a list of exportable items to the International Atomic Energy Agency (IAEA), which acts as a clearing-house for all nuclear transfers.[55] In 1989 the State Trading Corporation purchased 120 tonnes of thionyl chloride from Transpek, a chemicals company from Baroda, and attempted to ship it to Iran. Although the chemical is most widely employed in the production of pesticides, it is also used in the production of poison gas. Sources in Washington believe that India is becoming a major supplier of dual-use goods to countries such as Iran.[56] Similarly, the USA has recently accused the Indian Government of permitting the shipment of trimethyl phosphite to Syria.[57]

It seems unlikely that India will succeed in becoming a major exporter of defence equipment, for several reasons. First, the market is saturated. The international arms market is in a considerable slump, which ironically dates from around the time when the Indian Government decided upon the shift in policy. Particularly hard hit have been sales of major weapon systems, which is precisely what India wants and needs to sell to make the necessary gains in foreign exchange. Moreover, the market is now much more geared towards technology, which India would find difficult to supply. Second, India lacks the experience of its competitors and the necessary staying power. For example, attendance at the Asia Exhibition has been patchy, which amounts to poor marketing at the outset. By definition, both the sales pitch and the decision-making process are bureaucratized and might lack the flair and innovation of competitors from the private sector. Third, it is difficult to imagine a foreign country buying

---

[48] 'Retired Indian defense production units for Vietnam', *Strategic Digest (IDSA)*, vol. 20, no. 6 (June 1990), p. 2530.

[49] 'Bid to shore up defence exports', *Times of India*, 6 July 1991.

[50] 'Export successes for Bharat Electronics', *International Defense Review*, vol. 24, no. 1 (1991), p. 77.

[51] Habib, H., 'India to help modernise Bangladesh's defence forces', *The Hindu*, 23 July 1991.

[52] 'Mauritius seeks OPV supplier', *Jane's Defence Weekly*, vol. 16, no. 6 (10 Aug. 1991), p. 222.

[53] Nigudker, A., 'India puts surplus weapons up for sale', *Defence*, Mar. 1992, p. 7.

[54] 'N-accord signed with Vietnam', *Times of India*, 17 Aug. 1988.

[55] Balakrishna, K., 'India offers to export nuclear knowhow, products', *Economic Times*, 6 Aug. 1990.

[56] Hazarika, S., 'Lethal shipment', *Illustrated Weekly of India*, 23 Aug. 1989.

[57] Padmanabhan, 'Chemical Bogeys? US protest over an Indian export deal', *Frontline*, vol. 9, no. 21 (23 Oct. 1992), p. 128.

equipment which the Indian armed forces are so patently reluctant to absorb themselves. Fourth, the equipment—by global standards—is not of the highest quality and if a market niche does exist it is among the poor countries of, say, Africa and Central America where there is stiff competition from Brazil and China and counter-pressure from the World Bank and the IMF.

Finally, India does not really have a great deal to sell. Although there are many claims to indigenization, in reality foreign technology is present in many of the systems produced in India. Thus, although export prospects are often used as one justification for the the LCA, there will be several foreign governments to persuade before a sale can be approved, not least the USA if India fails to develop an indigenous engine. (Indians now joke that the only indigenous aspect of the LCA by the time it enters production will be the pilot.) The opposite is true in systems which India produces under licence but are no longer in production elsewhere. The MiG-21 and MiG-27 are examples from the USSR. The UK has recently stopped Jaguar production, which leaves HAL with the only production line in operation. However, HAL is currently holding back on the delivery of 15 Jaguar aircraft to the IAF because of the lack of foreign exchange which is needed to buy components. This makes the prospect for sales or supplies to other Jaguar operators—Ecuador, Nigeria and Oman— somewhat unlikely.[58]

Although talk of new procurement programmes continues, especially over the need for an advanced jet trainer, the reality of the situation is exceedingly stark. Having lost a valuable source of supply from the USSR, India must either produce the equipment itself or seek supplies from the West. Conceivably, in such a depressed market and given the need in many developed countries to keep production lines open, there may be some real bargains on offer. France has recently offered Pakistan generous credit terms to purchase the Mirage 2000, for example. Nevertheless, advanced military technology is rarely given away and it would be a surprise if India were allowed to proceed with the later stages of the defence modernization programme started in the early 1980s.

[58] 'Jaguar jumble', *Far Eastern Economic Review*, vol. 153, no. 28 (11 July 1991), p. 9.

7. Indigenous defence production: the failure of policy implementation

I. Indigenous defence production in the South

The process of absorbing and assimilating technology is considered fundamental to development. Through a range of complicated mechanisms involving bilateral arrangements and multilateral agencies and institutions, the technologically advanced countries either sell or transfer gratis under the right political conditions skills, production capability and capacity which in principle would permit developing countries to marry development needs to technology. Through these mechanisms developing countries are supposed to acquire the means of production on which to base agrarian and industrial development. In addition, the recipient countries may also enter into arrangements to import the managerial and administrative skills to organize and co-ordinate this process.

In the field of defence, the market is different in many ways, particularly with regard to restrictions on the nature and scale of the technology which is transferred, but the overall process is very much the same. If a country cannot produce for itself the systems and infrastructure considered essential for modern defence, it will be forced to look beyond its national industrial base for the relevant technology and expertise. Over the past 15 years, attempts to develop an indigenous defence capability have proceeded apace in several Third World countries. These efforts have led to a significant debate over whether or not this entails negative effects for the development process.

Developing countries become involved in defence production for different reasons.[1] Motivations tend to arise from a combination of political factors, existing and potential technological capability in both civilian and defence areas, and economic considerations. The configuration of indigenous defence industrial bases depends very much upon national strategies for industrialization, and this provides an initial explanation for the marked differences between, for example, the Brazilian and Indian defence industries. The former has been geared to export promotion, the latter towards import substitution.

From the strategic perspective, however, developing countries fit into one of three broad groups. First, there are those countries which see a defence industrial base as an essential part of an overall expression of regional dominance—India in South Asia, Brazil in Latin America, Indonesia in South-East Asia and,

---

[1] See Kwang-Il Baek, B. *et al.* (eds), *The Dilemma of Third World Defense Industries: Supplier Control or Recipient Autonomy?* Pacific and World Studies no. 3 (CIS-Inha University/Westview Press: Boulder, Colo., 1989); Brzoska, M. and Ohlson, T. (eds), SIPRI, *Arms Production in the Third World* (Taylor & Francis: London, 1986); Katz, J. E. (ed.), *Arms Production in Developing Countries: An Analysis of Decision Making* (Lexington Books: Lexington, Mass., 1984).

to a lesser extent, Egypt in the Middle East. Here, it is the threat of restrictions on the country's liberty of action and in the extreme case embargo which provides the primary political motivation for defence production. Prestige and status are also important. Just as it is difficult for a country to be considered a great power or superpower without nuclear weapons, so countries which aspire to regional hegemony and middle power status cannot convincingly do so without reducing their dependence upon external suppliers. The disparity between Japan's economic and political/military power is an instructive example.

Second, there are certain countries which are frequently or permanently ostracized by the international community, or parts of it, and as a consequence domestic production is often the only means of assuring a defence capability—there are limits to what can be bought with certainty on the black market. Countries such as Israel and South Africa fit into this category, the latter in particular. Iran and Iraq are current candidates. In difficult political or strategic circumstances, arms suppliers will operate a 'short-leash' policy which restricts the supply of spare parts and offers a degree of control over whether or not a conflict will continue. The USA has traditionally provided a 'leash' of about two weeks.

Third, some countries see economic advantages to be gained from encouraging local defence production, which may interface with the previous two motivations or, as in the case of Singapore, may simply be a means of generating export revenue.[2] The fact that many of the countries which have opted for defence production have ended up indebted, or with weakened economies, has contributed to linking this and other motivations—countries such as India and Brazil may have established an indigenous defence base for strategic reasons but have found themselves utilizing capacity for exports and foreign exchange reserves. Indeed, with limited domestic demand, exploiting the export market was virtually inevitable over the long term. Given the strength of evidence which shows a link between defence activity on the one hand and underdevelopment on the other, it could also be argued that a relationship between defence production, a weakening economy and defence exports is somewhat inevitable.

II. Making the commitment

In the case of India there are strong economic and political reasons for the considerable all-round investment in defence production. Economically, India is weak in many ways. The rupee is a 'soft' currency—although partial convertibility was attained in 1992 and full convertibility is expected as a part of the structural adjustment programme—and limitations on foreign exchange reserves have always been a constraint upon choice and source of technology. This was particularly the case in the 1970s. There is in this sense a high oppor-

---

[2] These arguments are more fully developed in Deger, S., *Military Expenditure in Third World Countries: The Economic Effects* (Routledge & Kegan Paul: London, 1986), pp. 152–55.

tunity cost to be considered. (It has often been argued that that there is little or no inherent opportunity cost as usually understood in defence production, since India's resource base is traditionally underutilized.[3]) In the late 1980s and 1990s the Indian economy was weak and the rupee fell against other 'hard' currencies.[4] Inflation (both within the defence industries and throughout the international economy) and the rate of technological change in the West forced up the price of defence systems, making continued reliance upon imports a costly and undesirable condition.

Politically, the arguments in favour of India developing an indigenous defence base are as persuasive as the economic ones. The need to become self-sufficient in defence production was first stated in 1926, well before independence, and was highlighted in the INC's Karachi Resolution, a political manifesto outlining the future shape of the Indian economy. Thereafter, the Bombay Plan of 1944 and the Industrial Policy Resolutions of 1948 and 1956 laid the basis for the creation of heavy industries and high technology skills based upon a system of state capitalism, the creation of 'mother industries' being a necessary prerequisite for an indigenous defence base.

From 1947 on there were few dissenting voices over the need for the country to develop an indigenous defence industry. Because indigenous production could save the country foreign exchange it was supported by those in favour of keeping defence expenditures low. It was also supported by those who favoured an industrial policy based upon import substitution, by those who did not want India to be bound by the ties of alignment and by those who saw India as an important regional power. The commitment to defence production increased significantly when the Indian Government responded to the US–Pakistani strategic relationship which started in 1954 and to defeat by the Chinese in the 1962 war.

Defence production was first started in 1801 when the East India Company established the Gun Carriage Agency outside Calcutta.[5] By chance but fortunately for India, partition left 16 of the ordnance factories established by the British inside India which gave a useful base upon which to build. Pakistan received none. Until the mid-1950s, during a period when defence policy was evolving slowly, defence production was limited to small arms and ordnance. In 1952 the Institute for Armament Studies was established at Kirki with the intention of familiarizing officers with military science and technology. In 1954 a new ordnance factory was set up at Ambarnath and Bharat Electronics was established in the same year as a limited company in the public sector under the control of the Ministry of Defence. Between 1955 and 1961 the ordnance factories were completely reorganized, which later permitted the absorption of

---

[3] Benoit, E., 'Growth and defence in developing countries', *Economic Development and Cultural Change,* vol. 26, no. 2 (1978).

[4] The actual cost of local defence production may greatly exceed the cost of 'off-the-shelf' import but this may be more than offset by foreign exchange savings, particularly during a period of declining terms of trade.

[5] Smith, C. and George, B., 'The defence of India', *Jane's Defence Weekly,* vol. 3, no. 2 (2 Mar. 1985), p. 366.

foreign technology in the form of licensed production agreements.[6] The agreement to produce Shaktiman trucks under licence from the German company MAN (Maschinenfabrik Augsburg-Nürnberg AG) in late 1958 is a case in point.

Also during the mid-1950s, soon after Pakistan had joined CENTO and SEATO, India entered into a licenced production deal with the UK to produce the Gnat and embarked upon a programme to build its first indigenous jet fighter, the HF-24 Marut. However, Krishna Menon's attempts to expand the potential for indigenous defence production during the late 1950s actually amounted to very little. Apart from the animosity which Menon created for other reasons within the defence community, India's small industrial base and the scarcity of resources, including foreign exchange, limited actual production and subsequent progress.[7]

The 1964 Defence Plan which was drawn up after the defeat by China called for an increased emphasis upon indigenous production. After the 1965 war with Pakistan and the experience of embargo by both the UK and the USA, the Defence Plan was realigned to run concurrently with the Five-Year Development Plan which required revision to cover the period 1966–71. A major objective was that by 1973–74 the country would be significantly less dependent upon arms imports. The ordnance factories performed reasonably well during the late 1960s, especially in the production of arms, ammunition and vehicles, but surprisingly much less well in the clothing and general stores sections. In addition, the public sector undertakings began to grow in size and output, HAL in particular.[8]

Successive Indian governments and the defence bureaucracy have fostered the idea, usually through the annual reports of the MoD, that defence production has been reasonably successful over the years and that slow but steady progress is being made towards self-sufficiency. In fact this is not the case. In many instances the public sector undertakings have either not performed well or been frustrated in their attempts to do so. Many of the claims that systems are 'indigenous' are in fact misrepresentations, as increasingly the term is being used to cover production which involves little more than assembly, where the local content is minimal. Although there have been some success stories the quest for self-sufficiency is far from fulfilled. The reasons for this are several.

III. Indigenous production for the Army

A major area of emphasis for the domestic defence industry has been the production of tanks. In 1961, against strong competition from the FRG, the British firm Vickers-Armstrong agreed to supply India with the manufacturing capabil-

[6] Kavic, L., *India's Quest for Security: Defence Policies 1947–1965* (University of California Press: Berkeley, Calif., 1967), pp. 128–29.

[7] Wulf, H., 'India: the unfulfilled quest for self-sufficiency', eds M. Brzoska and T. Ohlson, SIPRI, *Arms Production in the Third World* (Taylor & Francis: London, 1986), p. 127.

[8] SIPRI, *The Arms Trade with the Third World* (Almqvist & Wiksell: Stockholm, 1971), p. 742.

ity to produce a modified Chieftain tank at the Avadi heavy vehicle factory in Madras. The first tank, known as the Vijayanta, came off the production line in January 1965 and some three and a half years later 65 tanks had been received by the Army. However, although the indigenous content of the tank increased, reliance upon British design and know-how remained total. Production delays during the late 1960s led to the order of 75 T-55 tanks from the USSR.[9] Although the Vijayanta has experienced performance problems, particularly with the Leyland L-60 engine, the Avadi factory has successfully produced over 1000 units.[10] In the mid-1980s the decision was taken to equip the Vijayanta with a new engine. At the time it was alleged that the Army Base Workshop in the Delhi Cantonment was capable of uprating the engine for the period until a new indigenous MBT was ready. However, under pressure from a consultancy firm, Usha Services and Consultants, which employs several ex-service officers, the Government considered instead tenders from foreign defence contractors, including one from Rolls-Royce for the engine designed for the abandoned Shir II project.[11]

In the early 1970s the Indian Government decided that India's next MBT would be designed and produced indigenously. Both inside and outside India, the nation's progress in the field of tank production has been applauded. It is widely held that Avadi is a capable company and that the DRDO is equally capable of effecting innovations, witness the development of a mine-clearing device which is fitted to the front of some of the Vijayantas. On this basis, the R&D currently under way on the production of an indigenous MBT for deployment in the 1990s has been regarded with optimism. However, on closer inspection, there appears to be a host of managerial and technological problems associated with this project.

Plans to develop the Arjun, the MBT for the 1990s, first began in 1970 and the programme was approved in 1972 following the issue of the General Staff Qualitative Requirements. In May 1974 the Government sanctioned Rs.15.5 crores for the initial phase of the programme. Originally the programme envisaged that the engine, transmission and drive would be imported, understandably since the country has little indigenous capability in the motor industry. The DRDO was charged with the task of developing the hull, turret, running gear and gun. In 1976, when it became clear that attempts to acquire a powerpack from abroad were unlikely to succeed, the Combat Vehicle Research and Development Establishment was entrusted with the task of indigenous production. By 1982, it was apparent that little or no success had been achieved:

sources hasten to point out that a specialised process called Alphinbonding technique, in which the cylinder should have been cast, has not been used. Because of this, the present aluminium bonding used in the cylinder often gives way resulting in the establishment of communication between the inlet and exhaust ports which should never

[9] SIPRI (note 8), p. 743–44.

[10] 'India: indigenous programs flourish amid defense modernisation', *International Defense Review*, vol. 19, no. 4 (Apr. 1986), p. 437.

[11] Nayar, K., 'How armymen work against us', *Suyra,* vol. 11, no. 23 (8–11 Jan. 1984), p. 7.

occur . . . The poor casting, it is said, has resulted in a wastage of about Rs.5 lakh, as 50 cylinders had to be rejected. (Each cylinder costs nearly Rs.10 000) . . . Certain uncalled for modifications attempted on the tank have also put the clock back on its development. Masking the valves, using compressors to pressurise single cylinders, and ignoring the equilibrium condition have resulted in a wastage of time and money. It is now reported that top officials are toying with the idea of going in for the next advanced gas-turbine engine for the Chetak. . . . The wrongly-designed camshaft in the transmission group of the engine was also a contributory factor to the engine's low efficiency. The hydro-pneumatic suspension in the hull and turret were utter failures. Besides, the electrical system of the tank has not been fully implemented.[12]

In all other respects, the MBT was reasonably well on course during the early 1980s. A new form of armour, Kanchan, has been developed by the Defence Metallurgical Research Laboratory at Hyderabad (and is reputed to rate with the famous Chobham armour produced by the UK), the gun by the Armament Research and Development Establishment (ARDE) and the controls and instrumentation by the Instrument Research Development Establishment at Dehra Dun.

Even if the problems over a suitable powerpack for the MBT are resolved, there is no guarantee that the project will succeed thereafter within the given time projections. Thus, until the MBT enters both production and service, India will produce the Soviet T-72 or the T-80 under licence as a stop-gap measure, although for how long this will be necessary remains to be seen. When the MBT was due to go into production in the early 1990s the production plant in Madras should have been at the point of stabilizing production of the tanks produced under Soviet licence. The Avadi factory will not be capable of tooling up to produce both tanks without massive investment, the estimated cost being Rs.200 crores, with the bulk of the investment required by the end of the 1980s:

At present not much thought seems to have gone into the question of where the MBT will be produced, what sort of investment will be needed to manufacture it and other related questions. Unless these questions are examined in depth and the necessary decisions taken in time, we may find that although the MBT project achieves success as a design and development effort, other considerations may prevent it from getting off the drawing board.[13]

Recently, the programme has taken another step backwards. A new plan to spend $40 million upgrading the Vijayanta tanks could further delay the production of the Arjun. Effectively, a lack of funds has made an upgraded Vijayanta the cheapest option.[14] It may also be the case that spare parts supplies for the T-72 tanks are extremely unpredictable.

However, if the indigenous tank slips too far behind schedule, this may not be a serious problem. There are other questions to consider, in particular

[12] 'Insufficient progress on Main Battle Tank', *Indian Express* , 29 June 1982.

[13] Balachandran, G., 'MBT: attempting too much with too little', *The Hindu*, 6 Dec. 1983.

[14] Raghuvanshi, V., 'Upgrade may stall new Indian tank production: Army efforts to revamp aging Vijayanta fleet could postpone indigenous Arjun', *Defense News*, 30 Aug.–5 Sep. 1993.

whether or not the Arjun will be acceptable to the Army and whether or not the slow rate of progress will render the tank obsolete while it is still on the production line.

By the late 1980s, few of the production problems had been solved and more had emerged. Although a model prototype had been produced, the results of an examination by an expert committee was critical on eight specific points:

1. The turret and hull design are not suitable for smooth operation—the turret hits the driver when in an open-up position. The driver cannot enter or exit the tank when the turret is facing forwards.

2. The fire control system is neither integrated nor fitted.

3. The loading time of 15 seconds was unacceptably slow.

4. The air defence gun has to be operated by the loader, which means that when the tank is attacked from the air the main armament remains inoperative.

5. Only three ready rounds are in the turret area, as against the 12 rounds specified by the General Staff Qualitative Requirements.

6. The shape of the turret is a shell trap.

7. The width of the track has increased beyond the Army's specifications, further reducing the tank's mobility as it cannot now be transported on trains or indeed cross bridges in areas where it is likely to be deployed.

8. The seating positions are unsuitable.[15]

Furthermore, very little progress was reported on the continuing problems of finding a suitable engine. Of the six prototypes produced in 1987, all were fitted with MTU engines from the FRG. After agreement was reached on the importing of 42 engines costing Rs.220 million, it appeared that the order had failed to specify the requirements necessary for successful operations in Indian climatic conditions and that the overall cost of the tank has risen by a factor of 19.[16] By 1988, the Arjun had apparently fulfilled the Army's mobility requirements but problems with the 1500hp indigenous engine were persisting, to such an extent that a 1400hp MTU engine had been imported for use in the R&D process.[17]

By mid-1991 the situation had improved little, whether in relation to cost or to performance. On cost, it was admitted that 55 per cent of the budget was required in foreign exchange. Apart from belying all claims to indigenization— engine, transmission, primary sight and tracks amounting to 43 per cent of the tanks components are imported—this dependence would raise the overall cost of the project as the rupee falls in value. In fact, it is now known that only the

[15] Nigudker, A., 'The Arjuna MBT', *Defense and Armament Héraclès International*, no. 67 (Nov. 1987), p. 82. See also Bobb, D. *et al.*, 'Chinks in the armour', *India Today*, vol. 12, no. 13 (15 June 1987), pp. 52–53.

[16] Nigudker (note 15), p. 82.

[17] Mama, H. P., 'Indian tank developments', *International Defense Review,* vol. 21, no. 5 (May 1988), p. 578.

hull and the turret are indigenous.[18] A critical report on the project in 1990 listed the following areas which relied upon foreign technology:

(a) engine from MTU—from the FRG;
(b) transmission from RENK—also FRG;
(c) FWM fire control—FRG;
(d) primary sight OLDELFT—from the Netherlands;
(e) tracks from DIEHL—from the FRG;
(f) TCM hydronpneumatic system—from the USA; and
(g) communications equipment, yet to be decided.[19]

By the end of March 1991, the cost of the programme had risen dramatically but only 12 models had been produced. In 1989 the Comptroller and Auditor General estimated that over Rs.118 crores had been wasted on the project, the total cost of which had risen to Rs.280.8 crores.[20] Unit cost is estimated to be Rs.40 million.[21]

As in previous years, the Arjun has also been plagued by technical difficulties. Alhough it is expected that the MBT will be required primarily for use in the Rajasthan desert, the prototypes have performed badly in desert conditions. The engine is prone to ingest sand, which lowers an already sub-standard performance; optimum speed and load characteristics have not so far been attained. The cooling system is inadequate and the idler and bogey wheels, track links, hyperpneumatic suspension and rubber seals have failed quality control tests. The transmission cannot be married to the imported German engine. The equipment for maintenance and servicing is too bulky and the tank itself is overweight, which will inhibit mobility during an era when speed is of increasing importance.[22] It is also suspected that the Arjun fails to meet the required specifications on the engagement of moving targets and that the newly developed Fin Stabilized Armour Piercing Discarding Sabot is also a failure. User trials were once again put back, this time to 1993.[23] Nevertheless, by the turn of the century the Army hopes to have 1500 units in service.[24]

The shortfall engendered by the phasing out of the Vijayanta and the delay in producing the Arjun has forced India to rely upon licensed production of Soviet tanks. The T-72M (the most advanced version) is being produced at Avadi, costing $835 000 per unit, and with only 10 per cent local content, although it is understood that this figure will over time rise to 95 per cent. This programme is also under stress. While the modernization programmes for both the Vijayanta

---

[18] Popli, M. L., 'Project Arjun, a sitter for Pak's MBT Khalid', Link, 26 May 1991.

[19] 'India's main battle tank—Arjun', Indian Defence Review, Jan. 1990, p. 184. This article has two interesting features. First, it compares what the DRDO brochure has to say on the MBT with the available information on development and testing. Second, it is the most detailed critique yet available on the story of the MBT.

[20] 'Rs. 118 cr wasted on MBT: CAG', Times of India, 20 July 1989.

[21] 'Problems still plague MBT', Jane's Defence Weekly, vol. 16, no. 7 (17 Aug. 1991), p. 257.

[22] For a more detailed analysis see the report from the Indian Defence Review (note 19), pp. 184–87.

[23] 'Main battle tank reached nowhere after 17 years', The Statesman, 26 July 1991.

[24] 'Rs 300 cr sanctioned for battle tank project', Times of India, 4 Sep. 1988.

and the T-55 were due to be completed by 1990–91, completion is now set at 1996. Much of the trouble was alleged to stem from poor project management and development.[25]

In addition to experiencing problems with the MBT, the Combat Vehicle Research and Development Establishment (CVRDE) has also found it difficult to produce an infantry combat vehicle; this has led to the licensed production of the Soviet BMP–1. However, CVRDE has been able to develop ambulance and command post variants of the BMP–1. Finally, a licence to produce 200–300 amphibious tanks is being sought from Germany, Sweden or the USA.[26]

Although many of India's future artillery requirements will be met by the Bofors 155-mm field gun, even though production under licence is unlikely, other artillery projects are led by the 2300-kg 105-mm Indian Field Gun Mk II. This project, costing $1000 million, is also behind schedule: the Army had already formed several units to receive the guns by 1986. In 1989 Bharat Earth Movers were identified as the nodal agency for the gun's production, which is due to involve several public sector and ordnance factories and commence with the assembly of CKD kits.[27] The ARDE at Pune which is responsible for some aspects of the field gun is also producing new infantry weapons to replace the ageing Ishapore rifle. A variety of ammunition, propellants and explosives are being developed by the DRDO.[28] However, a much more innovative process is the development of a sophisticated C^3I system, the Army Radio Engineering Network (AREN). Development of this system has been under way for over 17 years and appeared to have been completed in 1988 at a cost of Rs.500 crores.[29] It is alleged that a follow-on system, the Integrated Services Digital Network, has already started.[30]

Although some of the projects earmarked for the Army have been badly delayed, indigenous defence production in this quarter appears to have run much more smoothly than in other areas, such as aerospace, albeit with traditional time and cost overruns. There are several possible reasons for this. First, the level of technology required by the Army may be easier for R&D establishments and the public sector enterprises to come to terms with and control than it is in the aeronautics sector, for example. Second, the degree of indigenous content may be relatively small, witness the mere 10 per cent involved in the production of the T-72M. Third, the Army could be a more compliant customer than the other two services and mind less accepting either Soviet-licensed or indigenous equipment.

Nevertheless, there are evident anomalies which suggest problems in the procurement process which militate against the further development of indigenous capability. Why have the ordnance factories failed to develop beyond the

[25] 'CAG flays army for inordinate delay', *Times of India,* 7 Aug. 1991.

[26] 'India: indigenous programs flourish amid defense modernisation' (note 10), p. 438.

[27] 'Plan to indigenise Bofors gun', *Times of India,* 14 Aug. 1989.

[28] *International Defense Review,* vol. 19, no. 4 (Apr. 1986), pp. 438–41.

[29] Mama, H. P., 'AREN network for Indian Army', *International Defense Review*, vol. 21, no. 3 (Mar. 1988), p. 259.

[30] Gupta, S., 'The new thrust', *India Today,* vol. 10, no. 21 (15 Nov. 1985), p. 58.

105-mm gun? Why when the 155-mm howitzers were deployed in Kashmir in mid-1990 were they so short of shells as to prevent normal shooting practice?[31] Why did India buy Rs.10 crores-worth of parachutes from France and South Korea when the same are manufactured in Kanpur? Why were 1.4 million blankets purchased from Australia in 1985 during a period when most Indian woollen mills had export capacity? Why were 1000 passive night goggles imported when the indigenous variety could have overcome the Army's objections by using a small imported component at a fraction the cost of the whole imported item? Similarly, why were 3000 pieces of illuminating ammunition for 81-mm mortars imported when the indigenous variety required only to have its fuse replaced by an imported one?[32] Why has the licensed production of Soviet equipment led to a cramping of indigenous capability, witness the 1984 agreement which allowed the USSR to take over many of India's Army base workshops to set up repair and manufacturing facilities for Soviet weaponry?[33] Could Indian technicians not have been trained for the task? Why has the decision been taken to procure a very large number of Soviet T-72 tanks if success with the indigenous MBT is on the horizon?

IV. Indigenous production for the Navy

Naval shipbuilding in India along with naval capacity in general was retarded during the early years of independence by financial stringency, although a design laboratory was set up in Bombay in 1949.[34] It was not until 1955 that the Government paid any real attention to naval construction, which came in the form of local orders for inshore minesweepers, seaward patrol craft and other minor vessels.[35] In 1960 the Government acquired a major shipyard, Mazagon Docks Ltd in Bombay, and the Garden Reach Workshop Ltd in Calcutta.[36] A more significant shipbuilding programme was eventually initiated in 1964 following an agreement with the UK which enabled India to construct the Leander Class frigate at facilities constructed at Mazagon Docks. The first vessel was laid down in 1966 and completed in 1976. The sixth and final vessel, INS *Vindhyagiri*, was completed in 1980. The experience gained on the Leander programme facilitated the development of the Godavari Class frigate which, at 3500 tons, is larger and better armed than its British counterpart. This

---

[31] 'Shell shock', *Far Eastern Economic Review,* vol. 148, no. 26 (28 June 1990), p. 8.

[32] All these examples from Gupta, S. and Chandran, R., 'The spending spree', *India Today,* vol. 11, no. 7 (15 Apr. 1986), p. 41.

[33] Bobb, D., 'Moscow's new offensive', *India Today,* vol. 9, no. 16 (31 Aug. 1984), p. 84.

[34] According to a Public Accounts Committee Report, this too was dogged by problems and delays: 'The Committee find that the major contract . . . for the expansion of Naval Dockyard at Bombay, conceived as far back as 1949, could be awarded only in September 1954 and even that was finally abandoned by the contractor in September 1956 after completing only 15 per cent of the work', India, Lok Sabha, *Naval Dockyard Expansion Scheme, 581st Report of the Public Accounts Committee (Ministry of Defence)* (Lok Sabha Secretariat: New Delhi, 20 Dec. 1977), pp. 3–4.

[35] Kavic (note 6), p. 135.

[36] Wulf (note 7), p. 139.

programme is for six frigates, all of which are heavily armed for their tonnage.[37] Although Mazagon dockyard built the hull and propulsion plant, the input from foreign designs is not clear. However, machinery, missiles and the fire control system have been imported. As a follow-on programme a new class of warship has been announced: 'Project 15' will design a 5000-ton frigate which will have an indigenous content of 85 per cent.[38] However, as with other areas of the Indian defence industry, it has never been made clear how the percentage of indigenous content is calculated.[39]

India is also anxious to acquire submarine technology and construction capability. To this end a deal was agreed with the FRG in December 1981 for two Type-209 submarines to be constructed at Kiel but with an option to build four additional vessels at Mazagon Docks. Construction of the required facilities began in January 1982 but was terminated by the Rajiv Gandhi Government because of West German dealings with South Africa. Of some interest was the rationale for the cancellation, which was based upon an Indian Ocean littoral state acquiring information about Indian naval capability:

The 60-page [West German] classified court document . . . states that all the documents of the Indian submarine are in possession of the South African Navy. Apart from the blueprints, the court notes that details about the vessel's viability and versatility, results from sea acceptance trials and details of the combat information centre will have been passed on to South Africa.[40]

In addition to Mazagon Docks, other public sector companies are the Garden Reach, Praga and Goa shipyards. The Indian Navy also has a significant shipbuilding capability. The 700-acre naval dockyard at Vishakhapatnam is the largest dry dock in south-west Asia with a workforce of over 7000 and the capacity to service 50 ships simultaneously. The USSR, which constructed the facility, was keen to keep it within its orbit but, in order to counter-balance Soviet investment, some Rs.300 crores is being invested by government into the dockyard to permit the repair of ships and, eventually, submarines which are not of Soviet or East European design.[41]

Also under construction near Karwar in Karnataka is a new naval base. Expected to cost around $2 billion and be operational by 1996, the base will cover 3650 km², have 4.5 km² of berthing space and involve the relocation of at least 30 000 local people. The base will be able to handle shipbuilding, maintenance and refitting facilities.[42] The bulk of the work would seem now to be in the hands of a Dutch–Australian conglomerate, Nedco-Redicon, which

[37] 'India selects turbine for new frigates', *International Defense Review*, vol. 19, no. 10 (Oct. 1986), p. 1563.

[38] 'New Indian warship class', *Jane's Defence Weekly*, vol. 8, no. 22 (5 Dec. 1987).

[39] For example, when the author visited a defence exhibition in Delhi he was informed that an anti-tank missile on display was 80 per cent indigenous. When the company representative was asked to point out the foreign components from the knocked-down version it appeared that at least half the components on display were imported.

[40] Subramaniam, C., 'Germans "forgot" to classify Indian list', *The Statesman,* 11 Oct. 1990.

[41] *Defence Market Report*, DMS Inc., Cheltenham, 1985, p. 9.

[42] 'New navy base for India', *Jane's Defence Weekly*, vol. 6, no. 19 (15 Nov. 1986), p. 1144.

has prevailed over 42 competitors.[43] However, it is possible that Karwar will not survive the latest budgetary crisis.

Since the acquisition of a second aircraft-carrier following the acceptance that a wider naval role is now called for, speculation is rising as to the future direction of procurement once the first aircraft-carrier, *Vikrant*, is retired before the end of the century. Providing the naval mission is maintained, and there seems no likelihood that India's naval presence in the Indian Ocean will be reduced, an additional one or possibly two aircraft-carriers will be required— the third to ensure continuity of presence given the amount of time these ships spend in dock. In 1987, Admiral Tahiliani, Chief of Naval Staff, stated that all future aircraft-carriers for the Indian Navy will be produced indigenously. Reports quoting former Defence Minister Arun Singh suggest that the Navy has already carried out preliminary design studies on a replacement for the *Vikrant,* but that the door has also been left ajar for a foreign design.[44] A likely place for construction is the shipyard at Cochin, and France appears to be the main contender for the role of prime foreign collaborator.[45] Under an MoU signed in 1989 help will be provided in the production of a 30 000–35 000-tonne carrier which would take four to five years in the design stage and, thereafter, six to seven years in production.[46] Much depends upon whether or not the Government presses ahead with its ambitious defence agenda and pursues a policy based on the control of the Indian Ocean as opposed to one based on sea denial.

The performance of the Mazagon Docks has not been spectacular. Part of this can be explained by the global recession in, and the traditional low profitability of, shipbuilding. However, it has also been the case that the inherent problems have been compounded by poor management, particularly during the period when N. K. Sawhney was the chairman and managing director, when productivity, efficiency and orders plummeted. In the space of two to three years the number of ships brought in for repair dropped from 3000 to 600.[47] In contracts with the Indian Navy, these problems have been particularly damaging. In the case of ship construction for the Navy, prices are fixed on a cost-plus basis giving 5 per cent profit on the original estimates. Any escalation of cost has the effect of reducing an already low percentage of profit, but, in the absence of any suitable system for supervision production planning, quality control and monitoring of costs, slippage is almost certain to occur. On the non-military working of the dock the Estimates Committee found that:

A detailed examination of an export order for six cargo vessels to a U.K. based shipping company during 1977 to 1979 revealed several deficiencies affecting cost efficiency and profitability. There was delay ranging from 12-15 months from the due dates in the delivery of these vessels and the company suffered a heavy loss of Rs.554.26 lakhs as against the anticipated profit of Rs.84.72 lakhs. The main factors

[43] 'Australian, Dutch cos to build Indian naval base', *The Telegraph* (India), 13 Mar. 1989.

[44] 'Indian Navy aircraft carrier plans', *International Defense Review*, vol. 20, no. 3 (Mar. 1987), p. 359.

[45] 'Pact with France on third aircraft carrier', *The Statesman*, 24 Feb. 1989.

[46] 'French help for third aircraft carrier', *The Hindu*, 31 Jan. 1989.

[47] 'Mazagon Docks: Red Sea', *India Today*, 31 Dec. 1986, p. 68.

responsible for this state of affairs were defective estimates, inadequacy of design capability, lack of proper production planning and control, inadequate supervision and deficiencies in quality control. Under-estimation of labour and materials resulted in a loss of about Rs.19 lakhs in one vessel alone. Further, lack of data bank for designing of various types and sizes of cargo vessels resulted in errors in working drawings which caused rework resulting in delay in execution as well as excess consumption of labour and materials.[48]

In 1985/86, the situation was little better. Mazagon Docks accrued a loss of Rs.389.7 million and Garden Reach and Mishra Dhatu Nigam[49] also returned losses of Rs.78.9 million and Rs.49.9 million respectively.[50]

There are four main reasons for the apparent lacklustre performance of the Indian naval construction programme. First, the Navy is a junior, not a senior service. Even though naval commitments have risen significantly, the emphasis upon indigenous production is of barely more than two decades' duration. While naval policy continues to be geared to blue water strategy, there are limitations upon how much the Government can commit to the naval programme given the competing claims of the more powerful Army programme and the more prestigious aeronautics programme. These issues are certain to become more acute given the dismal economic outlook for the 1990s and beyond. Inevitably, the naval construction yards will suffer from a lack of follow-on orders. Using the occasion of the launching of an inshore patrol vessel in 1985, the chairman of Garden Reach stated pointedly, 'Orders in the pipeline are poor . . . we keep reminding the government of this issue'.[51]

Second, the expense of setting up naval construction facilities should not be underestimated. The capital investments required for the basic infrastructure are very large, and combine with low profitability to reduce the appeal of an across-the-board commitment, witness the ongoing debates in the West regarding the viability of building and deploying large capital ships.

Third, advances in design and the attainment of technological change are not easy. Shipbuilding design is now more complex than ever and almost impossible to keep abreast of without, for example, computer-aided design facilities, and India does not possess the required sophistication in other sectors to provide such advanced capabilities.

Finally, the primary role in the past of the USSR as supplier of naval technology and weapon platforms has not provided the required impetus to the process of indigenization of defence production. As a rule, the USSR was reluctant to transfer technology and assistance to permit the full absorption of know-how, although this policy showed signs of change in recent years. This is cer-

---

[48] India, Lok Sabha, *Magazon Dock Ltd.—Shipbuilding. Seventy-Fourth Report of the Committee on Public Undertakings (Ministry of Defence–Department of Defence Production)* (Lok Sabha Secretariat: New Delhi, 1983), p. 18.

[49] This public sector enterprise is located in Hyderabad and major activities include gun barrel forgings, specialized metals and alloys for weapons systems and aerospace.

[50] Mukherjee, S. J., 'Further growth for Indian defence companies', *Jane's Defence Weekly*, vol. 7, no. 24 (20 June 1987)

[51] 'Indian IPV launch', *Jane's Defence Weekly*, vol. 4, no. 3 (20 July 1985).

tainly the case with the aeronautics industry—the Subramaniam Committee recommended that dependence upon the USSR for licensed production should end at the earliest possible time to facilitate a less pedestrian rate of indigenization. The committee also observed several deficiencies in the quality of the technical data and information offered by the USSR.[52]

In 1991 somewhat better news appeared from Mazagon Docks. In early 1991, INS *Delhi* was launched from Mazagon. This signified a quantum leap for the troubled naval production sector. *Delhi* is the lead ship of Project-15, the key to the Navy's blue water programme for the 1990s. *Delhi* will be commissioned in 1994/95, together with two other ships, each costing Rs.2 billion. However, as with other programmes, delays have been endemic, most recently because of resource shortages.[53]

V. Indigenous production for the Air Force

The majority of aeronautic defence production in India rests with HAL, the largest public sector enterprise which currently employs approximately one-third of the defence sector employees, about 42 000 people. The history of HAL dates back to the 1940s when Hindustan Aircraft was set up by Walchand Hirachand to repair and overhaul foreign aircraft. Soon after independence the company began building light trainers under licence before attempting the production of jet aircraft in the 1950s. In the early 1960s Hindustan Aircraft began the licensed production of the Folland Gnat and the Rolls-Royce Orpheus jet engine. Simultaneously, R&D on the Marut and Kiran began, these aircraft closely modelled on the Hawker Hunter and Hunting Jet Provost respectively.[54]

In 1964 Hindustan Aircraft merged with another Indian company, Aeronautics, to form HAL. Since that period there have been two major thrusts to the production work of the company with minimal linkage between the two. At the Nasik, Koraput and, to a lesser extent, Lucknow factories HAL produces what were Soviet aircraft under licence. At the other factories in Kanpur, Hyderabad and Bangalore the company produces the aircraft of several West European aerospace companies under licence and, in addition, undertakes R&D into aircraft and aeronautics design and development. The Bangalore complex is the main centre of R&D and the headquarters of the company.

One success story in HAL has been the production under licence of the MiG-21 series—the MiG-21FL interceptor, the MiG-21M ground attack aircraft and the MiG-21bis. By the time the production line was closed down in 1985 to make way for the production of the MiG-27M, over 500 units had been produced. In comparison with HAL's performance in other sectors, the progress on the MiG-21 has been relatively smooth. Production rates were consistently high and close to target and the IAF found the MiG-21 a dependable system. In

[52] Subramaniam Committee, 1968 (HAL archives, Bangalore).

[53] Wickramanayake, D., 'Biggest-ever Indian warship launched', *Defence,* vol. 22, no. 4 (Apr. 1991), p. 16.

[54] Velupellai, D., 'Hindustan aeronautics: India's aerospace giant', *Flight,* 8 Nov. 1980, p. 1179.

part the success can be explained by the fact that the MiG-21 is a relatively simple aircraft utilizing Soviet technology of the 1950s. In addition, the USSR agreed to a precise and even-handed process of technology transfer which took place in five stages. In the first stage all the aircraft were imported. In the second stage all the aircraft were tested in India. Third, all the equipment was assembled and tested in India and, fourth, sub-assembly was undertaken in India. Finally, attempts were made to reduce dependence upon raw materials. Eventually, only the designs, drawings and some of the more complicated materials were imported. This amounted to approximately 70 per cent indigenization in toolings and equipment with 20 per cent of that proportion supplied by ancillary industries under sub-contracting agreements. However, production of the MiG-21bis proved more difficult. It was selected in 1976 as a successor to the earlier MiGs, and tooling up for production started in 1977 with the objective of providing 150 units before the line was due to be closed in 1984.

It took until January 1983 for the first locally assembled aircraft to complete its flight tests.[55] Indigenous production of the MiG-21 series was an expensive venture for India. The cost of producing the MiG-21 in India was 193 per cent more than its imported cost, according to an estimate by SIPRI.[56]

A particular problem in the MiG agreement has been the supply of raw materials. In this area the USSR was frequently unwilling to supply raw materials in the relatively small quantities which are often required. Nor are there alternative suppliers of these materials in the West. The materials are also often extremely cheap, which acts as a disincentive to indigenization, the transfer to which is always expensive. HAL's attempts to nurture local industries have only been partially successful. Indian Aluminium Co. has been encouraged to take up the production of aluminium sheets which are required in large quantities; as yet there is no indigenous source for aluminium sheets of the required 2-metre width of sufficient quality. A factory has been set up in Hyderabad to produce approximately 30 types of material required by HAL, including stainless steel and nickel alloys; the USSR actively assisted in these developments. Another problem stemmed from those items which have a short life, such as adhesives and rubber items. It was difficult to persuade the USSR to export in the quantity and frequency required. The Indian MiGs are also used more frequently than their Soviet counterparts, and as a result the demand for brake pads, which require replacement after every 100 flights, is much higher. Therefore, whether too much or too little, materials and parts from the USSR have been extremely problematic and the future is even more uncertain.

These problems are relatively minor when compared with the overall success of the venture. Still more positive is the future of Indo-Soviet collaboration in the aeronautics field, providing it continues with Russia, the Ukraine and other CIS states. In July 1983 Defence Minister R. Venkataraman visited Moscow and returned with a commitment regarding licensed production of the MiG-27

[55] *MILAVNEWS,* Mar. 1983, p. 15.
[56] SIPRI (note 8), table 22.10, p. 739.

Flogger and the possibility of manufacturing rights for the MiG-29 Fulcrum. To the surprise of some, the offer was confirmed during the visit in March 1984 of a 70-strong, high-level Soviet defence team led by the former Defence Minister, Dmitri Ustinov. Some 300 units of both systems are expected to enter service with the IAF.

While the Soviet side of HAL appears to have met the expectations of all concerned, the same cannot be said of the other HAL complexes, for it is in these quarters that technological and managerial failures have been the most consistent and damaging. In the early period, between 1940 and 1956, India's aeronautic capability was understandably limited. The first licence agreement was for the production of the US Vultee Vengeance bomber. Between 1947 and 1950 about 50 UK Percival Prentice basic flight trainers were assembled at Bangalore. This was followed by the manufacture of Vampire jet aircraft and 150 DH-82 Tiger Moth primary trainers under an agreement with De Havilland of Canada.[57] Following agreements struck in 1956, India started to produce the Gnat lightweight fighter powered by the Orpheus-701 turbojet engine in 1959, and deliveries of the Gnat to the IAF commenced in 1963. The original idea came from Lord Mountbatten who suggested the possibility to Nehru after the Gnat had failed selection as a NATO fighter.[58]

Although the acquisition of the Gnat was widely held to be a good move for India, even though it had been rejected by NATO, negotiations with Folland were protracted. After a team of experts from the IAF and the MoD had inspected and approved of an initial procurement of 50–100 units, to be followed by licensed production, negotiations became increasingly slower and more complicated. At the same time a group of French intermediary negotiators had approached the managing director of Folland to offer their services for a payment of 2 per cent 'consideration money' of which 1 per cent would be given to the Indian negotiating team, in order to further the negotiations. Basically, the IAF had cooled towards the Gnat deal over the course of time, preferring instead the French Ouragan, perhaps because of the availability of 'consideration money' from another source. One year later the Gnat deal had still not been signed as officers in the MoD had held up the contract having been approached by a French firm which offered to sell India the Ouragan. Even after a strong intervention by Nehru the contact was still not signed for another six months. Nehru was disturbed by the suggestions of malpractice among senior IAF officers, and confused as well:

He [Nehru] said that it was surprising that whereas every country wanted to produce her own war material, in India even very senior officials and Ministers wanted to remain dependent on foreign countries and governments for military hardware and would not take any initiative for local production. These people did not understand that a country must not remain for ever dependent on another country for her military

[57] Thomas, R. G. C., *The Defence of India: A Budgetary Perspective of Strategy and Politics* (Macmillan: Delhi, 1978), p. 180.
[58] Mullik, B. N., *My Years With Nehru: 1948–1964* (Allied Publishers: Bombay, 1972), p. 125.

requirements as, in the event of a war breaking out, that country could stop supplies putting the receiving country in dire difficulties when her need was most acute.[59]

However, this was not a problem unique to the procurement of the Gnat; it has been a consistent factor in aircraft procurement.

The Gnat was a great success for both HAL and the IAF. During the 1965 war it performed extremely well, mainly because of its mobility, its small size and its utility at the forward edge of the battle area. A major advantage for India with the Gnat was that Folland went into liquidation in the late 1960s. The British RAF wanted the Gnat only for the Red Arrows, a non-combat display team, and so when Folland folded India was able to purchase most of the technology—the residual rights (80 per cent) went to the IAF. While the RAF kept the physical assets, India received the rest including the design jigs and the test facilities.[60] This success led to the production of over 200 units, allowing HAL to achieve economies of scale. Eventually 85 per cent of the airframe and 60 per cent of the engine were produced indigenously. Against this success must be set the high accident rate of the Gnat, probably because of the low-altitude problems with the longitudinal-control and hydraulic systems. These faults were rectified in the modified Gnat Mark I, the Ajeet, but not to the satisfaction of the IAF.[61] Production of the Ajeet was discontinued in the late 1980s, a decision which is less popular with civilian specialists than with the IAF—the Ajeet had a good reputation for combat performance and its low radar signature was increasingly valued. However the IAF did not like the Ajeet's relative lack of speed and the single engine.

HAL's major project in the 1960s was to produce indigenously a supersonic fighter, the HF-24 Marut. The project was conceived by Nehru and Menon as a means towards self-sufficiency. In this respect it was not dictated by military need and a qualitative assessment of Pakistan and Chinese capabilities. The project began in 1956 under the direction of an expatriate German, Kurt Tank, who was previously Focke-Wulf's war-time chief designer and responsible for the Kondor maritime bomber and the FW190 fighter.[62] The first stage of the project was to be the production of a supersonic fighter airframe to be followed in the second phase by the design and manufacture of an indigenous engine with a Mach capability. The aircraft was intended to satisfy the IAF's demand for a fighter-bomber. It was designed as a twin-engined aircraft with a 1.4/1.5 Mach speed capability.

Unfortunately, India's first attempt at joining the élite group of international aircraft producers did not proceed at all smoothly. The Marut was essentially a very long-drawn-out failure, for which there were four contributing reasons.

1. The Indian Government failed to strike a suitable agreement for the engine. The first four HF-24 Mk Is were handed over to the IAF in May 1964,

---

[59] Mullik (note 58), pp. 125–31.
[60] B. N. NagChaudhri, conversations with the author (15 Oct. 1984).
[61] Graham, T. W., 'India', ed. Katz (note 1), p. 171.
[62] SIPRI (note 8), p. 735.

an interim measure pending the production of three squadrons of HF-24 Mk IAs which were to be powered by the Bristol Orpheus 703 Reheat engine produced by HAL under licence.[63] However, in order to achieve supersonic speeds the Marut required a more powerful engine. India had hoped to purchase from Rolls-Royce the Bristol Orpheus 12, which was under development. In the event the aircraft for which this engine was being built was rejected by NATO and work on the project was curtailed.[64] The Indian Government then asked Rolls-Royce to upgrade the Orpheus 703 to supersonic capability. When the company requested £1 million for the project Menon refused.[65] The Government could not provide the additional finance to see the project through to completion and the contract did not provide sanctions to force completion.[66] There followed a number of frantic efforts to acquire a suitable engine. It has been suggested that Bristol Siddeley co-operated with the Indian Government on a scheme to modify the Orpheus 703 power plant by adding boosters from the Soviet VK-7 to achieve a substantial increase in thrust and a barely supersonic version of the HF-24 designated the HF-24 Mk IB.[67] Other attempts were made to acquire a suitable engine from the USSR (the RD 9-F) and from a German–Spanish–Egyptian consortium (the E-300), but both failed.[68] After the 1967 Arab–Israeli War, the Indian Government considered collaboration with Egypt to produce a supersonic engine. However, this too was a failed project, largely because of lack of interest on the part of the Egyptians.[69]

2. A fundamental tenet in aircraft design is that an airframe should always be designed around the engine and not vice versa. The decision to develop the Marut was a political one and the key decision makers were relatively unconcerned with the technical problems. Furthermore, Kurt Tank was an aircraft designer, not an engineer. Aircraft designers are trained in a systemic fashion and consider that a project is essentially the sum of its component parts. In the absence of strong direction from the MoD, problems of co-ordination and conception arose. Eventually, the problems in the design severely disadvantaged HAL's attempts to convince the IAF and the MoD that an acceptable system had been produced. There was a serious defect in the fuselage design which resulted in an unacceptable level of tail-drag. In the 1970s HAL attempted to update the Orpheus engine without outside assistance by adding an afterburner; developmental work was done by the Gas Turbine Research Establishment (GTRE). However, a mistake was made in not adding to the afterburner a bypass to provide additional air for the required mass, and the test plane exploded, killing the test pilot.[70]

[63] Kavic (note 6), pp. 197–98.
[64] Graham (note 61), p. 170.
[65] D. Raghunandan, conversations with the author (10 Oct. 1984, Delhi).
[66] Graham (note 61), p. 170.
[67] Kavic (note 6), p. 204, fn. 37.
[68] Graham (note 61), p. 170.
[69] B. N. NagChaudhri, conversations with the author (15 Oct. 1984, Delhi).
[70] B. N. NagChaudhri and D. Raghunandan, conversations with the author (15, 10 Oct. 1984, Delhi).

3. At no point is it possible to identify a well-orchestrated attempt to weigh the views of the military, politicians and industry on the project. Instead, progress was linear. As the project proceeded it passed from the hands of the politicians to the military and finally to industry. Or, to put it another way, the politicians defined the possibilities, the military defined the problem and industry was left to define the answer. The failure to acquire an appropriate engine was in part due to a series of unfortunate coincidences exacerbated by lack of foresight and financial stringency. It was also due to the Government's failure to sanction the development of an engine design team. Valuable experience had been acquired on the Gnat project through reverse engineering but it was not utilized for the Marut. In contrast to the cases of Brazil, China and Israel, for example, the Government had no confidence in HAL's reverse engineering capability, and at no point was HAL's capability assessed. These problems were compounded by the approach of the IAF to HAL's efforts. The IAF is well-trained at the operational level but is seemingly insufficiently conscious of technology. In the case of the Marut the IAF did little to assist with the design faults when they occurred.

In addition, the IAF appears to have little confidence or interest in indigenous technology, which was made very evident early on when the outright purchase of the French Ouragan was preferred to the licensed production of the Gnat. In many instances the preference has been to buy from abroad and, in all probability, the lack of faith in the HF-24 project is linked to this characteristic.[71]

4. Despite his confidence and talent, Kurt Tank was something of a failure in this project. He failed to gain the commitment of his design staff. Although he trained his designers well and gave them confidence in their capabilities, he was rigid in his approach to design. The IAF had no respect for his abilities and displayed little interest, for example, in co-ordinating work to solve the tail-drag problem on the Marut. Tank himself was more inclined to blame the lack of engine power rather than the tail-drag for the failure, and when the time came to lobby for more funds to rectify the aircraft's problems he procrastinated.[72] Eventually, production of the HF-24 did commence but only 145 instead of a projected 214 aircraft were built, and the Marut never flew at supersonic speed.[73] Although the Marut reached series production it never became a front-line aircraft and was quickly retired after an uneventful deployment.[74]

Another failure for HAL in the 1960s came in the attempt to produce under licence from Hawker-Siddeley the HS-748 transport plane. The aircraft performed badly, which led to reduced demand and high unit costs. Although Indian Airlines had agreed to a substantial intake, when the time came it

---

[71] D. Raghunandan, conversations with the author (10 Oct. 1984, Delhi).

[72] B. N. NagChaudhri, conversations with the author (18 Jan. 1984).

[73] Graham (note 61), p. 170.

[74] Karp, A., *The Light Combat Aircraft and the Insulation of Indian Weapons Procurement* (mimeo, Stockholm, Jan. 1991), p. 4.

refused to take up its promised order of 180 units and accepted only 17. The IAF was forced to take up the remaining 24 planes which were produced before the production line was closed down. The project resulted in the loss of Rs.3.4 crores.

Against these failures must be set the limited success of the HTJ-16 Kiran Mark I and II, a jet-engined trainer. Here the strategy was significantly different. Unlike the experience with the Marut, it was decided not to attempt to produce a state-of-the-art aircraft but instead to build upon past successes.[75]

Following the failure with the Marut, the fortunes of HAL changed significantly. Certainly, resources continued to be invested in the industry and, indeed, its scale of operations increased. However, neither the MoD nor the IAF were prepared to entrust any major project to the company. By the 1980s over 700 engineers were employed in the design sector, but the company's order books were lamentably empty. Many good employees left the company and a large proportion must have found jobs outside the country, thereby adding to the braindrain of the 1970s and 1980s:

Faced with limited job opportunities, the IIT [Indian Institute of Technology] . . . found some of its brightest graduates serving the needs of foreign aerospace establishments particularly in the US.

In India, till recently there were only licenced fighter aircraft programmes such as the Jaguar and the MiGs. This, quite understandably, failed to enthuse the IIT graduates. Statistics show that of the 90 aeronautical engineering graduates throughout the country, only a small percentage found jobs in the country's aerospace establishments. The Indian aeronautic industry lost 20 per cent to US aerospace establishments while a sizeable number ended up doing assignments which had nothing to do with their aeronautical background.[76]

At one point during the 1970s it seemed as if HAL's helicopter division in Bangalore would be more fortunate than its counterparts in the aircraft divisions. The question and possibility of an indigenous helicopter first emerged in 1969. In September 1970 the Government concluded a 10-year technology transfer agreement with the French firm, SNIAS, concerning the development and production of an Advanced Light Helicopter (ALH) for the 1980s. Naturally, the project was assigned to HAL, and 10 payments of $750 000 were made to SNIAS. Underpinning the collaboration agreement was the need to establish helicopter design and development facilities to ensure that the next generation of helicopters would be of Indian design and manufacture. It was part of the role of the SNIAS technical advisor to co-ordinate design concepts, undertake a training programme for designers and prepare joint feasibility studies and project reports.[77]

[75] Graham (note 61), p. 170.
[76] Laxman, S., 'DRDO gives aeronautics a massive boost', *Times of India*, 9 Oct. 1990.
[77] India, Lok Sabha, *Development of a Helicopter. 76th Report of the Public Accounts Committee (Ministry of Defence)* (Lok Sabha Sectretariat: New Delhi, 26 Mar. 1982), p. 18.

The helicopter division of HAL was established in 1974 and produced helicopters under licence, and by the mid-1980s had produced more than 400 Chetaks (Alouette III) and Chetahs (Lama). The agreement with SNIAS for the ALH was signed in September 1970, but the project was not sanctioned until February 1976. Part of the reason for the delay was the 1971 war which led to financial constraints in the years after. Although design work was initiated, the construction of the relevant facilities was held back for six years. Moreover, even after the project was sanctioned, delays and changes continued to occur. In 1977 the entire concept of the project was changed; a revised Air Staff Requirement (ASR) issued in February 1978 by Air Headquarters requested a radical change in configuration to a twin-engined model. This design change alone cost Rs.5.4 million and delayed procurement by at least 15 months. Moreover, 54.5 per cent of the French financial and technical assistance remained unutilized and only two-thirds of the 60 hours of free flying included in the contract were eventually taken up.[78] In 1982 the Public Accounts Committee (PAC) remarked with irritation that 'the project which was initially expected to fructify in the early 1980s is still at the drawing board'.[79] Although work would continue on the ALH within the HAL helicopter division, its configuration was still uncertain by 1984:

With a take-off weight given as 4,000kg (8,800lb) and a capacity of 10–12 passengers, the ALH is no longer 'light' (the original single-engined design had a maximum take-off weight of 2,500kg/5,500lb for the IAF and 3,000/6,600 for the navy version). Choice of powerplant is now stated to be two TM3333s or two PT6-35E/1s, which indicated that the Gem 43 is no longer in the running.[80]

In mid-1984 it was announced that a deal on technology transfer with the FRG was imminent.[81] MBB of the FRG were called in to provide technical assistance but, even so, first flights were again put back.[82] In August 1992 the first of four prototypes was unveiled. However, any euphoria associated with the occasion had been blunted by an earlier report of the Comptroller and Auditor General, which suggested that the helicopter would be surplus to requirements by the time it was made available to the armed forces: 'The ALH, which was being developed from 1970 onwards for meeting the multi-role requirements of the three services, including attack, air observation post and training would now be used only for utility services.'[83]

By mid-1993, the problems had still not been resolved. The French company, Turbomeca SA had supplied three sets of TM 333-2B engines and was set to supply another 50 sets. However, in early July 1993 US House Appropriations Committee (HAC) sources admitted that high costs were forc-

---

[78] *Development of a Helicopter* (note 77), pp. 19–21.

[79] *Development of a Helicopter* (note 77), p. 31.

[80] Mama, H. P., 'India's aerospace industry: impressive achievements by a developing country', *Interavia*, vol. 39, no. 2 (Feb. 1984), p. 151.

[81] *MILAVNEWS*, July 1984.

[82] 'HAL Advance Light Helicopter', *International Defense Review*, vol. 23, no. 10 (Oct. 1990).

[83] Ramachandran, R., 'Airborne in turbulent times', *Economic Times*, 5 Sep. 1992.

ing the company to look for another engine.[84] A helicopter which was first proposed in 1970 may now enter service in 1996 at the earliest, given the continuation of disputes over configurations—1995 was the starting date for production according to recent estimates, but this has now been put back another year.[85] However, there are growing signs that the armed forces are becoming disenchanted with the system. The IAF had wanted a small anti-tank system, the Army a larger system capable of carrying troops, and the Navy now feels that the system might not be capable of performing an adequate anti-submarine role. The waste of resources and opportunities has not been lost on the media:

This story about there being no indigenous buyers for an indigenous product has a familiar ring to it, in the context of defence R&D in particular. The ALH is yet another classic example of how an eminently sensible project can be undermined by lack of coordinated planning by the government that fails to extract a commitment from the potential end-users who themselves are not too keen about what they need.

If ALH's export potential is to be exploited the government would do well to ensure that the Services put ALH to use rather than go after fancy versions that are constantly entering the world market.[86]

The long, expensive history and the poor fortunes of the ALH were similarly reflected in the case of the HP-32, a single-piston-engined basic trainer. Although this aircraft is far from the cutting edge of aeronautic technology, the time lags and delays in defining IAF requirements were extensive. Despite the fact that expertise from the HT-2, the existing trainer, was readily available within HAL it took two and a half years (1965–68) for the IAF to identify the required changes to the new system and its operational requirements. It then took a further five and a half years for the Air Headquarters/Department of Defence Production (DoDP) to conclude that the Revethi Mk II under development by the Directorate General of Civil Aviation (DGCA) would not meet its requirements. Although HAL produced a feasibility report in February 1969 it was kept in cold storage until September 1974. Once again because of fluctuating Air Staff Requirements and minimal co-ordination between the DoDP, Air Headquarters, DGCA and HAL, further delays occurred.[87] In May 1985 the first HP-32 came off the production line at the HAL Kanpur division, seven years after the first prototype flew.

Similar problems have arisen with the recognition of the need for a more ad-vanced trainer in the 1980s, given the difficulties experienced by trainee pilots in graduating from the sub-sonic Kiran to the front-line aircraft. Essentially, the IAF was faced with three choices—indigenous production, import/licensed production from the West or import/licensed production from the USSR. The

---

[84] Raghavanshi, V., 'Engine debate stalls buy of copter in India', *Defense News*, 19–25 July 1993.

[85] 'Hindustan to fly ALH in September', *Flight International,* vol. 140, no. 4272 (26 June–2 July, 1991), p. 38.

[86] Ramachandran (note 83).

[87] *Development of a Helicopter* (note 77).

La Fontaine Committee, responsible for flight safety between 1977 and 1982, recommended the acquisition of the MiG-21 trainer, Mongol, as the most appropriate choice, a view apparently endorsed by Indira Gandhi. The wisdom behind this choice was considerable: (*a*) MiG cockpits, from the MiG-15 to the MiG-29, show generic similarities and India has procured several MiG versions; (*b*) India already had the ability to produce substantial parts of the aircraft and the additional plant could have been imported from the USSR, given that the model was no longer produced there; and (*c*) there were tangible export possibilities and obvious foreign exchange savings.[88] The IAF, however, favoured the import of either the BAe Hawk or the Dassault-Bréguet-Dornier Alphajet. By mid-1991, five years on, the issue had still not been resolved.[89] By August 1993 the Government had cleared the way for the purchase of 80 aircraft, down almost half from the original requirement for 150 aircraft. However, the choice between the Hawk and the Alpha had not been made. Instead the Cabinet directed the Defence Ministry to pursue detailed commercial and financial negotiations with the competing companies.[90]

Many of the problems which have occurred within the aeronautics sector have been identified and analysed in considerable detail. For example, in November 1967 the MoD appointed a committee under the chairmanship of C. Subramaniam, whose terms of reference were to assess Indian requirements in respect of aircraft and related equipment. In its report of the following year, the committee concentrated not just upon force levels but also upon the relationship between licensed and indigenous production. It is in this report that the inherent conflict between the two approaches to the acquisition of technology was made specific. The committee stressed a number of points which retard the growth and self-sufficiency of an aeronautics industry which, in the Indian case, is far from lacking in ability and enthusiasm. The committee was extremely critical of the IAF for its unwillingness to consider technological needs in relation to threat perceptions, a point made by Blackett two decades earlier and equally unpopular then with the armed forces:

The presentation by Air Headquarters did not include a statement of the tasks in terms of the threats faced by the country as determined by the Government and communicated to Air Headquarters. This is a basic requirement for any long term plans within the country. When this task was taken up with the Ministry of Defence in December, 1968, they took the view that the assessment of requirements for the Air Force was outside the terms of reference of the Aeronautics Committee. The Ministry of Defence stated, that given the requirements of the Air Force over a period of ten years, the Aeronautics Committee should recommend measures for the planned development of the Aeronautics Industry, so that these requirements be met by manufacture within the country, in the shortest possible time and in the most economical manner.[91]

[88] 'IAF pressing for jet trainer aircraft', *The Hindu,* 4 July 1990.
[89] Mahajan, V., 'IAF: pressing need for a trainer', *Times of India,* 16 Aug. 1991.
[90] 'Fewer Indian trainers given go-ahead', *Flight International,* 25–31 Aug. 1993.
[91] Subramaniam Committee (note 52), pp. 62–63.

Although the committee accepted the problem of threat assessment in principle, it was clearly put out by this apparent declaration of non-cooperation on the part of the Air Force:

The purpose of the critical assessment is to ensure that the requirements are reasonably spelt out and not likely to be changed easily; that they take account of resources; that they are moderated, to the extent feasible, by the technological capability of the country . . . Our defence posture, defence positions and defence priorities cannot be taken at present value even for the next decade. We have to deal with a changing situation. It is, therefore, important to recognize that the necessary exercises cannot be undertaken by any individual in any position. They have to be undertaken by organizations which have built up the necessary competence for the task. It is possible that the hesitation of the Ministry of Defence to explore the basis of the requirements arises from the handicap that none of the existing organizations has developed the competence to undertake the appropriate task.[92]

In its final recommendations the committee castigated the Air Force for imposing upon HAL in 1966 operational requirements for a ground attack fighter which were unrealistic in relation to industrial capacity and to cost.[93] On the role of the services in defining threats and requirements, the committee recommended the creation of expertise in research institutions outside the defence establishment to assist with assessing the relative costs and claims of defence requirements—a form of defence policy research institute.[94]

There were two other significant recommendations contained in the Subramaniam Committee report. First, it recognized that production under licence had meant that the design teams at Bangalore had not developed in step with production facilities: in 1968 the design team at Bangalore employed a staff of 335, a mere 20 per cent of the labour force and a much smaller percentage than obtained in the West European and North American defence industries. Moreover, the committee expressed grave reservations over the wisdom of production under licence as a means to technological self-sufficiency. On the issue of the choice of ground attack aircraft for the latter half of the 1970s, the committee was unequivocal:

One way would be to introduce a new ground attack aircraft through manufacture under licence. We do not favour it. This would be yet another type of aircraft to the five types which would be in service during [the] 1974–79 period. Secondly, such a decision would be based on inadequate appreciation of the HF-24Mk1.R under development or of the potential for further development in the HF-24 aircraft. *It is our finding that licenced production inhibits indigenous development; in the present case it would completely extinguish development.* [Emphasis added.] [95]

[92] Subramaniam Committee (note 52), pp. 63–65.
[93] Subramaniam Committee (note 52), p. 310.
[94] Subramaniam Committee (note 52), p. 83.
[95] Subramaniam Committee (note 52), pp. 67–68.

In the event, this is virtually what happened. Starved of major design projects for over 15 years, by 1982 some 70 per cent of production capacity at the Bangalore and Kanpur complexes had fallen idle.[96]

The second set of recommendations from the committee concerned management and organization, about which there was considerable criticism. At the wider level, the committee echoed the criticism of an earlier report prepared by a team of Swedish defence experts that research institutes were excluded from the planning process, that scientific expertise was not properly utilized and that productivity was low: 'Thus it was stated that 7500 manhours had been used to manufacture 18 tools for the HF-24—an average of about 400 hours per tool. The manufacturing time per tool for a corresponding type of aircraft in Sweden is about 40 hours per tool.'[97]

Elsewhere, the committee commented that 'if research establishments and the industry were involved in the formulation of weapons policy, their inventive skill could make a real contribution'[98]—a statement virtually identical to the one made by Patrick Blackett (see chapter 3, section IV) concerning defence science organization. Equally important, the committee was critical of the way in which policy making was executed. Its criticism of the Air Force has already been noted, but it also focused on the *ad hoc* nature of decision making beyond the political level and the extreme disaggregration between the research, manufacturing and military sectors:

The principal aircraft requirements relate to the Air Force. Hence, the relationship between the Air Force as the indentor and the industry is important; in fact, the success to meet the Air Force requirements by manufacture within the country depends upon complete understanding and [a] good working relationship between them.[99]

An earlier committee under the chairmanship of J. R. D. Tata had recommended in 1963 both centralization and rationalization in the aircraft industry to promote the orderly and co-ordinated development of aircraft, propulsion, armament (including missiles), electronics, testing and evaluation. Although the recommendation was accepted in principle by the MoD, it was later rejected on the grounds that the ministry did not want aeronautics R&D to be entrusted to an authority outside the R&D organization. The Subramaniam Committee reiterated Tata's recommendations by proposing a Requirement Policy Committee and better management practices.

The Subramaniam Committee report was never made available for wider comment and debate and it is fairly clear that its recommendations and those of previous committees and consultative bodies went relatively unheeded. Planning for aeronautic self-sufficiency remained disjointed and all too dependent upon the requirements of the IAF, which took little or no account of industrial capabilities and constraints.

[96] Sapru, S., 'HAL units remain idle for want of work', *Indian Express*, 28 June 1982.
[97] Subramaniam Committee (note 52), p. 183.
[98] Subramaniam Committee (note 52).
[99] Subramaniam Committee (note 52), p. 303.

VI. The light combat aircraft: forward to the past?

The long-term fortunes of HAL revived in the early 1980s after increased lobbying directly to the Prime Minister and her secretariat and the result was a rise in the level of commitment to indigenous development and production in the defence sector. The most important aspect of this was the proposal for development of a light combat aircraft (LCA), originally planned for production by 1994 with a prototype to be ready by 1990.

In mid-1983 reports first appeared regarding the Indian Government's commitment to the development of an LCA to be powered by an indigenous engine.[100] BAe emerged as the clear contender for the relatively limited collaboration envisaged by the decision makers given the complexity and ambitious nature of the project; by late 1984 reports continued to suggest that BAe would be a partner to the project.[101] Much of this optimism stemmed from BAe's continued presence in the Indian defence industry, through the Jaguar DSPA licensed production agreement, while experience with the French and the Mirage 2000 had been a disappointment. However, by early 1984 the Indian Government had invited foreign companies to prepare feasibility studies which would involve collaborative development even though all production and marketing was to take place in India. The technology required from abroad was considerable—composite material technology, cockpit displays and active controls with electronic sensing and signalling.[102] The significance of the commitment to indigenous capacity was reflected in the budgetary arrangements. By 1990 the project was expected to have cost Rs.12–15 billion, but only 10 per cent of the development budget was allocated for foreign consultants.[103] The response both inside and outside India to such an ambitious project was mixed, and before long the LCA became extremely controversial—experts questioned cost estimates, the aeronautic establishment's ability to deliver and the level of indigenous content.

In mid-1985 the project was adversely affected by the unexpected resignation of two of the key personnel within the Aeronautical Development Agency (ADA), the apex body set up to oversee the design and development of the LCA. The creation of the ADA itself had been a significant step and probably essential given the co-ordination and managerial problems which would inevitably emerge over the course of the programme. In other areas of big science, such as space research and nuclear energy, departments had been set up many years before in an attempt to co-ordinate diverse activities in a systematic manner and provide a recognized decision-making locus. In the field of aeronautics this did not occur, so that links between the R&D establishments

[100] *MILAVNEWS*, June 1983, p. 10.

[101] *MILAVNEWS*, Oct. 1984, p. 19.

[102] Wood, D., 'Proposals sought for Indian light fighter', *Jane's Defence Weekly*, vol. 3, no. 11 (14 Jan. 1984), p. 13.

[103] Mukherjee, S. J., 'Green light for Indian LCA', *Jane's Defence Weekly,* 16 Mar. 1985, p. 437.

and industry were severely hampered and the more general need for long-term planning and related decision making neglected:

The bureaucratic viewpoint was that in the absence of an aircraft development programme there was no need for technology development—a tragic error of judgment—which prevails even today. Any discussion on planning for LCA mission orientated R&D and technology development programmes and fall back positions invited sarcastic comments of planning for a fall back aircraft; any suggestions to plan for integration of R&D and the industry and referring to early committee recommendations were thought to be greed on the part of the people making such suggestions.[104]

The creation of the ADA should have been a step in the right direction and a means of channelling the country's R&D capabilities into a single project which involved 50 companies and over 600 work packages. Unfortunately, this proved not to be the case. Although the Agency was given the responsibility for setting up the LCA programme, the authority to ensure that its decisions were implemented was lacking. The very existence of the ADA was a considerable blow for HAL because it raised the profile of the National Aeronautics Laboratory (NAL) and indicated for the first time that the interests of government might differ from those of HAL.[105] The result was the resignation of two key figures, S. R. Valluri, the Director of the NAL in Bangalore and the Director General of the ADA, and India's chief aircraft designer and leader of the Agency design team, Raj Mahindra. Valluri had in fact been asked by the Chief Scientific Advisor to the MoD, V. S. Arunachalam, to remove Mahindra from the ADA following allegations in parliament relating to the latter's citizenship and patriotism, and Valluri also considered Arunachalam's apparent keenness to involve a number of younger designers in the project as an immense mistake. Aircraft design, he maintained, is in essence a product of accumulated experience which requires a person of experience at the top and a hierarchical organization, and Mahindra was the only person in India who could perform a similar role to that of the aircraft designer Mikoyan in the USSR, for instance.[106] Valluri's views on organization received considerable support. For example,

Valluri's views about organizational linkages between ADA and HAL were echoed by a HAL veteran who felt that the present organizational structure in the two was not conducive to design development. HAL is geared mainly to production, virtually a backyard workshop for the Air Force. Moreover, HAL's different wings reported to different departments: design and research to the DRDO and production to Defence production. 'I would put HAL's design and development wing under ADA', [Valluri] argued.[107]

---

[104] Valluri, S. R., 'Indian aeronautic scene: light combat aircraft', *Mainstream*, vol. 24, no. 27 (8 Mar. 1986), p. 12.

[105] Karp (note 74), p. 20.

[106] Valluri (note 104), p. 14.

[107] Singh, R., 'Light combat aircraft: trouble before take-off', *India Today,* vol. 9, no. 2 (31 Jan. 1986), p. 79.

Since then the development of the LCA has remained controversial. The loss of Valluri and Mahindra was certainly significant and must have affected the quality of technical decision making, particularly in relation to R&D and technology transfer. Throughout the mid- and late 1980s the LCA ran further and further into trouble as both government and industry prevaricated over the future direction of the project.

First and foremost it became unclear from which source the LCA engine would come, and until the capabilities of the engine were decided upon only limited progress could be made in other areas of design, unless of course the Marut failure was to be replicated. It was hoped during the early part of the project to utilize the GTX engine under development at the GTRE in Bangalore. However, the GTX is many, many years behind schedule and currently the main problems appear to be the production of an engine which can function very effectively in ambient temperatures of up to 45°C, which is essential for any advanced aircraft deployed in Indian conditions. By 1984 only two out of the 10 demonstrators had been produced and the requirement to demonstrate a thrust capability of 4500 kg and 6600 kg with afterburning had not materialized.[108] However, the scale of the task facing GTRE should not be underestimated; suggestions around 1987 that the GTX-35 would be ready by 1992 were extremely optimistic.[109] Indeed, Indian officials continue to maintain that the GTX-35, now named the Kivari, will power the LCA when it goes into production.[110]

Although the HAL Chairman, Air Marshal M. S. D. Wollen, stated in mid-1985 that India possessed the means to develop the LCA with one or more collaborative partners, despite the submission of design studies from BAe, MBB, Dornier and Aérospatiale (some at no charge), it became clear that this would not be the case; something beyond this type of collaboration was required.[111] In late 1985 the ADA met in Bangalore to review the design and development of the LCA and finalize the Air Staff Requirement, following which HAL could proceed to the definition stage.[112] It was probably during this meeting that the ADA decided that an interim measure had to be taken given the continuing delay of the GTX project and that collaboration was unavoidable.

In addition to the said European producers who were anxious to gain a toehold in the LCA project given the prevailing slump in the international combat-aircraft market elsewhere, the USA also appeared as a contender for collaboration, due entirely to Rajiv Gandhi's unsolicited willingness to do business with the USA and initiate a significant thaw in Indo-US relations. During a visit to the USA in January 1986, an agreement was reached over the export of the General Electric F404 engine, and the Prime Minister's visit was swiftly fol-

[108] *MILAVNEWS,* Apr. 1984, p. 6.
[109] Salvy, R., 'Light combat aircraft projects proliferate', *International Defense Review,* vol. 20, no. 12 (Dec. 1987), p. 1611.
[110] 'Hindustan begins building LCA prototypes', *Flight International,* vol. 40, no. 4272 (26 June–2 July 1991), p. 14.
[111] *MILAVNEWS,* Aug. 1985, p. 23.
[112] *MILAVNEWS,* Oct. 1985, p. 17.

lowed by a flood of US technicians to India. Thus, Grumman, Lockheed and Northrop added themselves to the list of contenders for collaboration. Meanwhile new costings for the LCA project took estimated expenditure from Rs.600 crores to Rs.1500 crores.[113]

By mid-1986 the LCA project had started to take shape following the issue of an Air Staff Requirement. The ADA had apparently decided upon a single-engined, single-seat aircraft with a maximum take-off weight of about 9000 kg. Primarily designed as a battlefield air superiority weapon system, with a secondary close support capability, it was to have a top speed of Mach 2. A decision on the interim engine was between the GE F404RM12 and the Rolls-Royce Turbo Union RB.199 Stage B, pending the successful development of the GTX. A prototype would fly by 1990 and the LCA would enter front-line service in the mid-1990s.

The political will of the Government to pursue the programme prompted many inside and outside India to consider the likely success of the project. In particular, consultants in the USA started to evaluate the project and HAL's capability given the likelihood of US involvement and the results were far from positive. Dr Steven Bryen, Head of the Strategic Trade Directorate in the Pentagon, considered the very basis of the project to be poorly conceived:

If India wants to go, suffer, spend a lot of money, in billions of dollars, that is your problem . . . But, there is a question about the economics of developing some of these products . . . [there] are no guarantees [it will work] . . . You are talking about inventing a new cadre of people to do that work . . . there is not enough rationale [for the LCA] . . . as it is [ultimately] an economic issue . . . because it starts to drag down where your talented people are going to spend their time, and I question those kinds of investments very closely.[114]

More to the point, for a US analyst, he also questioned the wisdom of US involvement in a project such as the LCA: 'The worse kind of project for us to get involved in is the one that fails, or, that gives opposition politicians a chance to stand up and say—you have been led up the garden path by the Americans.'[115]

Another respected US defence analyst, Jacques Gansler, considered the timing of the LCA project to be misconceived. In a similar interview he argued that India had embarked upon an extremely ambitious project but one which would only embody technology soon to be superseded by the coming generation. Thus, for example, the LCA is expected to incorporate a 'cranked arrow' configuration which calls for the leading edge of the wing to be angled with a resultant increase in lift for a given amount of power. However, the coming generation of fighter aircraft, notably the US Advanced Tactical Fighter (ATF),

---

[113] From this point on, costings for the LCA will be given in rupees only because of the severe depreciation of the rupee during this period. In 1983 the exchange value of the rupee was approximately Rs.14: £1.00 but the value in the early 1990s dropped to over Rs.50: £1. *MILAVNEWS*, Jan. 1986, p. 16.

[114] Quoted in Karnad, B., 'LCA venture expensive: US expert', *Hindustan Times*, 24 Feb. 1986.

[115] Karnad (note 114).

will incorporate vectored thrust technology which is much more advanced. The composite materials used to build the ATF and its avionics will also be far in advance of those of the LCA. Gansler's recommendation was for India to delay the project to make possible a limited acquisition of the emerging technologies.[116] However, Gansler did not discuss whether or not India could access such an advanced level of technology, afford the costs, or cope with and exploit such advances. In all three instances the answer would probably be negative.

Negotiations over defence technology transfer with the USA proceeded apace and were extended to cover not only LCA technology but also radar technology, anti-tank weaponry, night vision equipment, MBT fire control and transmission systems, ammunition and advanced materials.[117] A high point was reached in January 1987 when the US Secretary for Defense, Caspar Weinberger, visited India to promise publicly all the technical support the country required for the successful development of the LCA. At the same time, however, reports started to appear regarding future French involvement in the project. In October 1987 it was reported that Dassault-Breguet had signed an agreement worth $100 million with the Indian Government to supply 30 engineers to work in Bangalore under the auspices of the ADA. It therefore seemed that France had effectively won the design contract. Furthermore, it became evident that France wished for an even greater input into the project by seeking to turn the Government's head in the direction of the SNECMA M88 Mk II engine scheduled for use in the Rafale light combat aircraft.[118] In addition, at the same period an ADA team visited the Rolls-Royce Military Engine Group facilities in Bristol to view the Turbo-Union RB199 engine.[119]

Throughout 1987 interest in the LCA programme was overshadowed by the Bofors scandal and received much less media attention. However, by mid-1987 it seemed as though Saab had made a late bid to provide development assistance, probably on the grounds that the LCA would emerge as a close relation of the JAS-39 light combat aircraft. Although Saab did not contribute a feasibility study, it had held previous talks with the Indian Government on co-operation as early as 1980–81.[120] During the same period it was announced that General Electric (GE) had in fact won the order for 10 F404 turbofans for the prototype phase of the project, although this did not guarantee eventual incorporation at the production stage.[121]

Predictably enough, the project definition stage fell behind schedule by more than a year, and serious consideration was given to the future of the programme. One reason for the delay was a failure to agree upon the optimum

[116] Karnad, B., 'Light combat aircraft: the hi-tech factor', *Illustrated Weekly of India*, 8 June 1986, p. 45.

[117] 'LCA programme talks set as USA and India move closer', *Jane's Defence Weekly*, vol. 6, no. 8 (8 Nov. 1986), p. 1089.

[118] 'Dassault–Breguet to help design LCA for India', *Jane's Defence Weekly*, vol. 8, no. 17 (31 Oct. 1987), p. 976.

[119] 'LCA engines', *Defense and Foreign Affairs Weekly*, 27 Oct.–2 Nov. 1986, p. 3.

[120] *MILAVNEWS*, May 1987, p. 15.

[121] *MILAVNEWS*, June 1987, p. 14.

weight for the system which could in turn have been related to the delays encountered with the development of composite materials. Significantly, it was the IAF which was reported to be dissatisfied with progress and, furthermore, was actively considering abandoning the whole project in favour of joint development of the French Rafale. There would be several advantages for India in such a move. The GE F404 powers the Rafale prototype, which would not rule out an Indian version powered by the GTX-35, given that the engines are interchangeable. The multi-mode radar under development for the LCA could also be used in the Rafale. Finally, given the likelihood that the cost of the LCA would certainly spiral out of control with uncertain end results and timing, investment in the French system would be much safer and almost certainly cheaper.[122] Soon after it was reported that Dassault had succeeded in a bid to strike a 'company–company' agreement with HAL over the marketing of the LCA. In effect, Dassault had managed to introduce the LCA into its product spectrum alongside other systems in production and proposed—the Mirage 2000 and 4000, the Rafale and the Franco-German Alpha jet.[123] How much this represents the thin end of the wedge designed to assimilate finally the whole project remains to be seen.

During the same period a Letter of Offer and Acceptance was signed between the US Air Force and the Indian DRDO which allowed Indian technicians access to the four Air Force Wright Aeronautical Laboratories. This opened the way for collaboration and the participation of US industry in the project. The transfer of technology envisaged was unprecedented and covered avionics and flight controls, fly-by-wire systems, flight actuators and carbon composite materials.[124] Also, during the same period, the USSR started to display an interest in the ill-fated programme by offering New Delhi participation in a new single-engined combat aircraft, similar in capability to the US F-16, should the price tag for the LCA present further problems.

At the end of 1988 another peculiar twist was added to the LCA saga. In a bid to drive a wedge between New Delhi and both Washington and Paris, the USSR offered to improve radically the MiG-21, the aircraft the LCA is destined to replace. On offer for the MiG-21 was the MiG-29 engine, new wings and a modern avionics system. Since MiG-21 production facilities already existed in India the retrofitting could be done at a comparatively low cost. India could slow down the pace of LCA development and therefore distribute the escalating costs over a wider period of time or it could cancel what was rapidly becoming the biggest white elephant in the history of Indian defence production.[125] Furthermore, during a period when the country's foreign exchange reserves were becoming rapidly depleted, such an offer, if accepted, could also slow the import of other sophisticated aircraft and even provide India with a novel source of exports when many countries were finding it extremely difficult to

---

[122] De Briganti, G., 'India looks to Rafale after LCA lags', *Defence News,* 29 Aug. 1988.

[123] 'Dassault to market India's LCA', *Jane's Defence Weekly,* vol. 10, no. 11 (17 Sep. 1988), p. 607.

[124] *MILAVNEWS,* Oct. 1988, p. 19.

[125] Sharma, K. K., 'Moscow offers to upgrade Indian MiGs', *Financial Times,* 20 Dec. 1988.

afford state-of-the-art military technology. However, nothing more was heard of the offer.

By mid-1991 it appeared that the LCA was to be much more a hybrid of foreign technologies than ever imagined, with the inclusion of a US engine, Swedish avionics, a US or French fly-by-wire avionics system, and an airframe of which the main input has come from foreign consultants. From the original estimate of Rs.560 crores, the cost is now estimated to be Rs.1670 crores and production dates remain uncertain.[126] In addition, the configuration of the system changed markedly, specifically with regard to weight. From the lithe 5.5 tonne system originally planned, the LCA is now a more portly 8 tonnes and much closer to the F-16 it is intended to outperform. The fault has been the traditional tendency to add on technology, which has also ramified into price rises—cost estimates are now about $10 billion for a reduced number of 200 units.[127] However, a more optimistic note was sounded at the 1991 Paris Air Show when an HAL spokesman implied that the LCA production run could produce 500 aircraft.[128] This may tie in with the recent reports concerning a naval variant.[129] It is now unlikely that the LCA will be operational before the end of the century, and the number of prototypes has been cut from seven to two.[130]

The Indian LCA is beginning to appear in a similar light to other major aeronautics projects attempted by India—chaotic and subject to flux, cost overruns, technological slippage and time delays. There have even been reports that the programme has been shelved but this does not appear to be the case.[131] Above all it is possible that the IAF will eventually do what it appears to have done on numerous other occasions and effectively obstruct attempts at indigenization in an effort to ensure that foreign rather than indigenous systems prevail. Finally, in August 1992 the Indian Government at last took the inevitable step and opened the doors to full foreign collaboration, citing lack of funds as the primary reason.[132]

In the current climate the long- and short-term prospects for the Indian aeronautics industry look bleak. Hampered by bureaucratic infighting and rendered less capable than it really is by the unrealistic demands of the Air Force, deprived of an input into the decision making process and lacking the necessary political patronage, HAL is unlikely to develop its technological capabilities far enough to fulfil its undoubted potential. In this milieu there is no opportunity to close the gap between present levels of capability and the increasing rate of technological change in the defence industries of the West. Nor is the outlook

[126] Chadha, K. D., 'Time for introspection: the stakes in the DRDO's Light Combat Aircraft are far too high', *Hindustan Times*, 14 Apr. 1991.

[127] Karp (note 74), p. 23.

[128] Atwal, K., '500 LCAs for India?', *Defence*, vol. 22, no. 7 (July 1991), p. 8.

[129] Mama, H. P., 'India's light fighter will transform its aerospace industry', *Interavia*, no. 8 (Aug. 1990), p. 645.

[130] Karp (note 74), p. 24.

[131] 'India reviews LCA replacements', *Flight International*, no. 4229, vol. 138 (15–21 Aug. 1990), p. 12.

[132] 'Foreign collaboration on LCA', *Times of India*, 26 Aug. 1992.

helped by the severe downturn in the international aerospace market, which will hamper the company's attempts to attain rhythm and continuity. Given the way in which the technological needs for defence are defined, this is a pre-requisite.

The LCA project did to a certain extent reflect an understanding on the part of the Government that the opportunities for India to create a viable and credible aeronautic production capability based upon modern technologies were fast diminishing. If the Government had not proceeded with the LCA pro-gramme, the long-term prospects of HAL would have looked bleak indeed, not least in view of the development of HAL's technology base. However, sound decision making, effective management and co-ordinated support were equally important, and in this direction there are many questions. Why were two of the most effective members of the ADA allowed to resign without attempts at rec-onciliation, particularly given the peculiarities of the industry and the need for experienced leadership? Why were so many foreign technicians and consultants allowed on to the programme in such an *ad hoc* manner? No fewer than six countries made offers to India during the mid-1980s, which led to confusion and prevarication and must surely have hindered progress, resolve and morale. Why was the IAF allowed to court Dassault for the Rafale given the apparent resolve on the part of government to develop as much of an indigenous capacity as possible?

Equally relevant is the question why HAL was allowed to fall into such a parlous state in the late 1970s. During a period of rapid technological change why did government allow the industry to exist without projects and without significant R&D, thereby losing all the benefits of follow-on projects? This was the heart of the problems experienced over the course of the LCA programme. Under any circumstances it is both difficult and expensive for a country such as India to match the rate of technological change which obtains in the West or did obtain in the USSR. Any attempt, therefore, to leap one generation at least by moving from the HF-24 to the LCA when the industry has languished and many of the best and the brightest have left is bound to be time-consuming, costly and technically complex. Without effective management or government discipline over the role and input of all the relevant institutions, the failures and setbacks witnessed in recent years were probably inevitable.

However, in contrast to the situation in the 1970s, HAL now enjoys an unprecedented degree of political support. Although the LCA programme has been roundly criticized by pundits and watchdog committees alike, the LCA programme is now seen as a project of immense national importance and pres-tige. The facts that it is a white elephant, capable of inflicting severe opportu-nity costs on other areas of the defence budget, and that it will be virtually obsolete by the time it is produced and probably unexportable, have made little difference. What seems of greater importance is that India will be seen to pro-duce its own, indigenous advanced combat aircraft at some point in the future. By avoiding too much reference to foreign inputs, the myth of indigenization will be preserved. Quite where the LCA will figure in India's defence posture will depend very much upon the IAF.

VII. Indigenous defence production: unfulfilled expectations

Despite the views of the Indian Government, several Indian pundits and a good many external analysts, the Indian defence industry would seem to be in poor shape and clearly unable to reach the standards which its architects have envisaged. Indeed, India's ability to pass off equipment produced using copious amounts of foreign technology as home-grown is an extremely significant propaganda exercise.

Much of the blame for the lack-lustre performance, especially in the aeronautics sector, would seem to rest with the armed forces. Despite the political arguments in favour of indigenous production and the massive amounts of government finance which have been invested in the defence technology base, there would seem to be little interest in the development of this sector. The explanation for this antipathy may be quite simple—Indian officers are much less enamoured of Indian defence technology than might be expected. This observation makes some sense when placed in a wider context: the majority of Indians are rarely enamoured of indigenous products such as cars and electronics.[133] There has always been a tendency to favour Western military technology because of its position at the cutting edge of military technical change. Soviet technology was less acceptable but obviously unavoidable during the difficult 1970s. Whether justified or not, the comment of one officer on the reputation of the Marut is instructive: 'Pilots would lose weight flying that aircraft. Not that they lacked courage. But they simply did not have faith in the machine.'[134]

Second, the indigenous defence sector would not seem to have enjoyed the necessary support from central government, an idea which is explored further in chapter 9. Although successive reports and official statements have traditionally made much of this sector, the reality has been very different. While money has always been available to keep the infrastructure in place, the political commitment towards genuine progress has often been shallow.[135]

Third, success does not seem to have been apparent at the managerial levels. There appear to have been too many attempts to indigenize in the defence sector when it is perfectly clear that the expertise and technology are unavailable at the national level. Furthermore, Indian decision makers have always tended to pitch requirements far higher than industry is capable of delivering—this is a complaint heard frequently from foreign consultants. At the organizational level there are several shortcomings:

---

[133] During the early 1980s India commenced production of the Maruti car, under licence from Suzuki in Japan. As and when these models became available it was customary for new owners to give the car a Suzuki badge in place of the Maruti marque.

[134] Singh, G. K., 'Fighting fit?', *The Week* (Cochin), 9 Apr. 1989.

[135] Interview with senior ranking defence civil servant, Bangalore, Apr. 1984.

(a) The system lacks uniformity, in that the user has to look to three or four separate agencies for the development and production of the same commodity, (b) The existing control mechanism tends to break down, and failure to co-ordinate fully the efforts of all such agencies results in the lack of unified direction and integration of development and production effort, (c) Different contractual procedures and procurement practices confuse industry, and tend to encourage uneconomical practices.[136]

Above all, India would seem to have largely wasted a valuable opportunity to develop a defence industrial base of real, rather than illusory, independence. The large number of South Asian scientists and technologists now working abroad testifies graphically to the depth of talent and potential in the country.[137] Indeed, India's science and technology base has always been widely recognized. Success, however, has eluded the nation which formerly put forward the most ideologically persuasive argument in favour of eliminating the influence of major powers. The present situation is hardly what Nehru and Menon had in mind four decades earlier.

[136] Grant, N. B., 'What ails defence R&D units', *New Delhi*, 14 Nov. 1988.
[137] During Northrop's bid to sell India the F-20 under licence it was suggested at one point that the US team could be drawn exclusively from expatriate Indians, such is the number of South Asian workers in the US defence industry.

8. Nuclear weapons and delivery systems

I. India and nuclear weapons: the early years

Any discussion of India's defence policy since 1947 must highlight the significance and impact of deliberations over the direction of India's nuclear weapon programme. Equally, the decision to eschew one of the major multilateral arms control initiatives of the post-war period, the opening for signature of the NPT in 1968, should also be considered. Both affected India's foreign policy and its relations with foreign powers, especially the two superpowers. Moreover, both are driven more by internal, domestic considerations than anything else, including the putative capabilities of China and Pakistan.

Successive Indian governments have always displayed a distinct ambivalence about the question whether or not to include nuclear weapons in the country's national force structure. As indicated in chapter 3, Nehru was equivocal as to whether or not India should possess nuclear weapons; there is no suggestion that had he been confronted with a real option he would necessarily have accepted the need for a nuclear deterrent, but he recognized how much political power was commensurate with nuclear weapons. The extent of Nehru's ambivalence about the nuclear option was reflected in a statement he made to the Lok Sabha (the lower house of parliament) on 10 August 1960: 'So far as we are concerned, we are determined not to go in for making atomic bombs and the like. But we are equally determined not to be left behind in this advance in the use of this new power.'[1]

What Nehru wanted was somewhat contradictory. At one level, he firmly believed in nuclear disarmament, not least as a means of removing superpower control over the international system. In part, the paradox can be explained by understanding the considerable ignorance among policy makers throughout the world at that time—nuclear weapons were seen more as contiguous to large and powerful conventional weapons than as the qualitatively different, awesomely powerful and destructive weapons that we now more correctly consider them to be. His enthusiasm for the potential linkage between science and development also made the prospect of a nuclear energy programme a seductive possibility. After the 1962 war against China, the dichotomy in Nehru's thinking became more distinct. In a note to Homi Bhabha, Nehru mused, 'Apart from building power stations and developing electricity, there is always a built-in advantage of defence use if the need should arise'.[2]

---

[1] Quoted in Kapur, A., 'India's nuclear test: stretching out the options or the first step towards a weapons program?', Center for the Study of Armament and Disarmament Occasional Paper no. 4 (Center for the Study of Armament and Disarmament: Los Angeles, Calif., undated), p. 17.

[2] Kapur, A., *India's Nuclear Option: Atomic Diplomacy and Decision Making* (Praeger: New York, 1976), p. 194.

The change in Nehru's position on nuclear weapons was not purely the result of the threat from China; after all, the Chinese did not acquire nuclear weapons until late 1964, the year Nehru died. Homi Bhabha, a brilliant scientist and the father of India's nuclear weapon programme, used both his political power base, which stemmed from his pre-eminent position within the scientific bureaucracy during the 1960s, and his personal relationship with Nehru to advance the nuclear power programme and keep open the option to produce nuclear weapons. From 1948 until his death in an air crash in January 1966, Bhabha was the director of India's atomic energy programme and he ran the Department of Atomic Energy, of which Nehru was Minister. Bhabha was largely responsible for keeping the military option open during a period when internationalism rather than narrow self-interest dominated the opinion-shaping process in this area. The decision-making process allowed him a considerable and almost exclusive influence over Nehru's thinking on this matter. As was the case with conventional defence policy and posture, however, there was considerable ambiguity and variation between individual statements and viewpoints on the one hand, especially those of Nehru, and the direction of policy on the other.[3]

After Nehru's death and China's gate-crash entry into the nuclear club, Bhabha attempted to push India further towards the nuclear threshold. In Lal Bahadur Shastri, the new Prime Minister, and L. K. Jha, the Prime Minister's principal secretary, Bhabha found less opposition on the basis of ideology than with Nehru. In late 1965 Shastri approved in principle Bhabha's plan for an underground nuclear explosion. This also tied in with attempts to cajole Canada into accepting fewer safeguards on RAPP II (the Rajastani Atomic Power Plant) than on RAPP I.[4]

The deaths of Shastri and Bhabha in early 1966 deprived the Indian nuclear weapon programme of a considerable degree of momentum. Bhabha was intent on seeing India become the sixth member of the nuclear club and he also possessed the diplomatic, political and administrative skills on both the national and the international stage to succeed. His successor, Sarabhai, had neither quite the skill nor indeed the inclination and the new Prime Minister, Indira Gandhi, was too busy consolidating her political position within the Congress Party to concern herself unduly with such a risk-laden programme.

Three factors, therefore, influenced interest in nuclear weapons during the mid-1960s: (*a*) the 1962 war made its impact in this quarter, as it did in others, and serious thinking about the nuclear option coincided with the conventional defence buildup after 1962; (*b*) the death of Nehru permitted a new and more hawkish political debate on the defence options open to India, although this was weakened by the death of Bhabha; and (*c*) China's 1964 nuclear test offered the

---

[3] In Kapur's seminal study of India's nuclear decision making, his views on Nehru are close to my own in chapter 3: 'Did this mean that Nehru failed to think through the link between atomic energy for peaceful purposes and its possible defence use? Or did it mean that he thought about the link but failed only to articulate it publicly?' (note 2), p. 192.

[4] Kapur (note 2), p. 194.

Government a convenient argument for keeping open the nuclear option. Bhabha was quick to take the opportunity further to convince both government and the public that 'the explosion of a nuclear device by China is a signal that there is no time to be lost'.[5] The connection between the first explosion of China's H-bomb, on 1 July 1967, and the intensified interest in an Indian test, points to a close correlation at this time between Chinese and Indian nuclear policies, the latter reacting to developments in the former.

From this point on and up until the nuclear test in 1974, public opinion appeared to favour increasingly the pursuit of nuclear weapons. Indeed, in contrast to the majority of defence and foreign affairs issues, the bomb attracted an unusual degree of public interest during this period. According to public opinion surveys conducted in Delhi, Calcutta, Bombay and Madras throughout the late 1960s, strong support existed in favour of going nuclear. The urban-based, conservative party, the Jana Sangh (later the Bharatiya Janata Party, the BJP) was the most outspoken pro-bomb party—as it is now—and one which gained in popularity. Strength of feeling in favour of the bomb was particularly marked in Delhi.[6] In 1971, flushed with the success of the war against Pakistan, three-quarters of voters in these major cities supported the building of nuclear weapons, even if this led to a greater tax burden and drastic cuts in development expenditure.[7]

In a survey of the attitudes of Indian élites to both the bomb and the NPT, Ashis Nandy identified a stronger anti-bomb sentiment among the upper echelons of society (53.7 per cent) than existed among the wider public but, on the other hand, an extremely strong and unqualified antipathy (68.9 per cent) towards the NPT.[8] Although this may seem contradictory, it is not. For a politically aware Indian, it is perfectly feasible to be anti-nuclear and anti-NPT.

II. India and nuclear policy before the Non-Proliferation Treaty

Since the NPT opened for signature in 1968, India has been one of the most important 'hold-out' states. Quite distinct from the threat of nuclear proliferation to South Asian regional security, the threat India represents in this quarter stems from its highly articulate critique of the principles which underpin the NPT.

The starting point for understanding India's complex, and sometimes contradictory, stance on non-proliferation is the fundamental question of non-alignment. When India became independent Nehru was determined to avoid replacing the British Empire with another form of dependence—political, military or

[5] Jain, J. P., *Nuclear India* (Radiant Publishers: Delhi, 1974), p. 158, quoted in Jones, R. W, 'India', ed. J. Goldblat, *Non-Proliferation: The Why and Wherefore* (Taylor & Francis: London, 1985), p. 109.

[6] Jones (note 5), p. 108. Jones uses data from *Monthly Public Opinion Surveys*, 'Public opinion on India's nuclear device', vol. 19, no. 9 (June 1974), blue supplement, pp. I–XVI.

[7] Kapur (note 2), table 6, p. 181.

[8] Nandy, A., 'The bomb, the NPT and Indian elites', *Economic and Political Weekly*, vol. 7, nos 31–33, Special Number (Aug. 1972).

economic. Nuclear power, nuclear weapons and the grey area in between were a major concern for India in so far as they straddled key questions, such as energy supply and development, defence against China and India's role and voice on the international stage. Starting with the 1946 Baruch Plan for an independent international authority to own and manage all atomic materials, the USA had sought to tackle the problems of horizontal proliferation by curtailing the freedom of action of the non-nuclear states while nuclear weapons commanded a central and enduring position in its own force structure. Above all other states, India has offered an articulate and damaging—or successful, depending upon how the problem is understood—critique of the inevitable contradictions which have emerged.

In 1953, US President Eisenhower put forward his Atoms for Peace Plan, which originally envisaged a new UN agency taking control of fissionable material and using it to aid the developing countries in their search for nuclear energy. The refusal of the USSR to participate resulted in a series of bilateral initiatives between the USA and interested parties. The Indian Government was not able to respond incisively to the Baruch Plan, which came too early, but it could attack the Atoms for Peace proposal. First, for Nehru and Menon, the approach to non-proliferation was influenced by a strong desire on the part of the superpowers to influence and define the emerging rules and norms of how and when developing countries could acquire nuclear technology which hinted much too strongly of neo-colonialism. Second, India was keen to keep its own nuclear options as open as possible and not to allow the superpowers an opportunity to compromise either economic or political security—the question was not just one of sovereignty but one of development as well.[9] Third, India also maintained its principled support for global disarmament, which would include the elimination of superpower weapons, during a period when the superpowers were actively attempting to slip out from under the skirts of the UN to pursue more limited and self-interested arms control agreements. Ironically, the first example of this was the Partial Test Ban Treaty in 1963, an idea first mooted by Nehru in 1954.

In practical terms, India's response to the emerging set of norms over nuclear technology and material transfer took two forms. First, India argued stubbornly against the imposition of safeguards and the role of the IAEA, which were actively supported by both superpowers by the mid-1960s. The fact that Canadian foreign policy was in broad agreement with the Indian view on 'atomic colonialism' and, moreover, held an especially benign view of the needs of developing countries allowed officials in New Delhi to cajole Ottawa into a remarkably loose set of arrangements over the transfer of nuclear technology.[10]

Second, India dispatched V. C. Trivedi to Geneva to argue the Indian case in the Eighteen Nation Committee on Disarmament, a distant relative of the pre-

[9] Kapur (note 2), p. 99.
[10] Kapur (note 2), pp. 105–15.

sent Conference on Disarmament. Trivedi was an articulate expert on the areas which the Indian Government considered as critically important to the avoidance of a complete superpower duopoly over nuclear issues.

Under the guidance of Trivedi, India's nuclear diplomacy took shape between late 1963 and the opening of the NPT in 1968. In this task, Trivedi was well assisted by the Indian Ambassador to the UN, B. N. Chakravarty. What Indian diplomats attempted to do during this crucial period was to change the goalposts set up by the USA. First came an attempt to stand the emerging non-proliferation regime on its head by arguing that the crux of the proliferation problem lay with the nuclear weapon states, rather than with others which might display a future interest in nuclear weapon acquisition. Second, Trivedi argued that non-proliferation had to be accompanied by UN security guarantees for non-nuclear weapon states, presumably in the event of an attempt at nuclear blackmail. Also, in a statement which perhaps only a diplomat could make, Trivedi argued that a regime needed to make a 'clear and unambiguous distinction between the national decisions of countries on the one hand and the obligations to be assumed by them as signatories to an international instrument on the other'.[11] Overall, however, the central message from India was clear—nuclear disarmament by the minority had to be accompanied by nuclear abstention by the majority, and not vice versa.

By the time the NPT opened for signature, Ambassador Trivedi had left Geneva having scored a series of valuable political points which showed the emerging regime more in its true colours. The lack of meaningful movement by either superpower on disarmament commitments or security guarantees gave India two choices. First, it could turn its back on the NPT and walk away from the negative policies the regime represented. The second choice was to attempt to acquire nuclear weapons by instigating a crash plutonium programme or, at the very least, a peaceful nuclear explosion and enter the regime on another level, perhaps.[12] However, despite the best laid plans of Homi Bhabha and his efforts to create a symbiosis between the civil and military sides of the nuclear programme, India was not ready for a nuclear test, politically or technically. In 1972 India completed building the Purnima fast breeder reactor, which presupposes the existence of a plutonium separation plant. Whether or not the separated plutonium was to be used for military or civilian purposes became, from that point on, a political decision.

III. Rejecting the Non-Proliferation Treaty

Given the direction and the well-thought-out nature of India's anti-non-proliferation policy in the 1960s, outright refusal to sign the NPT should have been the natural course of policy, in keeping with the spirit of both sovereignty and non-alignment. Although India did not in the event sign the NPT, the issue

[11] Kapur (note 2), p. 136.
[12] Kapur (note 2), p. 145.

proved not to be so simple. As the treaty was being drawn up, Indian officials managed to instigate some important changes to the final text, which reflected the influence India might wield in the future by opting for a position on the inside of a non-proliferation regime. Many senior bureaucrats were in favour of the treaty and Indira Gandhi was genuinely undecided.[13] Furthermore, to join and then prevaricate over ratification could have expanded the Government's options and provided an effective platform for further anti-superpower statements.

What appears to have persuaded the Prime Minister, who chaired the all-important meetings of the Emergency Committee of the Cabinet (ECC), was that the majority of decision makers and opinion shapers did not want to sign the NPT, albeit for radically different reasons. On the one hand, a powerful group of hawks drawn from several different quarters were beginning to shape opinion in favour of the bomb: figures such as K. Subrahmanyam, Raj Krishna, Sisir Gupta, Y. B. Chavan, and Vikram Sarabhai.[14] On the other, the Gandhian pacifists, such as Morarji Desai, remained passionately in favour of India not developing nuclear weapons but equally firm in the belief that the NPT could not be signed because of its discriminatory nature. The Prime Minister would also have been acutely aware of the opinion polls which in 1968 showed a 79 per cent majority in favour of the nuclear option.[15] (Indeed, the very fact that opinion polls were concerned so much with the nuclear issue was evidence in itself of how important a question it was for the voting public.)

The eventual decision to remain outside the Non-Proliferation regime may well have been that of a young and inexperienced Prime Minister, taken for the reasons presented to her by the opinion polls and the inner sanctum of advisers. Indira Gandhi may have thought that the political cost and effort entailed in signing were not worth the time and trouble that would have been required to win over the electorate and the hawks in the interests of international peace and disarmament.

In addition, however pragmatic her decision may have been, it was also the combination of many years of sophisticated political debate pertaining to the nature of power and influence within the post-war international system. For India, the NPT was a microcosm of the imbalance and the ethnicity which pervaded thinking about international relations and, therefore, the structure of the international system. While the nuclear five had considered the nuclear option sufficiently tempting and useful to pursue with vigour during the immediate post-war period, the superpowers and the UK (China and France stayed outside the NPT until 1991) then demanded that the rest of the world eschew an option which still contained the same economic, military and political advantages. Furthermore, in the absence of a binding commitment to nuclear disarmament,

---

[13] Jones (note 5), p. 110.

[14] K. Subrahmanyam, founder member and Director of the Institute for Defence Studies and Analysis; Raj Krishna, prominent Indian economist and author of *Hindi Rate of Growth*; Sisir Gupta, Ambassador to North Viet Nam and international relations expert; Y. B. Chavan, Congress Party Minister of Home Affairs; and Vikram Sarabhai, Secretary for Atomic Energy and successor to Homi Bhabha.

[15] Jones (note 5), p. 108.

and with two of the five nuclear weapon states outside the regime, the effect of wholesale support for the regime would have been to endow the international, bipolar, system with a degree of rigidity that would have severely curtailed India's freedom of action. India, arguably sixth in line for nuclear status, could not agree to such a discriminatory policy; whether or not the nuclear option was to be pursued, it had to be kept open. Perhaps the most interesting and illustrative aspect of this perspective can be seen in those who adopted a stance which was anti-bomb on the one hand and anti-NPT on the other. The anti-bomb sentiment was most prevalent among élites and stemmed from several quarters, notably the Gandhian legacy of pacifism, the Nehru legacy of internationalism and the neo-Gandhian/neo-Marxist ideas which resulted. The middle classes have always been pro-bomb.

During the 1960s and 1970s, the NPT was something of an arms control flagship. It represented a carefully negotiated though highly compromised treaty designed to prevent the horizontal spread of nuclear weapons. Above all it possessed an element of meaning and reality which the rather cosmetic strategic arms limitation talks lacked.

Although the Indian Government did not accept the fundamental principles upon which the regime was founded, there was nevertheless a strong element of partnership and common cause which underpinned the Treaty, without which success in any shape or form would have been impossible. This rested on a fundamental clause which required the states in possession of nuclear weapons to make every effort at the earliest date to reduce their stockpiles of nuclear weapons.[16] Or, to put it another way, the non-nuclear weapon states would only forgo the option to go nuclear on the understanding that meaningful and discernible disarmament measures would be taken by China, France, the UK and the superpowers. The Treaty did also allow a signatory the right to withdraw if threats to national security made this necessary.[17]

Indian public opinion and voices within government doubted the sincerity of this commitment to partnership, a view which was more than vindicated in later years given the persistent prevarication over East–West arms control issues, recent agreements notwithstanding. The issue of reciprocity has always been a fundamental sticking-point in NPT review conferences, which are held every five years. Currently, concern over this issue centres upon the need for a Comprehensive Test Ban Treaty (CTBT). This was certainly the issue which prevented a satisfactory conclusion to the fourth Review Conference in 1990.[18]

---

[16] Article VI: 'Each of the parties to the treaty undertakes to pursue negotiations in good faith on effective measures relating to cessation of the nuclear arms race at an early date and to nuclear disarmament, and on a treaty on general and complete disarmament under strict and effective international control'.

[17] Article X.1: 'Each party shall in exercising its national sovereignty have the right to withdraw from the treaty if it decides that extraordinary events, related to the subject-matter of this Treaty, have jeopardized the supreme interests of its country.'

[18] For an excellent analysis of this conflict, see Fischer, D. and Müller, H., 'The fourth review of the Non-Proliferation Treaty', in *SIPRI Yearbook 1991*: *World Armaments and Disarmament* (Oxford University Press: Oxford, 1991), pp. 555–84.

However, given the changed international situation, it is unlikely to mar the 1995 Extension Conference as was once feared.

With the benefit of hindsight, therefore, it would seem that however logical the decision was to stay outside the regime, outside was to become an awkward place to be. At no point did this become more obvious than after the end of the cold war, when the USA decided that the way was clear to apply the maximum leverage against the 'hold-out' states.

IV. 'Pokhran'—India's nuclear test

On 18 May 1974 India exploded a plutonium device with a yield of 12–15 kilotons of TNT equivalent—approximately the same as the bomb dropped on Hiroshima. After the explosion the Ministry of Foreign Affairs received what became one of the more celebrated telegrams in international history which simply read, 'The Buddha is Smiling.' Prime Minister Gandhi was present at the test. It has perhaps had greater significance for the rest of the world than any other event in the country's independent history. It sent shock waves through the international system and radically altered India's relations with the superpowers.

There is no single explanation for the decision to carry out a nuclear test and the motivation was probably a mix of several factors. First, India had never really seemed to lose the political will to make a statement such as this, even after the death of Bhabha. Both inside and outside government it was an extremely popular decision because it displayed so much to the outside world— technological acumen, development and independence with the necessary degree of aggression. In a post-test opinion poll 90 per cent of respondents were proud of the event and thought that India's international prestige had been enhanced.[19] As the Prime Minister mused some years later, 'it was done despite the big powers trying to prevent India . . . The developing countries congratulated us'.[20]

Second, the mix of regional and international events which took place in the early 1970s made such a statement an appropriate gesture. Following the comprehensive defeat by India in 1971, Pakistan decided to pursue a nuclear weapon programme. Coupled with the US tilt towards Pakistan to facilitate elements of the new policy towards China, India needed to remind itself and the rest of the world that it was still an important actor in Asia.

Third, there may well have been a pronounced domestic angle to the test. Several considerations were of relevance here. During the early 1970s the Congress Party split, with Mrs Gandhi's faction—Congress(I)—emerging head and shoulders above the disaffected old guard, led by Morarji Desai, a seasoned anti-nuclear (and anti-NPT) supporter. With the Nehruvian group of equivocators discarded, the political cost of a nuclear test was greatly diminished. The

[19] Kaul, R., *India's Nuclear Spin Off* (Chanakya: Allahabad, 1974), p. 29.
[20] Rodney Jones, personal interview with Indira Gandhi, in Jones (note 5), p. 114.

decision as to timing could have been taken with a view to overshadowing political opposition: the decision in principle to conduct a test was taken in 1971, but there was no logical reason why May 1974 should be the preferred date except possibly that the Congress(I) Government was reeling under the effects of a national rail strike and centre–state tensions persisted with the governments of Bihar and Gujarat. Additional bureaucratic support may have stemmed from the desire not to eliminate a major counter-balance to the poor performance of the nuclear energy industry: while the bomb option is kept open the nuclear energy programme must continue.

The significance of the test was essentially political rather than military. Few pundits outside India doubted the country's ability to pursue a nuclear programme but the majority were surprised by the timing. On the international stage, the fall-out was considerable. The plutonium for the test could only have come from reprocessing spent fuel from the RAPP I reactor at the Tarapur reprocessing plant. India had acquired the CIRUS reactor in 1955 from Canada, on extremely beneficial terms, financial and otherwise.

The process by which Indian officials prised the technology out of Canada and then explained away the nuclear test was a diplomatic exercise of the highest order. From the outset, Homi Bhabha argued that India should attempt to obtain Canadian deuterium-uranium (CANDU) technology, which relied on natural uranium, whereas RAPP I, India's first atomic power station, relied on US-supplied enriched uranium and was therefore subject to safeguards. However, during the mid-1960s when a fault occurred with the Canadian-supplied fuel rods installed in RAPP I, Indian scientists managed to replace the defective rods with indigenous replacements.

Canada was extremely accommodating over the supply of nuclear technology. Athough Ottawa demanded safeguards, India managed to extract an agreement whereby only Canada could inspect RAPP I, and, moreover, the relationship would be reciprocal giving India the right to inspect certain Canadian facilities. The cost of the reactor, $5 million, was paid for under the Colombo Plan, a multilateral aid programme involving Canada, several other OECD countries and a number of states throughout Asia.

In the agreement between Canada and India, there were several references to the peaceful uses of nuclear technology. While India agreed to use the CANDU reactor for peaceful purposes only, it was only prepared to extend such an agreement to the pieces of the nuclear jigsaw supplied directly by Canada. This did not cover the plutonium separation plant built indigenously between 1961 and 1964 at the Bhabha Atomic Research Centre.[21] Nor, presumably, did this extend to the indigenous fuel rods.

Understandably, the Canadian Government felt deeply let down and humiliated by the Pokhran test, especially as Prime Minister Pierre Trudeau had gone to great pains during his 1971 visit to warn India against conducting a nuclear

[21] Kapur (note 2), pp. 105–15, 195–98; Hart, D., 'India', ed. H. Müller, *A European Non-Proliferation Policy* (Clarendon Press: Oxford, 1987), p. 138.

test. The Canadian voting public was also less than amused. Soon after the tes
the Canadian Secretary of State for External Affairs issued a firm statement o
protest which concluded:

[Canada] fully respects India's sovereignty and independence in all matters. It cannot
however, be expected to assist and subsidize, directly or indirectly, a nuclear pro
gramme which, in a key respect, undermines the position which Canada has for a lon{
time been firmly convinced is best for world peace and security.[22]

Two years later the Canadians withdrew all co-operation on and assistance tc
India's nuclear energy programme. Adverse reactions also came from severa.
other countries—Japan, the Netherlands, Sweden, the UK, the USA and, o{
course, Pakistan. In France, however, the Chairman of the Atomic Energy
Commission sent a telegram of congratulation to his Indian counterpart.
Surprisingly, China greeted the event with indifference.[23]

   The USA had trained more than 1300 nuclear scientists and technicians from
India and had also extended subsidized loans and research grants for both
applied and pure research in this area. The USA thereafter refused to supply
spare parts and enriched uranium for RAPP I, and in so doing revoked the
bilateral agreement of 1963 which extended US co-operation in nuclear energy
for 30 years, an issue which has conditioned the two countries' relations ever
since. France had also entered into similar agreements but showed altogether
less concern than the two North American states.[24]

   The Indian Government's somewhat weak protest that the test had been conducted without any form of foreign assistance made little difference. In the
space of two years India had lost most of the foreign assistance for its nuclear
energy programme. Although the programme continued, rigorous sanctions,
lack of sufficient foreign expertise, the dispersal of many bright young Indian
scientists to the West and pronounced managerial problems combined to slow
the pace of the Indian nuclear programme to a virtual standstill by the turn of
the decade.[25]

V. Nuclear policy under the Janata regime

During the Janata period a very different policy towards nuclear weapons was
articulated, although it is possible that this was more a matter of form than of
content. In keeping with the overall strategy of negating the policies adopted by
Indira Gandhi, Prime Minister Desai attempted initially to reject unequivocally
not just the nuclear option but nuclear testing as well. This was in part an
attempt to win back the technical co-operation lost from the USA, although

[22] SIPRI, 'Nuclear weapon proliferation', *SIPRI Yearbook 1975: World Armaments and Disarmament*
(MIT Press: London, 1975), p. 16–22.
[23] Hart (note 21), p. 144.
[24] Weissman, S. and Crossley, H., *The Islamic Bomb* (Times Books: New York, 1981), p. 131.
[25] In 1970 the Department of Atomic Energy estimated that India would have 2700 MW of installed
nuclear power capacity. By 1980 installed capacity was no more than 240 MW.

President Carter was less than accommodating on this issue. A second blow to the nuclear energy programme came in 1978 when the Carter Administration steered through the Nuclear Non-Proliferation Act which institutionalized his reservations and precluded the transfer of nuclear technology or material to countries which refused full-scope safeguards, namely, open inspection on all nuclear facilities at any time. Desai attempted to invoke the traditional framework through an offer to accept full-scope safeguards if the nuclear weapons states began to dismantle their nuclear weapons. Somewhat predictably, this led to a US ban on US nuclear supplies to India, although all were content to see France fill the gap.

The Janata Party's stance was also a reflection of Desai's deep commitment to the ideals of pacifism, internationalism and, perhaps, prudent housekeeping as well.[26] In June 1978 Desai announced that India would no longer engage in nuclear testing, whatever the policies of other countries—the 1974 test had prompted Pakistan to step up the military dimension of its nuclear programme, which had first become evident in 1971.[27] Strong political objections from within Janata and other political parties forced a volte-face, and a month later Desai was forced not to rule out the possibility of testing for peaceful purposes; three days later, however, he directly contradicted himself and gave assurances that under no circumstances would nuclear testing take place, at least while the Janata Party was in power.[28]

With the benefit of hindsight, the 1974 nuclear test was a major political mistake for India, although at the time the scale and intensity of international condemnation and the sanctions which followed could not have been clearly foreseen. It brought India dangerously close to pariah status and destroyed much of the country's credibility throughout the world, which Nehru had worked so hard to cultivate. This apart, however, it is apparent that the motivation behind the nuclear test was primarily if not exclusively political. At no point does it seem that military considerations and problems were considered and no discussion appears to have taken place between government and the military as to exactly what the country would do with such a capability once a positive decision had been taken to produce nuclear weapons. This was perhaps because the armed forces are less enthusiastic about a nuclear India than their civilian counterparts. Not only would a nuclear arsenal cut deep into the procurement budget and reduce the resources available for conventional defence, but, equally important, the military would effectively lose a degree of power, because the threat of or actual use of countervalue nuclear weapons is more a political than a military decision. Nor was there then or has there been since

[26] Subsequent estimates of the scale of financial resources required suggest that the government would have to find an extra $15 billion over a 10-year period to fund an unambiguous nuclear weapon programme. See Sen Gupta, B., *Nuclear Weapons: Policy Options for India* (Centre for Policy Research/Sage Publications: New Delhi, 1983), pp. 23–27.

[27] The literature on Pakistan's nuclear weapon programme is extensive. However, for a succinct review of the programme, see Kapur, A., *Pakistan's Nuclear Development* (Croom Helm: London, 1987) and the regular reports written by Leonard Spector of the Carnegie Endowment for International Peace.

[28] Thomas, R. G. C., *Indian Security Policy* (Princeton University Press: Princeton, N.J., 1986), p. 108.

any discussion concerning the assimilation of nuclear weapons into the Indian defence forces—which service would assume control, how conventional and nuclear forces would interface and how deterrent capability could be maximized.[29] Perhaps for this reason, some of the country's most senior Army officers have gone on record as saying that conventional forces alone can ensure India's security.[30] That is, of course, unless the IAF and/or the Navy have been quietly led to understand that they will control India's independent nuclear deterrent.

VI. Nuclear issues in the 1980s

India entered the 1980s with, in all probability, enough plutonium to provide the material for up to 80 nuclear warheads.[31] However, by the 1980s nuclear proliferation was no longer an issue just to use as a foreign policy tool. Over the 1970s and 1980s Pakistan made impressive strides towards acquiring its own nuclear capability through clandestine means. International concern gave India the opportunity to protest that it was Pakistan rather than India which was leading the nuclear arms race in the sub-continent. Beyond that, however, there was real concern in New Delhi about what these recent developments might mean.

The result was to pursue a policy of nuclear ambiguity, a policy much favoured by Israel and also adopted by Pakistan, to excellent effect.[32] Throughout the decade national leaders stated their personal willingness to sanction the nuclear option if it became clear that Pakistan was on the brink or worse. How long this would take is open to speculation, but most agree that India could assemble nuclear weapons in a very short space of time, given its apparent 'last wire unconnected' policy. Soon after her re-election in 1980 Prime Minister Gandhi told the Rajya Sabha (the upper house of parliament) that India would continue to test if such an activity were deemed to be in the national interest.[33] The *New York Times* of 28 April 1981 reported that India was planning a second test in response to Pakistan's nuclear activities. Soon after, however, in keeping with the requirement for a policy based upon ambiguity, Prime Minister Gandhi told a press conference that, first, 'we do not believe in the deterrent theory', and, second, 'we do not know how it would help if India is to have nuclear weapons'.[34] In 1983 the test issue was raised once again, this time by the *Washington Post*, which alleged that additional shafts had been prepared

---

[29] The concept of assimilation is explored in Dupoy, T. N., *The Evolution of Weapons and Warfare* (Hero Books: Fairfax, Va., 1984), p. 301.

[30] Hart (note 21), p. 143.

[31] Spector, L., *The Undeclared Bomb: The Spread of Nuclear Weapons, 1987–1988* (Ballinger Publishing Co.: New York, 1988), p. 93.

[32] For an analysis of the Pakistani approach to ambiguity, see Smith, C., 'A policy of ambiguity? Nuclear proliferation in South Asia', *ADIU Report,* vol. 9, no. 4 (July/Aug. 1987), pp. 1–4.

[33] Nayer, K., 'India would explode a nuclear device', *The Times,* 14 Mar. 1980.

[34] 'N.-deterrent policy not for India: Mrs Gandhi points to F-16 threat', *The Statesman,* 11 Aug. 1981.

at the Pokhran test site.[35] However, the commitment to reserve the right to continue tests was reiterated several years later, in 1986, for the same reasons.[36]

In 1987 the situation took a definitive turn with statements made by both A. Q. Khan, head of the Pakistan nuclear programme, and General Zia. The intimation that Pakistan possessed nuclear weapons and the fact that it was prepared to drop heavy hints to the international press to that effect were probably well-timed, daring moves to ensure maximum chaos, confusion and double-speak during a time when the US Congress was assessing Pakistan for additional military and economic aid.[37] Thereafter, received wisdom began confidently to predict that Pakistan was around or even over the nuclear threshold, which implied access to the necessary amount of highly enriched uranium from the Kahuta plant.

Throughout the 1980s, Prime Minister Gandhi, followed by her son Rajiv, seemed content to allow the proliferation question to move of its own accord and with its own momentum. The reason for this lacuna in policy was the clear advantage gained by both sides by tacitly advancing nuclear postures based upon ambiguity. In the aftermath of the Khan/Zia statements, Defence Minister K. C. Pant stated in April 1988 that India had not allowed a window of vulnerability to develop and that Indian armed forces would not be at a disadvantage in the face of a nuclear attack by Pakistan. This was followed by a similar statement from science bureaucrat Raja Ramanna to the effect that India could retaliate in kind if faced with a nuclear attack.[38] Beyond this, however, there was little to be gained. Assuming that both sides now possessed a nuclear capability, and given the reluctance to indicate to each other exactly how and when nuclear weapons might come into play (because this probably had not been thought through by either), the political costs of admission now massively outweighed the military benefits.

During the late 1980s Pakistan trod an extremely fine line by combining an aggressive nuclear policy with continued reliance upon the USA for military and economic aid, but not without success. In the near certain knowledge that Pakistan would slip down if not off the US strategic agenda once the USSR abandoned its hopeless mission in Afghanistan, minimizing thereby the possibility of making capital from those in Congress who felt that removing the USSR from Afghanistan should take precedence over horizontal nuclear proliferation, the Pakistan Government endeavoured successfully to gain wider acceptance of its ambiguous stance on nuclear weapons. This policy was also to the benefit of India. Statements to the effect that the nuclear weapon option was still open, or a new-found openness and confidence on the part of India's nuclear hawks, became increasingly accepted elements of the nuclear equation in South Asia and also justified to a certain degree India's refusal to enter into

[35] Balasubramaniam, V., 'India preparing for 2nd n-test, says US paper', *Hindustan Times*, 24 June 1983.

[36] *The Observer*, 11 May 1986.

[37] For an analysis of Pakistan's motivation for this new approach, see Smith (note 32).

[38] Vohra, A. M., 'Covert nuclear status suits India', *Times of India*, 24 Jan. 1991.

arms control talks with Pakistan. Yet, at the same time, India could avoid the act of final admission.

However, as the international system began to change dramatically towards the end of the decade, so did perceptions over the legitimacy of actions on the part of the hold-out states.

VII. India, nuclear proliferation and the new world order

India's nuclear weapon policy in the early 1990s should also be understood in the context of the momentous changes which occurred in the international system over this period. As the USSR effectively abandoned its role of major superpower, the implications for India, and other close Soviet allies in the Third World, were considerable. In effect, much of what has since happened in the Middle East and parts of Sub-Saharan Africa can be traced, directly or indirectly, to the diminution of the former USSR's global role. For India the collapse of the USSR has been a major consideration in terms of access to advanced military technology. For two decades the Kremlin had been the favoured source of advanced and affordable conventional military technology; no other supplier would be prepared to transfer nuclear-powered submarines or state-of-the-art front-line aircraft for so little remuneration and so few political returns. Politically, India is still coming to terms with the implications of the demise of the USSR. The most that can be said at this point is that the nuclear lobby seems somewhat chastened, unsure in which direction to go but certain that a new direction must be found sooner or later.

Alignment, it may be argued, was a genuine alternative to both overt nuclear proliferation and unacceptable levels of defence expenditure, particularly given Pakistan's relationship with the USA. Security guarantees, both explicit and implicit, were the key benefit to be reaped from alignment. For India and Pakistan, the involvement of China, the USSR and the USA in the South Asian security scenario provided the political equivalent of strategic deterrence—the underlying threat of massive retaliation. Without the USSR, India will consider itself more exposed and vulnerable, even though this might not be the case. Weapons of mass destruction are one means of filling this vacuum, albeit a negative one, but this may not be allowed by those who want India to stay a non-nuclear power.

Operation Desert Storm revealed just how far Iraq, a signatory of the NPT, had progressed down the path to a covert nuclear weapon capability. The world was shocked, and worried, not least because of the evidence of how complacent and maladroit France, Germany and others had been in the export of sensitive equipment to Baghdad. If, therefore, a signatory to the NPT could progress this far, how much less difficult had it been for the hold-out states, such as India and Pakistan?

This followed a more general pre-Persian Gulf War agreement within the US Administration to confront the nuclear proliferation problem with greater resolve. During the Reagan years, the Administration's attitude towards non-proliferation was decidely pessimistic, which led, in turn, to *laissez-faire* policies. The Bush Administration breathed new life into US non-proliferation policy, which became further energized after the end of the cold war and again after the Persian Gulf War.[39] Whether or not the Bush Administration really understood the problem is, however, open to question; evidence from several quarters suggests that while the spectre of proliferation remains a major threat to the stability and safety of the international system, the current situation is somewhat less portentous than was assumed throughout 1991. While Iraq had established a uranium enrichment programme, it had not yet reached the critical stage of enrichment cascading, namely, setting up a large number of centrifuges to operate in tandem.[40] Similarly, recent fears over the North Korean nuclear programme seem equally overstated, according to a recent evaluation within the USA.[41]

The combination of the USSR's collapse and all that the Allied victory in the Middle East implied was perceived by the Bush Administration as giving it authority to design and implement a new world order—Pax Americana—witness the tough policy adopted towards Israel in pursuit of a Middle East peace plan. In terms of conventional arms control, and given the evidence which the Iraqi example provides, the emphasis so far has been on an increased vigilance to prevent the 'right' military technology from reaching the 'wrong' arsenals. There is no intention here on the part of the USA to foreswear arms sales or halt the international arms trade, as the clear intention to sell Saudi Arabia the F-15 confirms. Instead the policy is geared to transparency and control and, specifically, the Bush Administration attempted to push members of the UN Security Council into a position which compelled them to hold 'meaningful consultation' on arms sales.[42]

In late 1993, after almost a year, President Clinton's foreign policy still appears to lack identity. In part, this is due to the new Administration's campaign promise to tackle head-on the country's escalating domestic problems. It is also due to a genuine confusion in the US Government over how to understand and interpret the evolving international order—witness the confusion in Bosnia and Somalia—and what type of resource the USA should commit to upholding its role as world policeman during a period when its own society is in desperate need of political and economic investment. On the question of arms sales, Clinton's policy will differ from that of his predecessor only in the number of countries likely to be restricted from receiving US defence technology. Recent defence cuts mean that the USA will have to maintain or even increase arms exports but not by so much as to return to the open season permitted by the Reagan Administration.

[39] Graham, T. W., 'Winning the nonproliferation battle', *Arms Control Today,* Sep. 1991, p. 9.
[40] *PPNN Newsbrief,* no. 17 (spring 1992), p. 13.
[41] Chanda, N., 'Atomic ambivalence', *Far Eastern Economic Review,* vol. 155, no. 39 (1 Oct. 1992), pp. 8–10.
[42] See '"Perm five" experts faced with difficult arms trade issues', BASIC Reports on European Arms Control, no. 20 (British American Security Information Council: London, 19 Feb. 1992).

However, it is not clear which countries are trustworthy and which might evolve as Iran and Iraq have done in the past, and this is of considerable importance for New Delhi. The fact that vast amounts of advanced weapons are flowing into the Gulf region and will continue to do so testifies to the problems and contradictions facing US policy makers, or to extraordinary faith in the longevity of the House of Saud. At the same time there is a growing suspicion against the majority of countries of what was the non-aligned Third World—all medium powers are potential Iraqs, and all national leaders are potential Saddams. The policy is a crude one and lends support to a long-held view that senior US policy makers care less than they should about the heterogeneity and inherent subtleties of the southern hemisphere.

In March 1992 the Indian Government attempted to open a bilateral dialogue with the USA over the nuclear question.[43] Talks did take place but the outcome seemed to be of little real use to either side. The rhetoric remained the same on the Indian side and progress is unlikely unless New Delhi is prepared to undertake a significant shift away from its traditional policies. Throughout 1992 US policy towards India became more focused, following on from the decision to block military and economic aid to Pakistan under the terms of the Pressler Amendment. The USA is keen to be seen to be even-handed, which further increases the momentum to pursue India on the nuclear question.

Given the clear intention of the USA to slow the Indian missile programme, primarily through the restriction of specific technologies in line with the principles of the Missile Technology Control Regime (MTCR), India turned to Russia to provide the space technology it required. In May 1992, after a series of shots across the bows, the USA moved against both India and Russia. The Indian Space Research Organisation (ISRO) was banned from receiving any imports or contracts from the USA and the same sanctions were applied to Glavkosmos of Russia.[44] In July 1993 the USA and Russia came to an agreement to break the impasse. Russia's future potential as as an independent defence exporter is of obvious concern during a period when the country has all too little to export. Therefore, it was always unlikely that Russia would concede to the demands from Washington. As a compromise the USA agreed to allow Russia to export the engines but not the technology. In return, to allay Russian fears that that the USA is attempting to diminish Russia's potential in the international technology and defence market, Russia has been allowed to bid competitively to provide services on as many as eight US-made satellite launchers.[45]

The ban on rocket technology was accompanied by a parallel move on the part of the USA to invoke US Trade Law Special 301, aimed at the protection of intellectual property rights, an issue which had been under close consideration for many months. The USA is arguing that the Indian Government has failed to protect US intellectual property rights. Indian patent legislation only

---

[43] McGirk, T., 'India woos US with promise of nuclear discussion', *The Independent* , 13 Mar. 1992.

[44] Adhikari, G., 'US slaps 2-year ban on ISRO, Glavkosmos', *Times of India,* 12 May 1992.

[45] Robbins, C. A. and Rosewicz, B., 'US and Russia settle dispute over missiles', *Wall Street Journal Europe*, 19 July 1993.

provides protection for between five and seven years for drugs and chemicals. Furthermore, pharmaceutical patents only cover the process by which drugs are produced, which allows Indian companies the opportunity to apply reverse engineering to produce cheap drugs by introducing a minimal change into the production process.[46] Indian companies are at liberty to produce and export goods in ways which would be illegal elsewhere. Effectively, India stands accused of stealing US intellectual property rights and exporting goods to the USA based upon this theft.[47] In late April 1992 the Bush Administration withdrew the duty-free generalized system of preferences accorded to the Indian pharmaceuticals and chemicals exported to the USA: these included antibiotic, chemotherapeutic and anti-parasitic drugs and represented a market worth about $60 million per annum to India. The Administration justified this step on the basis of India's continuing failure to legislate in favour of US patents. Shortly afterwards, the USA opposed India's application to the Asian Development Bank for a soft loan facility.[48]

The response of the Indian Government was uncompromising. US pressure on India became a major justification for the Agni test in May 1992. The Agni is an intermediate-range ballistic missile (IRBM) and the press and public opinion was wholly in favour of the move: 'The Narasimha Rao Government is not particularly brave, but faced with a barrage of criticism for going soft on the U.S., it considers it politically expedient to go ahead.'[49]

Quite how India will heal the growing rift with Washington remains to be seen. Publicly, and more so than ever before, the Government has no room for manœuvre—it cannot openly respond to US pressure. Behind the scenes, however, some form of compromise seems likely. This could possibly take the form of allowing outside observers access to nuclear facilities. The Clinton Administration may prove more forgiving—Democratic administrations tend to favour India over Pakistan—which could result in the whole issue being placed on the back burner. Conceivably, Prime Minister Narasimha Rao may have accepted that the traditional nuclear stance is not worth the political and economic cost, and he may be able to offer the USA enough under the table to defuse the situation, without being forced into a public admission. Nevertheless, Rao's hand would be strengthened enormously by positive movement at the international level, especially towards a CTBT.

Although the October 1993 Chinese nuclear test was a set-back for the prospects for a CTBT, because the USA is legally compelled to continue preparations for testing in the event of a development such as this, nevertheless, the future looks brighter under the Clinton Administration where there appears to be a sincere commitment to see the successful negotiation of a treaty.

---

[46] 'Warning shots', *The Economist*, vol. 323, no. 7758 (9–15 May 1992).

[47] Adhikari, G., 'Special 301: US retaliates against India', *Times of India,* 30 Apr. 1992.

[48] 'US opposed to ADB soft loan for India; Japan sympathetic', *Economic Times,* 4 May 1992.

[49] Joshi, M., 'A partial success: Agni's second test firing', *Frontline*, vol. 9, no. 12 (19 June 1992), p. 118.

VIII. India, nuclear weapons and the NPT in the 1990s

The NPT has been transformed in recent months. Up until late 1990 several key countries—Argentina, Brazil, China, France, Israel, India, Pakistan and South Africa—remained outside the NPT, and all bar China and France were widely thought to be keeping open the nuclear weapon option or engaging in clandestine development. Since then, this list has been shortened significantly. In July 1991 South Africa acceded to the NPT, which was followed one month later by a bilateral nuclear accounting and control agreement between Argentina and Brazil. Both have also agreed to full-scope safeguards.[50] Israel, it may be argued, has been constrained as never before by the Bush Administration's leverage over economic aid, particularly the amounts needed for the absorption of Russian Jews: quite what the ramifications of this will be for Israel's defence policy and posture remains to be seen.

Also during 1991 both France and China agreed to accede to the NPT, thereby placing all the nuclear powers and several new states under the terms of the Treaty. On the other hand, some of the fundamental problems underlying the regime have not been addressed. Initially, both the UK and the USA have stated without equivocation that a ban on testing is considered to be detrimental to their security which meant that a CTBT was some way off the agenda. Nor is France likely to cease testing now that it has become an NPT signatory. However, although significant progress towards a CTBT has been made by the new Clinton Administration it remains unclear whether these efforts will succeed and overcome both domestic and international pressures to slow the momentum.

Of greatest significance, perhaps, is the future of the NPT after the end of the system of bipolarity. Previously, any deviation by either superpower could be countered by the other. Now the situation is very different, witness the head of steam which built up temporarily in favour of military intervention in North Korea to destroy its nuclear weapon programme.[51] There is also a growing trend to link economic aid and accession to the NPT, a concept currently favoured by opinion shapers such as Robert McNamara and by Japan and Germany. Under the new regime, therefore, efforts to prevent the proliferation of nuclear weapons are likely to be based far more upon coercion, threat and denial, which will transform the regime into a very different animal. Key actors are currently talking much less about conflict resolution, confidence building and regional security accords. Never before has faith in political processes in the southern hemisphere been so low.

Although India continues to remain outside the NPT, events within that regime have a direct bearing upon its nuclear weapon and foreign policies.

---

[50] Fischer, D., 'Nuclear non-proliferation: the prospects for the non-proliferation regime after the Gulf War', *Energy Policy,* July 1992, pp. 672–82.

[51] See the tone and direction of the recent (21 Nov. 1991) House Foreign Affairs Committee, Asian and Pacific Affairs Subcommittee on North Korea's nuclear programme, which included statements in favour of outright intervention.

Certainly the Nehruvian basis of India's hold-out policy is now much less understood than it ever was—inside or outside India—and few now believe that India has any meaningful intention on arms control or disarmament. The tone of the editorials in the Indian newspapers in the early 1990s reflects an imperious attitude to the nuclear issue and would seem to confirm the pro-nuclear feeling in the country at large.

Recent changes in the international system have been far from benign for India. At the same time, India has for many years been its own worst enemy on the nuclear question, and it may soon pay the price of four decades of double-speak, power seeking and thinly veiled arrogance about whether or not to pursue the nuclear option. Basing a policy on ambiguity can be effective in the short term, as both India and Pakistan discovered in the 1980s. Over time, however, the USA became impatient with Pakistan, and when general conditions permitted aid was unceremoniously curtailed by the use of the Pressler Amendment, which is widely taken as confirmation that Pakistan had nuclear weapons. Since then, India has also come under the US spotlight and narrowly missed falling foul of the Foreign Assistance Authorization Bill. These developments have left India badly exposed. It cannot now reverse its ambiguity and call for a nuclear weapon-free zone in South Asia: rather it has had to advance its position and indicate to Pakistan and its own public that a form of parity still exists. This in turn offers the most conclusive proof that India has pursued one of three options: (*a*) it has possessed bombs 'in the basement' since 1974; (*b*) it went over the threshold in the late 1980s; or (*c*) it is actively connecting the last wires. Any one of these scenarios would be enough to justify US policy.

In the face of all these developments, India has very few policy options. It cannot now join the NPT: this would cause a public outcry and require an acceptance of full-scope safeguards, which India has spent decades arguing against. It cannot overtly pursue nuclear development: German and Japanese aid would be cut and multilateral aid placed in jeopardy. Such an act on the part of India would also be destabilizing *vis-à-vis* both China and Pakistan. Because India has consistently rejected bilateral or multilateral talks with Pakistan it will find it very difficult to initiate a regional solution, without serious loss of face and without arousing a great deal of suspicion. For example, over the course of non-official talks, involving intellectuals and opinion shapers from both sides, the feeling among the Pakistanis is that India is doing no more than stalling for time.

The chances of India acceding to the NPT being extremely remote, the alternative, in the interests of stability and of reducing pressure from the USA, could be a bilateral agreement with Pakistan, along the lines of the Argentina–Brazil solution. Although India may be forced to move in one or other direction in the future, and the demise of the USSR has been a genuine shock to the system, it has not been followed by anything like the hard thinking and collective soul-searching which is surely necessary to resolve this intensely complex problem. It may well be the case that India's refusal to accede to the NPT is primarily a problem for the West and not for India or other states in South Asia.

However, events are now moving quickly and in a decisive direction and New Delhi must be careful not to be wrong-footed.

Increasingly, India will find itself in an impossible position when it comes to confront the nuclear issue; the expression 'between a rock and a hard place' springs to mind. Without fundamental changes in foreign policy and public opinion, it cannot accede to the NPT. As the NPT changes further in character and intent, India's options will narrow and it may be given some very hard choices if Germany, Japan and the USA do link economic aid to the non-proliferation regime and reduce aid, and the economy continues to decline. India's central problem is one of possessing a nuclear capability but not knowing how to proceed from there. The root of the dilemma can be found in the past—equivocation, sharp practice and political petulance. Without doubt, the problems are mostly of the Indian élites' own making, as far back as Nehru.

Ironically, the nuclear ambition which was designed to place India at the top table may do the very opposite. If the number of permanent members of the Security Council is to be increased, the most favoured candidates are Brazil, Germany, India and Japan. If India cannot normalize the nuclear issue in the sub-continent, it will not be a popular choice for such a revered position. This would mean outright declaration of possession of nuclear weapons, which would be counter-productive as it would certainly preclude an early invitation from the Security Council. On the other hand, India could join the NPT and allow full inspection of its nuclear facilities, but in doing this it would pay a price other permanent members have so far avoided. Nor is there much chance that the world will sit idly by if India does declare itself the sixth nuclear power. Increasingly, steps towards renunciation at regional level and bilateral negotiations with Pakistan, coupled perhaps with covert verification, would be in India's best interests. In order to take these steps, however, Narasimha Rao or his successor must first orchestrate a major political debate aimed at reversing the tide of the pro-nuclear lobby. This will take time and political capital, and Rao has few reserves of either.

IX. Nuclear stability in South Asia

Despite the concern over the nuclear situation in South Asia, there is some evidence that the West has misunderstood the current situation in both India and Pakistan. On both sides of the divide, senior officials hold a relaxed view of the problem. For India, especially, the problem is pressure from the international community. K. Subrahmanyam wrily observed in early 1992: 'I find our politicians are more interested in not signing the NPT than in the Pakistani threat.'[52]

The reason for this relaxed view on both sides comes from the belief that both sides have stopped short of nuclear weaponization and assimilation, due either to technical shortcomings or to conscious decisions. Senior policy

[52] McDonald, H., 'Destroyer of worlds: concerns grow over nuclear arms potential', *Far Eastern Economic Review*, vol. 155, no. 17 (30 Apr. 1992), p. 24.

makers seem to take the view that a form of deterrence already exists but at the level of mutual capability rather than mutual assured destruction. Moreover, neither side really shows much enthusiasm—at this point—for weaponization.[53] From an economic point of view, the programme would be too expensive. Possibly there are technical constraints, particularly on the Pakistani side. There also seems to be an acceptance that the actual use of nuclear weapons would be of minimal military value at enormous political cost. India risks destroying sacred Sikh *gurwaras* (temples) and the birthplaces of Sikh leaders. The memory of pre-partition India is still alive and the links are considerable. How could Pakistan use nuclear weapons against fellow Muslims?—in Karachi, for example, 80 per cent of the population has familial ties with Indian Muslims.[54]

In addition, in neither country has the intellectual debate reached the point at which it is necessary to consider how and when nuclear weapons might be assimilated and used. Indeed, posing these questions directly to senior officials and researchers in both countries invariably meets with a revealing lack of interest. At present, paradoxically, this is a stable situation, but it is one that could change quickly and for the worse.

Assuming that India is able to seek a form of equilibrium with Pakistan based upon 'minimum nuclear deterrence', the prospect for long-term stability is negligible. Once a policy of formal nuclear deterrence is in place, pressure mounts for improvement and refinement—what else can explain India's long-range ballistic missile programme? That India has come as far as it has suggests strongly that the internal pressures from public opinion and the science bureaucracy have been considerable. If minimum deterrence becomes a policy, the armed forces will vie for this crucial mission and previous reticence will be forgotten. How long then until pressure mounts for a triad—ground-, sea- and air-based deterrence systems?

One of the obvious paths for both countries to take is a policy based upon transparency and verification. Unfortunately, in the meetings between the two sides, there is very little scope for departures of this magnitude, although the SAARC (South Asian Association for Regional Co-operation) process might offer one route, if the necessary confidence building can be achieved first.

Finally, it is worth considering where China fits into the South Asian nuclear equation. Since 1964, India has frequently used China as a major reason for rejecting overtures from Pakistan. In recent years, Sino-Indian relations have improved significantly—witness the September 1993 agreement over confidence-building measures. Increasingly—to some extent this has always been the case—China shows little concern over the South Asian nuclear problem. Equally, despite the brief deterioration in relations during the late 1980s, India seems relaxed over the erstwhile Chinese threat. Recently, in mid-1992,

[53] For a closely argued view of the policy implications which stem from an acceptance of the 'non-weaponization' view, and one which has gained a good deal of positive interest in New Delhi, see Perkovich, P., 'A nuclear third way in South Asia', *Foreign Policy*, no. 9 (summer 1993), pp. 85–104.

[54] Naim, R. A., *Asia's Day After: Nuclear War Between India and Pakistan?* (University of Illinois, Center for Arms Control, Disarmament and International Security: Urbana, Ill., undated), p. 564. Mimeograph.

the Chinese were tactless enough to conduct a nuclear test during a visit to Beijing by the Indian President. Contrary to expectations, the *faux pas* failed to deter both sides from increasing contacts at the ministerial level—the Venkataraman visit was followed in August by a visit by Defence Minister Sharad Pawar to further the Joint Working Group deliberations on issues surrounding the continuing border dispute.

While it would be an overstatement to say that neither side is worried about the nuclear deliberations of the other, relations between the two Asian giants are currently robust. Nuclear issues could unpick this carefully crafted relationship, but both sides seem content not to let this happen.

X. Delivery systems

One of the fundamental differences between a nuclear potential and a nuclear capability is the ability to deliver nuclear weapons. There are several ways in which nuclear weapons can be delivered—as missile warheads, free-fall bombs, depth charges or nuclear shells, for example.

Arguably, India has always possessed a nuclear delivery capability in the form of the Canberra fighter-bomber, procured from the UK in the 1950s. Given the fact that a nuclear strike would have been made at night, Pakistan's air defence would probably not have been adequate against the Canberra during the period since then.

Other nuclear-capable aircraft in the Indian inventory include the Jaguar and the Mirage 2000. Both are often touted as 'nuclear-capable' systems but few analysts make clear what is required for a nuclear capability. On the assumption that a 1-megaton nuclear bomb would weigh about 1000 lb—as is the case with NATO tactical nuclear bombs—neither of these systems would require special, structural modification. In all probability, what the exporting countries have denied India is the attack software for 'toss bombing'. As a plane flies in at low altitude, to avoid radar, the pilot faces the threat of collateral damage from the nuclear weapon and will turn and climb sharply before the bomb is released, and bank away from the trajectory of the bomb. For this type of manœuvre, complex software is required for auto-pilot, the use of which is considered rather too much for a single pilot to perform, which is why twin-seater Jaguar and Mirage aircraft are used by the France and the UK.[55] India does not have the two-seater nuclear-capable version.

It is certain, however, that India's missile programme is of far greater significance than its potential nuclear-strike aircraft. Arguably, the cost entailed in establishing an indigenous missile capability is far too great to justify anything less than a future nuclear ballistic weapon capability. True to form, the Government has consistently argued that successive missile tests have been nothing more than 'technology demonstrators'.

---

[55] The author is grateful to John Fricker for his advice on this point.

India's space programme was started in the early 1950s, soon after independence. In the early 1960s, before the Chinese nuclear test but in the wake of the 1962 war, India launched a 10-kg rocket within the atmosphere. From these modest beginnings, progress has been significant, which suggests a commendable level of success in a country where big science has received a great deal of criticism for poor performance and has suffered from outright duplicity in public relations.

In July 1975 a Soviet rocket launched the Aryabhata research satellite. There followed the INSAT programme, which relied upon collaboration and assistance from the USA. At the indigenous level, however, India elected to pursue the second generation of INSAT satellites alone, without inputs from the USA. More significant from a military perspective is India's indigenous space launch vehicle (SLV) programme. In 1980 an Indian launch of a four-stage rocket (SLV-3) reached beyond the Earth's atmosphere to place in orbit a 35-kg satellite.[56] The achievement was considerable; India had become the first developing country to launch a satellite into orbit on its own launch vehicle. The military implications of the space programme have never been denied. Following the successful launch of a 41.5-kg satellite in 1983 the Chairman of ISRO admitted soon after that the programme would lead to an intermediate-range ballistic missile (IRBM) capability. At that time, however, ISRO had probably not acquired the capability to produce the required heat shields or an inertial guidance system.

In the early 1980s the focus of the programme shifted to Hyderabad, where the Defence Research and Development Laboratory was instructed to undertake the Integrated Guided Missile Programme. At first there were failures, such as the augmented space launch vehicle (ASLV) which crashed into the Bay of Bengal in 1987. However, the space programme appeared to have the unequivocal support of Rajiv Gandhi, which assured money and continuity.

The first fruits of this programme, under the leadership of A. J. P. Abdul Kalam, became known in the late 1980s and were embodied in the successful launch of the Prithvi (February 1988), a 250-km range tactical surface-to-surface missile. Also on the programme was the development of the Trishul, a quick-reaction, low-level, surface-to-air missile (SAM), the medium-range Akash SAM and the Nag, a third-generation anti-tank missile.

Of these systems, Prithvi attracted the most attention. The overall indigenous content of the system was alleged to be considerable. In particular, the missile was alleged to incorporate a strap-down inertial guidance system, developed by the DRDO, with—allegedly—an accuracy of better than 1 per cent, which translates into a circular error probable (CEP) of less than 250 metres over a maximum range of 250 km.[57] Recently, however, the Army has expressed disquiet over its liquid propulsion, although a solid fuel version is said to be on the way. The Army also fears that even if deployed Prithvi could not be effectively

[56] Thomas (note 28), pp. 269–74.
[57] Mama, H. P., 'Progress on India's new tactical missiles', *International Defense Review*, vol. 22, no. 7 (July 1989), p. 963.

used because India lacks the communications infrastructure to transmit targeting information.[58]

In early 1989 it became apparent that India was on the verge of another test, this time on a surface-to-surface IRBM, the Agni. After some delay, a successful test was conducted on 22 May 1989. Although the test was over a range of 1000 km, the Agni reportedly has a much longer range, up to 2500 km. The missile can carry a 2.5-tonne payload, which lends itself to a conventional, nuclear or chemical payload. A second missile test took place in May 1992 and was, by and large, a failure but this did little to impinge upon the political and bureaucratic support for the programme.

Once deployed the missile will be mobile, transported by either road or rail. The only elements of the system which were not indigenous were the inertial guidance system and the carbon fibre used on the heat shield.[59] According to a July 1989 report in the *Wall Street Journal*, India imported the Agni's guidance system, its first-stage rocket and the nose cone (constructed from composite materials) from the FRG.[60] At the same time the US Central Intelligence Agency (CIA) reported that the USA was witholding space technology exports to India—the so-called 'shake and bake' system which simulates the heat and shock of re-entry.[61] It is of some interest that no investigation of the claims appeared subsequently, despite coverage in the Western technical defence journals. That in itself does not constitute reliable information. However, it does raise the possibility of self-censorship among the Indian press corps, witness the triumphant claim from one newspaper: 'Agni's success is due to two major technological breakthroughs: the designing of an ablative carbon re-entry shield and the development of an indigenous strapdown inertial navigation system.'[62]

In India, the response to the test was euphoric. India had become the sixth country to produce successfully an IRBM from indigenous technology. Although senior Indian politicians were quick to stress the non-nuclear potential in the development, opinion formers were less coy:

After Pokhran in 1974, the launch of the Agni to a triumphant splashdown in the Bay of Bengal is the biggest step forward in India's quest for a credible deterrent capability. The real success of such a capability is that it should never have to be used; it has to be achieved nevertheless. India cannot stop with just one testing of Agni. Any new missile system has to be tested repeatedly before any reliance can be placed upon it. These tests have necessarily to be carried out in the open because of the notification requirements at home and abroad, making a contrast with nuclear bombs that remain in the basement.[63]

[58] Sidhu, W. P. S., 'Prithvi missile—tactical gap: army has yet to find a role for the weapon', *India Today,* vol. 17, no. 17 (15 Sep. 1992), pp. 84–85.

[59] Gupta, A., 'Fire in the sky: the Indian missile programme', *Defense & Diplomacy*, vol. 8, no. 10 (Oct. 1990), p. 44.

[60] 'W. Germany refutes report on "Agni"', *Times of India,* 10 July 1989.

[61] 'CIA says Agni isn't indigenous', *Times of India*, 2 July 1989.

[62] Nanda, S. P. and Menon, M. C., 'Fire in the sky', *Sunday*, 4 June 1989.

[63] 'Triumphant splashdown', *Times of India* (editorial), 23 May 1989.

The Prithvi capability would seem to be an adequate system to deploy against Pakistan, in the early years at least, given the reasonable assumption that neither side could realistically target military installations or mobile units. Although the Agni test was popular, during a period of mixed fortunes for the Congress(I) Government, the rationale for it was somewhat speculative. The luxury of possessing a second echelon of missiles to back the shorter-range Prithvi seems excessive and the argument concerning the need to deter the Chinese missiles in the Kunlun Shan and Nan Shan ranges of Tibet is also debatable given the relatively successful diplomatic process which is proceeding apace. However, the deployment of the Agni is not certain, at this point, although it may be used to launch military satellites given the failure of the ASLV programme.[64] Indeed, whether or not the system is deployed will answer the question which pertains to much of India's defence capability, the degree to which it is an answer in search of a problem or vice versa.

[64] Gupta (note 59), p. 47.

9. Defence decision making in India: the policy-making process

I. The making of defence policy

The decision-making process is, in essence, the institutional course which any decision must run to become official policy. Before reaching this definitive stage, any potential policy change should be considered by all the relevant organizations to provide elected decision makers with sufficient information, data and advice to enable an informed and appropriate decision to be taken.

Unlike the case of many other countries in the South, the process of decision making in the Indian defence sector is reasonably well defined. Frequent descriptions appear in both official and unofficial published sources. Most appraisals of the process in India take one of two approaches to the issue. The first, adopted primarily by defence commentators and the Indian Government itself, places emphasis upon both the numerous stages in the process and the plethora of institutions which collectively shape policy. The intention behind this exercise is twofold. First, when publishing in Western technical journals, the purpose is to provide information for those outside the system, such as military attachés, who may have a professional interest in how the system works.[1] Both foreign and national bureaucratic and commercial interests will often need to know exactly how the decision-making process functions, where the primary actors are located and how to understand fully a system through which they might have to work either in order to secure a defence contract or for more general commercial intelligence purposes. Second, it is a means of reiterating the constitutional and democratic nature of the decision-making process, which is rare among developing countries and an aspect of governance of which India is quite correctly very proud.

The second approach is that of political scientists who seek to identify the role of the various decision makers and the organizations they represent. The value of this type of analysis comes from the stress upon the differing roles and perceptions of the individuals and institutions which formulate policy. However, this approach has concentrated primarily upon the workings of bureaucracies in the West, particularly the USA. A central purpose of these efforts in an Indian context is to underscore the country's continuing commitment to democracy and the role the legislature fulfils as an essential check and balance within the decision-making process, which includes the armed forces and the bureaucracy.

[1] See, for example, Singh, P., 'India's defence perspectives and the armed forces', *Asian Defence Review,* Oct. 1982, pp. 12–30.

Informative though these efforts may be, there is an underlying tendency to accept that, because these organizations exist, they are more or less key determinants in the policy-making process and function in practice as they should, according to the constitution. In other words, it is assumed that, by virtue of constitutional arrangements, the complex and sophisticated process of decision making is essentially democratic. This does not take account of a key factor thus far alluded to but not yet fully described, namely the way in which important decisions are made in relation to the distribution of information and knowledge. If one or more of the key actors or institutions misunderstands, does not have access to the information required, or is uninterested in the information available to influence the policy-making process, his ability to carry out his constitutional obligations will be reduced accordingly.

The responsibility for conventional defence in India, as established by the constitution, is vested in the Union Government which is responsible for all aspects of defence and national security. This includes not only the prosecution of war, but also defence preparedness and defence production.

The defence decision-making process in India has changed considerably since 1947. Originally, the structure was designed by Lord Ismay, who had previous experience in British defence decision making. He recommended the creation of a three-cornered system comprising the Defence Committee of the Cabinet (DCC), the Defence Minister's Committee (DMC) and the Chiefs of Staff Committee (CSC) (see figure 9.1). The logic behind this system was to provide equally weighted inputs from the Government (DCC), the bureaucracy (DMC) and the armed forces (CSC). These committees were assisted by smaller and more specialized committees, such as the Defence Science Advisory Committee. The DMC was by far the most important body and members of the other two key committees—the service chiefs, the Secretary of Defence and the Financial Adviser to the MoD—were in attendance at meetings.[2] Over time, however, the formal decision-making process was short-circuited and adhered to less and less. During the Nehru period decisions were taken on an *ad hoc* basis. Effectively, the DMC was bypassed, primarily as a result of the close working relationship between Krishna Menon and the Prime Minister (see chapter 3).[3]

During the 1962 war it became evident that the established formal peacetime decision-making process was inadequate for swift decision taking and wartime planning. This led to the creation of a series of emergency committees which met on a daily basis; the DCC became the Emergency Committee of the Cabinet (ECC) and the daily meetings were attended by several ministers (its composition changed over time). After the war it was decided that the daily meetings between the Defence Minister and the service chiefs should continue.

[2] Venkateswaran, A. L., *Defence Organisation in India: A Study of Major Developments in Organisation and Administration since Independence* (Ministry of Information and Broadcasting: Delhi, Jan. 1967), pp. 89-96.
[3] Thomas, R. G. C., *Indian Security Policy* (Princeton University Press: Princeton, N.J., 1986), p. 120.

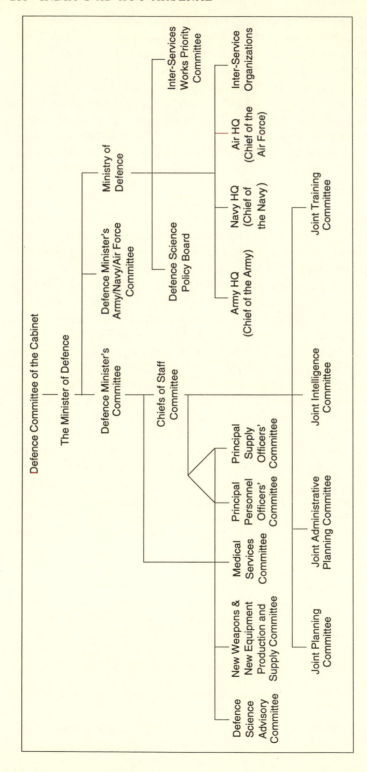

Figure 9.1. The decision-making process in India before 1966

Note: Only the more important of the committees have been included.

Source: Venkateswaran, A. L., *Defence Organisation in India: A Study of Major Developments in Organisation and Administration since Independence* (Ministry of Information and Broadcasting: Delhi, Jan. 1967).

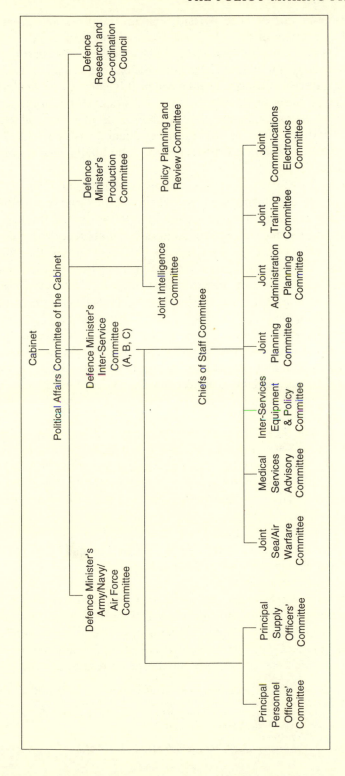

Figure 9.2. The decision-making process in India since 1966

Source: Venkateswaran, A. L., *Defence Organisation in India: A Study of Major Developments in Organisation and Administration since Independence* (Ministry of Information and Broadcasting: Delhi, Jan. 1967).

The starting point for defence decision making involves an appropriate definition and assessment of the actual and potential threat to India's security environment. This includes not only the country's borders and coastlines but also, and more recently, its airspace, island possessions and off-shore facilities.[4] Internal security issues will also be relevant in this context, particularly in relation to Sikh extremism in the Punjab and, to a lesser extent, terrorist activity in Tamil Nadu and, increasingly, the source and direction of communal tension. Since 1962 the starting points for preliminary evaluation have been the Policy Planning and Review Committee (PPRC) and the Joint Intelligence Committee (JIC) (see figure 9.2).

Set up in 1966, the PPRC is primarily a Ministry of External Affairs (MEA) committee, although a Defence Secretary was invited to join it in 1969. Its remit is to examine India's foreign policy in relation to the international environment, giving due regard to politico-military and politico-economic considerations.[5] The JIC originally comprised the Joint Secretary of the MEA as chairman, representatives of the MoD and the Ministry of Home Affairs and the Directors of Intelligence from the three services, and was a subsidiary body of the CSC, but it was reconstituted in 1965 following the dismal performance of Indian intelligence in 1962 and brought into the Cabinet Secretariat where an Additional Secretary is now the chairman.[6] It meets as often as necessary, even daily during times of crisis, and produces for the Cabinet swift assessments of changing situations and likely developments. Up until 1971, the JIC reported directly to the DCC, where all the major decisions on defence were taken.

The Political Affairs Committee of the Cabinet (PACC) was set up in 1971 to take quick political decisions, and has evolved into the major defence decision-making committee within the Cabinet, whereas the DCC has fallen by the wayside. This limits the Government's ability to consider long-term defence planning, and there is some pressure from parliament to see the DCC brought back.[7] The PACC is chaired by the Prime Minister and its usual members are the ministers for defence, external affairs, home affairs and finance. It is primarily the responsibility of the PACC to define defence policy in response to the assessments it receives from the JIC and the PPRC. Thereafter its directives must be both implemented and constitutionally legitimized, and this is the point at which security problems are translated into defence plans.

The implementation of defence policy is undertaken by the MoD, which is overseen by the Defence Minister, assisted by junior colleagues who run the four major departments within the Ministry—Defence, Defence Production, Supplies and Research and Development. The important committee here is the Minister's Inter-Service Committee (ISC) which deals with plans and papers on defence subjects which are not serious enough to be referred to the PACC.

---

[4] One of the major lessons which Indian defence planners drew from the Falklands/Malvinas War was the importance of protecting island possessions.

[5] Chari, P. R., 'The policy process', ed. J. M. Roherty, *Defence Policy Formulation: Towards Comparative Analysis* (Carolina Academic Press: Durham, N.C., 1980), p. 143.

[6] Venkateswaran (note 2), pp. 363–64.

[7] 'Reviving Cabinet panel on defence urged', *The Hindu,* 9 Apr. 1986.

Also, the DMC and the Defence Minister's (Production and Supply) Committee should be taken into account. The latter regulates the defence production effort and co-ordination with civilian industry. The Defence Research and Co-ordination Council directs and co-ordinates scientific research in relation to defence. A further division of labour occurs at the third echelon of the decision-making process involving bodies such as the Defence Electronics Committee and the Principal Supply Officers Committee.[8]

Between the PACC and the bodies which assess external threat, there is the CSC, comprising the three service chiefs and chaired by the member with the longest tenure. It deals with inter-service issues. By means of the morning meetings with the Defence Minister, through the ISC, the service chiefs are able to discuss any issue pertaining to defence, and this allows the military to communicate problems to government directly. Depending upon the decision taken, the Minister will delegate implementation to junior colleagues and departmental committees will take up the process and co-ordinate with all the necessary groups.

Each year the budgets for MoD and the armed forces are scrutinized by the legislature, upon whom responsibility rests for the future scale of defence operations and level of military expenditure. In principle, the legislature can demand that defence allocations are raised or lowered, for example, or the revised estimates from the previous year can be debated. Over the course of the annual debate in parliament on the defence budget, almost two days in April are given over to the discussion of defence and war preparedness. The documents placed before parliament by the MoD in the form of the *Defence Estimates* and the *Annual Report* together provide an overview of India's defence policy and posture which is fairly exhaustive, certainly more so than in many other countries. One noticeable omission from the information provided by the Government, however, is significant detail on where it stands at any given time on the nuclear weapon option.

In recent years there has been a strong lobby within the armed forces to create a Chief of Defence Staff (CDS), a post which existed under the British from the turn of the century through until independence.[9] It is currently argued that the armed forces are insufficiently integrated into the higher echelons of the decision-making process, and that the function of such a post would be to bring a military person much closer to the final centre of decision making, or that the present arrangement lacks an integrated approach to service requirements and involves the triplication of work because the same potential decision is examined by the military headquarters, the MoD and the latter's Financial Adviser. Those in favour of establishing such a post also point to India's developing military posture and the arcane defence decision-making process, and to the UK's success in the Falklands/Malvinas War which was the result in

---

[8] Chari (note 5), p. 133.
[9] Venkateswaran, A. L., 'Why a Defence Ministry?', *Indian Express,* 25 May 1984.

part of joint staff planning, better management practices and the elimination of inter-service rivalry.[10]

The CDS debate ebbs and flows with surprising regularity. It is doubtful that any Indian government would concede the creation of a CDS post, even though opposition parties have frequently raised the issue during the annual defence debate. There is no suggestion even that successive oppositions in parliament have been totally in favour of the post, and it may be that the notion of a CDS provides a debating point without much substance and may even be an object for filibuster.

Even if the CDS post made good bureaucratic and managerial sense, any government would still be likely to refuse the change. Those who argue against the post generally consider it pointless to add an additional echelon to an already cumbersome decision-making process. The creation of a post with such close access to the Prime Minister and Minister of Defence could diminish significantly the role of the MoD and effectively short-circuit rather than streamline the decision-making process. Nor have the implications of the concentration of such power and prestige in one military officer been overlooked, particularly given the history of the Pakistani military's involvement in politics. In addition to the disputes over bureaucratic turf and management efficiency, another reason for the antagonism to the proposal of successive governments may be the possibility that a CDS could reduce or complicate significantly the potential access to commissions for the major decision makers: the cake would have to be cut into more pieces. It is, therefore, somewhat unlikely that the system of defence decision making will change dramatically in the future.

Major change could occur if the country chose to take the nuclear weapon option. The changes here would be twofold. First, the decision to begin the production of nuclear weapons would require a different set of institutional actors. Although India demonstrated its ability to explode a nuclear 'device' in 1974, the transition from test to capability is a complicated one. Before developing a nuclear force capable of deterrence, the Government must be sure that the required amounts of unsafeguarded fissile materials are available. In addition, it must be equally clear that the missiles which India currently has under development and/or the nuclear-capable aircraft, such as the Mirage 2000 and the Jaguar, can deliver nuclear weapons of Indian size and design. Thus, a new set of decision makers drawn from the nuclear energy and space research establishments would of necessity be drawn into the inner decision-making circles. Furthermore, the MEA might be more prominent, given the need to assess the international reaction which would inevitably accompany the decision to go nuclear from individual countries and from the United Nations.

Second, the decisions to produce, deploy and use nuclear weapons are essentially political choices. Although the armed forces would be consulted, it would be in a technical capacity alone, for example, on how to interface conventional

[10] Elkin, J. F. and Ritezel, W. A., 'The debate on restructuring India's higher defense organisation', *Asian Survey*, vol. 24, no. 10 (Oct. 1984), pp. 1075, 1076–79.

and nuclear capabilities, targeting and delivery systems. The key actors would be the members of the PACC, or perhaps a more select body which does not as yet exist, and the armed forces would have a much smaller input than in the conventional sphere. This may be one reason why the military is less enthusiastic about the nuclear option than might be expected.

II. The decision-making process and the political backdrop

The annual defence debate in parliament is rarely if ever an indication that the watchdog and determining roles of the legislature are being adequately performed. Defence debates have been described as generating 'heat but never light'.[11] Recently, this criticism may be considered a relatively mild one: contemporary parliamentary debates tend to be extremely perfunctory and rarely illuminating or directive. Moreover, they are particularly badly attended:

Incredible though it may seem but [sic] the sad, indeed shameful truth is that there were three long stretches during the three day discussion on defence—which apart from being a matter of life and death costs the country close to Rs.6000 crores—when there was not even a quorum in the House. At times the number of those present did not exceed 20.[12]

There are two explanations for this lackadaisical approach on the part of the legislature. The first relates to the lack of information for the upper and lower houses. In comparison to many other countries, the information made available in India is substantial—the MoD, for example, frequently produces press releases when major new defence decisions are taken, as over military exercises or the purchase of a new defence system—but it is still insufficient for informed debate. The *Defence Estimates*, for example, which form the basis for the annual defence debate in the Lok Sabha, are inadequate. Procurement costs are put under one budget head, euphemistically entitled 'stores'. There is no indication of how much foreign exchange will be utilized for defence in any given year, so that it is difficult to estimate the full impact of defence expenditure upon the Indian economy in a given time-frame. Crude estimates could be made from evaluating the sources available outside India, such as commercial intelligence reports and technical journals, but this is a time-consuming and unsatisfactory exercise—the price paid for a weapon system may amount to less than 50 per cent of the total costs when training, technical advice, spare parts and maintenance are included.

When questions are tabled in parliament, which is not often, the Government frequently uses the excuse of 'national security' to avoid furnishing detailed information, even though on many occasions the information is publicly available outside and sometimes inside India.[13] Although there is a public and media

[11] Chari (note 5), p. 138.

[12] Malhotra, I., 'Defence debate paradox: confidence and apathy coexist', *Times of India*, 7 Apr. 1983.

[13] In fact, some of the more zealous Indian MPs have claimed that official information relating to national security should not be reproduced in the *Jane's* reference series.

defence debate, officials rarely intervene on anything more than a superficial level. Aided and abetted by nearly four decades of sophisticated propaganda against Pakistan, officials often retreat behind a smokescreen of 'gathering war clouds', the 'imminent threat of war', 'border movements' and the 'work of foreign hands'. Typically, the media react in a very passive way and tend not to move beyond the emotion generated by Pakistan or the USA or both; the constant references to the appearance of the USS *Enterprise* in the Bay of Bengal in 1971 are a case in point. Parliamentarians are thus neither encouraged nor cajoled by the press to debate key defence issues and military expenditure continues to be the exceptional 'holy cow'.

The second reason why parliament does not carry more weight on defence issues is the continuing hold of the Congress(I) Party on Indian political affairs. Except for 1977–80 either Congress or Congress(I) has held political power in India since 1947. This has had the effect of stifling debate and giving the Government a relatively free hand in the conduct of defence and other matters—internal security, space and nuclear power, for example. Together with the lack of parliamentary interest in defence, this has led to a situation in which the Government has little compunction in pursuing policies without legitimation, whatever the cost and impact. Nehru, Indira Gandhi and Rajiv Gandhi moreover all took up the defence portfolio, which further stifled debate: few Congress MPs would wish to challenge their party leader directly on such a sensitive issue. The continuing success of the Congress(I) Party severely damaged the fortunes of the political opposition parties. There is no nationally viable, single opposition party in India and the best that can be expected is a coalition of regional and factional interests. Even the Desai Government of 1978–80 was an unsatisfactory coalition inspired by a shared distaste for Indira Gandhi's style of government. There are consequently few politicians outside the ruling party with experience of office and no shadow Cabinet which could present a consistent critique of government policy;[14] no defence debate exists at present. It need not be the case that all opposition parties would be in favour of restraint. In some cases, opposition parties consider that the Government is lagging behind on defence preparedness. Recently the BJP, now a leading right-wing opposition party, criticized the Prime Minister for an inappropriate response to allegations regarding Pakistani developments in the nuclear field and adopted a resolution calling for the development and stockpiling of nuclear weapons by India.[15] It has some firm policies on non-nuclear issues and, if elected, would undertake a radical defence review.[16]

It can be argued, therefore, that although a democratic system exists in India it works imperfectly in the realm of defence. Primarily through the withholding of information, which is complemented by an advanced state of apathy on the part of politicians, the ability and interest of parliament to direct and monitor

[14] Chari (note 5), p. 140.

[15] *Journal of Defence and Diplomacy,* vol. 3, no. 10 (Oct. 1985).

[16] Conversations with the author, Delhi, Sep. 1992.

developments and progress in defence policy are severely limited. In principle, the PACC should formulate policy which should then be widely debated in parliament and beyond, assuming that the security issues at stake do not require an instant response, as the threat of invasion or war would. Information should be made more fully available and policy decisions defended at the formal committee level and in the debating chamber, as befits a democratic system. In practice, this appears not to be the case. The structures exist but they are not used.

Equally important in the analysis of the decision-making process is the degree to which the armed forces influence the choices open to the bureaucracy and legislature. The analysis of the decisive period between 1947 and 1962 in chapter 3 highlighted the inability of any individual or institution apart from the armed forces to define with authority the technological parameters of defence policy. Since the 1962 war, the decision-making process has changed significantly: the Cabinet—as opposed to parliament—is now better informed than hitherto and is able to make more informed judgements pertaining to procurement, and the MoD now has more expertise than it had in the Nehru era and is itself more capable of giving advice. However, an ability to counter-balance the institutional pressure of the armed forces is still not in evidence. Nowhere in India is there a recognized body capable of understanding fully the demands of the armed forces. The Defence Minister, with a tenure of limited length which is dependent in any case upon wider political circumstances, is hard pressed to come to terms fully with the complex world of defence, subject as it is to a rapid rate of technological change.

Much the same is true of the government-sponsored Institute for Defence Studies and Analysis (IDSA), the official defence think-tank. Certainly, the existence of this institution has fostered a more sophisticated public debate where before there was virtually none. However, on taking up the post the director becomes a civil servant (the present incumbent is a retired IAF officer), there are often retired military personnel on the staff and, consequently, the Institute is not entirely recognized either inside or outside India as an impartial source, although criticism of defence policy from within the IDSA is certainly tolerated. It is often and wrongly seen as little more than a means of articulating government defence policy both at home and abroad.

Another potential means of balance is to be found in the watchdog parliamentary committees. On the basis of the annual report and recommendations of the Comptroller and Auditor General, various areas of public policy implementation, including defence, are rigorously examined. The Public Accounts Committee (PAC) examines autonomous public sector defence enterprises and the Estimates Committee scrutinizes organizational efficiency. The published reports of these committees are often revealing. Nevertheless, all the PAC reports and most of the Estimates Committee reports are *ex post facto* (although the Estimates Committee is able to consider departmental estimates before they are presented to parliament).[17] They are, therefore, committees without teeth. Considering the serious nature of some of the allegations and the supporting evidence gathered by the watchdog committees, it is remarkable how little effect these hearings have, in stark contrast to the very different model of the congressional hearings in the USA, for example. Indeed, in 1989 the Government suppressed a PAC report alleging that the purchase of HDW submarines from the FRG was an 'outrageous mistake' and that the Navy's objections to the deal had been ignored.[18]

Equally, the expertise available to the legislature is not sufficiently impartial. Of particular importance is the fact that the JIC acts with a supporting staff drawn entirely from the military. The other body responsible for the assessment of threat, the PPRC, is serviced by the Policy Planning Division of the MEA which does not have a staff with a working knowledge of security affairs.[19] Its assessments of threat are thus bound to be heavily, if not exclusively, influenced by the armed forces.

When a problem requiring a decision has reached Cabinet level, the PACC will request advice from both the service chiefs and the MoD. The service chiefs are in attendance at PACC meetings to provide advice if required. In addition, they are able to use the 'morning meetings' to communicate with the Cabinet via the Defence Minister. Thus, although the military are not appointed to posts within the MoD, they do interject at several points in the policy-making process at the highest possible level.

In a relatively mature democracy such as exists in India, the MoD should have reached a much higher level of competence and proficiency since the 1950s when the power of decision making rested with the service chiefs, but this does not appear to have happened. Even though after 1962 the initiative for policy decisions was placed firmly with the MoD, the learning process did not go far enough, particularly on items requiring high expenditure. According to India's foremost defence bureaucracy analyst:

Proposals really connected with fighting efficiency or build-up of defence potential get through amazingly quickly irrespective of cost. The cases that drag on are those with amorphous fighting value—like creating additional posts of military attachés abroad, upgradation of ranks of individual posts for officers, construction of swimming pools and other amenities, etc. In fact Service HQs often buttress their proposals with stock phrases like 'operational preparedness' and 'maintenance of morale' and confuse the already baffled defence officials.

Recruitment, training, preparation of operational plans, location of troops, etc., have been entirely with the Service HQs. It would thus require a lot of imagination to suggest that the Defence Ministry functions as a super-military headquarters. Indeed Defence Ministry officials have no competence to be super-military staff, nor are they

[17] Chari (note 5) p. 139.
[18] Kumar, D. P., 'How critical PAC report was suppressed', *The Statesman,* 28 May 1989.
[19] Chari (note 5), p. 143.

required to be so. . . . the Service HQs seem to have consciously or otherwise a vested interest in keeping Defence Ministry officials in ignorance.[20]

In this overview of defence policy making, emphasis has been placed upon the ability of the military to influence the policy-making process. The need to solicit the views and advice of the military in the defence of the state cannot be disputed. However, one observation must follow if the armed forces are the primary force in shaping decisions: the policy-making process is at variance with the articles of the constitution, which place the main power of decision making in the hands of parliament. In the absence of non-military expertise to counter-balance the views of the military, the legislature is severely disadvantaged. This brings into question the claims of many commentators about the democratic nature of the defence decision-making process in India. However, it should be reiterated that this is not a problem unique to India, nor can it be argued that this anomaly has occurred as a result of subversive activity on the part of the military, bureaucracy or parliament. It is more the product of a failure, at a very early stage, to understand the degree to which the insufficient provision of information in a complex and sensitive area of decision making can seriously disadvantage the non-military decision makers.

Despite the evidence of the existence of a sophisticated machinery designed to facilitate a constitutional and rational decision-making process in India, the system does not work well in the realm of defence. In one sense this is a universal problem—democracy at work is always a complex and dynamic mix of power, opportunism, bureaucratic politics and pressure. In the absence of an informed and open process politicians are prone to rely too much upon power and pressure, and the merits of the system in principle become worthless. In a highly complex and sensitive area such as defence, with decisions involving large outlays with a commensurably long process of implementation, policy deviations are probably inevitable. In the case of India and other countries whose policy processes have been thoroughly studied, there is a universal problem of a relative lack of accountability and transparency.

However, it is necessary to distinguish between the inherent weakness of a system and subversion. The weakness of the policy process in the case of India is the inability of the legislature to counter the bargaining position of the armed forces and, to a lesser extent, of the MoD. While checks and balances exist in principle, in practice they are virtually meaningless. For example, a Ministry of Finance officer has a desk in the MoD to ensure that defence allocations are requested and disbursed in such a way as to prevent harm to other areas of the Indian economy. However, there is no evidence to suggest that this post, which effectively gives the Ministry of Finance the power of veto over the MoD when it comes to issues involving expenditure, is used in the way it could and should have been in recent years. There have been very few occasions when the equipment required by the armed forces has not been forthcoming because of high costs.

[20] Venkateswaran (note 9).

Although there are evident problems in the structure of policy making which have never been fully addressed by the governments, other aspects of Indian politics are also relevant. Towards the end of her life, Indira Gandhi met increasing criticism for her autocratic style of government and her propensity to develop a presidential style. From the time of her re-election in 1980, the over-all style of decision making changed dramatically, particularly in relation to defence. After a period of low activity in defence procurement, her return to power was swiftly followed by an open season for procurement and defence modernization. During the four-year period from 1980 until her death in October 1984, the basis of decision making was taken further away from the legislature. A small coterie of advisers drawn from the Prime Minister's secretariat and the so-called 'kitchen cabinet' (which took its name from the propensity of its members—the defence, finance and external affairs ministers and the Prime Minister—to conduct their business at the Prime Minister's residence) became responsible for the framing of important policy and, to a lesser extent, the monitoring of policy implementation.[21]

In the months before her death Indira Gandhi brought her son and heir apparent and his trusted advisers increasingly into the policy process. When Rajiv Gandhi took power the style of decision making changed very little, although there were enormous changes in the personnel involved and the distribution of power. Rajiv's first term of office was confused where decision making was concerned. Initially, he rejected most of the principal advisers used by his mother, such as G. Parthasarathy and R. K. Dhawan, and surrounded himself instead with younger people who lacked political experience but imbued the new Government with a new image based on technological development, 'clean' government, efficiency and dynamism. However, the dynamic atmosphere and the loyalty of the new advisers did not last long. Racked by incessant infighting and frequent threats to his authority, Rajiv Gandhi was forced into frequent Cabinet reshuffles to prevent the establishment of independent power bases and, eventually, sacked several of his erstwhile closest and most trusted advisers, such as his cousin, Arun Nehru. For several months he operated with an apparently ineffectual team which was unable to raise the level of the Government's performance. As the time for a general election drew nearer (elections had to be held before December 1989), Gandhi brought back many of his mother's trusted advisers.

In this way the defence policy process in India has reverted to what it was during the Nehru period. Debate on major decisions which date from the 1980 modernization programme was more incomplete than ever in an increasingly apathetic legislature. Congress(I) MPs became hamstrung by the growing use of patronage: rather than address themselves directly to the erosion of democracy, many chose instead to exploit the situation, and corruption and the abuse of power increased exponentially as they used their positions to amass the

[21] Sundar Rajan, K. R., 'Who runs India', *Gentleman*, Jan. 1984, pp. 48–54.

maximum wealth and power in the limited time available before the opportunities faded.

The prevailing style of decision making opened up a direct line of communication between the service chiefs and the Prime Minister via the Cabinet secretariat and the 'kitchen cabinet'. The domestic political crises which punctuated Indira Gandhi's last few years of power were hidden behind the thick smokescreen of a continuing security crisis. For the armed forces it was a halcyon period during which the importing of advanced military technology proceeded with unprecedented speed. In addition, the armed forces benefited from the increasing desire for India to become not just an undisputed regional power but also an internationally recognized military power. Supported by a belief that India was not a weak state but one that had yet to pull the correct levers to realize its vast potential wealth and power, they set out to challenge the *status quo* of the non-proliferation regime and to work towards superpower influence in the Indian Ocean and the outright control of the sub-continent itself.

In the legislature the concept of India becoming a major regional power, which required exponential rises in defence expenditure, was far from unpopular. First, there is a widespread desire on the part of Indian élites for their country to be taken more seriously within the international system. Since 1980, India's improved economic position and, until recently, the evident need to modernize at least some sections of the armed forces and the favourable terms to be found on the international arms market provided an opportunity which many had been waiting for since the 1971 war with Pakistan. Thus, a MEA official recently offered a Western diplomat the rather extended argument that one reason for the further development of a blue water Navy lay in the present and future turmoil within Southern Africa.[22] K. Subrahmanyam, the recognized spokesman for the hawkish element of the Indian élite, has argued that India should have a seat on the United Nations Security Council:

One out of every six people in the world is Indian. In any democratic structure, India would have an effective say. But you in the West devised a world order in which the second largest country isn't even a permanent member of the Security Council. That's a big omission.[23]

A retired Indian Navy admiral has been even more blunt: 'The world has learned to live with US power, Soviet power, even Chinese power, and it will have to learn to live with Indian power.'[24]

Second, the defence buildup is popular among the Indian middle classes, albeit at a level once removed from the concerns of the élites. Within India, the middle class, which numbers anything from 100 to 200 million, and the private sector have provided the economic dynamism which was evident in the early 1980s. They provide a form of national cement as they have a considerable vested interest in the Government's keeping the country together and preserv-

[22] Munro, R. H., 'Superpower rising', *Time*, no. 14 (3 Apr. 1989), p. 12.
[23] Munro (note 22), pp. 13–14.
[24] Munro (note 22), p. 13.

ing a single market. However, the liberalization programmes which gave India dynamism in the 1980s also begot regional disparities and increasing class differences.[25] The middle classes look to the ruling Congress(I) to maintain cohesion. Increasing the strength of the Centre can achieve these ends to a degree, but national unity, however cosmetic, cannot be achieved without a viable defence sector capable of providing external presence and internal security.

Nevertheless, it is somewhat curious that the PACC should have permitted the profligate expansionism of the 1980s. However much the process is in accord with the Government's view of the need to acquire great power status and the respect of other major powers, particularly the USA, the political cost of economic failure brought on by an excessive expansion of the defence sector and depleted foreign exchange reserves could only be borne by the incumbent ruling party. To this writer's knowledge, few requests from the armed forces during the 1980s were turned down, with the possible exception of the Tornado MRCA. This raises the question what the PACC members have to gain. Conceivably, the task of raising the country's international prestige could well have been achieved more economically. Or, to put it another way, how rational is it for a country to aspire to major power status and at the same time pay relatively little attention until recently to the fortunes and performance of the domestic defence industry? Why does India import when it could produce indigenously? Why are such lavish procurement programmes pushed through without reservations when the end, major power status, could be achieved at less political cost?

One explanation for the total rather than the measured acquiescence of the PACC may lie in the increasing evidence that most major defence deals between the arms exporters from the West and Third World countries, including India, are accompanied by sizeable commissions paid to those responsible for taking the final decisions. The costs incurred are then added to the total amounts paid for the defence equipment and may inflate prices by up to 50 per cent.[26]

Over the past few years allegations of corrupt practice in defence deals involving India have been commonplace. Indira Gandhi was alleged to have secured several million pounds in commission payments over the Jaguar DPSA deal and the 1985 Bofors case allegedly involved tens of millions of dollars in commissions. The influential Hindujah family was alleged to have received $500 million on behalf of unknown members of the Congress(I) Party responsible for taking the relevant decisions.[27]

Most senior military decision makers will admit that commissions have a significant influence on the decision-making process. Although allegations are

[25] Housego, D., 'A weaker rule for Mrs Gandhi's son', *Financial Times*, 28 Apr. 1989.

[26] Adam Raphael has this to say about recent British arms deals: 'All have been shrouded in secrecy, all involve large commission payments, which have inflated the Tornado sales price by between 30 and 50 per cent, and most involve barter arrangements with poor countries that cannot afford, and arguably do not need, such sophisticated weapons.' Raphael, A., 'Thatcher used aid to sell arms', *Sunday Times*, 7 May 1989.

[27] Gupte, P., 'The Hindujas', *Forbes*, Nov. 1987.

generally sensational, the greater part of the process is in fact quite mundane. A foreign exporter with an interest in selling equipment to India will 'employ' a low-level bureaucrat, via a retainer, to provide up-to-date information on future procurement plans. Thus, company representatives will be quickly aware when a certain type of weapon system becomes a gleam in the eye of the armed forces. From that point, the company will begin the process of competition with rival companies to win the covert side of the battle. From run-of-the-mill entertainment to placing substantial sums of money in Swiss bank accounts and paying college fees and medical bills, every effort will be made to win influence over those responsible for taking the final decisions, or influencing the final decision-making process.

The motivating forces behind corruption involving high-ranking politicians are several. Increasingly in India the benefits for the ruling party are personal and stem from the need for foreign exchange reserves which are held outside the country to cover luxury consumption, foreign health care, education and travel. A recognizable political function is also fulfilled by the ruling party's access to such reserves. In India elections are particularly expensive and labour-intensive. Bar the outright capturing of ballot boxes, it is extremely difficult for a ruling party to rig elections. In order to be successful, large sums of money are required to fund the 'carpet-bombing' style of election campaigning which the Indian electorate requires—the media do not offer an adequate source of communication as yet because the voting public demands to see the people it will elect, either on posters or in the flesh. Traditionally, the Congress Party has looked to landowners all over the country and commercial interests in Bombay to provide the vast amounts of finance required to fund election campaigns. There are inevitable political costs involved, many of which may directly contradict party manifestos. Thus, if the ruling party can use external contracts to enlarge its coffers, it will be less of a hostage to powerful domestic interest groups.

Once corruption enters the equation, the pattern of India's defence buildup in recent years begins to appear more understandable. The armed forces push and lobby for advanced military technology, which is commonplace in most countries. In one sense that is part of the professional role of the armed forces and part of ensuring that the country is as well defended as possible. Self-interest within the bureaucracy may endorse the military view of India's security problems. Increased allocations raise the relative status of the recipient departments, whether it be railways, education or defence. Senior representatives from the MoD and the MEA could also possibly fall into the élite group which considers India to be a major power in the making.

In principle, bureaucratic self-interest should be counter-balanced by both the PACC in the first instance and, via the annual parliamentary debate at least, the Lok Sabha. This does not happen. The Lok Sabha is generally starved of useful information from which it might mount a more searching policy debate than exists at present, and generally increase its ability to assess the situation. At the same time, Indian politicians do not seem particularly interested in taking up the relevant issues, either due to apathy, or from unwillingness to come close to criticizing their patrons, or because they too endorse the pursuit of great power status. Finally, the PACC and its advisers may have more than political status to gain from granting the requests made by the armed forces, especially if the source of defence equipment is the West.

10. Conclusion

In all probability, India will weather its current economic crisis, as it has so many others before. However, the fundamental changes institutionalized during the early 1990s by Manmohan Singh, the incumbent finance minister, will change the shape of the Indian economy in irreversible ways. Over the long term this may mean that the economy becomes much stronger, following the end of the 'licence raj'. Potentially, the reforms will unleash much of the suppressed economic talent and potential within the country, although there are certainly some hard times ahead which will especially affect the poor. The structural adjustment programme requested by the international finance organizations constitutes a considerable loss of economic sovereignty for India, however much the Narasimha Rao Government attempted to act independently as the crisis deepened: in mid-1992, for instance, government critics alleged the World Bank was shown the draft of the Eighth Five Year Plan before the Indian Parliament and commented upon many aspects of it.[1]

This is the reality of India's economic exposure and the extent of its political weakness. Whether on the question of future economic planning, state versus market or intellectual property rights, the Indian Government has less say over the direction and nature of public policy than at any point in its short history. Nothing could contrast more with the bold ideas of the founding fathers of the Indian nation state. Beyond rhetoric, little is left of the intellectual and ideological foundations which were intended to make India a strong yet independent state, free from the fetters of external interests.

The causes and consequences of this remarkable dénouement will provide a rich field for analysis and commentary in the future. Inevitably there will be those who choose to make a direct link between economic vulnerability and military expenditure, just as many before have looked at the relationship between military expenditure and underdevelopment. Although there have been exceptions, declared military expenditure for India has rarely exceeded 3 per cent of GNP. For a country as poor as India this may seem excessive, but this is not the point. A case can be made for saying that the structure and weakness of the economy would be much the same if military expenditure had been much lower: savings and additional resources would not necessarily have been directed into development projects but might instead have been used for other areas of big science designed to increase the country's international prestige. India's poverty is due to many factors, but increasingly to the lack of political will within the country to effect the kind of transformation and redistribution of resources that are required to bring development to the hundreds of millions who exist below

[1] Bushan, B., 'WB comments on plan before House sees it', *Indian Express*, 16 July 1992.

the poverty line. In contrast to the cases of Pakistan or the former USSR, the causal linkage between a strong defence posture and a weak economy is difficult to make in the case of India. Nevertheless, the defence sector stands as an excellent example of how an important public sector can be mismanaged and abused, as the preceding chapters attempt to explain.

First and foremost, India does have a number of important security problems. Arguably, however, too little attempt has been made to identify where the points of insecurity lie and in which direction defence efforts should be directed. The complexity of the situation is not in doubt, particularly in relation to the blurred division between internal and external security threats. However, there seem to have been too few attempts since 1947 to understand threat perceptions fully or to link these perceptions to defence needs. To put it another way, there appears to be a considerable gulf between defence and security—the country's perceived need to deploy two or even three aircraft-carriers is a case in point.

Second, mistakes were made during the early period of independence, between 1947 and 1962, which were of enormous importance for what came after. During this period, when Nehru controlled the defence portfolio, too little attention was paid to the way decisions were taken, who was taking them and whether or not they were appropriate. Consequently those most suited to match threat perceptions to military technological needs—the armed forces—were offered too much institutional freedom to expand their own roles; the traditional bureaucratic checks and balances appeared not to work at all well. As a result the country emerged with defence missions and, eventually, technological requirements and expenditures which it could have avoided.

Third, having advanced along the road towards a highly mechanized, diversified defence posture, governments directed too little effort to reducing dependence upon external suppliers and the drain on foreign exchange reserves, which served to exacerbate dependency and to keep defence costs high. India has over time failed to capitalize upon its manufacturing potential and build a defence production base which could have catered for a considerable proportion of the country's defence needs. Depending so much upon the USSR was only a partial solution to the need to avoid dependence upon the West. Although Soviet supplies allowed hard currency haemorrhages to be kept to a minimum until the 1980s, this relationship did little to expand production potential—the Soviet Union was habitually disinclined to release technology and know-how.

In part, the failure in defence production stems from a degree of hubris, typified by what will probably be HAL's last major programme, the LCA. Despite the fact that India has significant capabilities, it would never have been possible for it to attain the technological levels and rates of technical change which obtained in the West throughout the cold war. What decision makers failed to do was to enforce the design and production of weapon systems which were within the capability of industry. It is true that the quality–quantity, high technology–low technology debate is a great deal more complex than was understood before the Persian Gulf War. Nevertheless, no such debate appears to have taken place since the efforts of Patrick Blackett came to so little. Under what circumstances did those who took decisions on the LCA programme really think that India could leap generations of aeronautic technology without enormous cost and foreign involvement?

The Indian defence industry has been consistently retarded by a fifth column. The country's decision makers have consistently allowed the armed forces, especially the IAF, effectively to sabotage indigenous efforts in favour of imported equipment. Over time, India could have built up a significant defence production base which would have become increasingly independent and self-supporting. Because they required Western levels of technology, projects were bound either to fail or to require increasing inputs and assistance from foreign sources. Had the defence industry taken a similar view to that of its Brazilian counterparts, for example, the situation could have been very different.

That this situation persisted through several parliaments raises many questions about the motivations and awareness of the nation's leaders. Indian élites have always harboured a deep-seated desire for their country to be taken seriously by the West. The possession of a nuclear capability, advanced nuclear delivery systems and a broad array of conventional options has eventually done the trick, though this may yet cost the country a permanent seat on the Security Council. India is now a recognized military power. Few outside India really believe that the country has not taken the option to produce nuclear weapons, even though the evidence is too thin to state the case with certainty. If India can resist pressures to join the NPT, which grows less relevant by the year for both India and Pakistan, the political gains will be seen as worthwhile: after nearly half a century, India is beginning to command attention, if not respect, on the international stage. Nevertheless, they have been expensive gains and look increasingly nugatory as the post-cold war world begins to unfold.

Finally, India's defence posture is as unstructured and anarchic as it is profligate. Arguably, India commands much less defence capability than might have been expected following the massive investment programme of the 1980s. The available evidence of logistical shortcomings may only tell a fraction of the story. Weaponry has been imported and produced under licence from a considerable array of suppliers. This in itself would provide a logistical nightmare, in terms of spare parts supply, maintenance and training—problems severely compounded by recent economic setbacks.

The explanation is in part to do with government aversion to defence dependence and the need to avoid allowing a single external power the possibility to influence foreign and defence policy through the withholding of spare parts and technical assistance. However, it would also seem to be heavily influenced by the financial opportunities which are always presented in the form of commissions and which have played an influential role in deciding the shape and scope of India's defence posture. A plethora of suppliers increases the competition for India's defence market and therefore the prospect of better commissions as suppliers struggle to secure a niche.

Without doubt, the outcome could have been very different. With the benefit of hindsight, India could have achieved adequate defence at much less cost. In addition, quite apart from the chaotic nature of defence procurement and posture, the overall programme has failed to a greater degree than is immediately obvious. India may be less well defended than it could have been if different decisions had been taken. The procurement programme over time and the failure to take indigenization seriously have also contributed to a decline in economic security. With this has come a loss of sovereignty which will take many years to redress.

Appendix A. Security Council resolutions and decisions on India–Pakistan in 1948

38 (1948). Resolution of 17 January 1948 (S/651)

The Security Council,
Having heard statements on the situation in Kashmir from representatives of the Governments of India and Pakistan,

Recognizing the urgency of the situation,

Taking note of the telegram addressed on 6 January 1948 by its President to each of the parties[1] and of their replies thereto,[2] in which they affirmed their intention to conform to the Charter of the United Nations,

1. *Calls upon* both the Government of India and the Government of Pakistan to take immediately all measures within their power (including public appeals to their people) calculated to improve the situation, and to refrain from making any statements and from doing or causing to be done or permitting any acts which might aggravate the situation;

2. *Further requests* each of those Governments to inform the Council immediately of any material change in the situation which occurs or appears to either of them to be about to occur while the matter is under consideration by the Council, and consult with the Council thereon.

Adopted at the 229th meeting by 9 votes to none, with 2 abstentions (Ukrainian Soviet Socialist Republic, Union of Soviet Socialist Republics).

Decision

At its 229th meeting, on 17 January 1948, the Council decided that the President should invite the representatives of India and Pakistan to take part in direct talks under his guidance in an effort to find some common ground on which the structure of a settlement might be built.

---

[1] See *Official Records of the Security Council, Third Year*, Nos 1–15, 226th meeting, pp. 4–5 (Document S/636).

[2] *Ibid., Third Year, Supplement for January, February and March 1948*, Documents S/639 and S/640.

39 (1948). Resolution of 20 January 1948 (S/654)

The Security Council,
Considering that it may investigate any dispute or any situation which might, by its continuance, endanger the maintenance of international peace and security and that, in the existing state of affairs between India and Pakistan, such an investigation is a matter of urgency,

Adopts the following resolution:

A. A Commission of the Security Council is hereby established, composed of representatives of three Members of the United Nations, one to be selected by India, one to be selected by Pakistan, and the third to be designated by the two so selected.

Each representative on the Commission shall be entitled to select his alternates and assistants.

B. The Commission shall proceed to the spot as quickly as possible. It shall act under the authority of the Security Council and in accordance with the direction it may receive from it. It shall keep the Security Council currently informed of its activities and of the development of the situation. It shall report to the Security Council regularly, submitting its conclusions and proposals.

C. The Commission is invested with a dual function:

(1) To investigate the facts pursuant to Article 34 of the Charter of the United Nations;

(2) To exercise, without interrupting the work of the Security Council, any mediatory influence likely to smooth away difficulties; to carry out the directions given to it by the Security Council; and to report how far the advice and directions, if any, of the Security Council have been carried out.

D. The Commission shall perform the functions described in Clause C: (1) In regard to the situation in the Jammu and Kashmir State set out in the letter of the representative of India addressed to the President of the Security Council, dated 1 January 1948,[1] and in the letter from the Minister of Foreign Affairs of Pakistan addressed to the Secretary-General, dated 15 January 1948;[2] and (2) In regard to other situations set out in the letter from the Minister of Foreign Affairs of Pakistan addressed to the Secretary-General, dated 15 January 1948, when the Security Council so directs.

E. The Commission shall take its decision by majority vote. It may allocate among its members, alternate members, their assistants, and its personnel such duties as may have to be fulfilled for the realization of its mission and the reaching of its conclusions.

F. The Commission, its members, alternate members, their assistants and its personnel shall be entitled to journey, separately or together, wherever the necessities of their tasks may require, and, in particular, within those territories which are the theatre of the events of which the Security Council is seized.

G. The Secretary-General of the United Nations shall furnish the Commission with such personnel and assistance as it may consider necessary.

---

[1] *Official Records of the Security Council, Third Year, Supplement for November 1948,* document S/1100, annex 28.

[2] *Ibid.,* annex 6.

---

47 (1948). Resolution of 21 April 1948 (S/726)

The Security Council,
Having considered the complaint of the Government of India concerning the dispute over the State of Jammu and Kashmir,

Having heard the representative of India in support of that complaint and the reply and counter-complaints of the representative of Pakistan,

Being strongly of the opinion that the early restoration of peace and order in Jammu and Kashmir is essential and that India and Pakistan should do their utmost to bring about a cessation of all fighting,

Noting with satisfaction that both India and Pakistan desire that the question of the accession of Jammu and Kashmir to India or Pakistan should be decided through the democratic method of a free and impartial plebiscite,

Considering that the continuation of the dispute is likely to endanger international peace and security,

Reaffirms its resolution 38 (1948) of 17 January 1948;

Resolves that the membership of the Commission established by its resolution 39 (1948) of 20 January 1948 shall be increased to five and shall include, in addition to the membership mentioned in that resolution, representatives of . . . and . . . , and that if the membership of the Commission has not been completed within ten days from the date of the adoption of this resolution the President of the Council may designate such other Member or Members of the United Nations as are required to complete the membership of five;

Instructs the Commission to proceed at once to the Indian subcontinent and there place its good offices and mediation at the disposal of the Governments of India and Pakistan with a view to facilitating the taking of the necessary measures, both with respect to the restoration of peace and order and to the holding of a plebiscite, by the two Governments, acting in co-operation with one another and with the Commission, and further instructs the Commission to keep the Council informed of the action taken under the resolution; and, to this end,

Recommends to the Governments of India and Pakistan the following measures as those which in the opinion of the Council are appropriate to bring about a cessation of the fighting and to create proper conditions for a free and impartial plebiscite to decide whether the State of Jammu and Kashmir is to accede to India or Pakistan:

A. *Restoration of peace and order*

1. The Government of Pakistan should undertake to use its best endeavours:

(*a*) To secure the withdrawal from the State of Jammu and Kashmir of tribesmen and Pakistani nationals not normally resident therein who have entered the State for the purpose of fighting, and to prevent any intrusion into the State of such elements and any furnishing of material aid to those fighting in the State;

(*b*) To make known to all concerned that the measures indicated in this and the following paragraphs provide full freedom to all subjects of the State, regardless of creed, caste, or party, to express their views and to vote on the question of the accession of the State, and that therefore they should co-operate in the maintenance of peace and order.

2. The Government of India should:

(*a*) When it is established to the satisfaction of the Commission set up in accordance with the Council's resolution 39 (1948) that the tribesmen are withdrawing and that arrangements for the cessation of the fighting have become effective, put into operation in consultation with the Commission a plan for withdrawing their own forces from Jammu and Kashmir and reducing them progressively to the minimum strength required for the support of the civil power in the maintenance of law and order,

(*b*) Make known that the withdrawal is taking place in stages and announce the completion of each stage;

(*c*) When the Indian forces have been reduced to the minimum strength mentioned in (*a*) above, arrange in consultation with the Commission a plan for stationing of the remaining forces to be carried out in accordance with the following principles:

(i) That the presence of troops should not afford any intimidation or appearance of intimidation to the inhabitants of the State;

(ii) That as small a number as possible should be retained in forward areas;

(iii) That any reserve of troops which may be included in the total strength should be located within their present base area.

3. The Government of India should agree that until such time as the Plebiscite Administration referred to below finds it necessary to exercise the powers of direction and supervision over the State forces and police provided for in paragraph 8, they will be held in areas to be agreed upon with the Plebiscite Administrator.

4. After the plan referred to in paragraph 2 (a) above has been put into operation, personnel recruited locally in each district should so far as possible be utilized for the re-establishment and maintenance of law and order with due regard to protection of minorities, subject to such additional requirements as may be specified by the Plebiscite Administration in paragraph 7.

5. If these local forces should be found to be inadequate, the Commission, subject to the agreement of both the Government of India and the Government of Pakistan, should arrange for the use of such forces of either Dominion as it deems effective for the purpose of pacification.

B. *Plebiscite*

6. The Government of India should undertake to ensure that the Government of the State invite the major political groups to designate responsible representatives to share equitably and fully in the conduct of the administration at the ministerial level while the plebiscite is being prepared and carried out.

7. The Government of India should undertake that there will be established in Jammu and Kashmir a Plebiscite Administration to hold a plebiscite as soon as possible on the question of the accession of the State to India or Pakistan.

8. The Government of India should undertake that there will be delegated by the State to the Plebiscite Administration such powers as the latter considers necessary for holding a fair and impartial plebiscite including, for that purpose only, the direction and supervision of the State forces and police.

9. The Government of India should, at the request of the Plebiscite Administration, make available from the Indian forces such assistance as the Plebiscite Administration may require for the performance of its functions.

10. (a) The Government of India should agree that a nominee of the Secretary-General of the United Nations will be appointed to be the Plebiscite Administrator.

(*b*) The Plebiscite Administrator, acting as an officer of the State of Jammu and Kashmir, should have authority to nominate his assistants and other subordinates and to draft regulations governing the plebiscite. Such nominees should be formally appointed and such draft regulations should be formally promulgated by the State of Jammu and Kashmir.

(*c*) The Government of India should undertake that the Government of Jammu and Kashmir will appoint fully qualified persons nominated by the Plebiscite Administrator to act as special magistrates within the State judicial system to hear cases which in the opinion of the Plebiscite Administrator have a serious bearing on the preparation for and the conduct of a free and impartial plebiscite.

(*d*) The terms of service of the Administrator should form the subject of a separate negotiation between the Secretary-General of the United Nations and the Government of India. The Administrator should fix the terms of service for his assistants and subordinates.

(*e*) The Administrator should have the right to communicate directly with the Government of the State and with the Commission of the Security Council and, through the Commission, with the Security Council, with the Governments of India and Pakistan and with their representative with the Commission. It would be his duty to bring to the notice of any or all of the foregoing (as he in his discretion may decide) any circumstances arising which may tend, in his opinion, to interfere with the freedom of the plebiscite.

11. The Government of India should undertake to prevent, and to give full support to the Administrator and his staff in preventing, any threat, coercion or intimidation, bribery or other undue influence on the voters in the plebiscite, and the Government of India should publicly announce and should cause the Government of the State to announce this undertaking as an international obligation binding on all public authorities and officials in Jammu and Kashmir.

12. The Government of India should themselves and through the Government of the State declare and make known that all subjects of the State of Jammu and Kashmir, regardless of creed, caste or party, will be safe and free in expressing their views, and in voting on the question of the accession of the State and that there will be freedom of the press, speech and assembly and freedom of travel in the State, including freedom of lawful entry and exit.

13. The Government of India should use and should ensure that the Government of the State also use their best endeavours to effect the withdrawal from the State of all Indian nationals other than those who are normally resident therein or who on or since 15 August 1947 have entered it for a lawful purpose.

14. The Government of India should ensure that the Government of the State releases all political prisoners and take all possible steps so that:

(*a*) All citizens of the State who have left it on account of disturbances are invited, and are free, to return to their homes and to exercise their rights as such citizens;

(*b*) There is no victimization;

(*c*) Minorities in all parts of the State are accorded adequate protection.

15. The Commission of the Security Council should at the end of the plebiscite certify to the Council whether the plebiscite has or has not been really free and impartial.

C. *General provisions*

16. The Governments of India and Pakistan should each be invited to nominate a representative to be attached to the Commission for such assistance as it may require in the performance of its task.

17. The Commission should establish in Jammu and Kashmir such observers as it may require of any of the proceedings in pursuance of the measures indicated in the foregoing paragraphs.

18. The Security Council Commission should carry out the task assigned to it herein.

Adopted at the 286th meeting.[1]

The five members of the United Nations Commission for India and Pakistan were: Czechoslovakia (nominated by India on 10 February 1948); Belgium and Colombia (appointed by the Council on 23 April 1948; Argentina (nominated by Pakistan on 30 April 1948); United States of America (designated by the President of the Council on 7 May 1948, in the absence of agreement between Argentina and Czechoslovakia on the member to be designated by them).

Decision

At its 287th meeting, on 23 April 1948, the Council, pursuant to its resolution 47 (1948), appointed Belgium and Columbia as the additional members of the United Nations Commission for India and Pakistan.

Adopted by 7 votes to none, with 4 abstentions (Belgium, Colombia, Ukrainian Soviet Socialist Republic, Union of Soviet Socialist Republics).

---

[1] The draft resolution was voted on paragraph by paragraph. No vote was taken on the text as a whole.

Appendix B. Agreement on bilateral relations between the Government of India and the Government of Pakistan

1. The Government of India and the Government of Pakistan are resolved that the two countries put an end to the conflict and confrontation that have hitherto marred their relations and work for the promotion of a friendly and harmonious relationship and the establishment of durable peace in the sub-continent, so that both countries may henceforth devote their resources and energies to the pressing task of advancing the welfare of their peoples.

In order to achieve this objective, the Government of India and the Government of Pakistan have agreed as follows:-

(i) That the principles and purposes of the Charter of the United Nations shall govern the relations between the two countries;

(ii) That the two countries are resolved to settle their differences by peaceful means through bilateral negotiations or by any other peaceful means mutually agreed upon between them. Pending the final settlement of any of the problems between the two countries, neither side shall unilaterally alter the situation and both shall prevent the organisation, assistance or encouragement of any acts detrimental to the maintenance of peaceful and harmonious relations;

(iii) That the pre-requisite for reconciliation, good neighbourliness and durable peace between them is a commitment by both the countries to peaceful co-existence, respect for each other's territorial integrity and sovereignty and non-interference in each others internal affairs, on the basis of equality and mutual benefit;

(iv) That the basic issues and causes of conflict which have bedevilled the relations between the two countries for the last 25 years shall be resolved by peaceful means;

(v) That they shall always respect each other's national unity, territorial integrity, political independence and sovereign equality;

(vi) That in accordance with the Charter of the United Nations they will refrain from the threat or use of force against the territorial integrity or political independence of each other.

2. Both Governments will take all steps within their power to prevent hostile propaganda directed against each other. Both countries will encourage the dissemination of such information as would promote the development of friendly relations between them.

3. In order progressively to restore and normalise relations between the two countries step by step, it was agreed that:

(i) Steps shall be taken to resume communications, postal, telegraphic, sea, land including border posts, and air links including over-flights.

(ii) Appropriate steps shall be taken to promote travel facilities for the nationals of the other country.

(iii) Trade and co-operation in economic and other agreed fields will be resumed as far as possible.

(iv) Exchange in the fields of science and culture will be promoted.

In this connection delegations from the two countries will meet from time to time to work out the necessary details.

4. In order to initiate the process of the establishment of durable peace, both the Governments agree that:

(i) Indian and Pakistani forces shall be withdrawn to their side of the international border.

(ii) In Jammu and Kashmir, the line of control resulting from the cease-fire of December 17, 1971 shall be respected by both sides without prejudice to the recognised position of either side. Neither side shall seek to alter it unilaterally, irrespective of mutual differences and legal interpretations. Both sides further undertake to refrain from the threat or the use of force in violation of this Line.

(iii) The withdrawals shall commence upon entry into force of this Agreement and shall be completed within a period of 30 days thereof.

5. This Agreement will be subject to ratification by both countries in accordance with their respective constitutional procedures, and will come into force with effect from the date on which the Instruments of Ratification are exchanged.

6. Both Governments agree that their respective Heads will meet again at a mutually convenient time in the future and that, in the meanwhile, the representatives of the two sides will meet to discuss further the modalities and arrangements for the establishment of durable peace and normalisation of relations, including the questions of repatriation of prisoners of war and civilian internees, a final settlement of Jammu and Kashmir and the resumption of diplomatic relations.

(Indira Gandhi)   (Zulfikar Ali Bhutto)
Prime Minister   President
Republic of India   Islamic Republic
                                          of Pakistan

Simla, the 2nd July, 1972

Appendix C. Trade in and licensed production of major conventional weapons: imports by India and Pakistan, 1950–92

This register lists major weapons on order or under delivery, or for which the licence was bought and production was under way or completed, during the period 1950–92. The column 'Year(s) of deliveries' includes aggregates of all deliveries and licensed production since the beginning of the contract. Sources and methods for the data collection are explained in *SIPRI Yearbooks*. Abbreviations, acronyms and conventions are listed at the end of the register. Entries are alphabetical, by supplier and licenser.

Recipient/ supplier or licenser	No. ordered	Weapon designation	Weapon description	Year of order/ licence	Year(s) of deliveries	No. delivered/ produced	Comments
India							
Supplier:							
Australia	5	N-24A Nomad	Transport	1977	1977	5	
Canada	6	C-47 Dakota	Transport	1963	1963	6	
	(20)	DHC-1 Chipmunk	Trainer	(1949)	1950–51	(20)	
	26	DHC-3 Otter	Transport	(1955)	1957–58	26	
	5	DHC-3 Otter	Transport	(1962)	1963	5	
	4	DHC-4 Caribou	Transport	(1967)	1968	4	
	16	DHC-4 Caribou	Transport	(1963)	1963–64	16	
	36	T-6 Harvard	Trainer	1962	1963	36	
Czechoslovakia	(300)	OT-62	APC	(1967)	1969–72	(300)	
	(300)	OT-64	APC	(1969)	1971–74	(300)	
	225	T-54	Main battle tank	(1967)	1968–71	(225)	
France	12	Alizé	ASW aircraft	1977	1978	12	For Navy
	3	Alizé	ASW aircraft	(1967)	1968	3	For Navy
	15	Alizé	ASW aircraft	(1959)	1961	15	For Navy
	33	MD-450 Ouragan	Fighter/bomber	(1955)	1957	33	
	71	MD-450 Ouragan	Fighter/bomber	(1952)	1953–54	(71)	
	40	Mirage-2000	Fighter	1982	1985–86	(40)	Incl 4 Mirage-2000TH trainer version; Indian designation: Vajra
	9	Mirage-2000	Fighter	1986	1987	9	Incl 3 Mirage-2000TH trainer version; Indian designation: Vajra
	110	Mystere-4A	Fighter	(1956)	1957–59	(110)	
	20	SA-316B	Helicopter	(1962)	1963	20	
	(150)	AMX-13	Light tank	(1956)	1957–58	(150)	
	. .	PSM-33	Surveillance radar	1988	1990–92	(3)	
	4	TRS-2100	Surveillance radar	(1983)	1984–85	(4)	
	4	TRS-2100	Surveillance radar	(1983)	1984–85	(4)	
	(98)	ARMAT	Anti-radar missile	1984	1986–87	(98)	For 49 Mirage-2000 fighters

Recipient/ supplier (S) or licenser (L)	No. ordered	Weapon designation	Weapon description	Year of order/ licence	Year(s) of deliveries	No. delivered/ produced	Comments
	(50)	AS-30	ASM	(1966)	1968	(50)	
	50	ENTAC	Anti-tank missile	(1967)	1969	(50)	
	(1 800)	Milan	Anti-tank missile	(1980)	1982–84	(1 800)	Prior to licensed production
	(48)	R-550 Magic	Air-to-air missile	(1983)	1983–84	(48)	For Navy Sea Harrier fighters
	(558)	R-550 Magic	Air-to-air missile	(1979)	1981–87	(558)	For 93 Jaguar fighters
	(196)	R-550 Magic	Air-to-air missile	(1984)	1987–88	(196)	For 49 Mirage-2000 fighters
	(392)	R-550 Magic-2	Air-to-air missile	(1984)	1986–87	(392)	For 49 Mirage-2000 fighters
	(3 600)	SS-11	Anti-tank missile	(1967)	1968–70	(3 600)	Prior to licensed production; deal worth $7.5 m
	(294)	Super-530	Air-to-air missile	1984	1986–87	(294)	For 49 Mirage-2000 fighters
Germany, FR	3	Do-228-200MP	Maritime patrol	1983	1986–87	(3)	For Coast Guard; prior to licensed production
	24	Sea Hawk	Fighter	(1965)	1966	24	Ex-FRG Navy; for Navy
	2	Deepak Class	Support ship	(1965)	1967–75	2	Shipping company Mogul Lines paid for construction and has part-time use of the vessel
	1	Aditya Class	Support ship	1987			Option on 1 more
Indonesia	2	Type 1500	Submarine	1981	1986	2	Prior to licensed production
	8	Vampire T-55	Fighter/trainer	(1961)	1962	8	
Italy	(50)	Model 56 105mm	Towed gun	(1969)	1971	(50)	Some probably shipped on to Bangladesh
Japan	1	Type 956	Patrol craft	(1982)	1983	1	For Coast Guard; prior to licensed production
Korea, South	3	Sukanya Class	OPV	1987	1989–90	3	
Netherlands	(40)	Flycatcher	Fire control radar	1987	1989	(40)	Prior to licensed production
Poland	50	TS-11 Iskra	Jet trainer	1975	1976–77	(50)	
	(200)	T-54	Main battle tank	(1971)	1972–73	(200)	
	2	Polnocny Class	Landing ship	(1984)	1985–86	2	
	2	Polnocny Class	Landing ship	(1964)	1966	2	
	8	Polnocny Class	Landing ship	(1973)	1975–86	8	
Russia	(20)	MiG-29 Fulcrum		1992			Deal worth $500 m; incl 6 MiG-29UB trainer versions
	..	2S6	AAV(M)	1992	1993	(30)	Part of larger deal incl aircraft and tanks
	..	SA-11 SAMS	SAM system	1992	1993	(1)	Part of larger deal incl aircraft and tanks; $830 m extended in credits for total deal
	..	SA-11 Gadfly	SAM	1992	1993	(1)	Part of larger deal incl aircraft and tanks; $830 m extended in credits for total deal
	..	SA-19	SAM	1992			For 2S6 AAV(G/M); part of larger deal incl aircraft and tanks
Singapore	2	Jija Bai Class	Patrol craft	1986	1987	2	For Coast Guard; prior to licensed production
Sweden	410	FH-77 155mm	Towed gun	1986	1986–91	(410)	Deal worth $1300 m; planned licensed production abandoned
UK	5	AOP-9	Lightplane	(1962)	1963	5	
	30	AOP-9	Lightplane	(1954)	1955–56	30	

No. ordered	Designation	Description	Year of order	Year of delivery	No. produced	Comments
5	BN-2A Defender	Transport	(1975)	1976	5	In addition to 5 delivered 1976
4	BN-2A Defender	Transport	(1980)	1980	4	In addition to 9 in service
9	BN-2A Defender	Transport	(1983)	1983	9	
12	Canberra B-15	Bomber	(1968)	1970–71	12	
10	Canberra B-I-12	Bomber	(1968)	1970–71	10	
6	Canberra B-I-8	Bomber	(1964)	1965	6	
66	Canberra B-I-8	Bomber	(1957)	1958	66	
8	Canberra PR-57	Reconnaissance plane	(1957)	1958	8	
6	Canberra T-4	Bomber/trainer	(1957)	1958	6	
6	Commando Mk-3	Helicopter	(1984)	1986–88	(6)	Sea King Mk 42C version; part of deal worth $900m incl 20 Sea King ASW version and Sea Eagle anti-ship missiles
5	Firefly	Fighter/ground attack	(1957)	1958	5	
5	Firefly	Fighter/ground attack	(1952)	1953	5	
25	Gnat	Fighter	(1956)	1958	25	
15	Gnat	Fighter	(1957)	1959	15	Locally assembled
36	Hunter F-56	Fighter	(1965)	1967	36	
160	Hunter F-56	Fighter	1957	1957–61	(160)	
5	Hunter F-6	Fighter	(1970)	1972	5	
12	Hunter T-66	Fighter/trainer	(1965)	1967	12	
22	Hunter T-66	Fighter/trainer	1957	1959–61	(22)	Prior to licensed production; incl trainer version; Indian designation: Shamsher
40	Jaguar	Fighter	(1979)	1981–82	(40)	18 delivered on loan from RAF in 1980; 8 returned 1982; 1 to Oman; 1 crashed; rest offered to Indian AF
8	Jaguar	Fighter	(1982)	1982	8	
10	SA-6 Sealand	Transport	(1949)	1950	10	
6	Sea Harrier	Fighter	1979	1983–84	6	For use on aircraft-carrier Vikrant
10	Sea Harrier	Fighter	1985	1990–92	10	Deal worth $230 m incl 1 trainer
7	Sea Harrier	Fighter	1986	1988	(7)	In addition to 19 ordered earlier
2	Sea Harrier T-4	Fighter/trainer	1979	1984	2	
1	Sea Harrier T-4	Fighter/trainer	1985	1987	1	
1	Sea Harrier T-4	Fighter/trainer	1986	1989	1	For Navy
24	Sea Hawk	Fighter	(1959)	1960–63	24	
6	Sea King HAS-1	Helicopter	(1972)	1973–74	(6)	For Navy
6	Sea King HAS-1	Helicopter	(1970)	1971	6	For Navy
3	Sea King HAS-2	Helicopter	1977	1980	(3)	For Navy
20	Sea King HAS-5	Helicopter	(1984)	1985–90	(20)	Deal worth $900 m incl 6 unarmed transport versions and Sea Eagle anti-ship missiles
(10)	Vampire FB-5	Fighter	(1952)	1953	(10)	
(52)	Vampire FB-9	Fighter	(1949)	1950–53	(52)	
(300)	Vampire FB-9	Fighter	(1952)	1954–59	(300)	Also incl trainer versions; locally assembled

Recipient/ supplier (S) or licenser (L)	No. ordered	Weapon designation	Weapon description	Year of order/ licence	Year(s) of deliveries	No. delivered/ produced	Comments
	2	Viscount-700	Transport	(1954)	1955	2	For VIP transport
	21	Westland 30	Helicopter	1986	1988–89	(21)	Negotiations resumed late 1985; cost covered by British grant
	68	Abbot 105mm	Self-propelled gun	(1968)	1969–71	(68)	
	(160)	Medium Gun 5.5	Towed gun	(1950)	1951–54	(160)	
	210	Centurion Mk-5	Main battle tank	(1955)	1956–57	(210)	
	15	FV-180 CET	AEV	1986	1988–90	(15)	First 9 upgraded ex-British Army stocks; option on more
	(50)	FV-712 Ferret	Scout car	(1955)	1956–57	(50)	
	(12)	FV-432	APC	(1968)	1969–71	(12)	Command post version for use with Abbot 105mm
	(120)	FV-1611 Humber	APC	(1948)	1950	(120)	
	(24)	FV-105 Sultan	APC/command post	(1979)	1980–81	(24)	
	10	Seacat Launcher	ShAM launcher	1972	1972–81	10	Arming Nilgiri Class frigates
	(2)	Seacat Launcher	ShAM launcher	(1986)	1987	(2)	Arming aircraft-carrier *INS Viraat*
	(10)	Tigercat SAMS	SAM system	(1971)	1972–73	(10)	Unconfirmed
	(5)	Watchman	Surveillance radar	(1987)	1987–88	(5)	For surveillance of missile test range
	(84)	Sea Eagle	Anti-ship missile	1983	1987–88	(84)	Arming Sea King helicopters
	(48)	Sea Eagle	Anti-ship missile	1985	1987–88	(48)	Arming Sea Harrier fighters
	(24)	Sea Eagle	Anti-ship missile	(1986)	1987–88	(24)	Arming 8 Jaguar aircraft converted to maritime strike role
	(156)	Sea Skua	Anti-ship missile	(1985)	1987–89	(54)	Arming Navy and Coast Guard Do-228 aircraft
	(160)	Seacat	ShAM	1972	1972–81	(160)	Arming Nilgiri Class frigates
	(24)	Seacat	ShAM	(1986)	1987	(24)	Arming aircraft-carrier *INS Viraat*
	(120)	Tigercat	SAM	(1971)	1972–73	(120)	
	3	Blackwood Class	Frigate	1954	1958–59	3	
	1	Fiji Class	Cruiser	1954	1957	1	Ex-RN *HMS Nigeria*; renamed *Mysore*
	2	Ham Class	Minesweeper	(1954)	1955	2	
	1	Hermes Class	Aircraft carrier	1986	1987	1	Deal worth approx $74 m
	3	Hunt Class	Frigate	(1952)	1953	3	Type 2
	3	Leopard Class	Frigate	1954	1958–60	3	
	1	Majestic Class	Aircraft carrier	(1957)	1961	1	Ex-RN *HMS Hercules*; renamed *Vikrant*; carries Sea Harrier fighters
	3	R-Q Class	Destroyer	(1948)	1950	3	
	4	Ton Class	MCM	(1956)	1956	4	
	2	Whitby Class	Frigate	1956	1960	2	Refitted with Styx ShShMs from Osa Class FACs during 1975–78
USA	2	Boeing 737-100	Transport	1977	1978	2	
	2	Boeing 737-200L	Transport	1980	1983	2	
	24	C-119G Packet	Transport	(1962)	1963	24	
	29	C-119G Packet	Transport	(1960)	1961	29	
	26	C-119G Packet	Transport	(1952)	1954	26	

2	DHC-4 Caribou	Transport	(1962)	1963	2	For evaluation; aid
9	L-1049	Transport	(1960)	1961–63	(9)	5 for Navy, 4 for AF
10	Model 300	Helicopter	(1969)	1971–72	10	For Navy
12	Model 47G	Helicopter	(1960)	1961–62	12	
4	Model 47G	Helicopter	(1956)	1957	4	
6	S-55 Chickasaw	Helicopter	(1952)	1954	6	
2	S-55 Chickasaw	Helicopter	(1956)	1957	2	
2	S-62A	Helicopter	(1959)	1960	2	For evaluation
30	T-6G Texan	Trainer	(1955)	1956	30	
(250)	M-4 Sherman	Main battle tank	(1948)	1949–53	(250)	
2	AN/TPQ-37	Tracking radar	(1990)	1992	(2)	Deal worth $22 m
USSR						
10	An-12 Cub-A	Transport	(1965)	1966	10	
24	An-12 Cub-A	Transport	(1960)	1961–63	24	
95	An-32 Cline	Transport	1980	1984–87	(95)	Some Western avionics integrated
28	An-32 Cline	Transport	1985	1987–88	28	
24	Il-14 Crate	Transport	(1960)	1961	24	
2	Il-14 Crate	Transport	(1954)	1955	2	
5	Il-38 May	ASW/maritime patrol	1975	1977	5	For Navy
24	Il-76 Candid	Transport	(1977)	1985–89	(24)	Order increased from 20 to 24 in 1987
7	Ka-25 Hormone	Helicopter	(1977)	1980	7	For use on 5 Kashin (Rajput) Class destroyers
13	Ka-27 Helix	Helicopter	(1985)	1985–90	(13)	Ka-28 export version
(100)	Mi-17 Hip-H	Helicopter	(1984)	1984–89	(100)	Replacing Mi-8s
12	Mi-24 Hind-D	Helicopter	(1982)	1983	(12)	Unconfirmed
(10)	Mi-26 Halo	Helicopter	(1985)	1986–88	(10)	
10	Mi-26 Halo	Helicopter	1988	1992	1	
20	Mi-35 Hind	Helicopter	1988	1989	20	Deal worth $172 m incl spares and support equipment
32	Mi-4 Hound	Helicopter	(1960)	1961–63	32	
76	Mi-4 Hound	Helicopter	(1964)	1965–66	76	
(80)	Mi-8 Hip	Helicopter	1979	1980–81	(80)	
20	Mi-8 Hip	Helicopter	(1969)	1971	20	
(75)	MiG-21bis	Fighter	1976	1976–77	(75)	
21	MiG-21F	Fighter	(1963)	1964–65	(21)	
75	MiG-21FL	Fighter	1971	1972–73	(75)	
(20)	MiG-21MF	Fighter	(1971)	1972	(20)	
14	MiG-21UTI	Fighter/trainer	(1965)	1966	14	
80	MiG-23BN	Fighter/ground attack	(1979)	1980–83	(80)	In addition to 140 licence-produced
40	MiG-23M Flogger	Fighter	1983	1983–84	(40)	
15	MiG-23U Flogger	Fighter/trainer	(1979)	1980–82	(15)	
(8)	MiG-25R Foxbat	Reconnaissance plane	(1980)	1981	(8)	

Recipient/ supplier (S) or licenser (L)	No. ordered	Weapon designation	Weapon description	Year of order/ licence	Year(s) of deliveries	No. delivered/ produced	Comments
	50	MiG-29 Fulcrum	Fighter	1984	1986–87	(50)	Initial delivery incl 42 single-seater trainers and 8 two-seaters; further requirements may reach 150
	(15)	MiG-29 Fulcrum	Fighter	1988	1989	15	Order number may be 20
	140	Su-7B Fitter-A	Fighter/ground attack	(1967)	1967–69	(140)	
	10	Tu-142 Bear	Reconnaissance plane	1984	1988–89	(10)	For Navy
	(150)	BM-21 122mm	MRL	(1974)	1975–77	(150)	Unconfirmed
	(100)	D-20 152mm	Towed gun	1965	1966–67	(100)	
	(550)	D-30 122mm	Towed gun	(1969)	1970–74	(550)	
	(350)	M-1944 100mm	Towed gun	(1965)	1966–69	(350)	
	(600)	M-46 130mm	Towed gun	(1967)	1968–75	(600)	
	(40)	S-23 180mm	Towed gun	(1974)	1975–76	(40)	
	(650)	BMP-1	AIFV	(1982)	1983–89	(650)	Prior to licensed production
	...	BRDM-2 Gaskin	AAV(M)	(1981)	1981–83	(12)	Unconfirmed
	(250)	BTR-152	APC	(1971)	1972–73	(250)	
	(200)	BTR-50P	APC	(1977)	1978–79	(200)	
	(25)	BTR-60P	APC	(1979)	1980	(25)	
	178	PT-76	Light tank	(1962)	1964–65	(178)	
	225	T-55	Main battle tank	(1967)	1968–71	(225)	
	(450)	T-55	Main battle tank	1971	1972–74	(450)	Indian designation: Ajeya
	(500)	T-72	Main battle tank	1980	1981–83	(500)	
	(60)	ZSU-23-4 Shilka	AAV(G)	(1975)	1977	(60)	
	8	Bass Tilt	Fire control radar	1983	1989–91	4	For Khukri Class corvettes
	7	P-15 Flat Face	Surveillance radar	1977	1977–78	(7)	
	(6)	FROG Launcher	Mobile SSM system	(1980)	1982	(6)	Unconfirmed; FROG-7
	16	Long Track	Surveillance radar	1976	1976–79	(16)	
	(10)	SA-11 SAMS	SAM system	(1984)	1987–88	(10)	
	(40)	SA-2 SAMS	SAM system	(1964)	1965–66	(40)	
	(20)	SA-3 SAMS	SAM system	(1967)	1969–72	(20)	
	(30)	SA-6 SAMS	SAM system	1977	1977–78	(30)	
	(36)	SA-8 SAMS	SAM system	1976	1977–79	(36)	Some 180 launchers in approx 36 btys
	..	SA-N-1 Launcher	ShAM launcher	(1982)	1984–89	(48)	
	(6)	SA-N-1 Launcher	ShAM launcher	(1977)	1980–83	6	Arming 3 Kashin Class destroyers
	4	SA-N-1 Launcher	ShAM launcher	1982	1986–88	4	Arming 2 Kashin Classs destroyers
	3	SA-N-4 Launcher	ShAM launcher	1975	1977–78	3	Arming 3 Nanuchka Class corvettes
	3	SA-N-4 Launcher	ShAM launcher	(1978)	1983–87	(3)	Arming 3 Godavari Class frigates
	7	PRV-11 Side Net	Surveillance radar	1977	1977–78	(7)	

7	P-12 Spoon Rest	Surveillance radar	(1977)	1977–78	(7)	
8	SS-N-2 Styx L	ShShM launcher	1975	1976–77	(8)	Arming 8 Osa-2 Class fast attack craft
3	SS-N-2 Styx L	ShShM launcher	(1976)	1977–78	3	Arming 3 Nanuchka Class corvettes
3	SS-N-2 Styx L	ShShM launcher	(1977)	1980–83	3	Arming 3 Kashin Class destroyers
(6)	SS-N-2 Styx L	ShShM launcher	(1978)	1983–87	(6)	Arming Godavari Class frigates
8	SS-N-2 Styx L	ShShM launcher	(1970)	1971	8	Arming 8 Osa-1 Class fast attack craft
3	SS-N-2 Styx L	ShShM launcher	1982	1986–88	(2)	Arming Kashin Class destroyers
8	SS-N-2 Styx L	ShShM launcher	1987	1987–91	6	Arming Tarantul Class corvettes
8	SS-N-2 Styx L	ShShM launcher	1983	1989–91	4	For Khukri Class corvettes
6	SS-N-2 Styx L	ShShM launcher	1987	1991–92	2	Arming Vibhuti Class corvettes
8	Thin Skin	Surveillance radar	1976	1976–79	(8)	
(63)	AA-2 Atoll	Air-to-air missile	(1963)	1964–65	(63)	Arming MiG-21s
480	AA-5 Ash	Air-to-air missile	1980	1980–83	(480)	For MiG-23s
(320)	AA-7 Apex	Air-to-air missile	(1979)	1980–83	(320)	Arming MiG-23s
(576)	AA-7 Apex	Air-to-air missile	(1984)	1987	(576)	Arming MiG-29s; designation unknown, may be AA-10 Alamos
(240)	AA-8 Aphid	Air-to-air missile	(1983)	1983–84	(240)	Arming 40 MiG-23Ms
(386)	AA-8 Aphid	Air-to-air missile	(1984)	1987	(386)	Arming MiG-29s
(1 200)	AT-3 Sagger	Anti-tank missile	1980	1981–84	(1 200)	Possibly on BRDM-2 vehicles
	AT-4 Spigot	Anti-tank missile	1983	1991–92	(600)	For BMP-2 armoured vehicles
	FROG-7	SSM	1980	1982	(20)	Probably version 7; unconfirmed
(20)	SA-11 Gadfly	SAM	(1984)	1987–88	(100)	
(480)	SA-14 Gremlin	Portable SAM	(1985)	1985	(400)	
..	SA-16 Gimlet	Portable SAM	(1990)	1991–92	(480)	
(400)	SA-2 Guideline	SAM	(1967)	1969–72	(240)	
(480)	SA-2 Guideline	SAM	(1964)	1965–66	600	
(240)	SA-3 Goa	SAM	1977	1977–78	(1 050)	
(600)	SA-6 Gainful	SAM	1976	1977–79	(400)	
(1 050)	SA-7 Grail	Portable SAM	1981	1982–83	(768)	
(400)	SA-8 Gecko	SAM	(1982)	1984–89	(300)	
..	SA-9 Gaskin	SAM	(1981)	1981–83	(132)	
(300)	SA-N-1 Goa	ShAM	(1977)	1980–83	(88)	Arming 3 Kashin Class destroyers
(72)	SA-N-1 Goa	ShAM	1982	1986–88	(60)	Arming 2 Kashin Class destroyers
(88)	SA-N-4 Gecko	ShAM	1975	1977–78	(60)	Arming 3 Nanuchka Class corvettes
(60)	SA-N-4 Gecko	ShAM	(1978)	1983–87	(160)	Arming Godavari Class frigates
(60)	SA-N-5 Grail	ShAM	(1983)	1989–91	(80)	Arming Khukri Class corvettes
..	SA-N-5 Grail	ShAM	1987	1991–92	(72)	Arming Vibhuti Class corvettes
(72)	SA-N-5 Grail	ShAM	1987	1987–91	(160)	Arming Tarantul Class corvettes
(200)	SA-N-5 Grail	ShAM	1983	1989–91	(40)	Arming 5 Pauk Class patrol craft
(40)	SS-N-2 Styx	ShShM	1975	1976–77	(36)	Arming 8 Osa-2 Class FACs
(36)	SS-N-2 Styx	ShShM	(1976)	1977–78		Arming 3 Nanuchka Class corvettes

Recipient/ supplier (S) or licenser (L)	No. ordered	Weapon designation	Weapon description	Year of order/ licence	Year(s) of deliveries	No. delivered/ produced	Comments
	(36)	SS-N-2 Styx	ShShM	(1977)	1980–83	(36)	Arming 3 Kashin Class destroyers
	(36)	SS-N-2 Styx	ShShM	(1978)	1983–87	(36)	Arming Godavari Class frigates
	(40)	SS-N-2 Styx	ShShM	(1970)	1971	(40)	Arming 8 Osa-1 Class FACs
	(36)	SS-N-2 Styx	ShShM	1982	1986–88	(24)	Arming Kashin Class destroyers
	..	SS-N-2 Styx	ShShM	1987	1987–90	(60)	Arming Tarantul Class corvettes
	..	SS-N-2 Styx	ShShM	1983	1989–91	(48)	Arming Khukri Class corvettes
	..	SS-N-2 Styx	ShShM	1987	1991–92	(24)	Arming Vibhuti Class corvettes
	1	Charlie-1 Class	Nuclear submarine	(1985)	1988	1	Returned to USSR in 1990
	8	Foxtrot Class	Submarine	(1967)	1968–74	8	
	3	Kashin Class	Destroyer	1976	1980–83	3	Modified Kashin Class version
	2	Kashin Class	Destroyer	1982	1986–88	2	In addition to 3 delivered earlier
	8	Kilo Class	Submarine	(1984)	1986–91	8	
	3	Nanuchka-2 Class	Corvette	(1975)	1976–78	3	
	6	Natya-1 Class	Minesweeper	(1972)	1978–80	6	
	6	Natya-1 Class	Minesweeper	1982	1986–89	6	In addition to 6 delivered earlier
	8	Osa-1 Class	Fast attack craft	(1970)	1971	8	
	8	Osa-2 Class	Fast attack craft	1975	1976–77	(8)	
	5	Pauk-2 Class	Fast attack craft	1983	1989–91	4	Indian designation: Abhay Class
	10	Petya-2 Class	Corvette	(1967)	1969–74	10	
	1	T-58 Class	Minesweeper	(1970)	1971	1	Converted to submarine rescue ship
	5	Tarantul-1 Class	Fast attack craft	1987	1987–90	5	Prior to licensed production; Indian designation: Veer Class
	1	Ugra Class	Support ship	(1967)	1968	1	
	6	Yevgenia Class	MCM	(1983)	1983–84	6	
Yugoslavia	(200)	M-48 76mm	Towed gun	(1960)	1962–63	(200)	
Licenser:							
France	(140)	SA-315B Lama	Helicopter	1971	1973–85	(140)	First 40 assembly only; also for civilian use
	..	SA-316B Chetak	Helicopter	(1962)	1964–92	(209)	Also produced for civilian use
	5	TRS-2215	Surveillance radar	(1983)	1988–90	(5)	In addition to 4 supplied directly
	27 112	Milan	Anti-tank missile	1982	1985–92	(27 112)	Production switched to Milan-2
	(15 000)	Milan-2	Anti-tank missile	1992			
	(10 400)	SS-11	Anti-tank missile	(1970)	1971–83	(10 400)	70% indigenous
Germany, FR	103	Do-228	Transport	1983	1987–92	(46)	Incl maritme patrol and armed anti-ship versions
	2	Type 1500	Submarine	1981	1992	(1)	In addition to 2 delivered direct
Korea, South	7	Sukanya Class	OPV	1987	1990–92	(4)	In addition to 3 delivered direct
Netherlands	212	Flycatcher	Fire control radar	(1987)	1988–92	(82)	In addition to direct deliveries

Supplier	No.	Weapon	Type	Year of order	Year(s) of deliveries	No. delivered	Comments
Singapore	9	Jija Bai Class	Patrol craft	1986	1989–92	(6)	In addition to 2 delivered direct from Singapore, for Coast Guard
Switzerland	..	Fledermaus II	Fire control radar	(1967)	1970–80	(44)	
UK	215	Gnat	Fighter	1956	1963–74	(215)	
	..	HS-748	Transport	(1960)	1964–84	(64)	
	45	Jaguar	Fighter/ground attack	1978	1982–87	(45)	In addition to 40 delivered direct; incl trainer version; Indian designation: Shamsher
	46	Jaguar	Fighter/ground attack	1982	1985–89	(46)	Incl trainer version; Indian designation: Shamsher
	62	Prentice-1	Trainer	(1948)	1949–53	(62)	
	(1 425)	Vijayanta	Main battle tank	1961	1965–84	(1 425)	
	2	Ham Class	Minesweeper	(1966)	1968–70	(2)	In addition to 2 purchased directly in early 1950s
	2	Magar Class	Landing ship	(1979)	1987–92	(2)	
	6	Nilgiri Class	Frigate	1964	1972–81	(6)	Similar to British Leander Class
USSR	(220)	MiG-21bis	Fighter	1976	1979–87	(220)	Indian production phased out 1987 in favour of MiG-27
	140	MiG-21FL	Fighter	(1962)	1967–74	(140)	First MiG version produced in India
	(150)	MiG-21MF	Fighter	1972	1973–81	(150)	
	(200)	MiG-27	Fighter/ground attack	1983	1984–92	(200)	
	..	BMP-2	APC	1983	1987–92	(184)	Indian designation: Sarath
	500	T-72	Main battle tank	(1980)	1987–92	(346)	Including 175 knocked-down kits with very low Indian content; in addition to 500 delivered direct
	(2 200)	AA-2 Atoll	Air-to-air missile	(1963)	1968–87	(2 200)	For MiG fighters
	..	Astra	Air-to-air missile	(1986)			Indian designation: Astra
	6	Tarantul-1 Class	Fast attack craft	1987	1991–92	(2)	Order may reach 15

Pakistan
Supplier:

Supplier	No.	Weapon	Type	Year of order	Year(s) of deliveries	No. delivered	Comments
Afghanistan	(2)	Mi-24 Hind-D	Helicopter	1986			Inadvertently put down in Pakistan and re-sold by Pakistani Government, 1 to the UK, the other probably to the USA
Australia	50	Mirage-3O	Fighter	1990	1990–91	(50)	Deal worth $28 m
Belgium	3	TF-104G	Fighter/trainer	(1966)	1968	(3)	
China	98	A-5 Fantan-A	Fighter/ground attack	1984			Second order
	52	A-5C Fantan	Fighter	1981	1983–84	(52)	
	(24)	F-4	Fighter	(1978)	1978	(24)	Unconfirmed
	(20)	F-6	Fighter	1979	1980–81	(20)	Probably FT-6 trainers
	(15)	F-6	Fighter	(1972)	1974	(15)	
	(80)	F-6	Fighter	(1969)	1971–72	(80)	Incl some FT-5 trainers
	60	F-6	Fighter	(1965)	1966–67	(60)	Incl some FT-5 trainers
	20	F-7M Airguard	Fighter	1983	1986–87	(20)	
	40	F-7M Airguard	Fighter	1988	1992	(20)	Incl 20 trainer versions
	95	F-7P Skybolt	Fighter	1988	1990–91	(95)	Incl 15 FT-7P trainer versions
	80	F-7P Skybolt	Fighter	1992			

Recipient/ supplier (S) or licenser (L)	No. ordered	Weapon designation	Weapon description	Year of order/ licence	Year(s) of deliveries	No. delivered/ produced	Comments
	4	Il-28 Beagle	Bomber	(1965)	1966	4	
	25	Karakorum-8	Jet trainer	1987			
	4	MiG-15UTI	Fighter/trainer	(1964)	1965	4	
	(50)	Type 54 122mm	Self-propelled gun	(1977)	1978–79	(50)	
	(200)	Type 59-1 130mm	Towed gun	1974	1976–80	(200)	
	(50)	Type 81 122mm	MRL	(1981)	1982–83	(50)	
	..	Type 59	Main battle tank	(1975)	1978–88	(825)	Seller unconfirmed
	159	Type 59	Main battle tank	(1973)	1974	159	Many upgraded to T-69 standard
	210	Type 59	Main battle tank	(1968)	1970–72	(210)	
	(80)	Type 59	Main battle tank	(1964)	1965–66	(80)	
	(50)	Type 60	Light tank	(1980)	1981–82	(50)	
	(50)	Type 63	Light tank	(1971)	1972–73	(50)	
	..	Type 69	Main battle tank	1988	1989–91	(275)	Prior to licensed production of up to 1000
	(200)	YW-531	APC	1972	1973–76	(200)	
	4	Hai Ying-2 L	ShShM launcher	1980	1981	4	Arming 4 Hegu Class FACs
	4	Hai Ying-2 L	ShShM launcher	1983	1984	4	Arming 4 Huangfen (Osa-2) Class FACs
	(2)	HQ-2B SAMS	SAM system	(1985)	1985	(2)	Unconfirmed
	20	M-11 launcher	SSM launcher	1991	1991	20	Pakistani designation: Hatf-3
	(6)	SA-2 SAMS	SAM system	1979	1980	(6)	
	(8)	Hai Ying-2	ShShM	1980	1981	(8)	Arming 4 Hegu Class FACs
	(16)	Hai Ying-2	ShShM	1983	1984	(16)	Arming 4 Huangfen (Osa-2) Class FACs
	(20)	HQ-2B	SAM	(1985)	1985	(20)	Unconfirmed; copy of SA-2 SAM
	(55)	M-11	SSM	1991	1991	(55)	Pakistani designation: Hatf-3; designation and number uncertain
	(54)	SA-2 Guideline	SAM	(1979)	1980	(54)	SAMs deployed Jul 1980; designation unconfirmed
	1	Fuqing Class	Support ship	(1985)	1987	1	
	2	Hainan Class	Patrol craft	1979	1980	2	In addition to 2 delivered 1976
	2	Hainan Class	Patrol craft	1975	1976	2	
	4	Hegu Class	Fast attack craft	(1980)	1981	4	
	4	Huangfen Class	Fast attack craft	(1983)	1984	4	Chinese-built version of Osa-2 Class
	4	Huchuan Class	Fast attack craft	1972	1973	4	
	12	Shanghai Class	Patrol craft	(1970)	1972–73	(12)	
France	4	Type P58A	Patrol craft	(1988)	1989–90	4	Two more on option
	3	Atlantic-1	ASW/maritime patrol	1974	1975–76	3	
	1	Atlantic-1	ASW/maritime patrol	1988	1988	1	Joins 3 Atlantics already in PAF service
	(2)	Falcon-20G	Maritime patrol	(1986)	1988	(2)	
	3	Mirage-3D	Fighter/trainer	1967	1968	3	

Supplier	No. ordered	Item	Description	Year of order	Year of delivery	No. delivered	Comments
	18	Mirage-3E	Fighter	1967	1968	18	
	3	Mirage-3R	Reconnaissance plane	1967	1968	3	
	2	Mirage-5DP	Fighter/trainer	1979	1980	2	
	2	Mirage-5DP	Fighter/trainer	1970	1971	2	
	30	Mirage-5P	Fighter/ground attack	1979	1980–83	(30)	
	28	Mirage-5P	Fighter/ground attack	1970	1971–72	(28)	
	10	Mirage-5R	Reconnaissance plane	1975	1977	10	
	1	Mystere 20	Transport	(1970)	1972	1	For VIP transport
	12	SA-315B Lama	Helicopter	1992	1992		Deal worth FFR 100 m
	36	SA-316B	Helicopter	(1972)	1972–75	(36)	For AF and Army
	4	SA-316B	Helicopter	(1967)	1968	4	
	35	SA-330L Puma	Helicopter	1977	1978–79	(35)	For Army
	4	Super Frelon	Helicopter	(1975)	1975	(4)	Unconfirmed
	(36)	Crotale SAMS	SAM system	1975	1977–78	(36)	6 btys with 6 launchers each
	6	Rasit E	Battlefield radar	1988	1989–91	(6)	
	(36)	AM-39 Exocet	Anti-ship missile	(1980)	1982–83	(36)	Arming some of 32 Mirage-5s delivered 1980–83
	(36)	AM-39 Exocet	Anti-ship missile	(1974)	1975–76	(36)	Arming Breguet Atlantic ASW aircraft
	36	AM-39 Exocet	Anti-ship missile	(1974)		(36)	Arming 6 Sea King helicopters
	(432)	R-440 Crotale	SAM	(1975)	1977–78	(432)	
	(128)	R-530	Air-to-air missile	1979	1980–83	(128)	Arming 32 Mirage-5s
	(216)	R-530	Air-to-air missile	(1967)	1968–72	(216)	Arming Mirage-3/5s
	(60)	R-550 Magic	Air-to-air missile	(1975)	1977	(60)	Arming Mirage-5s
	(192)	R-550 Magic	Air-to-air missile	1979	1980–83	(192)	Arming 32 Mirage-5s
	2	Agosta Class	Submarine	1978	1979–80	2	
	3	Daphne Class	Submarine	(1967)	1970	3	Built for South Africa but embargoed Jan. 1978
	1	Eridan Class	MCM	1992	1992	1	Ex-French Navy
		Eridan Class	MCM	1992	1992		In addition to one second-hand and one built locally
Germany, FR	(50)	UR-416	APC	(1972)	1975–76	(50)	
	(1 000)	Cobra-2000	Anti-tank missile	1963	1965–68	(1 000)	
Iran	4	C-130B Hercules	Transport	(1966)	1967	4	
	5	C-130E Hercules	Transport	(1974)	1974	5	
	90	CL-13 Sabre	Fighter	(1965)	1966	90	
Italy	(10)	Skyguard	Fire control radar	1981	1983	(10)	Fire control for AAGs and Sparrow SAMs
Jordan	10	F-104A	Fighter	(1970)	1971	10	Reportedly returned after 1971 war with India
Netherlands	1	F-27 Maritime	Maritime patrol	(1984)	1985	1	
	1	F-27 Mk-100	Transport	(1963)	1965	1	F-27 refurbished by Fokker to F-27 Maritime
Portugal	1	Daphne Class	Submarine	1975	1975	1	
Romania	4	SA-316B	Helicopter	(1982)	1983	4	
	6	SA-316B	Helicopter	(1987)	1988	6	
Sweden	15	Supporter	Trainer	1974	1974–76	(15)	Prior to licensed production; Pakistani designation: Mushshak

Recipient/ supplier (S) or licenser (L)	No. ordered	Weapon designation	Weapon description	Year of order/ licence	Year(s) of deliveries	No. delivered/ produced	Comments
UK	800	RBS-70	Portable SAM	1984	1986–87	(800)	Version RBS-70+; deal includes Giraffe radars
	36	Attacker F-1	Fighter	(1949)	1951–53	(36)	
	62	Bristol-170	Transport	(1949)	1950–55	(62)	
	(2)	Lynx	Helicopter	1988	1988	(2)	For 2 Leander Class frigates
	5	SA-6 Sealand	Transport	(1949)	1950–52	(5)	
	(30)	Sea Fury	Fighter	(1949)	1950–51	(30)	
	6	Sea King HAS-1	Helicopter	(1973)	1974–75	(6)	For Navy; not fitted with ASW equipment
	1	Sea King HAS-2	Helicopter	1989	1989	1	Attrition replacement
	1	Trident	Transport	(1966)	1967	1	
	1	Viscount-700	Transport	(1956)	1957	1	For VIP transport
	(10)	FV-701 Ferret	Scout car	(1953)	1954	(10)	
	20	Transac GS	APC	(1987)	1988	20	
	2	Seacat Launcher	ShAM launcher	(1981)	1982	2	Arming County Class destroyer
	(2)	Seacat Launcher	ShAM launcher	1988	1988	(2)	Arming 2 Leander Class frigates
	(24)	Seacat	ShAM	(1981)	1982	(24)	Arming County Class destroyer
	(24)	Seacat	ShAM	1988	1988	(24)	Arming 2 Leander Class frigates
	1	Battle Class	Destroyer	(1955)	1957	1	
	1	Bellona Class	Cruiser	1955	1956	1	
	1	County Class	Destroyer	1981	1982	1	Ex-Royal Navy *HMS London*
	3	CR Class	Destroyer	1956	1958	3	
	2	Leander Class	Frigate	1988	1988	2	Ex-Royal Navy ships *HMS Diomede* and *HMS Apollo*
	3	O Class	Destroyer	1949	1949–51	3	
	4	Town Class	Patrol craft	1963	1965	4	3 destroyed in 1971 war with India
USA	3	Boeing 707	Transport	(1985)	1985–89	(3)	
	1	Baron	Lightplane	(1963)	1965	1	
	1	Model 35	Lightplane	(1959)	1960	1	
	3	C-130B Hercules	Transport	(1979)	1979–81	3	
	2	C-130B Hercules	Transport	(1973)	1974–75	2	
	4	C-130B Hercules	Transport	(1962)	1963	4	
	2	C-130E Hercules	Transport	1965	1966	2	Bought from civilian airline
	26	Canberra B-57BD	Bomber	(1957)	1958	26	
	1	Commander-560	Transport	(1959)	1960	1	
	1	Commander-680	Transport	1960	1961	1	
	12	F-104A	Fighter	(1960)	1962	12	
	3	F-104B	Fighter	(1960)	1962	3	
	28	F-16A	Fighter	1981	1982–86	(28)	Deal worth $1.1 b incl 28 fighters and 12 trainers

12	F-16B	Fighter/trainer	1981	1982–84	(12)	Part of deal incl 28 F-16A fighters
100	F-86F Sabre	Fighter	(1955)	1956–57	100	
25	F-86F Sabre	Fighter	1959	1960–61	25	
4	HH-43B Huskie	Helicopter	(1962)	1963–64	4	
1	Hiller 360	Helicopter	1951	1952	1	
5	HU-16A Albatros	Maritime patrol	(1958)	1959	5	
1	King Air C-90	Trainer	(1978)	1979	1	
3	Model 204 UH-1B	Helicopter	(1986)	1987	3	
6	Model 205 UH-1H	Helicopter	(1976)	1977	6	For Army
5	Model 206A	Helicopter	1975	1976	5	For Army
10	Model 209 AH-1S	Helicopter	1981	1984–85	10	Part of deal incl TOW missiles, tanks, ARVs, tank destroyers and artillery
10	Model 209 AH-1S	Helicopter	1982	1986	10	
32	Model 47	Helicopter	(1960)	1962–64	(32)	
(5)	O-1 Bird Dog	Lightplane	(1971)	1972	(5)	Assembled from parts
60	O-1 Bird Dog	Lightplane	(1957)	1957–58	60	
2	PA-34 Seneca-2	Transport	(1977)	1978	2	
2	Queen Air A65	Transport	(1962)	1963	2	For Army
3	RT-33A T-Bird	Reconnaissance plane	(1955)	1957	3	
4	S-55 Chickasaw	Helicopter	1960	1961	4	
12	S-55 Chickasaw	Helicopter	1956	1957	12	
6	SH-2F Seasprite	Helicopter	1989	1989	3	Incl 3 SH-2F versions and 3 SH-2Gs
21	T-33A T-Bird	Jet trainer	(1954)	1955–57	21	
25	T-37B	Jet trainer	(1961)	1963–65	25	
30	T-37C	Jet trainer	1977	1978	30	
4	T-37C	Jet trainer	(1970)	1971	4	
24	T-6 Texan	Trainer	1953	1954–55	(24)	
(250)	M-101A1 105mm	Towed gun	1955	1956–57	(250)	
(40)	M-109 155mm	Self-propelled gun	1963	1964–65	(40)	
64	M-109A2 155mm	Self-propelled gun	1981	1983–84	(64)	In addition to 64 ordered 1981
36	M-109A2 155mm	Self-propelled gun	1982	1984–85	(36)	Deal worth $78 m
88	M-109A2 155mm	Self-propelled gun	(1985)	1986–89	(88)	Deal worth $40 m incl M-198 howitzers and support equipment
(20)	M-109A2 155mm	Self-propelled gun	1988	1989		
40	M-110A2 203mm	Self-propelled gun	1981	1984–85	(40)	
(200)	M-114 155mm	Towed gun	(1960)	1960–63	(200)	
(40)	M-115 203mm	Towed gun	(1954)	1955–58	(40)	
75	M-198 155mm	Towed gun	1981	1984–86	(75)	
(20)	M-198 155mm	Towed gun	1988	1989	(20)	Deal worth $40 m incl M-109-A2 howitzers and support equipment
(200)	M-59 155mm	Towed gun	(1954)	1954–57	(200)	
(150)	M-7 105mm	Self-propelled gun	(1954)	1955–56	(150)	
300	M-113	APC	(1972)	1973	300	

Recipient/ supplier (S) or licenser (L)	No. ordered	Weapon designation	Weapon description	Year of order/ licence	Year(s) of deliveries	No. delivered/ produced	Comments
	300	M-113	APC	(1959)	1960–64	(300)	US LoO Sep. 1985; total value: $25 m
	110	M-113A2	APC	(1985)	1986–87	(110)	
	(150)	M-24 Chaffee	Light tank	(1953)	1954–55	(150)	
	(20)	M-36 Jackson	Tank destroyer	(1956)	1958	(20)	
	200	M-4 Sherman	Main battle tank	(1953)	1954–55	(200)	
	50	M-41 Bulldog	Light tank	(1953)	1954–55	(50)	
	(200)	M-47 Patton	Main battle tank	(1954)	1955–60	(200)	
	(200)	M-48 Patton	Main battle tank	(1954)	1955–60	(200)	
	100	M-48A5 Patton	Main battle tank	1981	1982–83	(100)	
	35	M-48A5 Patton	Main battle tank	(1984)	1985	35	
	145	M-48A5 Patton	Main battle tank	1968	1968–69	(145)	
	35	M-88A1	ARV	1981	1984–85	(35)	
	24	M-901 ITV	Tank destroyer	1981	1984–85	(24)	
	1	AN/FPS-20	Surveillance radar	(1960)	1961	(1)	Under MAP programme at Sarghoda air base
	..	AN/TPQ-36	Tracking radar	(1982)	1984–85	(9)	
	5	AN/TPQ-36	Tracking radar	1988	1989	5	
	..	AN/TPQ-36	Tracking radar	(1990)			Deal worth $65 m
	4	AN/TPQ-37	Tracking radar	(1985)	1987–89	(3)	
	6	Phalanx	CIWS	(1987)	1987–88	(6)	Arming Gearing Class destroyers
	4	Phalanx	CIWS	1989	1989	(4)	Arming Garcia Class frigates
	1	Phalanx	CIWS	(1988)	1988	1	Arming Country Class destroyer
	1	RGM-84A Launcher	ShShM launcher	1985	1986	1	Re-fitted into *PNS Babur*
	1	RGM-84A Launcher	ShShM launcher	1988	1990	1	Arming *PNS Shahjahan*
	(4)	RIM-67A Launcher	ShAM launcher	1988	1989	4	Arming 4 Brooke Class frigates leased from US Navy; deal worth $40m incl 64 MK 46 torpedoes
	(500)	AIM-9B	Air-to-air missile	1974	1974	(500)	Converted to AIM-9J standard in Pakistan
	(400)	AIM-9B	Air-to-air missile	(1960)	1961–64	(400)	Arming F-86s, F-104s and F-6s; being converted to AIM-9J standard
	500	AIM-9M	Air-to-air missile	1985	1985–87	(500)	Arming F-16 fighters; total cost: $50 m; quick delivery of first 100
	1005	BGM-71A TOW	Anti-tank missile	1981	1983–86	(1 005)	Arming Model-209 helicopters and M-901 AVs
	2030	BGM-71C I-TOW	Anti-tank missile	1986	1987–90	(2 030)	Deal worth $20 m
	2386	BGM-71D TOW-2	Anti-tank missile	1987			First Pakistani TOW-2 order; with 144 launchers
	(100)	FIM-92A Stinger	Portable SAM	1985	1985	(100)	Undisclosed number delivered
	..	FIM-92A Stinger	Portable SAM	(1987)	1987	(150)	Unconfirmed; diverted from Afghan Mujahideen
	16	RGM-84A Harpoon	ShShM	(1985)	1986	(16)	Arming *PNS Babur*, plans for refits of Gearing Class destroyers
	(20)	RGM-84A Harpoon	ShShM	(1987)	1987–88	20	
	(18)	RGM-84A Harpoon	ShShM	1988	1990	(18)	Arming *PNS Shahjahan*

No. ordered	Weapon designation	Weapon description	Year of order	Year(s) of deliveries	No. delivered	Comments
USSR						
64	RIM-67A/SM-1	ShAM	1988	1989	64	Arming 4 Brooke Class frigates leased from US Navy
..	UGM-84A Harpoon	SuShM	1988	1989	(8)	Arming Agosta Class submarines
1	Ajax Class	Support ship	1989	1989	1	Ex-US Navy
8	Bluebird Class	Minesweeper	1955	1955–63	8	Also designated Adjutant Class
4	Brooke Class	Frigate	1988	1989	4	Lease not renewed; to be returned to the USA
4	Garcia Class	Frigate	1988	1989	4	Lease not renewed; to be returned to the USA
2	Gearing Class	Destroyer	1976	1977	2	
2	Gearing Class	Destroyer	1980	1980	2	In addition to 2 delivered 1977
2	Gearing Class	Destroyer	(1982)	1982–83	2	In addition to 4 in service
1	Mission Class	Tanker	(1962)	1963	1	On loan until 1975 when purchased
1	Tench Class	Submarine	(1963)	1964	1	Sunk in 1971 war with India
12	Mi-8 Hip	Helicopter	(1967)	1968–71	(12)	For Army
(50)	M-1937 152mm	Towed gun	(1968)	1969–70	(50)	Possibly bought from China
(100)	M-46 130mm	Towed gun	(1968)	1969–70	(100)	Possibly bought from China
(20)	PT-76	Light tank	(1968)	1969–70	(20)	
(100)	T-54	Main battle tank	(1968)	1969	(100)	
(50)	T-55	Main battle tank	(1968)	1969	(50)	
3	P-37 Barlock A	Surveillance radar	1968	1968	3	
Licenser:						
China						
..	Karakorum-8	Jet trainer	1993	1993	160	Following direct delivery/local assembly of 25 aircraft
..	T-69II	Main battle tank	(1989)	1991–92	350	Deal worth $1.2 b
..	Anza	Portable SAM	(1988)	1989–92	150	
..	Red Arrow-8	Anti-tank missile	1989	1990–92		
France						
1	Eridan Class	MCM	1992	1992		In addition to 2 built in France
Germany, FR						
..	Cobra-2000	Anti-tank missile	1963	1978–79	200	West German Government claims no licence-production contract exists
Italy						
..	Skyguard	Fire control radar	(1988)	1989	4	
Sweden						
..	Supporter	Trainer	1974	1975–92	212	Pakistani designations: Mushshak, Shahbaz; first 92 assembled from kits
..	Giraffe	Surveillance radar	(1985)	1987–88	8	
(125)	RBS-70	Portable SAM	(1985)	1988–91	125	Part of deal incl licensed production of RBS-70 portable SAMs
USA						
775	M-113A2	APC	1989	1990–91	775	
..	LAADS	Surveillance radar	(1989)	1989		Lead items delivered from 1989

Abbreviations and acronyms:

AAV(G)	Anti-aircraft vehicle (gun-armed)
AAV(M)	Anti-aircraft vehicle (missile-armed)
AEV	Armoured engineering vehicle
AIFV	Armoured infantry fighting vehicle
APC	Armoured personnel carrier
ARV	Armoured recovery vehicle
ASM	Air-to-surface missile
ASW	Anti-submarine warfare
Bty	Battery
CIWS	Close-in support system
FAC	Fast attack craft
incl	Including/includes
LoO	Letter of Offer
MAP	Military Assistance Program
MCM	Mine countermeasures (ship)
MRL	Multiple rocket launcher

OPV	Offshore patrol vessel
SAM	Surface-to-air missile
ShAM	Ship-to-air missile
ShShM	Ship-to-ship missile
SSM	Surface-to-surface missile
TOW	Tube-launched, optical, wire guided
VIP	Very important person
VLS	Vertical launch system

Conventions:

. .	Data not available or not applicable
–	Negligible figure (< 0.5) or none
( )	Uncertain data or SIPRI estimate
b	billion
m	million

Source: Prepared by Siemon T. Wezeman from the SIPRI arms trade data base.

Appendix D. Bibliography

Primary sources

Blackett, P. M. S., *Scientific Problem of Defence in Relation to the Indian Armed Forces: A Report to the Hon'ble the Defence Minister* (Defence Ministry: New Delhi, 10 Sep. 1948), p. 1.

India, Lok Sabha, *Development of a Helicopter. 76th Report of the Public Accounts Committee (Ministry of Defence)* (Lok Sabha Secretariat: New Delhi, 26 Mar. 1982).

India, Lok Sabha, *Magazon Dock Ltd—Shipbuilding. 74th Report of the Committee on Public Undertakings (Ministry of Defence–Department of Defence Production)* (Lok Sabha Secretariat: New Delhi, 1983).

India, Lok Sabha, *Replacement of a Basic Trainer Aircraft. 87th Report of the Public Accounts Committee (Ministry of Defence)*, (Lok Sabha Secretariat: New Delhi, 16 Apr. 1982).

India, Ministry of External Affairs, *Report 1980–81* (Ministry of External Affairs: New Delhi, 1981), pp. iv–v.

UK, Parliament, *Statement on the Defence Estimates 1986* (HMSO: London, 1986) Cmnd. 9763-I.

UK, War Office, *Statistics of the Military Effort of the British Empire During the Great War* (War Office: London, 1922).

USA, Department of State, *Warsaw Pact Economic Aid Programs in Non-Communist LDCs: Holding Their Own in 1986* (US Government Printing Office: Washington, DC, Aug. 1988).

Library of Congress, Congressional Research Service, *The Soviet Union in the Third World, 1980–85: An Imperial Burden or Political Asset?* Report prepared for the Committee on Foreign Affairs, US House of Representatives (Library of Congress, Congressional Research Service: Washington, DC, 23 Sep. 1985).

Secondary sources

'Air defence regiments to be modernised', *Times of India*, 13 Aug. 1981.

Albrecht, U. and Kaldor, M., 'Introduction', eds M. Kaldor and A. Eide, *World Military Order: The Impact of Military Technology on the Third World* (Macmillan: London, 1979), pp. 1–16.

Alker, H. R. Jr and Biersteker, T. J., 'The dialectics of world order: notes for a future archaeologist of international savoir faire', *International Studies Quarterly*, vol. 28, no. 2 (1984), pp. 121–42.

Allison, G. T., *Essence of Decision: Explaining the Cuban Missile Crisis* (Little Brown & Co.: Boston, Mass., 1971).

Amita, S., 'Subhas Chandra Bose: a light on his political ideas as related to the problem of Indian defence', *Asian Affairs*, vol. 6, no. 1 (Jan.–Mar. 1984).

Andoni, L., 'Jordan calls in IMF assistance on foreign debt', *Financial Times*, 17 Mar. 1989.

Anthony, I., 'Soviet–Indian defence cooperation', *Royal United Services Institute and Brassey's Defence Yearbook* (Brassey's: London, 1988).

'Armed forces modernisation', *India Backgrounder*, vol. 4, no. 17 (173), (23 July 1979).

Balachandran, G., 'MBT: attempting too much with too little', *The Hindu*, 6 Dec. 1983.

Ball, N., 'Defence and development: a critique of the Benoit study', *Economic Development and Cultural Change*, vol. 31 (Apr. 1983).

—*The Military in the Development Process* (Regina Books: Claremont, Calif., 1981).

—'Third World militaries and politics: an introductory essay', *Cooperation and Conflict*, vol. 17 (1982).

Baran, P. A. and Sweezy, P. M., *Monopoly Capital: An Essay on the American Economic and Social Order* (Pelican: Harmondsworth, 1968).

Barraclough, G., *An Introduction to Contemporary History* (Pelican: Harmondsworth, 1967).

Bedard, P., 'Overseas markets drying up for US arms makers', *Defense Week*, vol. 7, no. 35 (8 Sep. 1986), pp. 1, 12.

Benoit, E., *Defence and Economic Growth in Developing Countries* (Lexington Books: Lexington, Mass., 1973).

—'Growth and defence in developing countries', *Economic Development and Cultural Change*, vol. 26, no. 2 (1978).

Bhargava, G. S., *South Asian Security after Afghanistan* (Lexington Books: Lexington, Mass., 1983).

'Big role for the navy envisaged', *Times of India*, 9 Aug. 1981.

Blechman, B. M. and Kaplan, S. S., *Force Without War: U.S. Armed Forces as a Political Instrument* (Brookings Institution: Washington, DC, 1978).

Blechman, B. M., Nolan, J. and Platt, A., 'Pushing arms', *Foreign Policy*, no. 46 (spring 1982), pp. 138–54.

Blomström M. and Hettne, B., *Development Theory in Transition* (Zed Books: London, 1984).

Bobb, D., 'The message from Moscow', *India Today*, 15 Aug. 1983.

—'Moscow's new offensive', *India Today*, vol. 9, no. 16 (31 Aug. 1984), p. 84.

Bobb, D. *et al.*, 'The Bofors blast', *India Today*, vol. 12, no. 9 (15 May 1987).

—'Chinks in the armour', *India Today*, vol. 12, no. 13 (15 June 1987).

Booth, K., *Strategy and Ethnocentrism* (Croom Helm: London, 1979).

Bose, S. C., *The Indian Struggle* (Asia Publishing House: New Delhi, 1964).

Bright, J. (ed.), *The Speeches of Jawaharlal Nehru* (Indian Printing Works: Lahore, 1946).

'Britain poised to win £1bn. Jaguar order from India', *Financial Times*, 28 June 1977.

British Aerospace Dynamics Group, 'First export sale of Sea Eagle new generation anti-ship missile', News Release, 20 July 1983.

Brown, N., *The Future Global Challenge: A Predictive Study of World Security, 1977–1990* (RUSI/Crane, Russak & Co.: New York, 1977).

—*The Future of Air Power* (Croom Helm: London, 1986).

Brzoska, M. and Ohlson, T. (eds), SIPRI, *Arms Production in the Third World* (Taylor & Francis: London, 1986).

Builder, C. H., 'The prospects and implications of non-nuclear means for strategic conflict', Adelphi Paper no. 200 (International Institute for Strategic Studies: London, 1985).

Buzan, B., 'Common security, non-provocative defence and the future of Western Europe', *Review of International Studies*, vol. 13 (1987), pp. 265–79.

—*An Introduction to Strategic Studies* (Macmillan/International Institute for Strategic Studies: London, 1987).

—'Power, peace and security: contending relations in international security', *Bulletin of Peace Proposals,* vol. 21, no. 22 (1984), pp. 109–25.

Buzan, B. and Rizvi, G. (eds), *South Asian Insecurity and the Great Powers* (Macmillan: London, 1986).

Calvocoressi, P., *World Politics Since 1945* (Longman: London, 1977).

Chari, P. R., 'The policy process', ed. J. M. Roherty, *Defence Policy Formulation: Towards Comparative Analysis* (Carolina Academic Press: Durham, N.C., 1980).

Chaudhuri, P., *The Indian Economy: Poverty and Development* (Crosby Lockwood Staples: London, 1978).

Chuter, A., 'Indian navy to purchase anti-ship missile', *Jane's Defence Weekly,* vol. 4, no. 12 (21 Sep. 1985), p. 601.

Clark, M., 'The alternative defence debate: non-nuclear defence policies for Europe', ADIU Occasional Paper no. 3 (University of Sussex, Armament and Disarmament Information Unit: Falmer, Aug. 1985).

Cohen, S., *The Indian Army: Its Contribution to the Development of a Nation* (University of California Press: London, 1971).

Cohen, S., *The Pakistan Army* (University of California Press: Berkeley, Calif., 1984).

Cohen, S. P., *The Security of South Asia: American and Asian Perspectives* (University of Illinois Press: Chicago, Ill., 1987).

'Conflict in India over naval policy', *The Times,* 13 May 1969.

Cronin, R. P., 'Pakistan: US Foreign Assistance facts', Congressional Research Assistance Issue Brief (Library of Congress, Congressional Research Service: Washington, DC, Mar. 1987).

Curnow, R. *et al.*, 'General and complete disarmament: a systems-analysis approach', *Futures*, vol. 8, no. 5 (Oct. 1976).

'Dassault-Breguet to help design LCA for India', *Jane's Defence Weekly,* vol. 8, no. 17 (31 Oct. 1987), p. 676.

'Dassault to market India's LCA', *Jane's Defence Weekly,* vol. 10, no. 11 (17 Sep. 1988).

de Briganti, G., 'India looks to Rafale after LCA lags', *Defense News,* 29 Aug. 1988.

Defence Industry Review (Fielding, Newson-Smith & Co.: London, 1986).

Deger, S., *Military Expenditure in Third World Countries: The Economic Effects* (Routledge and Kegan Paul: London, 1986).

Deitchman, S., *Military Power and the Advance of Technology: General Purpose Military Forces for the 1980s and Beyond* (Westview: Boulder, Colo., 1983).

de Riencourt, A., 'India and Pakistan in the shadow of Afghanistan', *Foreign Affairs,* vol. 61, no. 2 (Mar. 1982).

Deshingkar, G., 'Can Pakistan take us on?', *The Illustrated Weekly of India*, 5 Aug. 1984.

—'Civilisation concerns', *Seminar,* no. 256 (1980).

—'People's security versus national security', *Seminar,* no. 280 (Dec. 1982).

Dua, H. K., 'Navy may get new aircraft carrier', *Indian Express,* 7 May 1981.

Dupoy, T. N., *The Evolution of Weapons and Warfare* (Hero Books: Fairfax, Va., 1984).

Economist Intelligence Unit, *India, Nepal: Country Profile 1986–87* (Economist Publications: London, 1986).

Elkin, J. F., 'New Delhi's Indian Ocean policy', *Naval War College Review,* vol. 15, no. 4/3 (autumn 1987).

Elkin, J. F. and Ritezel, W. A., 'The debate on restructuring India's higher defense organisation', *Asian Survey,* vol. 24, no. 10 (Oct. 1984), pp. 1069–85.

Ember, L. R., 'Worldwide spread of chemical arms receiving increased attention', *Chemical and Engineering News,* 14 Apr. 1986, pp. 8–16.

'First view of INS Ranvir with Ka-28', *Jane's Defence Weekly,* vol. 6, no. 21 (29 Nov. 1986), p. 1260.

Frank, A. G., 'Arms economy and welfare in the Third World', *Third World Quarterly,* vol. 2, no. 2 (1980), p. 228.

'French arms supply to Indian sub-Continent', *India Backgrounder,* vol. 4, no. 31 (187), (29 Oct. 1979).

Furdson, E. (Maj.-Gen.), 'Huge order by India for Soviet arms', *Daily Telegraph,* 19 Jan. 1984.

Gardner, L. C., *et al., Creation of the American Empire: U.S. Diplomatic History* (Rand McNally & Co.: London, 1973).

George, T., Litwak, R. and Chubin, S., 'The place of India in US foreign policy', in International Institute for Strategic Studies, *India and the Great Powers* (Gower/ IISS: Aldershot, 1984).

Goldblat, J. and Milan, V., 'Militarization and arms control in Latin America', *SIPRI Yearbook 1982*: *World Armaments and Disarmament* (Taylor & Francis: London, 1982), pp. 393–416.

Goldschmidt, B., 'India's nuclear problems', *Strategic Digest,* vol. 12, no. 7 (July 1983), p. 465.

Goody, J., *Technology, Tradition and the State in Africa* (Oxford University Press: Oxford, 1971).

'Govt cancels sale of Centurions', *Indian Express,* 10 Dec. 1980.

Graham, M., 'The Conference on Disarmament', ADIU Fact Sheet no. 2 (University of Sussex, Armament and Disarmament Information Unit: Falmer, May 1984).

—*Determinants of the Arms Race: A Review of the Literature Relating to the Armament Process in the United States since the Second World War* (University of Sussex, History & Social Studies of Science, Mar. 1981). Mimeograph.

Green, R. H., *Neo Liberalism and the Political Economy of War: SSA as a Case Study of a Vacuum* (University of Sussex, Institute of Development Studies, Dec. 1988). Mimeograph.

'Green light for Indian LCA', *Jane's Defence Weekly,* vol. 3, no. 11 (16 Mar. 1985), p. 437.

'Gunfire on the Glacier', *India Today,* 31 July 1985, p. 79.

Gupta, S., *Kashmir: A Study in India–Pakistan Relations* (Asia Publishing House: Bombay, 1966).

Gupta, S. and Chandran, R., 'The spending spree', *India Today,* vol. 11, no. 7 (15 Apr. 1986).

Gupta, S. and Thakurta, P. G. 'Defence forces: heading for a crisis', *India Today,* vol. 14, no. 4 (28 Feb. 1989), pp. 42–50.

Gupta, 'The new thrust', *India Today,* vol. 10, no. 21 (15 Nov. 1985).

—'The Indian Army: asking for more', *India Today,* vol. 10, no. 2 (31 Jan. 1985), pp. 94–99.

Gupte, P., 'The Hindujas', *Forbes,* Nov. 1987.

Halpern, M., *The Politics of Social Change in the Middle East and North Africa* (Princeton University Press: Princeton, N.J., 1963).

Harrigan, A., 'India's maritime posture', *Military Review,* Apr. 1969.

'Hermes for scrap if India says no', *Jane's Defence Weekly,* vol. 3, no. 25 (22 June 1985), p. 1197.

Honsa, C., 'India gets USSR arms at bargain-basement prices', *Christian Science Monitor,* 30 May 1980.

Horn, R. C., *Soviet–Indian Relations: Issues and Influence* (Praeger: New York, 1982).

Housego, D., 'Gandhi's moment for steel nerves', *Financial Times,* 27 Feb. 1989.

—'A weaker rule for Mrs Gandhi's son', *Financial Times,* 28 Apr. 1989.

Huntington, S. P., *Political Order in Changing Societies* (Yale University Press: New Haven, Conn., 1968).

Independent Commission on Disarmament and Security Issues, *Common Security: A Programme for Disarmament* [Palme Report] (Pan Books: London, 1982).

'India II', Defence Market Report, DMS Inc.: Cheltenham, 1985.

'India as a prospective partner', *US Naval Institute Proceedings,* vol. 90, no. 9 (Sep. 1964).

'India begins Army modernisation', *Jane's Defence Weekly,* vol. 9, no. 9 (5 Mar. 1988), p. 390.

'India buys Dutch radar system', *The Statesman,* 1 Jan. 1986.

'India considering Jaguar production', *Flight International,* 8 Aug. 1968.

'India considers Vickers self-propelled howitzer', *Jane's Defence Weekly,* vol. 6, no. 25 (27 Dec. 1986), p. 1472.

'India decides to rely more on Russians as source of its weapons', *Washington Times,* 5 July 1984.

'India: indigenous programs flourish amid defense modernisation', *International Defense Review,* vol. 19, no. 4 (Apr. 1986), p. 437.

'India receives first "Kilo" class submarine', *Jane's Defence Weekly,* vol. 6, no. 12 (27 Sep. 1986), p. 670.

'India selects Jaguar International', *Aviation Week & Space Technology,* 16 Oct. 1978, p. 26.

'India selects turbine for new frigates', *International Defense Review,* vol. 19, no. 10 (Oct. 1986), p. 1563.

'India still undecided about aircraft proposals', *Jane's Defence Weekly,* vol. 4, no. 1 (6 July 1985), p. 14.

'Indian Army to upgrade the tank units', *Asian Defence Journal,* Nov. 1981, p. 36.

'Indian defence spending', *Financial Times,* 1 Mar. 1982.

'Indian follow-on order for Sea Harriers "imminent"', *Jane's Defence Weekly,* vol. 4, no. 12 (21 Sep. 1985), p. 605.

'Indian IPV Launch', *Jane's Defence Weekly,* vol. 4, no. 3 (20 July 1985), p. 111.

Indian National Congress, *Resolutions on Economic Policy and Programme: 1924–54* (All India Congress Committee: New Delhi, 1954).

'Indian naval construction set for major expansion', *International Defense Review*, no. 3 (Mar. 1986), p. 369.

'Indian Navy aircraft carrier plans', *International Defense Review*, vol. 20, no. 3 (Mar. 1987), p. 359.

'Indian Navy buys British carrier', *Navy News and Undersea Technology*, vol. 3, no. 10 (9 May 1986).

'Indian Navy to receive Dorniers with Sea Skua', *Jane's Defence Weekly,* vol. 6, no. 12 (19 July 1986).

'Indian Navy to replace corvettes', *Jane's Defence Weekly,* vol. 6, no. 11 (20 Sep. 1986), p. 622.

'Indian purchase of Jaguar jet raises hot issue', *International Herald Tribune,* 11–12 Aug. 1979.

'Indians ready to ditch low flying Jaguar', *The Guardian,* 12 Aug. 1980.

'Indian SSN departs Vladivostok submarine base', *Jane's Defence Weekly,* vol. 9, no. 3 (23 Jan. 1988), p. 116.

'Indian submarine joins fleet', *Jane's Defence Weekly,* vol. 7, no. 10 (14 Mar. 1987).

'India's naval role takes shape', *US Naval Institute Proceedings*, vol. 94, no. 9 (Aug. 1968).

'India's Soviet windfall?', *Aerospace Daily*, 24 Oct. 1983, p. 282.

'India's SSGN identified', *Jane's Defence Weekly,* vol. 9, no. 5 (6 Feb. 1988), p. 199.

'Insufficient progress on Main Battle Tank', *Indian Express*, 29 June 1982.

'Intelligence', *Far Eastern Economic Review,* 17 Feb. 1978, p. 5.

International Institute for Strategic Studies, *The Military Balance 1979–1980* (International Institute for Strategic Studies: London, 1980).

—*The Military Balance 1986–1987* (International Institute for Strategic Studies: London, 1986).

'Italian–Indian Pact', *Jane's Defence Weekly,* vol. 2, no. 15 (20 Oct. 1984), p. 681.

Jacobs, G., 'India's army', *Asia Defence Journal,* no. 9 (Sep. 1985), pp. 4–7.

—'India's navy and the Soviet Union', *Jane's Defence Review,* vol. 4, no. 9 (Aug. 1983).

Jain, J. P., *Nuclear India* (Radiant Publishers: Delhi, 1974).

Janowitz, M., *The Military in the Political Development of New Nations: An Essay in Comparative Analysis* (University of Chicago Press: Chicago, Ill., 1964).

Jha, P. S., *India: A Political Economy of Stagnation* (Oxford University Press: Bombay, 1980).

Johnson, J. J., *The Role of the Military in Underdeveloped Countries* (Princeton University Press: Princeton, N.J., 1962).

Jones, R. W, 'India', ed. J. Goldblat, SIPRI, *Non-Proliferation: The Why and The Wherefore* (Taylor & Francis: London, 1985).

Journal of Defence and Diplomacy, vol. 3, no. 10 (Oct. 1985).

Kaldor, M., 'The military in Third World development', eds M. Graham, R. Jolly and C. Smith, *Disarmament and World Development* (Pergamon: Oxford, 1986).

—'The role of arms in capitalist economies: the process of overdevelopment and underdevelopment', eds D. Carleton and C. Schaerf, *Arms Control and Technological Innovation* (Croom Helm: London, 1977), pp. 322–41.

—*Towards a Theory of the Arms Trade* (University of Sussex, Institute of Development Studies: Falmer, 1977). Mimeograph.

Kaldor, M. and Eide, A., *World Military Order: The Impact of Military Technology on the Third World* (Macmillan: London, 1979).

Kapur, A., *India's Nuclear Option: Atomic Diplomacy and Decision Making* (Praeger: New York, 1976).

—'India's nuclear test: stretching out the options or the first step towards a weapons program?', Center for the Study of Armament and Disarmament Occasional Paper no. 4 (California State University, Center for the Study of Armament and Disarmament: Los Angeles, undated [?1974]).

—*Pakistan's Nuclear Development* (Croom Helm: London, 1987).

Karnad, B., 'LCA venture expensive: US expert', *Hindustan Times*, 24 Feb. 1986.

—'Light combat aircraft: the hi-tech factor', *Illustrated Weekly of India*, 8 June 1986.

—'Sub-standard sub for the navy', *Hindustan Times*, 21 Nov. 1981.

Kathari, R. D. (Admiral), *A Sailor Remembers* (Vikas: New Delhi, 1982).

Katz, J. E. (ed.), *Arms Production in Developing Countries: An Analysis of Decision Making* (Lexington Books: Lexington, Mass., 1984)

Kaul, B. M. (Lt-Gen.), *The Untold Story* (Allied Publishers: New Delhi, 1967).

Kavic, L., *India's Quest for Security: Defence Policies 1947–1965* (University of California Press: Berkeley, Calif., 1967).

Kennedy, G., *The Economics of Defence* (Faber and Faber: London, 1975).

Khera, S. S., *India's Defence Problems* (Orient Longman: New Delhi, 1968).

Kidron, M., *Western Capitalism Since the War* (Weidenfeld and Nicolson: London, 1968).

Kitchenman, W. F., *Arms Transfers and the Indebtedness of Less Developed Countries*, N-2020-FF (Rand Corporation: Santa Monica, Calif., Dec. 1983).

Klare, M. T., *War Without End: American Planning for the Next Vietnam* (Alfred A. Knopf: New York, 1972).

Larus, J., 'The Indian Navy: the neglected service expands, modernizes and faces the future.' Paper presented to Foreign Policy Perspectives, US and India Seminar, Bangalore, 25–29 June, 1978.

'LCA engines', *Defense and Foreign Affairs Weekly,* 27 Oct.–2 Nov. 1986, p. 3.

'LCA programme talks set as USA and India move closer', *Jane's Defence Weekly,* vol. 6, no. 18 (8 Nov. 1986), p. 1089.

Locke, P. and Wulf, H., 'Consequences of the transfer of technology on the development process', Paper prepared for the 27th Pugwash symposium on problems of military orientated transfer of technology in developed countries, FELDAFING, 22–26 Nov. 1976.

—'The economic consequences of the transfer of military-oriented technology', eds M. Kaldor and A. Eide, *World Military Order: The Impact of Military Technology on the Third World* (Macmillan: London, 1979).

Luckham, R., *The Militarisation of Development: Alternative Frames of Analysis* (University of Sussex, Institute of Development Studies: Falmer, Aug. 1988). Mimeograph.

—'Militarisation: the new international anarchy', *Third World Quarterly*, vol. 6, no. 2 (1985), pp. 351–73.

—'Militarism and international dependence: a framework for analysis', ed. J. J. Villami, *Transnational Capitalism and National Development* (University of Sussex, Institute of Development Studies: Falmer, 1978), p. 179.

—'Militarism and international economic dependence', eds M. Graham, R. Jolly and C. Smith, *Disarmament and World Development* (Pergamon: Oxford, 1986).

MacLachlan, A., 'Dassault wins Indian order for Mirage jets', *Defense Week*, vol. 2, no. 25 (26 May 1981), p. 1.

'Major Indian arms contract goes to Soviets', *Defense Week*, vol. 5, no. 8 (3 Feb. 1984), p. 6.

Malhotra, I., 'Defence debate paradox: confidence and apathy coexist', *Times of India*, 7 Apr. 1983.

—'Hankering after the Harrier: wrong approach to naval defence', *Times of India*, 6 Sep. 1973.

—'India finally signs deal for Mirages', *The Guardian*, 13 Feb. 1982.

Mama, H. P., 'AREN network for Indian Army', *International Defense Review*, vol. 21, no. 3 (Mar. 1988), p. 259.

—'Indian tank developments', *International Defense Review*, vol. 21, no. 5 (May 1988), p. 578.

—'India's aerospace industry: impressive achievements by a developing country', *Interavia*, vol. 39, no. 2 (Feb. 1984).

'Marked slow-down in Indian defense spending', *International Defense Review*, vol. 21, no. 5 (May 1988), p. 478.

Marshall, P., 'India is shopping for arms with list totaling $4 billion', *Washington Star* (9 July 1979).

Mascarenhas, A., 'India lets Harrier option drop', *Sunday Times*, 20 July 1980.

'Mazagon Docks: Red Sea', *India Today*, 31 Dec. 1986, p. 68.

Mellor, J. W., 'The Indian economy: objectives, performance and prospects', ed. J. W. Mellor, *India: A Rising Middle Power* (Selectbook Service Syndicate: Delhi, 1981).

Menon, K. P. S., *The Flying Troika* (Oxford University Press: London, 1963).

'Mi-24 helicopters for the IAF', *Asian Defence Journal*, Nov. 1981, pp. 36, 38.

Mukherjee, S. J., 'Further growth for Indian defence companies', *Jane's Defence Weekly*, vol. 7, no. 24 (20 June 1987).

Müller, R., 'The multinational corporation and the underdevelopment of the Third World', in C. K. Wilber, *The Political Economy of Development and Underdevelopment* (Random House: New York, 1973).

Mullik, B. N., *My Years With Nehru: 1948–1964* (Allied Publishers: Bombay, 1972).

Munro, R. H., 'Superpower rising', *Time*, no. 14 (3 Apr. 1989), pp. 10–17.

Nandy, A., 'The bomb, the NPT and Indian elites', *Economic and Political Weekly*, vol. 7, nos 31–33, Special Number (Aug. 1972).

Nations, R., 'Pride and paranoia: a Hindu resurgence inspires the "Indira Doctrine"', *Far Eastern Economic Review*, no. 33 (16 Aug. 1984), pp. 23–28.

Nayar, K., 'How armymen work against us', *Suyra*, vol. 11, no. 23 (8–11 Jan. 1984), p. 7.

Nehru, J., *India and the World* (Allen and Unwin: London, 1936).

Neuman, S., 'Offsets in the international arms market', *World Military Expenditures and Arms Transfers* (US Arms Control and Disarmament Agency: Washington, DC, 1985), pp. 35–40.

'New destroyer for Indian Navy', *Jane's Defence Weekly*, vol. 6, no. 11 (20 Sep. 1986), p. 618.

'New Indian warship class', *Jane's Defence Weekly*, vol. 8, no. 22 (5 Dec. 1987).

'New navy base for India', *Jane's Defence Weekly*, vol. 6, no. 19 (15 Nov. 1986), p. 1144.

Nigudker, A., 'The Arjuna MBT', *Defense and Armament Héraclès International*, no. 67 (Nov. 1987), p. 82.

'No Indian Jaguar probe', *Flight International*, 5 Apr. 1980, p. 1048.

Pacific Defence Reporter 1985 Annual Reference Edition (Dec. 1984/Jan. 1985).

'Pakistan: living on the edge', *The Economist*, 17 Jan. 1987.

Palit, D. K. (Maj.-Gen., ret'd), 'Mirage deal needs careful thought', *Times of India*, 30 Oct. 1981.

Palma, G., 'Dependency: a formal theory of underdevelopment or a methodology for the analysis of concrete situations of underdevelopment?', eds P. Streeten and R. Jolly, *Recent Issues in World Development: A Collection of Survey Articles* (Pergamon Press: Oxford, 1981).

'PM to probe defence "degradation"', *Indian Express*, 3 Mar. 1986.

'Public opinion on India's nuclear device', *Monthly Public Opinion Surveys*, vol. 19, no. 9 (June 1974), Blue Supplement, pp. I–XVI.

Ram, A., 'A few thoughts on applied science in India', *CGCRI Bulletin*, vol. 13, no. 4 (1966), pp. 1–8.

Ram, M., 'India goes shopping', *Far Eastern Economic Review*, 16 Oct. 1981, p. 27.

—'Planes and boats and guns—the bill is growing', *Far Eastern Economic Review*, 31 May 1984, pp. 26–27.

Rao, P. V. R., *Defence Without Drift* (Popular Prakashan: Bombay, 1970).

Raphael, A., 'Thatcher used aid to sell arms', *Sunday Times*, 7 May 1989.

Rashid, A., 'Apocalypse now for Pakistan's melting pot', *The Independent*, 30 Jan. 1987.

Rasor, D. (ed.), *More Bucks, Less Bang: How the Pentagon Buys Ineffective Weapons* (Fund for Constitutional Government/Project on Military Procurement: Washington, DC, 1983).

Reiss, M., 'Beyond the 1985 NPT Review Conference: learning to live with uncertainty', *Survival*, vol. 27, no. 5 (Sep./Oct. 1985), pp. 226–34.

'Reviving Cabinet panel on defence urged', *The Hindu*, 9 Apr. 1986.

'Revolution in Tibet and Nehru's philosophy', *Jen-Min Jih-pao* (Peking), 6 May 1959, p. 12.

Rikhye, R., 'India unhappy over Soviet arms', *Armed Forces Journal International*, Mar. 1975, p. 14.

—*The Indo-Pakistan Ground Balance: A Preliminary Analysis* (Centre for the Study of Developing Societies: Delhi, 1984), p. 124. Mimeograph.

—*The War That Never Was: The Story of India's Strategic Failures* (Chanakya Publications: Delhi, 1988).

Robertson, B. A., 'South Asia and the Gulf complex', in Buzan and Rizvi.

Roxborough, I., *Theories of Underdevelopment* (Macmillan: London, 1979).

'Royal Ordnance awarded £40m Indian order', *Financial Times*, 22 Jan. 1987.

Rubin, B. R., *Private Power and Public Investment in India: A Study in the Political Economy of Development* (Unpublished PhD dissertation, University of Chicago, 1982).

Rudolph, L. I. and S. H. *In Pursuit of Lakshmi: The Political Economy of the Indian State* (University of Chicago Press: Chicago, Ill., 1987).

Saigal, J. R. (Lt Col), *The Unfought War of 1962: The NEFA Debacle* (Allied Publishers: New Delhi, 1979).

Salvy, R., 'Light combat aircraft projects proliferate', *International Defense Review,* vol. 20, no. 12 (Dec. 1987).

Sandhu, B., *Unresolved Conflict: India and China* (Sangam Books: London, 1988).

Sapru, S., 'HAL units remain idle for want of work', *Indian Express* (28 June 1982).

Sardesai, D. R., 'India and Southeast Asia', in Nanda, B. R., *Indian Foreign Policy: The Nehru Years* (Vikas: Delhi, 1976).

'A sea change: the navy has ambitious expansion plans', *India Today,* vol. 12, no. 24 (31 Dec. 1987), p. 72.

Sen Gupta, B., *Nuclear Weapons: Policy Options for India* (Centre for Policy Research/Sage Publications: New Delhi, 1983).

Sharma, K. K., 'Gandhi confirms Jaguar deal', *Financial Times*, 14 Mar. 1980.
—'Gandhi hints at heavier Indian defence spending', *Financial Times*, 11 Aug. 1981.
—'Jaguar deal "pay-off" claim', *Financial Times*, 17 Aug. 1979.
—'Modernising the military: Indian defence requirements' *Financial Times*, 12 Apr. 1979.
—'Moscow offers to upgrade Indian MiGs', *Financial Times*, 20 Dec. 1988.

Singh, P., 'India's defence perspectives and the armed forces', *Asian Defence Review,* Oct. 1982, pp. 12–30.

Singh, R., 'Light combat aircraft: trouble before take-off', *India Today,* vol. 9, no. 2 (31 Jan. 1986), p. 79.

SIPRI, *Arms Trade Registers: The Arms Trade with the Third World* (MIT Press and Almqvist & Wiksell: Cambridge, Mass. &c., 1975).
—*The Arms Trade with the Third World* (Almqvist & Wiksell and Humanities Press: Stockholm &c., 1971).
—'The Indian nuclear explosion', *SIPRI Yearbook 1975: World Armaments and Disarmament* (MIT Press and Almqvist & Wiksell: Cambridge., Mass. &c., 1975), pp. 16–20.
—*World Armaments and Disarmament 1969–70* (Almqvist & Wiksell: Cambridge., Mass. &c., 1970).

Sivard, R. L., *World Military and Social Expenditures: 1986* (World Priorities: Washington, DC, 1986).
—*World Military and Social Expenditures: 1987–8* (World Priorities: Washington, DC, 1987).

Smith, C., 'The Pokharan test ten years after', *ADIU Report,* vol. 6, no. 3 (May–June 1984), pp. 6–9.
—'A policy of ambiguity? Nuclear proliferation in South Asia', *ADIU Report,* vol. 9, no. 4 (July–Aug. 1987), pp. 1–4.

Smith, C. and George, B., 'The defence of India', *Jane's Defence Weekly,* vol. 3, no. 9 (2 Mar. 1985), pp. 365–70.

Smith, D. and R., *The Economics of Militarism* (Pluto Press: London, 1983).

Smith, S., 'The development of international relations as a social science', *Millennium: Journal of International Studies*, vol. 16, no. 2 (summer 1987).

Socialist International Committee on Economic Policy, *Global Challenge: From Crisis to Co-operation, Breaking the North–South Stalemate* [Manley Report] (Pan Books: London, 1985), p. 196.

'Soviet arms leave gap for India', *The Times,* 3 July 1970.

Spear, P., *A History of India,* vol. 2 (Penguin: Harmondsworth, 1965).

Spinney, F. C., *Defense Facts of Life: The Plans/Reality Mismatch* (Westview Press: London, 1985).

'The stakes in Siachin', *The Hindu* (International Edition), 22 June 1985.

Stuadenmaier, W. O., 'Iran–Iraq (1980–)', eds R. E. Harkavy and S. G. Neuman, *The Lessons of Recent Wars in the Third World: Approaches and Case Studies, Vol. 1* (Gower/Lexington: Aldershot, 1985).

Subrahmanyam, K., *Indian Security Perspectives* (ABC Publishers: Delhi, 1982).

—'Nehru and the India–China conflict of 1962', in B. R. Nanda, *Indian Foreign Policy: The Nehru Years* (Vikas: Delhi, 1976).

Sundar Rajan, K. R., 'Who runs India', *Gentleman,* Jan. 1984.

Taibo, X. I., 'Talks on Spanish–Indian ventures', *Jane's Defence Weekly,* vol. 3, no. 10 (9 Mar. 1985), p. 402.

Tandon, B., 'Kremlin in chase for navy deals', *Daily Telegraph,* 5 Mar. 1984.

Tellis, A., 'Aircraft carriers and the Indian Navy: assessing the present, discerning the future', *Journal of Strategic Studies,* vol. 10, no. 2 (June 1987), pp. 141–67.

—'India's naval expansion: reflections on history and strategy', *Comparative Strategy,* vol. 6, no. 2 (1987).

Terhal, P., 'Foreign exchange costs of the Indian military, 1950–1972', *Journal of Peace Research,* vol. 19, no. 3 (1982).

—'Preliminary estimate of foreign exchange use of the Indian military, 1950–1972', Discussion Paper no. 63 (Centre for Development Planning, Erasmus University: Rotterdam, 1982).

Thakurta, P. J., 'Up, up and away: pros and cons of a fresh IMF loan are debated', *India Today,* vol. 14, no. 8 (15 May 1989), pp. 68–69.

Thomas, R., *India's Emergence as an Industrial Power—Middle Eastern Contracts* (C. Hurst: London, 1982).

Thomas, R. G. C., *The Defence of India: A Budgetary Perspective of Strategy and Politics* (Macmillan: Delhi, 1978).

—*Indian Security Policy* (Princeton University Press: Princeton, N.J., 1986).

'Tornado sales team in India', *Asian Defence Journal,* Nov. 1981, p. 38.

Toye, J., *Dilemmas of Development: Reflections on the Counter Revolution in Development Theory and Policy* (Basil Blackwell: Oxford, 1987).

Ullman, H. K., 'Profound or perfunctory: observations on the South Atlantic conflict', eds R. E. Harkavy and S. G. Neuman, *The Lessons of Recent Wars in the Third World: Approaches and Case Studies, Vol. 1* (Gower/ Lexington: Aldershot, 1985).

United Nations, *Economic and Social Consequences of the Arms Race and of Military Expenditures* (United Nations: New York, 1962).

—*Economic and Social Consequences of the Arms Race and of Military Expenditures.* UN document A/8469/Rev. 1 (United Nations: New York, 1972).

—'The reduction of military budgets', Disarmament Study Series no. 10 (United Nations: New York, 1983).

—'The relationship between disarmament and development', Disarmament Study Series no. 5 (United Nations: New York, 1982), pp. 136–38.

Valluri, S. R., 'Indian aeronautic scene: light combat aircraft', *Mainstream*, vol. 24, no. 27 (8 Mar. 1986).

Velupellai, D., 'Hindustan Aeronautics: India's aerospace giant', *Flight,* 8 Nov. 1980, p. 1179.

Venkateswaran, A. L., *Defence Organisation in India: A Study of Major Developments in Organisation and Administration Since Independence* (Ministry of Information and Broadcasting: Delhi, Jan. 1967).

—'Why a defence ministry?', *Indian Express*, 25 May 1984.

Vertzberger, Y., 'Bureaucratic-organizational politics and information processing in a developing state', *International Studies Quarterly*, vol. 28, no. 1 (Mar. 1984).

Vertzberger, Y., 'India's strategic posture and the border war defeat of 1962: a case study of miscalculation', *Strategic Studies,* vol. 5, no. 3 (Sep. 1982), pp. 370–92.

Vishvanathan, S., *Organizing for Science: The Making of an Industrial Research Laboratory* (Oxford University Press: Delhi, 1985).

Vlahos, M., 'Designing a Third World navy', *Journal of Defense and Diplomacy*, vol. 3, no. 3 (Mar. 1985), pp. 39–42, 62.

'War plane order lost', *Sunday Times*, 22 June 1980.

Weiner, M., 'Assessing the political impact of foreign assistance', ed. J. Mellor, *India: A Rising Middle Power* (Selectbook Service Syndicate: Delhi, 1981).

Weissman, S. and Crossley, H., *The Islamic Bomb* (Times Books: New York, 1981).

Who's Who in the World, 1982–83 (Marquis Who's Who Inc.: Chicago, Ill., 1982).

Wigg, R., 'Mrs Gandhi defends her policy on Afghanistan', *The Times* (3 Apr. 1980).

Wood, D., 'Proposals sought for Indian light fighter', *Jane's Defence Weekly*, vol. 1, no. 1 (14 Jan. 1984), p. 13.

Worldwatch Institute, *State of the World* (Norton: New York, 1986).

Wulf, H., 'India: the unfulfilled quest for self-sufficiency', eds M. Brzoska and T. Ohlson, SIPRI, *Arms Production in the Third World* (Taylor & Francis: London, 1986).

Zuckerman, S., *Nuclear Illusions and Reality* (Collins: London, 1982).

Index